A HANDBOOK FOR
TEACHING & LEARNING
IN HIGHER EDUCATION

ENHANCING ACADEMIC PRACTICE

HEATHER FRY   STEVE KETTERIDGE   STEPHANIE MARSHALL

KOGAN PAGE

ACKNOWLEDGEMENTS

The editors wish to acknowledge all those who have assisted in the production of this book. We are especially grateful to our team of contributing authors and those who have supplied case studies.
The encouragement and support of Professor Gus Pennington is warmly acknowledged by the editors.
The editors particularly wish to thank Mrs Brenda Wilson, University of York, for her professional assistance in all stages of development of the handbook.
Finally, we thank Jonathan Simpson of Kogan Page for his help in the management of this project.

Heather Fry
Steve Ketteridge
Stephanie Marshall
Summer 1999

First published 1999

Kogan Page Limited
120 Pentonville Road
London N1 9JN

British Library Cataloguing in Publication Data

A CIP record for this book is available from the British Library.

ISBN 0 7494 2948 8

Typeset by Kogan Page
Printed and bound in Great Britian by Bell & Bain Ltd, Glasgow

Contents

Contributors

THE EDITORS

Ms Heather Fry is Senior Lecturer in Medical and Dental Education at St Bartholomew's and the Royal London School of Medicine and Dentistry, Queen Mary and Westfield College, University of London. She was formerly lecturer in higher education at the Institute of Education, London. She has also taught history in an overseas university. She now researches, publishes, and teaches across a range of areas, including teaching, learning and assessment, quality matters, curriculum change and policy in higher and professional education.

Dr Steve Ketteridge is Head of Staff Development at Queen Mary and Westfield College, University of London, where he was formerly a lecturer in microbiology. He has extensive experience of teaching at BSc and Masters levels, working with students from across the life sciences and from civil engineering. He now works in staff and educational development with a main interest in the development of academic practice. With Heather Fry he directs the College's Postgraduate Certificate in Academic Practice. He is also involved in teaching quality enhancement and the development of key skills in undergraduate curricula.

Dr Stephanie Marshall is Director of Staff Development and Provost of Goodricke College at the University of York. She is an historian by training and prior to her current post she was a lecturer in educational studies. She has many years of experience of staff and educational development work and of involvement in quality matters. She recently introduced the York Certificate of Academic Practice for newly appointed academic staff. She takes a particular interest in discipline-specific training, particularly in the arts and humanities.

THE AUTHORS

Dr Liz Beaty is Head of Learning Development at Coventry University. She is responsible for courses for teaching staff and for projects to develop new approaches to teaching and higher education research. She is a member of the Higher Education Funding Council for England Learning and Teaching Committee and co-Chair of the Staff and Educational Development Association (SEDA).

Margot Brown is National Co-ordinator at the Centre for Global Education, College of Ripon and York St John. She has worked with teachers and student teachers in developing global perspectives and active learning strategies for use in classroom and college courses.

Dr Krista Cowman is lecturer in history in the School of Cultural Studies, Leeds Metropolitan University. She has wide experience of teaching history, both in schools and at other universities in the United Kingdom. Her main area of research and publication is British women's history.

Dr Vaneeta-Marie D'Andrea is Director of Educational Development, Policy and Standards at the Roehampton Institute, London. Since 1976 she has been involved with, and published on, professional development programmes on teaching and learning in higher education both in the United Kingdom and abroad.

Dr Kate Exley is course director of the Postgraduate Certificate in Academic Practice at the University of Nottingham and was formerly a lecturer in genetics. She publishes widely on teaching, learning, assessment and research supervision, particularly in relation to science, engineering and medicine.

Dr Adam Feather is a lecturer in medical and dental education at St Bartholomew's and the Royal London School of Medicine and Dentistry, Queen Mary and Westfield College, University of London. He is also a Specialist Registrar in Care of the Elderly Medicine at the Homerton Hospital in London.

Dr Judith Foreman is Programme Director of the Masters in Managing Organisational Change in the Department of Management, Hospitality and Leisure Studies at Bradford and Ilkley Community College. Her current research and teaching interests are in race, ethnicity, gender, sexuality and organization.

Hazel Fullerton is Head of Educational Development Services at the University of Plymouth. She trains new teachers, supports teaching and learning innovations and carries out observation of teaching. She has wide experience of teaching and staff development across several sectors of education.

Sue Grace works in the Staff Development Office at the University of York. She co-ordinates the Certificate in Academic Practice and provides training for postgraduate arts students. She has taught English, History and Women's Studies for a number of years and continues to research criminal history.

Dr Carol Gray is Lecturer in Modern Languages in Education, University of Birmingham. She is involved in the development of initial and in-service training for modern language teachers and publishes on a range of related topics.

Helen Garrett is a Senior Lecturer in educational and staff development at London Guildhall University and was formerly Staff and Training Officer at City University in London. One of her main interests is in disciplinary differences in teaching and learning.

Sandra Griffiths is Director of the Educational Development Unit at the University of Ulster. With a background in teaching in several sectors of education, she has been much involved in developing and teaching on a postgraduate certificate for university teachers.

Dr Jennifer Horgan is Director of Staff Development at the University of Wales, Aberystwyth. She was previously involved in initial teacher training for science teachers and has taught across many sectors of education, including for the Open University.

Dr Sherria Hoskins is a research fellow at the University of Plymouth. Her research focuses on the effect of learning environments on learning. She is particularly interested in the development of approaches to learning in students who have prolonged exposure to higher education.

Dr Dai Hounsell is Head of the Department of Higher and Further Education at the University of Edinburgh. He is a member of two funding council advisory groups and editor of the international journal *Higher Education*. He publishes widely on teaching, learning and assessment in universities and colleges.

Dr Tom Johnston is Head of the Department of Management, Hospitality and Leisure Studies at Bradford and Ilkley Community College. He trained as a teacher and taught in primary schools and in teacher education before switching to occupational psychology.

Dr John Klapper is Senior Lecturer in German and Director of the Modern Languages Unit, University of Birmingham. He produces and publishes materials for the teaching of German and Russian and publishes on second language learning.

Professor Robin Middlehurst is Director of the Centre for Continuing Education at the University of Surrey. Before this, she was Director of the Quality Enhancement Group at the Higher Education Quality Council. She has taught at all levels of education from primary to adult and publishes extensively on leadership, quality matters and policy and change in higher education.

Professor Stephen E Newstead holds a chair at the University of Plymouth and was President of the British Psychological Society from 1995–96. His research interests include the psychology of assessment and learning in higher education, as well as thinking and problem solving. He has published extensively on all these areas.

Dr Margaret Noble is Director of Lifelong Learning at the University of Teesside. She was previously Head of Educational Development at the University of Lincolnshire and Humberside. She develops, researches and publishes across a range of areas, including key skills, modularity and credit frameworks.

Professor Patricia Partington now works as a consultant on quality review and other continuing professional development matters at The Nottingham Trent University. She was the first chief executive of the Universities and Colleges Staff Development Association (formerly the Universities Staff Development and Training Unit) and is an established figure in staff and educational development.

Professor Gus Pennington is Chief Executive of the Universities and Colleges Staff Development Association (UCoSDA) and Chair of the Institute for Learning and Teaching's Accreditation Committee. In these roles, he is committed to supporting the establishment of a UK-wide framework for higher education teaching. He publishes widely on learning and teaching matters.

Richard Wakeford is Staff Development Officer at the University of Cambridge. He is an experienced researcher, teacher and presenter who has worked in the fields of education, psychology and medicine. He is best known for his work and publication in the fields of assessment and medical education.

Jenni Wallace is the part-time coordinator on the Teaching and Learning Certificate at the University of North London. She also works as a teaching and learning consultant and is the Certified Trainer in the United Kingdom for Supplemental Instruction.

Dr Su White is Learning Technologies Coordinator at the University of Southampton. Originally a lecturer in computer science, she went on to become responsible for IT across the curriculum. She is a member of the UK Teaching and Learning Technology Support Network.

1 | A User's Guide

Heather Fry, Steve Ketteridge and
Stephanie Marshall

PURPOSE OF THIS BOOK

This book is intended primarily for new lecturers in higher education. Established
lecturers interested in exploring recent developments in teaching, learning and
assessment will find the book valuable. It has much to offer other staff in higher
education with roles in support of teaching and learning, such as computing and
information technology staff, librarians, technical staff, researchers, graduate
teaching assistants and foreign language assistants. The book is informed by best
practice in teaching, learning and assessment from across the higher education sector, underpinned by appropriate reference to research findings. The focus is primarily on the undergraduate level in the United Kingdom. Clearly, the handbook
has much to offer others working with adult learners and similar staff working in
education in other countries. A particular strength of this book is that it reviews
generic issues in teaching and learning that will be common to most practitioners,
and also explores practices in a range of major disciplines.

An underlying strategy in writing this handbook has been to ensure that the
book supports all those staff who may wish to become members and associate
members of the Institute for Learning and Teaching.

The book draws together the accumulated knowledge and wisdom of many
practitioners, researchers and educational developers in the sector. Authors
come from a range of disciplinary backgrounds, from a range of higher
educational institutions, and from across the United Kingdom. They have
taken care in writing to avoid over-use of jargon, to introduce key terminology, and to make the text readily accessible to staff from all disciplines. The
handbook aims to take a scholarly and rigorous approach, while maintaining a
user-friendly format.

A basic theme of the handbook is that the purpose of teaching, of whatever type
and in whatever discipline, is to bring about learning. This message is reflected in

the prominence given to Understanding Student Learning (Chapter 3). We recommend all readers engage with this chapter at an early stage.

For the purposes of the handbook the terms 'academic', 'lecturer', 'teacher' and 'tutor' are used interchangeably and should be taken to include anyone engaged in the support of student learning in higher education.

THE CONCEPT OF ACADEMIC PRACTICE

This book is premised on the recognition of the multifaceted and complex role of all those working in higher education. It acknowledges and recognizes that academics have contractual obligations to pursue excellence in several directions at the same time, most notably in research and scholarship, teaching, academic management and, for many, maintenance of standing and provision of service in a profession (such as teaching or nursing). Academic practice is a term used throughout that encompasses all of these facets. Hence teaching is recognized as being only one of the roles that readers of this book will be undertaking.

The authors recognize the changing nature of higher education in the United Kingdom. Recent years have seen a significant increase in student numbers, greater diversity in the undergraduate student body, pressure on resources, requirements for income generation, improved flexibility in modes of study and delivery, and new imperatives related to quality and standards. Another challenge facing the sector is a growing expectation for the preparation of students for the world of work. At the same time the pressures of research assessment have become even more acute for many in the sector. All of these features have implications for the nature of teaching in higher education, and all have brought increased stress and demands on staff time.

USING THE HANDBOOK

The handbook has five sections. The introductory section, with two chapters, sets out the purpose of the book and examines the changing role and place of teaching in universities, especially in the United Kingdom. It notes the changing policy and national imperatives which are affecting the way in which higher education practitioners are prepared for their role in teaching and learning and expected to maintain and enhance good practice throughout a lifetime of teaching.

Following the introductory section, the book is divided into three parts. Part 1, the Development of Practice, contains 13 chapters, each of which explores a major facet of teaching and/or learning. Each aspect is considered from a broad perspective, rather than adopting the view or emphasis of a particular discipline. These chapters cover most of the repertoire required for undergraduate teaching, learning and assessment.

Part 2, the Development of the Academic for Teaching and Learning, addresses the development of the academic as a teacher. It is concerned with how teachers can learn, explore, develop and enhance their practice. It provides guidance to help teachers scrutinize their understanding of underpinning theory and of practice. There are suggestions for giving and receiving feedback, and for self-auditing one's own progress. This section provides the building blocks for continuing professional development.

Part 3, Working in Discipline-Specific Areas, considers teaching and learning from the perspective of different fields of study. It seeks to draw out, for several major disciplinary groupings, the characteristic features of teaching, learning and assessment.

The final section is a glossary of technical terms.

DISTINCTIVE FEATURES

The book has several distinctive features. Each chapter is written so that it can be read independently of others, and in any order. Readers can select and prioritize, according to need.

Chapters feature one or more instances where readers are invited to consider a feature of their own institution, department, courses, students or practice: this is done by posing questions to the reader under the heading 'Interrogating Practice'. This feature has several purposes. First, to encourage the reader to audit practice with a view to improvement. Second, to challenge the reader to examine critically their conceptions of teaching and workplace practice. Third, to ensure the reader is familiar with their institutional and departmental policies and practices. The reader is free to choose how they engage with these queries, and may consider them either at the time of reading or later.

In each part of the book the chapters include case studies. The case studies exemplify issues, practice, and research findings mentioned in the body of the chapters. They are real cases and examples drawn from a wealth of institutions, involving the everyday practice of authors and colleagues, to demonstrate how particular approaches have been used successfully. Some are at the leading edge of teaching in their discipline, others report on authors' own research.

Each chapter has its own reference section and recommended further reading. In some instances readers are referred to web sites, resource materials, videos, etc.

A further distinctive feature is the glossary. It contains the main terms encountered in teaching and learning in higher education and some commonly used acronyms. In the text such 'technical terms' are indicated in bold type. All of these are succinctly explained in the glossary at the end of the book. This may be used as a dictionary independent of any chapter.

This handbook has been written on the premise that readers will strive to extend and develop their academic practice. It endeavours to offer a starting point for teaching: provoking thought, giving rationales and examples, encouraging reflective practice and prompting action to improve and enhance one's role as a teacher in higher education.

2 Towards a New Professionalism: Accrediting Higher Education Teaching

Gus Pennington

INTRODUCTION: SOME STARTING PROPOSITIONS

Effective teaching in higher education matters greatly – it always has – and although fashions, forms, and techniques of teaching may alter over time and between locations and disciplines, there is no reason to believe that this will not continue long to be the case. Building on foundations laid in primary and secondary education, teachers in universities and colleges engage with a vital educative process directed towards a variety of intellectual, professional and economic ends. At a macro level, higher education teachers contribute significantly to the formation of the next generation of workers, equipping them with the requisite knowledge and generic skills necessary to sustain and develop the national economy (Williams and Fry, 1994). At a micro level, these same teachers help shape the cognitive, emotional and moral development of individual adult learners for their multiple roles as citizens, parents and community members (Knowles, 1990). In short, effective teachers are a scarce and valuable resource and should be treated as a national asset; and effective teaching (the process) forms the bedrock of a dynamic culture and society. It is a central proposition of this chapter that these interdependent elements (people and processes) require investigation, investment and nurturing to maintain their impact and relevance.

Although teaching forms the major concern of this book, and this chapter, and is important and intrinsically valuable, it represents only one of the key functions of universities, alongside research and broader service to the community. Ideally, a balanced and contextually appropriate development of all these elements should be encouraged as they are equally essential to the fulfilment of the mission of higher education. In reality, forces in the present British higher education environment have tended to drive these activities apart, and many institutions (and individual staff) have found themselves in a situation of managing them as separate entities with varied status and priority. This need not be the case. Moreover, each element of academic practice is underpinned by its own form of learning and each is sustained by its own separate, but equally valid form of scholarship (Boyer, 1990a).

In the United Kingdom during the early and mid 1990s 'the scholarships of discovery' and 'integration' (ie research) have generally occupied a more prominent and prestigious position on the national agenda than 'the scholarships of application and teaching'. As Boyer reminds us:

> ...the *scholarship of teaching* affirms the fact that the work of the professor is consequential only as it is understood by others. Today, teaching is often viewed as a routine function, tacked on, something almost anyone can do. When defined as *scholarship*, however, teaching both educates and entices future scholars. Great teachers create a common ground of intellectual commitment. They stimulate active, not passive, learning and encourage students to be critical, creative thinkers, with the capacity to go on learning.... Indeed, as Aristotle said, 'Teaching is the highest form of understanding'.
>
> *(Boyer, 1990b: 13)*

Boyer's view is still relevant as we approach the millennium and now is the time for teaching to assume its former equal standing with research as a number of sector-wide initiatives coincide.

There are, of course, differences between learning and understanding in the context of studying or as a form of professional development, and learning in the context of groundbreaking research. One yields knowledge that is new for that individual, the other generates knowledge that is new in an absolute sense. Reconceptualizing a university's core mission around learning (Bowden and Marton, 1998) and accepting Boyer's paradigm of scholarship enables us to create a more relevant, non-hierarchical relationship between these activities. In essence, it is learning that links research and teaching to the benefit of both activities and the mutual satisfaction of teacher and learner (Moses, 1990; Rowland, 1996).

What follows starts from the premises above and conceives the processes we call 'teaching' as a scholarship enterprise involving the development of a knowledge of practice through:

● building of bridges between teacher's understandings and students' learning (Marton and Booth, 1997);

- teachers learning from students about their learning;
- teachers researching their own practice with a view to its improvement (Zuber-Skerritt, 1992);
- teachers engaging with the kinds of critical self-reflection, critical reason and critical action identified by Barnett (1997);
- teachers understanding research on student learning and deploying this knowledge in their approaches to teaching (Entwistle, 1998).

This view of teaching is fundamental to a new professionalism in higher education teaching and must form the core of any process that aims to recognize and accredit teachers. In the absence of such an approach, academics tend to reproduce in their own practice processes they were subjected to themselves as learners.

WHY PROFESSIONALISM? THE CONTEXT

'Professionalism at all levels', and a need for substantial investment in staff training and development, is a major theme running through the **Dearing Report** (NCIHE, 1997). Dearing states uncompromisingly that 'Institutions and their staff face a great challenge if our vision that the UK should be at the forefront of world practice in learning and teaching in higher education is to be realized' (paragraph 8.56). This theme is expanded further with the view that '…forms of professional development should not be restricted to those at the beginning of their careers, or to those groups with a formal responsibility for teaching'. In short, only career-long, **continuous professional development** (CPD) and systematic updating in the discipline and in pedagogy can equip teachers, and others who support learning, with the expertise and understanding to support student learning. Given the half-life of knowledge, the changing profile of students, the demands of lifelong learning and the potential of information technology, there are compelling reasons why CPD is , if not more important, then equal to initial professional formation. Dearing's contention is that a major, strategic commitment to upgrading, extending and retraining of teaching skills is an important element in institutions' capacities to respond to changing work environments and to remaining competitive at a regional, national and international level.

Pressure to adopt a more systematic approach to the preparation of staff for their teaching role arises from both the wider socio-political environment and from within the higher education sector itself (Connor *et al*, 1996; Pennington, 1997). Given the politicized nature of much contemporary decision making, however, analyses of higher education developments frequently ignore or play down the extent to which the latter force shapes events, and the degree to which academic and institutional leaders, through their own work and activities, influence major shifts in attitude and practice. Over the last decade fundamental change has occurred in the sector and a significant feature of reform has been the increasing importance placed on the development of high quality and innovative teaching and learning strategies. With regard to effective teaching and professional preparation for this, two particular strands can be identified.

First, significant advances have been made in **adult learning theory** and a growing volume of researched good practice about teaching is now available at generic, subject and methodological levels (for example: Biggs, 1994; Hazel, 1995; Marton and Booth, 1997). This contrasts starkly with the situation even a decade ago when the number of researchers interested in student learning and effective teaching was small. It is not unkind to suggest that this small band generally discussed their findings with each other, discussion was relatively closed and there was unsystematic dissemination to a wider audience. Today, there are many hundreds of individuals within the UK and elsewhere who are using research frameworks and research tools to make sense of teaching, student learning and the effective delivery of course programmes (see Gibbs, 1994; Wright, 1995; Marton, Hounsell and Entwistle, 1997). More importantly, the results of research are being used to enhance educational quality and to shape institutional practices for the delivery and evaluation of teaching (Entwistle, 1995).

Second, there is now more widespread acceptance among academic staff (and, significantly, their professional and subject associations) that a more supported and structured induction to, and career-long development of, teaching expertise is required to establish good practice, excellence and consistent standards (AUT, 1996). A number of developments can be summarized as follows:

- A wider range of UK institutions has developed programmes for induction into teaching, although this provision is still aimed mainly at new staff and could, indeed must, in a suitably modified form, be extended to more experienced staff and those in mid-career (see Griffiths, 1996; Luby, 1997). Some of this provision is award-bearing and has been developed over a period of a decade or more (Pennington and Calderon, 1994); some is new and highly sensitive to demands in the present environment (Pyle, 1999).
- A small but growing number of institutions are beginning to link proficiency (excellence, even) in teaching to rewards and promotion procedures (see Elton and Partington, 1993; Gibbs, 1996; Hounsell, 1996). Although more and urgent thought needs to be directed to the development of effective reward systems as a means for improving the quality of university teaching in the UK, formative work in Australia provides an interesting starting point for making rapid progress if circumstances prove right (Ramsden *et al*, 1995).
- A limited number of institutions have introduced formal, mandatory schemes for peer observation of teaching (Pennington, 1994), with even more encouraging peer feedback and collaborative **reflection** on an informal basis. When

effectively managed, there is great power in such schemes as they focus on specific incidents, enhance and extend teaching techniques and help develop professionally relevant skills such as self-reflection and critical dialogue with colleagues in a subject context (Martin and Double, 1998).

- More institutions now recognize the importance of managing organizational change and of developing coherent, strategic staff development strategies which are integrated with co-related policies to sustain advances in teaching, the use of learning technology and the development of the learning environment (Nightingale and O'Neil, 1994). Turning these interrelated strategies into effective, coordinated curriculum provision and effective teaching practices remains a challenge both here and abroad (Alexander and McKenzie, 1998). However, evidence exists that many institutions are responding well to such pressures, as evaluations of funding council projects testify (Smith, 1998).

WHAT DO WE MEAN BY PROFESSIONALISM IN TEACHING?

Many staff in higher education display an exemplary commitment to and proficiency in teaching. More importantly, it is highly likely that such staff form a substantial core of the current academic workforce. There is little evidence after four years of national teaching quality assessments in higher education to suggest that poor teachers constitute a higher proportion of practitioners than in other comparable occupations (Warwick, 1999). Placing higher education teaching on a more professional basis, however, will entail more than the elimination of weak performance (so-called 'weeding out the incompetent') or systematic remedial provision for those who fail to deliver teaching to an acceptable level. Nor will it be achieved through a compulsory national 'training scheme' or even the conferring of Qualified Teacher Status through a recognized formal award as is the case for primary and secondary school teachers.

If **competence** is to be promoted and incompetence avoided then it must be addressed directly. We are reminded that competence in teaching is not measured by academic achievement and is certainly not the same as excellence: 'Pursuing excellence in teaching, worthy though that is, does not produce a trickle down to the generality of teachers. The experience of the majority of students will not be with the small minority of truly excellent teachers…if we are to enhance their experience we must concern ourselves with the competence of the majority…' (Randall, 1998: 19).

Competence is at the heart of professionalism. A key task for a professional body of the kind proposed by Dearing (recommendation 14) is to identify (a) the practical skills and techniques, together with underpinning subject and pedagogical knowledge, associated with competent teaching, and (b) the behaviours, values and protocols associated with professional conduct. Registered members of a professional body are typically required to be 'trained' and educated to a level where they can demonstrate the required competence and conduct to a common standard at both 'entry' and higher levels. And while the identification and assessment of progressive levels of professional competence is a technically demanding activity with a number of potential pitfalls, the task is not beyond us and has already been accomplished in a number of fields (Eraut, 1994).

It would be naive to believe that professionalism of the kind outlined here will be achieved solely through the creation of a new organization and the establishment of a national framework against which to accredit initial and CPD for teaching. Central action must be matched by local effort and the wholehearted commitment of individual and institutional resources to career-long learning supportive of competent teaching. Thus, beside an explicit sector-wide commitment to teaching, and to raising the status of effective teachers through the creation of appropriate rewards and pathways, institutions will also need to establish the right culture and organizational conditions to support the growth of professionalism. A managed, strategic approach in this area might be expected to include:

- development and implementation of an institutional policy for CPD focused on teaching;
- provision of varied and appropriate opportunities for engagement with development activities;
- committing targeted resources to support delivery of 'training' programmes and other forms of development such as peer observation schemes;
- ensuring a sufficiency of appropriately trained and committed professional tutors and mentors to support development work at both a generic and subject level;
- ensuring that well-informed judgements about individual teaching competence inform career progression decisions such as satisfactory completion of **probation**, appraisal, promotion and reward;
- ensuring individuals have sufficient and appropriately scheduled time to engage seriously with development activities;
- establishing formal means for recording this engagement and noting progression (for example through the use of **portfolios** or other professional development records).

IMPLEMENTING DEARING'S VISION

Many of these proposals are not new and the Dearing Report (NCIHE, 1997) explicitly recommends several. What is new in the present context, however, is that proposals of this kind are now 'going with the grain', command widespread agreement, and are able to draw on models of proven good practice both within the United Kingdom and elsewhere. Indeed, interest in the theory and practice of university level teaching and its improvement is now global. The result is that universities and colleges are better placed to design and deliver effective development programmes for new staff and to assess the prior work-based learning of those with more experience (Nyquist, 1996).

Despite the assessment of practice often being uncomfortable, approximate and problematic, it is not an issue that can be evaded if we are serious about the **accreditation** of learning aimed at the professional development for teaching. The development and assessment of portfolios of evidence and records of professional development is central to the notion of competence, as Jessup (1991) reminds us. Well-structured and reflective portfolios provide information about an individual's abilities across the range of demands appropriate to the effective performance of their role. More importantly, they focus on the outcomes and application of learning, rather than a simple record of events, and present sufficient convincing work-based examples to demonstrate achievement. The most compelling portfolios draw together learning from a wide range of activities and emphasize the integration of this learning within individuals' work contexts and current responsibilities.

ESTABLISHING AN ACCREDITATION FRAMEWORK

Accreditation of higher education teaching (AUT, 1996; Gregory, 1998) is seen as a means of stemming public (frequently ill-informed) concerns about 'poor teaching' and providing an overarching national framework which identifies a set of core elements academics must demonstrate in order to be recognized as competent teachers. Although accreditation is a controversial and complex area, many academics are already familiar with its demands through their subject-related professional practice in (say) law, engineering, accountancy and computing. Since Dearing reported, sector-wide acceptance of the need for a national academic scheme for higher education teaching has strengthened and a wide range of constituencies perceive benefits in such an initiative. The major professional benefit is that those with a teaching role in universities and colleges would be able to provide evidence of their competence, commitment and continued development in this field, and thereby assure students, the general public, and statutory and regulatory bodies that teaching standards and practices are secure.

Establishment and operation of a national accreditation scheme will generate a number of potentially radical changes. One such shift will be to move debate from the question 'what is effective teaching?' to the more threatening 'who is an effective teacher?' However uncomfortable this second question is, now is the time to ask it, for while we have a growing base of evidence to answer the first query, responses to the second are frequently rooted in partial, out-of-date, anecdotal (dubiously come by) evidence. This situation cannot continue; it is unfair to those teachers who are effective and does little to lift the general level of debate.

Part of the process of putting Dearing's recommendations into practice involved the creation of an Institute for Learning and Teaching Planning Group (ILTPG), with responsibility for further development of a national accreditation scheme. This group brought together a broadly based collection of representative and statutory bodies, development agencies and professional associations with a view to translating into reality Dearing's recommendation (NCIHE, 1997, paragraph 8.61) that a new independent accrediting body with national standing be created. In tackling its agenda, the ILTPG identified a number of principles which would need to be satisfied if a national accreditation scheme were to operate in a flexible, light-touch and effective way (Pennington, 1998):

- whatever form the Institute's proposals and guidelines ultimately took, they must be capable of generating commitment and ownership across the whole of the sector;
- accreditation procedures would need to recognize institutional diversity in mission, programmes and approaches to teaching and learning;
- the Institute of Learning and Teaching's (**ILT**) modes of operating should encourage variety and innovation in meeting a set of common national standards or outcomes;
- accredited provision within institutions should focus on effective subject teaching;
- a national accreditation scheme should acknowledge the contribution made to learning of a broad constituency of staff who support students in a variety of modes, as well as full-time academic staff;
- the scheme should be relevant and attractive to staff at different career stages and with different levels of experience;
- the scheme should not prescribe either the content or format of provision (which are properly matters for academic and professional judgement at an institutional level) but should emphasize consistency of outcomes in key domains.

THE NATURE OF THE NATIONAL FRAMEWORK

Notwithstanding our present knowledge of what effective teachers do, any attempt to describe a national framework for higher education teaching is bound to be contentious. The field itself is complex, there are competing epistemologies and multiple variables operating in different teaching-learning contexts. To these imperatives must be added a diverse range of institutional, subject and personal views with regard to teaching (Trigwell, Prosser and Taylor, 1994). Moreover, given the ILT's view that effective higher education teaching is subject-based, any generic descriptions of professional competence must be capable of informing and being translated into discipline-based practice.

The character of the national accreditation framework is based on five major categories or areas of outcome:

- designing and planning a curriculum;
- teaching and supporting learning in the subject field;
- assessing students' learning achievements;
- maintaining institutional systems for supporting students;
- evaluating and improving the teaching-learning process.

Sub-outcomes are identified within the five domains, and the expectation is that teachers will demonstrate the majority of these as a condition of registration with the ILT. Insofar as it is compatible with the maintenance of a common standard, it is vitally important that the national framework is not interpreted in a crude and mechanistic way, and that its diagnostic and developmental potential is exploited alongside its assessment function.

EMERGING ISSUES

Establishing a new UK-wide approach to professional development for university level teaching is fraught with technical difficulties and political pitfalls. In a sector which rightly guards its autonomy, there is an inevitable tension between institutions' wishes to develop programmes which suit their own particular needs and the ILT's need to operate a common national framework which commands wide acceptance among a diverse range of institutions. A number of other key issues also present themselves.

- In recognizing institutional provision to satisfy its accreditation process, the ILT will wish to maintain a distinction between accredited programmes and accredited pathways as separate, but equally valid, vehicles to gain ILT membership. There is a likelihood that the former will be directed in the main (but not exclusively) towards meeting the initial professional development needs of relatively new teachers and 'supporters of learning'. By contrast, the establishment of accredited pathways will be a major route through which experienced staff can demonstrate competence in teaching via the assessment of a portfolio of evidence. A 'pathways' approach will entail developing clear procedures for determining 'advanced standing' and for the application of rigorous processes to identify and give credit for prior learning, be this certificated or based on experience. It is highly likely that many individuals will require a mixed mode of development involving some elements of a programme plus credit for prior experience. The professional challenge for academic and staff developers, therefore, will be to create flexible provision that maintains transparent comparability of standards. While the national 'standard' will remain constant, the means of approaching and satisfying it must be appropriately varied.

- Throughout the ILT's proposals there is an underlying and fundamental assumption that both initial and CPD will involve a wide range of independent and supported work-based learning as opposed to narrowly conceived classroom-based experiences comprising high contact hours. It would be a travesty if staff wishing to improve their teaching performance were subjected to high dosages of didactic teaching about effective teaching and learning methods. Planning groups for the ILT have wished to encourage institutions to exploit a variety of means to enhance conceptual understanding and classroom performance. These have included: exposure to good models of professional conduct; familiarity with the scholarship and research of higher education learning and teaching; guided practice; peer observation; self-assessment; work-based exercises and expert mentoring. Elements of these kinds will need to be woven into coherent initial and CPD programmes, the best of which will be paradigmatic of what is presently known about effective in-service and post-experience learning. This is the kernel of a demanding task for those responsible for designing, delivering and assessing their institution's provision. If ILT accreditation is to proceed at an even pace on a broad front, some development of staff developers may be necessary. Indeed, registration of staff developers themselves against a modified set of national outcomes may well be a further phase of development the ILT wishes to promote.

- Development and embedding of a national scheme based on accredited local provision will not be successful without continued, and in some cases new, forms of institutional support. Some universities and colleges have already invested in staffing and structures for the development of individuals' expertise in teaching and, moreover, have seen this as a necessary component of their commitment to effective delivery of academic programmes. Other institutions have been less active, with the result that national provision is patchy and characterized by variability in the amount, level and duration of initial and CPD provision. It is clear that a number of institutions will need to invest more heavily in this area than they have hitherto, or will need to seek forms of collaboration which will deliver mutual benefits. Even the widespread availability of good provision, however, will not in itself ensure a tangible advance in university teaching and the quality of students' learning. This goal will only be achieved when comprehensive opportunities for professional development are an integral part of a coherent and systemic institutional CPD strategy. This strategy will need to be skilfully managed and carefully articulated with a range of other initiatives for curriculum change, development of the learning environment and greater, integrated use of communication and information technology to boost learning and teaching. In the short term we might expect to see a national 'filling in' of provision, and this is a necessary condition for further advance. Once there is a sufficiency of good provision, however, the medium-term goal must be to align procedures for induction, probation, appraisal, reward, progression and performance management. Only at this point can the sector truly claim to have committed itself to professionalism in teaching.

- We should also recognize the imperative facing the ILT in its first years of operation to attract and build a 'critical mass' of competent, registered members from all parts of the United Kingdom and from a range of institutions with different approaches to teaching. Processes need to be established at an institutional and national level to attract new and experienced staff to accredited provision at the same time, and from the very beginning of the Institute's existence. Although much of the early emphasis has been on accredited programmes for staff at the start of their careers, a key constituency to establish the credibility of the Institute are experienced teachers who wish to have their existing competence and expertise recognized. There is also a case for creating an additional level of 'advanced' membership that would require high levels of scholarship in teaching as well as personal competence.

Those in mid-career form the core of professional competence within the sector and represent in aggregate the accumulated wisdom of effective practice. This group, to achieve membership, will need to be actively supported through individualized portfolio building and the assessment of prior learning. Nor should it be forgotten that there will be a need to recognize, value and build on staffs' concern for their discipline. Responding to this challenge could have considerable implications of the kinds described by Jenkins (1996).

BEYOND COMPULSION

There will be those who, for a variety of reasons, wish to represent a national initiative to encourage and recognize teaching competence as heralding a new era of regulation and intervention. Initiatives of this kind inevitably generate intense political interest, but this should not distract us from the core intention of this particular enterprise. A more accurate and less alarmist view would be that the establishment of a national framework for higher education teaching represents a drawing together of many elements which have arisen as good practice within the sector itself over at least two decades of evolutionary change.

Encouraging the systematic development of teaching competence, especially at the outset of an individual's career, is intended to accelerate the acquisition of skills and understandings necessary for proper engagement with the responsibility placed upon them. Effective professional induction for the teaching role lays down practical approaches, values and frameworks capable of further development, and provides tools for the analysis of complex situations and changing circumstances. Periodic enhancement of these conceptual tools and performance skills throughout a career helps ensure that individuals continue to be effective in the face of new demands and rising public expectations. The fact that many academic staff have developed competence in teaching in the absence of such systematic induction, upgrading and updating is a weak justification to preserve the status quo.

Finally, it needs to be acknowledged that professionals in all walks of life engage with career-long development of their knowledge and practice base because it is a necessary component in the maintenance of quality, standards and service. As many in higher education already know, self-regulation and a degree of professional autonomy flourish where there is widespread confidence that teachers fulfil their responsibilities to learners. In this form of social contract, critical dialogue, peer appraisal and voluntary professional development for teaching are key elements in building a shared community of interests. Over a working lifetime a competent teacher will influence many hundreds of students and his or her ability to teach well represents an incalculable investment in human capital. That capital lives on in the attitudes, actions and thinking of the next generation; its formation cannot be left to happenstance.

REFERENCES

Alexander, S and McKenzie, J (1998) *An Evaluation of Information Technology Projects for University Learning*, Committee for University Teaching and Staff Development, Canberra, Australia

AUT (Association of University Teachers) (1996) *Professional Accreditation of University Teachers: A Discussion Document*, (November) AUT, London

Barnett, R (1997) *Higher Education: A Critical Business*, SRHE/OU, Buckingham

Biggs, J (1994) Student learning research and theory: where do we stand? in *Improving Student Learning: Theory and Practice* ed G Gibbs, pp 1–19, Oxford Centre for Staff Development, Oxford

Bowden, J and Marton, F (1998) *The University of Learning: Beyond Quality and Competence in Higher Education*, Kogan Page, London

Boyer, EL (1990a) *Scholarship Reconsidered: Priorities for the Professoriate*, Carnegie Foundation, Princeton NJ

Boyer, EL (1990b) Teaching's renewed role in evaluation of learning, *Times Higher Education Supplement*, p13, 21/12/90

Connor, H, Pearson, R, Court, G and Jagger, N (1996) *University Challenges: Student Choices in the 21st Century*, a report to CVCP, Institute for Employment Studies, Brighton

Elton, L and Partington, P (1993) *Teaching Standards and Excellence in Higher Education: Developing a Culture for Quality*, 2nd edn, CVCP/USD, Sheffield

Entwistle, N (1994) The use of research on student learning in quality assessment, in *Improving Student Learning: Theory and Practice*, ed G Gibbs, pp 24–43, Oxford Centre for Staff Development, Oxford

Entwistle, N (1998) Conceptions of teaching for academic development: the role of research, in *Development Training for Academic Staff*, ed KJ Gregory, pp 23–32, Goldsmiths College, London

Eraut, M (1994) *Developing Professional Knowledge and Competence*, Falmer, London

Gibbs, G (1994) *Improving Student Learning: Theory and Practice*, Oxford Centre for Staff Development, Oxford

Gibbs, G (1996) Promoting excellent teachers at Oxford Brookes University: from profiles to peer review in ten years, in *Evaluating Teacher Quality in Higher Education*, eds R Aylett and K Gregory, pp 42–66, Falmer, London

Gregory, K (1998) (ed) *Development Training for Academic Staff*, Goldsmiths College, London

Griffiths, S (1996) *The Professional Development of Academic Staff in their Role as Teachers*, Universities and Colleges Staff Development Agency, Sheffield

Hazel, E (1995) Improving laboratory teaching, in *Teaching Improvement Practices: Successful Strategies for Higher Education*, ed A Wright, pp 155–79, Anker Publishing Co, Bolton, MA

Hounsell, D (1996) Documenting and assessing excellent teachers, in *Evaluating Teacher Quality in Higher Education*, ed R Aylett and K Gregory, pp 72–76, Falmer, London

Jenkins, A (1996) Discipline-based educational development, *The International Journal for Academic Development* **1** (1), pp 50–62

Jessup, G (1991) *Outcomes: NVQs and the Emerging Model of Education and Training*, Falmer, London

Knowles, M (1990) *The Adult Learner: A Neglected Species*, 4th ed, Gulf Publishing Co, Houston

Luby, A (1997) T*owards an Accreditation System for Professional Development for Academic Practice in Higher Education*, COSHEP/SHEFC/UCoSDA

Martin, G and Double, JM (1998) Developing higher education teaching skills through peer observation and collaborative reflection, *Innovations in Education and Training International*, **35** (2), pp 161–69

Marton, F and Booth, S (1997) *Learning and Awareness*, Laurence Erlbaum, NJ

Marton, F, Hounsell, D, Entwistle, N (eds) (1997) *The Experience of Learning: Implications for Teaching and Studying in Higher Education*, 2nd ed, Scottish Academic Press, Edinburgh

Moses, I (1990) Teaching, research and scholarship in different disciplines, *Higher Education*, **19** (3), pp 351–75

NCIHE (1997) (Dearing Report) *Higher Education in the Learning Society*, National Committee of Inquiry into Higher Education, HMSO, London

Nightingale, P and O'Neil, M (1994) *Achieving Quality Learning in Higher Education*, Kogan Page, London

Nyquist, JD (1996) *Working Effectively with Graduate Assistants*, Sage, London

Pennington, G (1994) Developing learning agents, in *Achieving Quality Learning in Higher Education*, eds P Nightingale and M O'Neil, pp 41–52, Kogan Page, London

Pennington, G (1997) Quality assessment of higher education practice: Scylla or Charybdis?, *Psychology Teaching Review*, **6** (1), pp 5–13

Pennington, G (1998) Towards a national accreditation framework for higher education teaching, in *Evaluating Teacher Quality in Higher Education*, eds R Aylett and K Gregory, pp 13–18, Falmer, London

Pennington, G and Calderon, D (1994) *Improving Learning in Higher Education*, Universities Staff Development Unit, Sheffield

Pyle, D (1999) *Supporting the Development of a National Institute for Learning and Teaching: A Report to the DfEE (NTO) Division*, Universities and Colleges Staff Development Agency, Sheffield

Ramsden, P, Margetson, D, Martin, E and Clarke, S (1995) *Recognising and Rewarding Good Teaching in Australian Higher Education*, Committee for University Teaching and Staff Development, Canberra, Australia

Randall, J (1998) Developing academic staff: the role of national standards of competent performance, in *Evaluating Teacher Quality in Higher Education*, eds R Aylett and K Gregory, pp 19–21, Falmer, London

Rowland, S (1996) Relationships between teaching and research, *Teaching in Higher Education*, **1** (1), pp 7-20

Smith, B (1998) *Report of the FDTL Project 'Sharing Excellence'*, Nottingham Trent University

Trigwell, K, Prosser, M and Taylor, P (1994) Qualitative differences in approaches to teaching first year university science, *Higher Education*, **27** pp 78–82

Warwick, D (1999) Does more mean worse? *The Guardian, Education Guardian*, 16 February, p iii

Williams, G and Fry, H (1994) *Longer Term Prospects for British Higher Education*, Committee of Vice-Chancellors and Principals, London

Wright, AW (1995) *Teaching Improvement Practices: Successful Strategies for Higher Education*, Anker Publishing Co, Boston, USA

Zuber-Skerrit, O (1992) *Professional Development in Higher Education: A Theoretical Framework for Action Research*, Kogan Page, London

Part 1
Development
of Practice

3 Understanding Student Learning

Heather Fry, Steve Ketteridge and
Stephanie Marshall

INTRODUCTION

It is unfortunate, but true, that some academics teach students without having much formal knowledge of how students learn. Many lecturers know how *they* learn best, but do not necessarily consider how *their students* learn and if the way they teach is predicated on enabling learning to happen.

Learning is about how we perceive and understand the world, about making meaning (Marton and Booth, 1997). It can be about abstract principles, factual information, the acquisition of methods, techniques and approaches, about ideas, behaviour appropriate to types of situations, recognition, and finally, about reasoning.

Despite many years of research into learning, it is not easy to translate this knowledge into practical implications for teaching. This is because education deals with students as people, who are diverse in all respects, and ever changing. Not everyone learns in the same way, or equally readily about all types of material. The discipline and level of material to be learnt also have an influence on learning. Students bring different backgrounds and expectations to learning. There are no simple answers to the questions 'how do we learn?' and 'how as teachers can we bring about learning?' Our knowledge about the relationship between teaching and learning is still incomplete, but we do know enough about learning to be able to make some firm statements about types of action that will usually be helpful in enabling learning to happen.

Most teachers will recognize that motivation and assessment both play a large part in student learning in higher education and these are considered, particularly, in Chapter 6.

We draw on research specific to students in higher education and also mention some aspects of **adult learning**. However, higher education teachers need to be aware that less mature students (in age or behaviour) may not be 'adult learners' and that some of the evidence about adult learning is less than robust.

This chapter is not written for (or by) academic psychologists but is intended to give a simplified overview of what we know about student learning and the implications this has for teaching. It sets out to (a) present and review some of the common models and ideas related to learning in higher education; and (b) indicate the broad implications of these ideas for selecting teaching and assessment methods and strategies.

Interrogating Practice

As you read this chapter, note down, from what it says about learning, what the implications for teaching might be in your discipline. When you reach the last section of the chapter, compare your list with the general suggestions you will find there.

VIEWS OF LEARNING

In the literature there are three main schools of thought about how learning takes place. Of these the most prominent is constructivism.

Constructivism

Most contemporary psychologists use constructivist theories of one type or another to explain how human beings learn. The idea rests on the notion of continuous building and amending of previous structures, or schemata, as new experience, actions and knowledge are assimilated and accommodated. **Constructivism** stems in part from the work done by Kant over 200 years ago, who thought that experience leads to the formation of general conceptions or constructs that are models of reality. Unless schemata are amended, learning will not occur. Learning (whether in **cognitive, affective, interpersonal** or **psychomotor domains**) involves a process of individual transformation. Thus people actively construct their knowledge (Biggs and Moore, 1993). Piaget (1950) and Bruner (1960, 1966) are two of the 20th century's most prominent constructivists. For example, Bruner's ideas relating to inducting students into the modes of thinking in individual disciplines and his notion of revisiting knowledge at ever-higher levels of understanding, leading to the idea of a spiral curriculum, have been very influential. In the discipline of history, for instance, Bruner is often cited as the inspiration for changing the focus of history teaching in schools. This shifted the balance from regurgitation of factual information to understanding. Some of the ways in which this was done were to encourage learners to understand how the past is reconstructed and understood, for example by learning how to empathize and to work from primary sources. Most of the current ideas about student learning, including **experiential learning**, the use of **reflection**, etc, are based in constructivism.

Constructivism tells us that we learn by fitting new understanding and knowledge into, with, extending and supplanting, old understanding and knowledge. As lecturers we need to be aware that we are rarely if ever 'writing on a blank slate', however rudimentary or wrong pre-existing related knowledge and understanding are. Without changes or additions to pre-existing knowledge and understanding, no learning will have occurred.

Very frequently learning is thought of in terms of adding more knowledge, whereas teachers should be thinking of bringing about change or transformation to pre-existing knowledge (Mezirow, 1991). Additions to knowledge, in the sense of accumulated 'fact', may be possible without substantial change, any learning of a higher order, involving understanding or creativity, for example, can usually only happen when the underlying schemata are themselves changed to incorporate this new understanding. Such change will itself facilitate retention of facts for the longer term (see approaches to study, below). Chalmers and Fuller (1996) provide a succinct and useful account of some of these ideas.

Interrogating Practice

Think of one or two occasions when you feel you have gained real mastery or insight into a particular aspect of your discipline. Would you say that this was only by addition, or involved a change of pre-existing understanding?

Other views of learning

Rationalism (or idealism) is an alternative school, or pole, of learning theory still with some vogue. It is based on the idea of a biological plan being in existence that unfolds in very determined directions. Chomsky is a foremost proponent of this pole. Associatism, a third pole, centres on the idea of forming associations between stimuli and responses. Pavlov and Skinner belong to this pole. Further details of such theories may be found in Richardson (1985).

Case Study 1: Programme in Academic Practice

Queen Mary and Westfield College, University of London

Below are some statements about student learning. We use these to challenge attitudes of new staff and help them unpack their perceptions of learning. Staff (during a workshop in the induction phase) are asked for their reaction to each statement.

Student learning is:

- quantitative increase in factual knowledge;
- memorization and reproduction;
- applying and using knowledge;
- acquisition of skills and methods;
- making sense and understanding;
- abstracting meaning;
- understanding or comprehending the world in a different way;
- performing well in assessment;
- solving problems;
- developing creativity;
- extending imagination;
- developing an analytical approach;
- changing within oneself as a consequence of understanding the world differently.

We ask staff to think about their own views, to discuss them with their neighbours and then to participate in a whole group discussion. Initially, discussion usually highlights some differences between disciplines in the importance attached to individual statements. However, as discussion progresses, usually a consensus view emerges in which most staff, irrespective of discipline, strongly support the view that student learning involves most of these things.

(Heather Fry and Steve Ketteridge)

ADULT LEARNING THEORY

It is questionable how far there really are theories of adult learning. On one hand it is debatable how far the learning of adults is sufficiently distinct from the learning of others, and on the other hand, some of the axioms of adult learning are indeed axioms rather than theory (see Bright, 1989, especially Brookfield). Despite this, there are propositions concerning the learning of adults which have had much influence on higher education, if only to cause teachers in that sector to reexamine their premises and adjust some of their views. Adult learning theories have also been thought by some to be increasingly relevant as non-traditional participants (whether considered by age, mode of study or ethnic, economic or educational background) increase as a proportion of traditional students.

Malcolm Knowles is associated with the use of the term **andragogy** (despite its much earlier aetiology) to refer to this area. His most quoted definition of andragogy is as the 'art and science of helping adults learn' (Knowles, 1984). One of the complications of the area is that he has changed his definition over time. From his work spanning more than 30 years, andragogy is considered to have five principles:

1. As a person matures they become more self-directed.
2. Adults have accumulated experiences which can be a rich resource for learning.
3. Adults become ready to learn when they experience a need to know something.
4. Adults tend to be less subject-centred than children; they are increasingly problem-centred.
5. For adults the most potent motivators are internal.

There is a lack of empirical evidence to support these views. Despite many critiques of andragogy and the problems of its definition (eg, see Davenport, 1993) it has had considerable influence. Many 'types' of learning that are much used and discussed in higher education, including experiential learning, student **autonomy** in learning and **self-directed learning**, belong in the tradition of adult education. (Furthermore, considerable areas of work in higher education around the student experience, supporting students, and widening participation are also closely linked to work which has its origins in adult education, eg barriers to entry and progression.)

EXPERIENTIAL LEARNING

It is self-evident that experience gained through life, education and work plays a central role in the process of learning and this perspective on learning is called 'experiential learning' or 'learning by doing' (see also Chapter 11). Probably the most popular theory of learning from experience can be attributed to David Kolb (1984) who progressed ideas from other models of experiential learning.

An appreciation of experiential learning is necessary to underpin many of the different types of teaching activity discussed elsewhere in this book, including **work-based learning**, teaching **laboratory** and practical work, **action learning**, **role play** and many types of **small group teaching**. The Kolb model frequently appears in the literature, often modified to accommodate particular types of learning (or training) experiences and using alternative or simplified terminology (eg Coles, 1998; Race, 1994 and 1996).

Experiential learning is based on the notion that ideas are not fixed or unchangeable elements of thought but are formed and re-formed through 'experience'. It is also a continuous process, often represented as cyclical, and, being based on experience, implies that we all bring to learning situations our own ideas and beliefs at different levels of elaboration.

The cyclical model of learning that has become known as the 'Kolb Learning Cycle' (see Figure 3.1) requires four kinds of abilities/undertaking if learning is to be successful. Learning requires:

- concrete experience (CE);
- reflective observation (RO);
- abstract conceptualization (AC);
- active experimentation (AE).

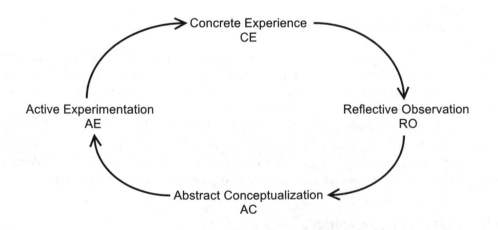

Figure 3.1 The Kolb Learning Cycle

But what do these terms mean? First, learners are involved fully and freely in new experiences (CE). Second, they must make/have the time and space to be able to reflect (RO) on their experience from different perspectives. It is this element in the cycle that will be strongly influenced by **feedback** from others. Third, learners must be able to form and re-form, process their ideas, take ownership of them and integrate their new ideas into sound, logical theories (AC). This moves towards the fourth point (AE), using theories to make decisions and problem-solve, test implications in new situations, all of which generate material for the starting point for the next round, the concrete experience again. Thus the experiential cycle does not simply involve doing, but also reflecting, processing, thinking and understanding. By extension, this cyclical process has a part to play in even the most abstract and theoretical disciplines where the academic is concerned to help the learner acquire the 'tools of the trade' or the modes of thinking central to the discipline, such as in philosophy or literary criticism.

All four stages of the process are necessary for effective learning to be achieved. This leads to the question: is it possible to be at two points in the cycle at one time? For example, can one act and reflect at the same time? Is it possible to be at the concrete experience stage in the cycle and be undertaking abstract conceptualization together? These are pairs of very different types of ability, described by some as polar opposites in the learning process, and the learner may have to choose which one to allow to dominate in the particular learning situation (see Chapter 16). The way in which the learner resolves these tensions will have an effect on the learning outcome and the development of different types of strength in the learner and, as will be seen, may pertain to personality traits and/or disciplinary differences.

Wolf and Kolb (1984) have suggested that learners develop different learning styles that emphasize preference for some modes of learning over others, leading to the following characteristics.

Table 3.1 Learning styles (based on Wolf and Kolb, 1984)

Learning style	Strengths	Dominant learning ability
Convergent	Practical application of ideas	AC and AE
Divergent	Imaginative ability and generation of ideas	CE and RO
Assimilation	Creating theoretical models and making sense of disparate observations	AC and RO
Accommodative	Carrying out plans and tasks that involve them in new experiences	CE and AE

Clearly those responsible for organizing learning need to be able to create opportunities for learning that are sensitive to these different styles of learning. However, it should not be forgotten that even though learners may have different preferences, for effective learning, they will need to be encouraged to move through all the constituent elements in the learning cycle.

The preferred learning style of an individual may bear some relationship to the particular disciplinary framework in which the learning is taking place. Becher (1989) brings together the work of two principal authors as the 'Kolb-Biglan Classification of Academic Knowledge'. This classification would seem to suggest that the preferred learning style might be attributable to a relationship with a particular disciplinary framework. Accepting this classification implies that encouragement in different elements of the learning cycle needs to be taken into account when planning experiential learning opportunities in different disciplines.

Table 3.2 Classification of academic knowledge

[1] Abstract Reflective	[2] Concrete Reflective
AC–RO	CE–RO
Hard Pure	*Soft Pure*
Natural Sciences	Humanities
Mathematics	Social Sciences

[3] Abstract Active	[4] Concrete Active
AC–AE	CE-AE
Hard Applied	*Soft Applied*
Science-based professions, Engineering,	Social professions
Medicine and other health care	Education, Social Work
professions	Law

Based on Kolb-Biglan Model described by Becher (1989).

The distribution in the four quadrants is interesting, in that those in quadrants 1 and 2 are described as showing some preference for reflective practice. However, we must ask ourselves, noting that some of the disciplines mentioned in quadrants 3 and 4 are now strongly associated with reflective practice, just how useful this classification really is. Perhaps the lesson to learn is that there are likely to be disciplinary differences in these characteristics that may be difficult to classify. How far students acquire, are attracted to, or bring with them to a subject any of the associated ways of thinking, or 'frames of mind', is a difficult matter (see Gardner's classic work, 1985). There is another issue concerning transitions in students' learning styles and Nulty and Barrett (1996) present some recent research findings in this area.

Reflection and **reflective practice** are not easy concepts for the lecturer in higher education, either in respect of their own professional development or the learning of their students. Support in their development is often necessary (see Chapters 11 and 16).

Schon (1987), in examining the relationship between professional knowledge and professional **competence**, suggests that rather than looking to another body of research knowledge, practitioners should become more adept at observing and learning through reflection on the artistry of their own particular profession. Reflection on practice (on experience) is central to the development of professions for two reasons: first, recognized 'experts' in the field exhibit distinct artistry and, second, this artistry cannot be learned through traditional models – it can only be learned through observation of competent practitioners, through practice and reflection.

Interrogating Practice

Call to mind three occasions when conscious reflection on something you have experienced (in the street, the laboratory, on the television, from reading, etc) has enhanced your understanding or ability to carry out a particular task.

APPROACHES TO STUDY AND LEARNING STYLES

Approaches to study

In the 1970s, Marton (1975) conducted empirical work that has subsequently gained much credibility and currency in higher education. Considerable subsequent work has taken place since then (eg Marton and Saljo, 1984). This research, investigating the interaction between student and a set learning task, led to the conclusion that students' approaches to the task (their intention) determined the extent to which they engaged with their subject and thus affected the quality of outcomes. These approaches to study/learning were classified as deep or surface.

The former, the **deep approach** to learning, is typified as an intention to understand and seek meaning, leading students to attempt to relate concepts to existing experience, distinguishing between new ideas and existing knowledge, and critically evaluating and determining key themes and concepts. In summary, such an approach results from the students' intention to gain maximum meaning from their studying, which they achieve through high levels of cognitive processing throughout the learning activity. Facts are learnt in the context of meaning.

The latter, the **surface approach** to learning, is typified as an intention to complete the task, memorize information, make no distinction between new ideas and existing knowledge; and to treat the task as externally imposed (as extrinsic). Rote learning is the typical surface approach. In summary, such an approach results from the students' intention to offer the impression that maximum learning has taken place, which they achieve through superficial levels of cognitive processing. Facts are learned outwith a meaningful framework.

An illustration provides illumination of these concepts. The learning outcomes for, say, social science students, who adopt a deep approach to the task of reading a set text, would include full engagement with the central theme of the text and an understanding of contributing arguments. In contrast, those who adopt a surface approach would fail to identify the central themes primarily because they would be engrossed in progressing through the text sequentially, attempting to remember the flat landscape of facts.

The conceptions of deep and surface learning have increased in sophistication with further research, most notably the work of Biggs (1987) and Ramsden (1988). Ramsden (1992: 47–48) gives useful examples of statements from students in different disciplines exhibiting deep and surface approaches.

Biggs and Ramsden turned learning theory on its head in that rather than drawing on the work of philosophers or cognitive psychologists, they looked to the students themselves for a distinctive perspective. Ramsden (1988) suggested that approach to learning was not implicit in the make-up of the student, but something between the student and the task and thus was both personal and situational. An approach to learning should not, therefore, be seen as an individual characteristic but rather a response to the teaching environment in which the student is expected to learn. Biggs (1987) identified a third approach to study – the **strategic**, or **achieving approach**. Here the emphasis is on organizing learning specifically to obtain a high grade. With this intention, a deep learner may adopt some of the techniques of the surface learner to meet the requirements of a specific activity such as a test. Thus taking a deep approach is not a fixed and unchanging characteristic. The achieving approach is intimately associated with assessment.

One of the greatest misconceptions on the part of many students is their belief that a subject consists of large amounts of factual knowledge and, to become the expert, all one need do is add this knowledge to one's existing store. It is the responsibility of the teacher to challenge and change such conceptions and to ensure that their teaching, the curricula they design, and the assessments they set, do not seem to echo this perspective. Biggs and Moore (1993: 314) are firmly of the view that approaches to learning can be modified by the teaching and learning context, and are themselves learnt. They contrast approaches to learning (modifiable) with learning styles (fixed and part of personality characteristics and traits). There has been much debate and publication in this area in recent years. For further discussion and consideration of the implications see Prosser and Trigwell (1999). In these circumstances the current state of play dictates that neither should be regarded as fixed, but both the approach to learning and learning style may be habituated and may not be easy to change.

Learning styles

There have been several different categorizations of learning style. That of Wolf and Kolb is described above, another categorization is described in Chapter 16, and many readers will have heard of a third which opposes serialist and holist learning styles (Pask, 1976). A serialist is said to prefer a step-by-step approach and a narrow focus while holists prefer to obtain the 'big picture' and work with illustrations and analogies.

However, perhaps the best known categorization of learning style is that of Honey and Mumford (1982). They offer a four-fold classification of activist, pragmatist, reflector, and theorist:

- Activists respond most positively to learning situations offering challenge, to include new experiences and problems, excitement and freedom in their learning.
- Reflectors respond most positively to structured learning activities where they are provided with time to observe, reflect and think, and allowed to work in a detailed manner.
- Theorists respond well to logical, rational structure and clear aims, where they are given time for methodical exploration and opportunities to question and stretch their intellect.
- Pragmatists respond most positively to practically-based, immediately relevant learning activities, which allow scope for practice and using theory.

It is anticipated that the preferred learning style of any individual will include elements from two or more of these four categories.

An awareness of learning styles is important for the teacher planning a course module, as a variety of strategies to promote learning should be considered.

Teachers also need to be aware that changing firmly-established patterns of behaviour and views of the world can prove destabilizing for the learner who is then engaged in something rather more than cognitive restructuring (Perry, 1979).

Approaches and styles

Many of those who have worked with learning styles and approaches to learning have developed questionnaire-type taxonomies, or inventories, for identifying the approach or style being used by the learner. These have limited use if one regards the underlying concepts, and understanding of whether the characteristics are learnt or inherent, as in a state of flux. This has not prevented lecturers using them to 'diagnose' student learning. Their use does have the advantage of helping students to think about how they best learn and whether they would benefit from trying to modify their behaviour. Those who are interested might wish to see the 'Approaches to Study Inventory' (Entwistle and Ramsden,1983) or Honey and Mumford (1982).

Whenever encountering the term 'learning style', it is important to be clear about which categorization is being referred to and not to confuse learning style with approaches to study/learning.

Interrogating Practice

Think of occasions when you have chosen to use a deep approach to learning. Think of other occasions when you have used a surface approach and consider how many of these involved an achieving intention.

TEACHING FOR LEARNING

'It is important to remember that what the student does is actually more important in determining what is learned than what the teacher does.' (Sheull, cited in Biggs 1993.) This statement is congruent with a constructivist view and reminds us that students in higher education must engage with and take some responsibility for their learning. The teacher cannot do all the work if learning is to be the outcome. As designers of courses and as teachers, if we want to 'produce' graduates of higher education able to think, act, create and innovate at a relatively high level, then we need to consider how we lead learners beyond being regurgitator, copyist or operative. These and many more related issues have been highlighted by Ronald Barnett over the last decade (see, for example Barnett, 1994, 1997). These imperatives, coupled with those of our discipline, should affect our view of what constitutes good teaching in higher education.

> ## Case Study 2: Survey of Views of Good Teaching in Higher Education

Queen Mary and Westfield College, University of London, and the University of York.

Two of the authors, in ongoing work, have collected the perceptions of 55 staff new to teaching at two traditional universities The survey has been administered to staff attending teaching and learning induction programmes since 1997. The part of the work reported here consisted of providing new teachers with a list of 35 statements describing what good teaching might be and asking them to indicate:

- which of the statements they agreed to be a component of good teaching in higher education; and
- to select five of the statements which taken together represented most closely their view of what good teaching in their discipline was.

Table 3.3   What is good teaching in higher education?

Good teaching is:	Per cent of respondents selecting each statement (n=55)	Overall rank order of statements	Rank order as one of five statements to best describe personal teaching stance in relation to discipline
1. Making the material you are teaching stimulating and interesting	96	1	1
2. Engaging the students at their level of understanding	71	18=	14=

Table 3.3 continued

3. Explaining the material plainly	62	22=	7=
4. Making it clear what has to be understood, at what level and why	76	10=	10=
5. Showing concern for your students	66	21	16=
6. Showing respect for your students	91	5	14=
7. Taking account of students with different abilities	89	6	13
8. Facilitating students to draw upon their own experience	60	24	20=
9. Improving and adapting when the immediate situation demands	75	12=	31=
10. Updating and responding to new demands	75	12=	7=
11. Inducting students into a discipline	44	33	26=
12. Using teaching methods and academic tasks that require students to think for themselves	95	2=	2
13. Using teaching methods and academic tasks that require students to work together co-operatively	58	25=	23=

Table 3.3 continued

14. Using teaching methods and academic tasks that require students to take responsibility for their own learning	84	7	6
15. Raising ethical considerations when appropriate	55	28=	31=
16. Helping students to engage actively with what is being learned	75	12=	4
17. Making sure learners know what we expect them to achieve	76	10=	10=
18. Using appropriate assessment methods	78	8=	20=
19. Sharing your love of the subject with your students	58	25=	16=
20. Developing student skills for the workplace	49	32	16=
21. Stretching your students	58	25=	16=
22. Focusing on key concepts	73	16=	7=
23. Promoting students' understanding	75	12=	10=
24. Covering the ground	35	35	0
25. Motivating your students	93	4	3

Table 3.3 continued

26. Enabling students to take away good sets of lecture notes	40	34	23=
27. Giving prompt feedback to students on their work	73	16=	20=
28. Transmitting information	53	30	0
29. Learning from students	55	28=	28=
30. Understanding students' needs	62	22=	28=
31. Getting it better next time round	71	18=	23=
32. Remembering equal opportunities are important	51	31	0
33. Developing creativity in students	67	20	28=
34. Being available to students at times you have agreed	78	8=	26=
35. Being well prepared for the session	95	2=	5

Participants came from a range of disciplines, including arts and humanities, languages, social sciences, science and engineering, and health professions. Numbers are insufficient to warrant analysis on a disciplinary basis, nevertheless some interesting features emerge. In particular, 'explaining the material plainly' (statement 3), 'helping students to engage actively with what is being learned' (16), 'developing student skills for the workplace' (20), and 'focusing on key concepts' (22), were selected by relatively fewer respondents in a global ordering of components of good teaching, but selected by a relatively larger proportion of respondents as being a key part of their view of what teaching in their discipline is about. Conversely 'showing respect for your students' (6), 'improving and adapting when the immediate situation demands' (9), 'using appropriate assessment methods' (18) and 'being available to students at times you have agreed' (34) were statements selected by a large proportion of respondents as being elements of good teaching, but only highly ranked by a few as being one of five selected statements to best describe their view of what good teaching is. Three statements were not selected as a key part of personal views of what good teaching is, numbers 24, 28 and 32.

The survey shows that new academics regarded as highly important and ranked highly on both scales:

- 'making the material you are teaching stimulating and interesting' (1);
- 'using teaching methods and academic tasks that require students to think for themselves' (12);
- 'being well prepared for the session' (35);
- 'motivating your students' (25).

The results of the survey provide evidence that many new staff bring with them an awareness of some of the key components of teaching that are likely to promote effective learning.

(Heather Fry and Steve Ketteridge)

All too often, discussions of teaching in higher education centre on the premise that learning is only, or primarily, about the acquisition of more and more factual information. The onus is on us to be discriminating in selecting methods of teaching, assessment and course design to bring about the types of learning we desire. General advice about teaching should not be plucked out of thin air, but grounded in theories about learning. Notable among the precepts that emerge from what we understand about how students learn are the following:

- Learners experience the same teaching in different ways.
- Learners will approach learning in a variety of ways and the ways we teach may modify their approaches.
- Teachers may need to extend/modify the approach of many learners.
- Learners have to be brought to 'engage' with what they are learning so that transformation and internalization can occur.

- Learners bring valuable experience to learning.
- Learners may be more motivated when offered an element of choice.
- Learners need to be able to explain their answers and answer 'why' questions.
- Learners taking a discipline that is new to them may struggle to think in the appropriate manner (an important point in modular programmes).
- Teachers need to understand where learners are starting from so that they can get the correct level and seek to correct underlying misconceptions or gaps.
- Teachers and learners are both responsible for learning happening and students must take/have some responsibility for learning.
- Teachers need to be aware of the impact of cultural background and beliefs on learner behaviour, interpretation and understanding.
- Feedback is important in enabling the teacher and learner to check that accommodations of new understanding are 'correct' (peer feedback can be very important here too).
- Prior knowledge needs to be activated.
- Learning best takes place in a relevant context (to facilitate the 'making of meaning').
- When planning, specifying outcomes, teaching or assessing, teachers need to consider all appropriate domains and to be aware of the level of operations being asked for.
- The learning climate/environment in which learners learn affects the outcomes (eg, motivation, interaction, support, etc).
- Reduce the amount of didactic teaching.
- Avoid content overload, too much material will encourage a surface approach.
- Basic principles and concepts provide the basis for further learning.
- Assessment has a powerful impact on student behaviour.

OVERVIEW

What is important about teaching is what it helps the learner to do, know or understand. There are different models of learning that teachers need to be aware of. What we do as teachers must take into account what we know about how students learn.

REFERENCES

Barnett, R (1994) *The Limits of Competence*, Society for Research into Higher Education/ Open University Press, Buckingham

Barnett, R (1997) *Higher Education: A Critical Business*, Society for Research into Higher Education/Open University Press, Buckingham

Becher, T (1989) *Academic Tribes and Territories*, Society for Research in Higher Education/Open University Press, Buckingham

Biggs, J (1987) *Student Approaches to Learning and Studying*, Australian Council for Educational Research, Hawthorn, Victoria

Biggs, J (1993) From theory to practice: a cognitive systems approach, *Higher Education Research and Development* (Australia), **12** (1), pp 73–85

Biggs, J and Moore, P (1993) *The Process of Learning*, Prentice-Hall, New York

Bright, B (ed) (1989) *Theory and Practice in the Study of Adult Education: The Epistemological Debate*, Routledge, London

Brookfield, S (1989) The epistemology of adult education in the United States and Great Britain: a cross-cultural analysis, in *Theory and Practice in the Study of Adult Education: The Epistemological Debate*, ed B Bright, pp 141–73, Routledge, London

Bruner, JS (1960) *The Process of Education*, Harvard University Press, Cambridge, Mass

Bruner, JS (1966) *Towards a Theory of Instruction*, Harvard University Press, Cambridge, Mass

Chalmers, D and Fuller, R (1996) *Teaching for Learning at University*, Kogan Page, London

Coles, C (1998) The process of learning, in *Medical Education in the Millennium*, eds B Jolly and L Rees, pp 63–82, Oxford University Press, Oxford

Davenport, J (1993) Is there any way out of the andragogy morass?, in *Culture and Processes of Adult Learning*, eds M Thorpe, R Edwards, and A Hanson, pp 109–17, Routledge, London

Entwistle, N and Ramsden, P (1983) *Understanding Student Learning*, Croom Helm, London

Gardner, H (1985) *Frames of Mind*, Paladin, London

Honey, P and Mumford, A (1982) *The Manual of Learning Styles*, Peter Honey, Maidenhead

Knowles, M and Associates (1984) *Andragogy in Action*, Gulf Publishing Co, Houston

Kolb, DA (1984) *Experiential Learning*, Prentice-Hall, Englewood Cliffs, New Jersey

Marton, F (1975) On non-verbatim learning – 1: level of processing and level of outcome, *Scandinavian Journal of Psychology*, **16**, pp 273–79

Marton, F and Booth, S (1997) *Learning and Awareness*, Lawrence Erlbaum Associates, Mihwah, New Jersey

Marton, F and Saljo, R (1984) Approaches to learning, in *The Experiences of Learning*, eds F Marton, D Hounsell, and N Entwistle, Scottish Academic Press, Edinburgh

Mezirow, J (1991) *Transformative Dimensions of Adult Learning*, Jossey-Bass Publishers, San Francisco

Nulty, DD and Barrett, MA (1996) Transitions in students' learning styles, *Studies in Higher Education*, **21**, pp 333–44

Pask, G (1976) Learning styles and strategies, *British Journal of Educational Psychology*, **46**, pp 4–11

Perry, W (1979) *Forms of Intellectual and Ethical Development in the College Years*, Holt, Rinehart and Winston, New York

Piaget, J (1950) *The Psychology of Intelligence*, Routledge and Kegan Paul, London

Prosser, M and Trigwell, K (1999) *Understanding Learning and Teaching: The Experience in Higher Education*, Society for Research into Higher Education/Open University Press, Buckingham

Race, P (1994) *The Open Learning Handbook*, 2nd edn, Kogan Page, London

Race, P (1996) How does learning happen best? Deliberations website at http://www.lgu.ac.uk/deliberations/eff.learning/

Ramsden, P (1988) *Improving Learning: New Perspectives*, Kogan Page, London
Ramsden, P (1992) *Learning to Teach in Higher Education*, Routledge, London
Richardson, K (1985) *Personality, Development and Learning: Unit 8/9 Learning Theories*, Open University Press, Milton Keynes
Schon, D (1987) *Educating the Reflective Practitioner: Toward a New Design for Teaching and Learning in the Professionss*, Jossey-Bass Publishers, San Francisco
Wolf, DM and Kolb, DA (1984) Career development, personal growth and experiential learning, in *Organisational Psychology: Readings on Human Behaviour*, 4th edn, eds D Kolb, I Rubin, and J McIntyre, Prentice-Hall, Englewood Cliffs, New Jersey

FURTHER READING

Biggs, J (1999) *Teaching for Quality Learning at University*, Society for Research into Higher Education/Open University Press, Buckingham. A well regarded author in the field.
Chalmers, D and Fuller, R (1996) *Teaching for Learning at University*, Kogan Page, London. Part One is a useful introduction to student learning and its impact on teaching and assessment. The rest of the book considers the teaching of learning skills.
Gibbs, G (1994) (ed) *Improving Student Learning*, Oxford Centre for Staff Development, Oxford. Many contributions from leading authorities on student learning.
Ramsden, P (1992) *Learning to Teach in Higher Education*, Routledge, London. Still much valuable discussion of student learning, despite date.

Organizing Teaching and Learning: Outcomes-based Planning

Vaneeta-Marie D'Andrea

ORGANIZING TEACHING AND LEARNING

Organizing teaching is really about designing learning. Designing learning is one of the most fundamental activities of a university teacher. Often, due to pressures of time, preparing to teach is given less time and consideration than implementing and evaluating the teaching/learning process. Furthermore, the language of pedagogic design has historically been off-putting to most academics, seeming little more than educational jargon at best, and 'mumbo-jumbo' at worst. Despite the jargon, the aim of pedagogic design to assist in the development of conscious and purposeful teaching and learning is a laudable one, especially if the learning outcomes achieved are improved by so doing.

Teaching involves helping students to know something not known before, it constitutes a process of change. These intentions are most often implicit or inferred. The conscious planning of teaching and learning make these intentions explicit. As will be discussed, making teaching/learning intentions more explicit improves the learning experience of students. The current terminology for approaching the design of teaching and learning in this fashion is 'outcomes-based planning'. The discussion that follows will focus on the use of this approach for the organization of teaching and learning in higher education.

Aims, objectives and outcomes of this chapter

The primary **aim** of this chapter is to review the principles and practices of **course/module** design in order to provide higher education staff, with teaching responsibilities, with a foundation for developing an outcomes-based planning approach to the organization of teaching and learning.

The **objectives/outcomes** of this chapter can be specified as follows. It is expected that as a result of working through this chapter, the reader will be able to:

- state the rationale for using an outcomes-based approach to organizing teaching and learning in higher education;
- write learning objectives/outcomes for a course/module that clearly communicate to those with responsibilities for teaching and to students and other interested parties, the explicit intention of a teaching and learning experience;
- identify the links between objectives/outcomes, student characteristics, course/module content, teaching and learning strategies, course/module assessment methods;
- evaluate the usefulness of an outcomes-based approach to teaching and learning, for students, themselves, their subject, and other interested benefactors of higher education provision.

OUTCOMES-BASED PLANNING: THE BACKGROUND

The findings of the Higher Education Quality Council (HEQC) Graduate Standards Programme (1997) and the Dearing Report (NCIHE, 1997) echo decades of debate, both in the United Kingdom and abroad, on the importance of making the teaching and learning process more explicit and transparent to both teacher and students alike and, most recently, other benefactors of higher education provision. The earliest discussions of making teaching and learning more explicit centred on the development of learning objectives. These originated in the field of behavioural psychology. The debates surrounding the use of behavioural objectives in higher education have been ongoing for several decades and at times have been quite vociferous (Mager, 1962). Arguments for and against their use are listed in Table 4.1.

Table 4.1 Teaching and learning objectives: pros and cons

Pros	Cons
make learning focused and achievable	focus too narrowly on minutiae, which can trivialize learning
give direction to student learning	focus on measurable objectives to the neglect of attitudes, values, motivation and interests
provide a positive contract between the teacher and student, avoiding digressions	difficult and time-consuming to write
allow for specific intervention if objectives not met	teacher-centred
allow for flexibility in learning activities	limits opportunities from spontaneous unintended outcomes occurring during learning experiences
help to focus on essential concepts and skills in the subject	educational achievements confounded by issues of accountability
literature suggests possible increase in learning	

Defining learning objectives requires teachers to make conscious choices about a wide range of teaching and learning considerations. The process of identifying teaching/learning objectives essentially defines what it is the teacher wants the student to learn. The focus of this planning is on the inputs to the learning experience and can be described as teacher-centred. For educators who subscribe to a learner-centred pedagogy, learning objectives are less acceptable than the notion of learning outcomes. In this case the outcomes equal outputs and focus on what the student will be able to do at the end of their programme of study (Otter, 1992; Walker, 1994).

References to learning outcomes, per se, are becoming more and more prevalent in higher education literature, especially with regard to recent developments related to the recommendations of the Dearing Report (NCIHE, 1997), eg **programme specifications**. Outcomes are viewed as a middle ground between statements of learning which are considered over-generalized (learning aims) and those which are over-specified (learning objectives) (Walker, 1994).

It is not uncommon when reading the literature on organizing learning in higher education to find the terms 'objectives' and 'outcomes' used interchangeably or together, as objectives/outcomes. The distinctions are frequently overlooked because, despite the variations in how they have been defined, when used, both require greater explicitness and transparency with regard to planning the teaching/learning process. The pedagogic value of objectives/outcomes for planning is discussed in the section to follow.

MODELS OF COURSE/MODULE DESIGN

When asked how they go about planning, academics often identify a process described as the 'intellectual approach'. That is, they start by listing topics they wish to cover in a course/module, placing primary emphasis on disciplinary content (see Table 4.2). Subject specialists in the arts and humanities often report using the 'experiential approach' to planning and those in the physical sciences and medicine tend to report using a 'problem-based approach'. Others may use a combination of approaches when planning courses. Knowledge of the various approaches to learning design is useful when reviewing and assessing teaching practice.

Table 4.2   Five approaches to course/module design

Systematic	Proceeds from identifiable needs to predictable outcomes. It follows a planning sequence with a feedback loop for changing and improving the design each time the course is taught.
Intellectual	Examines the subject matter in terms of assumptions held in the discipline with regard to a particular body of information, attitudes and skills. It asks questions such as: should the course be taught at the macro- or micro-level of conceptual analysis?
Problem-based	Identifies one or more specific problems to be addressed. It is not objective-defined but objective-based through inference. It eventually gets to a systematic approach but not sequentially. It places an emphasis on process of understanding the problem.

Creative/experiential	Involves teaching/learning by experience and generally through the dynamics of a group process. Outcomes are defined in the existential moment of learning.
Training/workshop-based	Outcomes are defined by the skills acquired through the training workshop.

Interrogating Practice

If you have had some teaching experience, a good place to start when thinking about reviewing your present approach to course/module planning is to answer the questions below. (If you are just starting to think about this area, then put the questions in the future tense.)

- How do you typically go about planning a course/module?
- Why do you do it the way you do?
- How satisfied are you with your approach?
- How successful is it for your students' learning?

(based on Young, 1978)

Systematic approach and outcomes-based planning

Among the various planning approaches commonly used in higher education, the systematic approach to course/module planning is most closely linked to the outcomes approach to teaching and learning. In fact, the specification of outcomes is the first step in the systematic approach. Figure 4.1 illustrates each of the component parts of a systematic approach to course/module design. It demonstrates that integral to this approach is the interrelationship of the various steps, ie each part links to and informs the others in an iterative fashion. Because the first step in this planning process starts by stating the objectives/outcomes, followed by the second step of identifying and sequencing the topics to be considered, the emphasis of this model is clearly on the outcomes to be achieved by the student, not the content to be imparted. It also shifts the focus used by the intellectual model of course/module planning from the knowledge base of the teacher to the knowledge needs of the student, thus creating a more learner-centred educational experience.

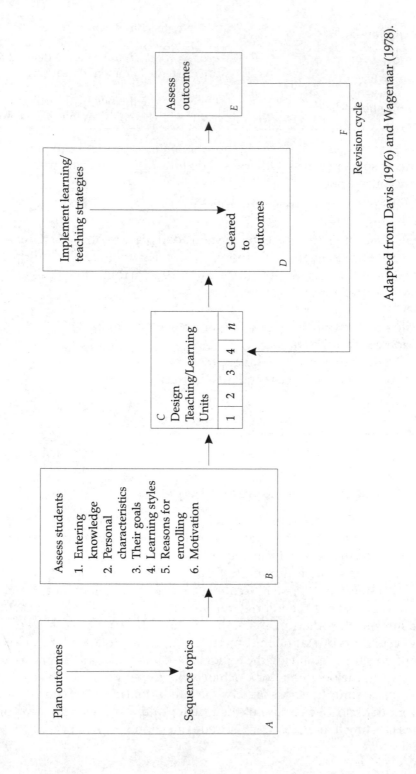

Figure 4.1 Systematic approach to course/module planning

In addition to shifting the focus of the course/module planning to the needs of students, another advantage of this model is that by following the sequence of tasks outlined in the systematic model, planning occurs in incremental steps. It addresses the complex task of course/module planning by helping to organize a body of knowledge into manageable components, thus making a challenging activity one which is eminently more achievable. As one staff member in higher education stated: 'When starting to plan a course I tend to look at everything at once, which can be overwhelming. By using the systematic approach I can pinpoint my focus and make some progress. Otherwise I do little or nothing constructive about planning my course/module.'

Because the systematic planning model is both helpful to the process of organizing teaching and learning, and promotes the implementation of an outcomes-based approach to course/module development, the remainder of this chapter focuses on a consideration of each of the steps in the systematic approach. However, for some models of teaching, parts of the process may occur in a slightly different order and/or receive different emphasis, such as courses using problem-based learning or work in some of the creative arts.

Step A: plan outcomes – sequence topics

Learning outcome statements have some degree of flexibility when compared to the rigid rules for writing learning objectives as outlined by Mager (1962). The expectations for writing learning objectives included defining:

- who is to perform the desired behaviour (eg, the student)
- what the actual behaviour would be to demonstrate the objective (eg, to write)
- result of the behaviour (eg, the product)
- conditions under which the behaviour would be performed (eg, in a two-hour exam)
- standard used to evaluate the success of the product (eg, 70 per cent correct). (Goldsmid, 1976; Robert Gordon University, 1996)

Effective **learning outcomes** are less prescriptive and are meant to facilitate the student's orientation to the subject being studied as well as guiding the choice of teaching/learning/assessment strategies for the course/module. They are meant to communicate course/module expectations to the student, so they should be stated in language that the student would understand (Case Study 1).

Case Study 1: Writing Learning Outcomes

Oxford Brookes University

Well-written learning outcomes will need to satisfy a number of key criteria and should:

- be written in the future tense;
- identify important learning requirements;
- be achievable and assessable;
- use language which students can understand;
- relate to explicit statements of achievement.

Some examples of learning outcomes:

History

- provide causal analysis of particular events or issues that presuppose a familiarity with the major historical processes which have shaped modern British and European societies;
- use a wide range of potential historical resources, and avoid the pitfalls which these may present.

Occupational Therapy

- explain your own responsibilities under Health and Safety at Work legislation and act accordingly;
- recognize and apply the implications of professional ethics (for example, in relation to confidentiality, plagiarism, syndication and copyright)

(Walker 1994: 5–7)

Levels of outcomes

Concern for levels of achievement as an element of stated learning outcomes was considered by Bloom as early as 1956 and preceded the current debate in the United Kingdom on levels descriptors by decades. Bloom's taxonomy of learning objectives (outcomes) is considered a major work in this field of inquiry. His original taxonomy was focused on what he called the **cognitive domain** of learning. Bloom suggested that in the cognitive domain understanding ranged over six levels of learning, from the lowest level which he termed factual knowledge to increasingly more difficult cognitive tasks, through comprehension, application, to analysis and synthesis, up to the highest level, evaluation of information.

This taxonomy, although useful for planning and writing learning outcomes, was criticized because it excluded other domains of learning. Bloom and his colleagues (Krathwohl *et al*, 1964) and Kibler (1970) set out to extend the taxonomy to include what they called the **affective** and **psychomotor** domains as well. Others have extended them further and there are now taxonomies of the perceptual, experiential and interpersonal domains (Moore, 1967; Steinaker and Bell, 1965; Menges and McGaghie, 1974).

More recently (NCIHE, 1997, recommendation 21) four 'domains' of intended learning outcomes for programmes of study in higher education in the United Kingdom have been proposed:

1. Knowledge and understanding;
2. Key skills: communication, numeracy, IT, learning to learn;
3. Cognitive skills (eg, ability in critical analysis);
4. Subject specific skills (eg, laboratory skills).

For some disciplines and in some universities, specification based on these four 'domains' would present no problem because current practice is not dissimilar. For others this would mean radical change and would raise issues of acceptability in relation to the teaching of discipline. Understanding the domains of learning, whatever the classification, is the first step in establishing levels of learning outcomes, but more important are the levels themselves.

Research on **deep** and **surface approaches** (eg Biggs, 1987) to learning (Chapter 3) has also influenced thinking on levels of outcomes and views all learning as having five levels delineated as:

1. An increase in knowledge;
2. Memorizing;
3. The acquisition of procedures;
4. The abstraction of meaning;
5. Understanding reality.

When the teaching and learning outcomes focus on the first three levels, this is called a 'surface' approach to learning. When they focus on the last two levels, this is called a 'deep' approach to learning. The major difference between the two types of learning are the levels of meaning placed by the student on knowledge acquisition. Bloom's taxonomies of learning are useful in helping to write outcomes that also take into account deep and surface approaches to learning.

Practical advice for writing learning outcomes

In order to assist the student produce the result which is appropriate for the level of achievement intended, it is important to word outcomes carefully. Table 4.3 lists some of the possible words that have been identified as useful for this purpose. It is easy to see that a common characteristic of all of these words, no matter what the level, is that they are unambiguous action verbs.

Table 4.3 Suggested words for outcome level statements (cognitive domain)

Level	Suggested words
Evaluation	judge, appraise, evaluate, compare, assess
Synthesis	design, organize, formulate, propose
Analysis	distinguish, analyse, calculate, test, inspect
Application	apply, use, demonstrate, illustrate, practice
Comprehension	describe, explain, discuss, recognize
Knowledge	define, list, name, recall, record

(Adapted from Bloom, 1956)

Some systematic course/module planning models include defining the broader aims of teaching and learning in advance of defining the outcomes. When this is done, words such as understand, appreciate, and grasp are used. A comparison of words commonly used in writing aims and those that may be used in writing outcomes are given in Table 4.4. The two lists help to identify the differences between aims and outcomes and their use in planning and designing learning.

Table 4.4 Comparison of words used in writing aims and outcomes statements

Aims	Outcomes
Know	Distinguish between
Understand	Choose
Determine	Assemble
Appreciate	Adjust
Grasp	Identify
Become familiar	Solve, apply, list

Interrogating Practice

Writing learning outcomes:

1. You are teaching a foundation course and you want your students to remember some important terms. Write a learning outcome statement that you hope will achieve this and involve a deep approach to learning.
2. You are teaching about a specific concept in your subject area. You want your students to reach an analytical level in their thinking. Choose one outcome that you want students to accomplish and write a learning outcome for this session.
3. You are teaching at the foundation level about a theoretical area important to understanding your subject. What you want your students to be able to do is to reach the level of evaluation. Write a learning outcome for this session.

(based on D'Andrea, 1996; Schnable, 1993)

Sequencing topics

Once the outcomes are written, the remainder of the systematic approach is fairly straightforward and involves more of a matching exercise than anything else. The match must be made between the stated outcomes and all subsequent stages. First, the topics chosen need to match the outcomes before they are organized into the sequence which will be followed during the period of study.

Course/module aims:

_____

Associated objective/outcome:

_____

Teaching/learning strategy:

_____

Assessment Strategy:

Figure 4.2   Framework for linking aims, outcomes and strategy

---

Interrogating Practice

Using the format illustrated in Figure 4.2, start by completing the first two sections for a unit of your teaching. Then, following the description of Steps C, D and E which follow, complete the rest of the sections. Once completed, check to see that the various sections match against each other, both in terms of inherent logic and their relationship to each other, particularly in contributing to the achievement of the outcomes stated.

Step B: assessing student characteristics

The next step in the systematic approach to organizing teaching and learning is to identify the major categories of student characteristics that affect the learning experience of students. Some of the characteristics that have been found useful to the planning process include: knowledge on entry, personal characteristics, demographics, variables and **learning style** (Table 4.5). Once identified, a match can be made between student needs and learning outcomes. For example, knowledge on entry will clearly help determine the topics to be examined and the depth of their consideration in a course/module. If getting information on the students for your specific course is difficult, aggregate information on students at the institution can prove quite useful. Some institutions are well-equipped to provide a wide range of information on students enrolled on specific programmes; others are not.

If all available information is taken into account when designing the teaching/learning units and choosing the strategies to implement them, it is much more likely that effective strategies will be employed to enhance the students' learning experience.

Interrogating Practice

Table 4.5 lists a few examples of student characteristics that can be used to assist with the planning of a course/module. It also suggests sources of information and how they can be used in the planning process. Using this as a guide: (1) identify the sources of information on students available at your institution; and (2) specify how the information available could be used in your course/module planning.

Table 4.5 Categories of student characteristics

---

1. **Knowledge on entry**

    (i)   Knowledge and skills relevant to the outcomes of the course/module (eg, IT skills for a statistics course).

    (ii)   Possible source of information: student self-report, pre-test (**diagnostic test**), result of previous course(s)/module(s).

    (iii) Use of information: alter outcomes, provide learning development activities, decide on concrete versus abstract presentation of information, pace of presentation.

2. **Personal characteristics**

    (i)   Characteristics which result in orientation to subject matter and work habits which influence learning. Examples: academic self-concept, 'beliefs' about the subject, course, unit/lesson's relevance and worth to a student. (eg, two-year experience as a juvenile case worker prior to a course in juvenile justice system).

    (ii)   Possible source of information: student self-report, interview, observation, standardized and self-developed instruments, beginning of course questionnaire, informal conversations.

    (iii) Use of information: assessment and development of affective objectives. Special attention to some students. Relate course material to experiences, interests, and aspirations as a way to make it meaningful, ensure concrete experience before presenting abstractions, use skills and experiences in the course.

3. **Demographic information**

    (i)   Examples: age, academic status, work status, residence, degree programme, class/work schedule.

    (ii)   Possible source of information: self-report questionnaire, oral introduction at first class session.

    (iii) Use of information: assess teaching/learning methods and activities.

4. **Learning style**

    (i)   Characteristic way a student processes information and/or participates in learning activities. Example: as a learner, a student might be independent, collaborative, dependent, avoidant, competitive or participative.

    (ii) Possible source of information: student self-report, observation, learning style inventory (Chapters 3 and 16).

    (iii) Use of information: understanding of student behaviour, design methods of teaching and learning to use, or to alter student's preferred style.

Interrogating Practice

Using the classification in Table 4.3, determine which levels could be achieved in: a lecture, small group teaching session, practical work, field-work or project work in your discipline.

Steps C, D and E: designing teaching/learning units, implementing teaching/learning strategies and assessing outcomes

In a systematic approach to course/module planning, designing the teaching and learning units, choosing and implementing teaching and learning strategies, and assessing the teaching and learning are the critical steps which need to be directly linked to the outcomes planned. Each unit should be related to at least one outcome and the teaching, learning and assessment methods should be chosen so that the outcomes can be achieved. For example, a course with practical outcomes should adopt practical methods of teaching and learning and assess students' learning in practical situations. On the other hand, courses with the aims to develop students' ability to undertake independent studies within a discipline should include significant elements of independent study assessed by project work, rather than a lecture-based course assessed by unseen exams (D'Andrea, 1996). There is no correct teaching and learning strategy and there may be many possible routes to this end. Whatever is chosen, it should be the one that can help students achieve the stated outcomes for the course/module.

Step F: revision cycle

The systematic approach also includes a revision cycle. This is meant to allow for the improvement of the course/module delivery and achievements of students' learning. In this case, results of students' assessments are used to inform the changes to be made. Again, these would of necessity be directly linked back to the outcomes stated in Step A. It is also important to reappraise the learning outcomes themselves at regular intervals in order to establish whether they continue to reflect the needs of the subject and/or the students. If not, then it is time to revisit them in order to renew and update them and to begin the systematic planning cycle again (Robert Gordon University, 1996).

OVERVIEW

Using an outcomes-based approach to organizing teaching serves a multitude of purposes. It allows teachers to clarify for themselves the implicit outcomes that are always part of any teaching and learning activity. It allows for a reflective interrogation of all aspects of the pedagogical practice and assists in the selection of appropriate teaching/learning and assessment strategies. It allows students to have a clearer understanding of what they can expect from their educational pursuits and avoids any unnecessary guessing games about what is important to learn. Both these last points will assist students through potentially greater motivation to learn, which in turn can lead to improved performance in the process of learning. Collectively such approaches should foster and facilitate improved communication between teachers and students.

REFERENCES

Biggs, JB (1987) *Student Approaches to Learning and Studying*, Australian Council for Educational Research, Melbourne

Bloom, B (1956) *Taxonomy of Educational Objectives Handbook I: Cognitive Domain*, McGraw-Hill, New York

D'Andrea, V (1996) *Course design workshop materials*, Roehampton Institute, London

Davis, JR (1974) *Learning Systems Design*, McGraw-Hill Co, New York

Gaymer, S (1997) *Levels, Credits and Learning Outcomes Article*, Higher Education Quality Council, Quality Enhancement Group Memorandum, London.

Goldsmid, CA, and Wilson, E (1980) *Passing on Sociology*, Wadsworth, Belmont, California.

Goldsmid, CA (1976) *Components/Characteristics of Instructional Objectives*, American Sociological Association Projects on Teaching Undergraduate Sociology, Oberlin, Ohio

Higher Education Quality Council (1997) *Graduate Standards Programme Final Report*, Volumes 1 and 2, Higher Education Quality Council, London

Kibler, RJ (1970) *Behaviorial Objectives and Instruction*, Allyn and Bacon, Boston

Krathwohl, DR, Bloom, BS, and Masica, BB (1964) *Taxonomy of Educational Objectives: Handbook II: Affective Domain*, David McKay, New York

Mager, RF (1962) *Preparing Instructional Objectives*, Fearon, Palo Alto, California

Moore, JW (1969) Instructional design: after behavioural objectives what? *Educational Technology*, **9**, pp 45–48

Menges, RJ, and McGaghie, WC (1974) Learning in group settings: towards a classification of outcomes, *Educational Technology*, **14**, pp 56–60

NCIHE (1997) (Dearing Report) *Higher Education in the Learning Society*, National Committee of Inquiry into Higher Education, HMSO, London

Otter, S (1992) *Learning Outcomes in Higher Education*, Unit for the Development of Adult and Continuing Education, London

Robert Gordon University (1996) *Specifying the Outcomes of Student Learning: a course booklet for the postgraduate certificate in Tertiary Level Teaching*, Educational Development Unit, The Robert Gordon University, Aberdeen

Schnable, J (1993) *Exercise on Writing Learning Objectives*, American Sociological Association, Teaching Techniques and Strategies: How to Revive the Classroom, Cincinnati, Ohio

Steinaker, NN, and Bell, MB (1979) *The Experiential Taxonomy: A New Approach to Teaching and Learning*, Academic Press, New York

Wagenaar, TC (1978) *Curriculum Workshop Materials*, American Sociological Projects on Teaching Undergraduate Sociology, Oberlin, Ohio

Walker, L (1994) *Guidance for Writing Learning Outcomes*, Oxford Brookes University, Oxford

Young, RE (1978) *Course Planning: A Workable Approach to Course Design*, Virginia Commonwealth University, Richmond, Virginia

FURTHER READING

Allan, J (1996) Learning outcomes in higher education, *Studies in Higher Education*, **21** (1), pp 93–108. A very useful summary on the history of learning objectives/outcomes.

Entwistle, N (1992) *The Impact of Teaching on Learning Outcomes in Higher Education, A Literature Review*, UCoSDA,CVCP, Sheffield. A useful reference list on the subject of learning outcomes.

Mager, RF (1962) See above. Essential reading for anyone wishing to start at the beginning of the objectives/outcomes debate.

Walker, L (1994) See above. For practical advice on writing learning objectives/outcomes, including examples from a range of subjects.

5 Principles of Assessment

Richard Wakeford

INTRODUCTION

The **assessment** of students' learning is an under-discussed and, in most disciplines, an under-researched aspect of higher education. This is understandable – teachers may feel that their educational energy is being sapped by curricular and pedagogical demands, and what's wrong with the present assessment system, anyway? – but it is not tolerable. Why not? Why is it important to include a discussion of student assessment in a handbook for teachers in higher education?

It is important for two quite different reasons. First, assessment is an integral component of the teaching and learning system. Assessment may be used explicitly to guide students in their study. But also, student perceptions of what is rewarded and what is ignored by more formal examination procedures will have a substantial impact upon their learning behaviour and thus upon the outcomes of a course.

Second, for a variety of reasons, assessment needs to be accurate – and if it is not itself examined, then we cannot know how accurate it is. We need assessment to be accurate because it is pointless and unfair to students if it is otherwise. We need it to be accurate for internal and external quality assurance purposes; and we need it to be accurate to defend the increasingly likely legal challenges from disaffected students who feel they have been unfairly judged, classified or even excluded.

Thus assessment may be seen as informal and **formative**, within the teaching process, or **summative**, making formal decisions about progress and level of achievement. While the distinction may not always be a true one – less formal assessments may be summated and included in summative assessment, and failing a summative assessment may be most formative – this chapter concentrates on the formal, summative assessment and the principles underpinning it.

As part of its current (1998–2000) round of **subject reviews**, the Quality Assurance Agency for Higher Education (**QAA**) will ask the following questions within its inspections (QAA, 1997), making it clear that it regards assessment as a central component of the teaching and learning process.

How effective are assessment design and practice in terms of:

- clarity, and students' understanding of assessment criteria and assignments;
- promoting learning (including the quality of feedback to students);
- measuring attainment of the intended learning outcomes;
- appropriateness to the student profile, level and mode of study;
- consistency and rigour of marking;
- evidence of internal moderation and scrutiny by external examiners?

Such external interest may well cause assessment procedures, customs even, to be re-examined and evaluated. A few years ago, a senior examiner in an old university wrote to his examiners as follows about changes to degree classification conventions: 'May I emphasize that this year beta/alpha, alpha/beta and alpha/alpha/beta are functioning, respectively, almost exactly as beta/beta/alpha, beta/alpha and alpha/beta did last year. Markers familiar with last year's conventions should adapt to the new nomenclature (designed to make Firsts look more like Firsts to outsiders) and not stint their leading alphas.' Unfortunately for him, the memorandum fell into the hands of *Private Eye*, resulting in freedom for this small but telling piece of information. The assumption is that all those being communicated with would automatically understand the arcane secret language of examination procedures.

In UK medical schools, the interest of an external accrediting body, the General Medical Council, has resulted in almost wholesale reform of curricula and examinations. So the QAA's interest will certainly cause higher education institutions and their staff to take a greater interest in the topic, and may reduce the 'if it ain't broke, don't fix it' attitude of many, which can extend to a presumption that if a system has been in existence for decades (or even centuries), then it must be all right. Assessment procedures for many are simply part of the academic wallpaper.

ASSESSMENT CONCEPTS AND ISSUES

Depending upon the aims of assessment policies of an individual institution or department, effective assessment will reflect truthfully some combination of an individual's abilities, achievement, skills and potential. Ideally it will permit predictions about future behaviour. To be effective, assessment will need to reflect programme content, and be **valid**, **reliable** and **fair**.

In the past, tests have often been constructed by the fairly haphazard compilation of a set of questions, using whatever assessment method(s) existed. It is now recognized that assessment needs to reflect programme content accurately by being blueprinted onto it, at both a general and detailed level. At a general level, the nature of assessment will reflect the general **objectives** (or intended outcomes) of a teaching programme. For example, a course designed to teach problem-solving skills would use approaches to assessment which permit assessment of problem-solving abilities, not knowledge recall; a course emphasizing cooperative activities and personal presentation skills would probably need to utilize testing techniques other than written ones. At a more detailed level, the questions or items used within an assessment component need to be created according to some form of blueprint. The nature of the blueprint will depend upon the subject, but might look something like the example in Table 5.1, where a test item is to be generated for each cell in the table.

Table 5.1 Blueprinting assessment

	Teaching content as specified in Course Handbook					
	Topic A.1	Sub-topic A.11	Sub-topic A.12	Topic A.2	Topic A.3	Topic B.1
Knowledge recall (multi-choice test)						
Application to professional practice (short answer questions)						
Technical problem-solving (computer-based test)						
Critical evaluation of theories (essay)						

Effective assessment procedures need to be at once valid (or appropriate) and reliable (or accurate and consistent). Validity can be seen as having three aspects: face validity, construct validity and impact validity. Face validity is to do with the appropriateness of the content of a test for the audience and level used. Construct validity concerns the nature of the broader constructs tested – for example, recall of knowledge, demonstration of teamwork skills, oratorical persuasive powers. A carefully blueprinted test should have good face and construct validity. Impact validity is about the impact which an assessment procedure has upon the behaviour of the learners, and is probably closely related to students' perceptions of what is rewarded by the test methods used. For example, in a postgraduate examination, an essay test was modified so as explicitly to assess candidates' ability to evaluate published research papers: very significant changes in learner behaviour took place, emphasizing group discussions of primary source material.

Thus validity is judged largely qualitatively; but the reliability of an assessment procedure is calculated mathematically. Depending upon the nature of the assessment method, there are many sources of unreliability in assessment: these include inadequate test length, inconsistency of individual examiners (poor intra-examiner reliability), inconsistencies across examiners (poor inter-examiner reliability), and inadequacies of individual test items used. Inter- and intra-examiner reliabilities can be evaluated straightforwardly, given the raw data. Correlation matrices will enable test item performance to be evaluated when using open-ended written tests; commercial software exists to enable examiners to evaluate the performance of items in computer-marked tests such as multiple-choice tests. The more open-ended assessment is, in general the harder it is to determine reliability in these ways.

Such techniques will permit judgements about aspects or components of a test (eg, 'Dr X marks differently to all his colleagues'; 'The question on the rise of Irish nationalism needs re-thinking'), but examination boards will increasingly need some overall evaluation of the reliability of a test. What is needed is an answer to the question: to what extent would the same results have been achieved with a similar, parallel form of the same test? A statistical technique that estimates this for most types of test is known as Cronbach's alpha (see Further Reading, page 69). A correlation coefficient ranging from 0 (bad) to 1 (very good), it will give an indication of the robustness of the rank order of candidates produced by a test: any modern statistical software package will compute it. Other statistics can be used to assess the robustness of pass/fail decisions or degree classifications.

An assessment can be well blueprinted, valid and reliable, but care must be taken to ensure that it is fair both to all individuals and to groups of individuals. For example, it is well known that individual examiners may have varying, idiosyncratic and often consistent marking tendencies: there are hawks and doves, theatrical and restrained markers, despite the possible existence of marking schedules and model answers. Individual candidates are likely to be unfairly treated in open-ended written tests if the marking arrangements pretend that such differences are insignificant.

There is also evidence that different groups may perform differentially according to assessment methods used. Overall, women appear to perform less well than men in multiple-choice type tests, for example, with the reverse difference for free response items, such as essays. Consider the following unpublished data (Table 5.2) from a national postgraduate examination in medicine, involving a free-response essay-type paper and a multiple true/false multiple-choice question (MCQ) paper.

Table 5.2 Differences in test scores by gender and type of test

	Mean MCQ mark	Mean essay mark	Number of candidates
Men	50.11	48.20	1609
Women	48.78	51.69	1482

The men/women differences are statistically highly significant ($p < .00001$ in each case), but differences will not inevitably always follow this pattern. In Cambridge University, an ongoing research project seeks to understand the apparent under-performance of women in the Tripos examinations which is manifest in many though by no means all subjects. The implication is that all examination boards would be well advised to set in place appropriate quality assurance monitoring procedures and never rely upon a single examination modality.

ASSESSMENT METHODS

A large number of assessment methods are available for use in higher education. They are listed and described in detail in the principal texts on assessment (see Further Reading, page 69). Those most likely to confront new university teachers are long essay questions, short answer questions, MCQs of many varieties, the assessment of practical or laboratory exercises and quite possibly oral examinations.

Essay questions

Description: Questions inviting extended written responses (each taking from half-an-hour to an hour or more to answer).
Variations: Varying approach to content – legion, subject only to imagination. Article with an audience in mind (eg, an article explaining a current controversy or scientific development for the *Telegraph*, the *Sun*). Book review. Grant application. Method may be varied by setting topics in advance (the '168-hour examination' (Gibbs, Habeshaw and Habeshaw, 1988)) or using the open book approach, whereby a limited number of texts are permitted to be brought into the examination room.

Marking systems: Traditionally marked by academic instinct. More recently it has been found that the use of model answers may make for more consistent and fair marks, but this may also overemphasize what is omitted, not rewarding clever ideas not thought of by the question-setter, and encourage 'grapeshot' answering approaches (ie, flinging everything faintly relevant onto the page in the hope of occasionally hitting the examiner's model). A compromise may be better, where examiners agree a list of five to six themes or constructs for an essay question, on each of which each candidate's essay is rated on a standard scale.

Advantages: Readily set. Should be able to test high level cognitive skills (eg ability to bring different ideas or theories together and create a synthesis).

Drawbacks: It may be difficult to permit enough essays to reflect realistically the examination blueprint. To achieve adequate reliability, testing time needs to be long (eg, three hours) and multiple marking may be required. Poor exam questions may be unclear ('Write a letter to Wundt's grandson' – Wundt, in case you didn't know, was a turn-of-the-century phrenologist) or, even if clear, simply invite/reward regurgitation of lectures. Candidates may interpret the question in different ways, making fair marking difficult. Fair marking is difficult, anyway. Choice of question makes fair marking almost impossible. May enhance impact of differential examiner marking tendencies.

Interrogating Practice

What criteria do you use in essay marking? Are these criteria freely available to and clear to your students?

Short answer questions

Description: Questions inviting limited written responses, not normally more than a page in length and often less; can be short notes or diagrammatic in nature. Response time: five to ten minutes per item.

Variations: Limited. Open book approach possible with reference materials permitted to be brought in to the examination room.

Marking systems: Model answer systems typically used (answer supplied by question-setter), but no guarantee of accurate or consistent marking. 'Theme/construct' again recommended.

Advantages: Readily set, reasonably quick to mark. Can cover a broad test blueprint. Number of questions can give adequate reliability in (often) one or two hours of testing time.

Drawbacks: It takes effort to produce items which test at cognitive levels higher than simple recall.

Multiple-choice questions

Description: Classically, an item stem with four or five completions, with the candidate being invited to identify the most correct one (the 'single correct response' type). Generally, responses are entered on a computer-readable card.

Variations: Many. Multiple true/false items are common in some disciplines in the United Kingdom (each item must be identified true or false). 'Extended matching items' (**EMIs**) are the current vogue in medicine, with a more or less extended stem being followed by a number of linked and sophisticated MCQ completion items (Case and Swanson, 1998).

Marking systems: Different approaches imply different systems. Controversy over whether there should be penalties for incorrect responses ('students shouldn't be encouraged to guess') or whether there should not ('otherwise we test confidence/personality as well as what we're trying to test'). Such issues are discussed in detail elsewhere (Case and Swanson, 1998).

Advantages: Quick coverage of broad test blueprint. Results available quickly. Removes marking error and encourages examiner pre-agreement over correct/incorrect responses. Items can be banked for future use.

Drawbacks: Often fierce hostility of traditionalists, 'dumbing down assessment'. Hard to write good items and to develop approaches which test at higher cognitive levels. True/false items impossible in some disciplines. Must be monitored statistically (when it is frequently found that technical errors have been made). Need for security with respect to item bank.

Assessment of laboratory/practical work

Description: The use of a laboratory situation to assess aspects of a student's work that may not appropriately be assessed by regular paper-based tests. A wide variety of testing objectives are possible and Brown, Bull and Pendlebury (1997) offer a long list of potential objectives which may need to be included in assessment. As a result of deciding what exactly it is that needs to be assessed, the teacher must decide whether any simple paper-and-pencil test method is adequate, or whether the laboratory needs to be the venue for assessment. Typically, students are required to perform some experimental procedure, note the results and evaluate their findings (see Chapter 21).

Variations: Many, including 'dry practicals', where the results of a laboratory experiment are presented and students are required simply to analyse them and to evaluate and comment on them. Group work is increasingly a feature of many undergraduate programmes, reflecting the importance of collaboration skills as a course aim. But the assessment of group work brings a variety of problems (Wood, 1991).

Marking systems: Variable, depending upon the approach. Main problems surround how to balance assessment of process versus outcome/analysis/evaluation and standardizing this. Work in the assessment of medical students using objective, standardized approaches may be helpful (Harden and Gleeson, 1979).

Advantages: Assessment of a uniquely important aspect of many subjects, the 'real world' of scientific enquiry.

Drawbacks: Practical difficulties towards making assessment equitable for all students: what happens if a student's experiment 'goes wrong'. Cost. Determining assessment priorities (eg process versus outcome) and rewards.

Orals

Oral or **viva voce** examinations, though commonly used in professional and post-graduate assessment, are the subject of great concern to test developers and psychometricians. They have their attractions, but are subject to all the well-known biases and problems of selection interviews, and should only be used in the full knowledge of these problems and how their effects may be minimized. The new practitioner in higher education is counselled to beware of and avoid orals, certainly until he or she has read some of the literature (eg Wakeford, Southgate and Wass, 1995).

BECOMING AN EXAMINER YOURSELF

Most university teachers rapidly find themselves required to take part in their university's formal assessment procedures, often more rapidly than they feel comfortable with. What guidance might they be offered?

The most important and general point is to refuse to be intimidated and to join a conspiracy of misunderstanding and silence. When told that you are to be an examiner, request direction towards:

- any university information for examiners, including relevant rules and regulations, appeals procedures, policies on unfair practices by candidates, codes of practice, and any general guidance;
- similar departmental or faculty information;
- course and programme details (including what the students are told to expect about assessment);
- marking schemes, assessment criteria and guidelines for honours classifications (as appropriate).

So do not be afraid to ask for help as you start to grapple with the practical realities of examining. And if you can observe examples of some of the harder assessment techniques such as oral examinations, do so before attempting them.

Interrogating Practice

Look carefully through the list above. What university and/or departmental guidelines, or other documentation, do you currently have?

MAKING ASSESSMENT DECISIONS DEFENSIBLE

UK universities have yet to experience substantial challenges by students to their assessment decisions, but there are signs that this may change. With payment of fees, students are increasingly starting to look like customers, and may well start to behave like them. Academics themselves, moreover, are starting to challenge university decisions made about them on matters such as promotion (Evans, 1999).

With little 'case law' available in the United Kingdom, we can do little but look to North America to see what the bases of such challenge may be. McManus (1998) has summarized the bases of candidates' successful legal challenges there:

- being denied the possibility of re-sitting an assessment because of an arbitrary limit on the number of attempts allowed;
- arguing that they were not, as learners, in a position to learn the things which the assessment procedures assessed;
- asserting that the test was not valid for the purpose for which it was being used (and possibly had been devised in an inadequate way);
- asserting that the test had inadequate reliability;
- arguing that the test was discriminating unfairly against some group (to which the plaintiff belonged);
- stating that due process had not taken place (ie rules and regulations had not been properly observed);
- arguing that the pass mark had been set inadequately.

Towards better, more defensible assessment procedures

The North American evidence (Mehrens and Popham, 1992; Downing and Haladynia, 1997) comes from countries with different legal traditions to the United Kingdom and should thus be treated cautiously, as it itself suggests, especially for 'high stakes' examinations such as vocational qualifications and assessments contributing to degree classifications. For example, the North American literature goes so far as to recommend the use of fearsome procedures such as routine 'bias-sensitivity review', for which UK academics may not yet be ready. Translated into the local culture, the implications are that, for assessment in higher education:

- contemporary good practice in assessment should be adopted (or at least pursued) generally;
- the function of different components of an assessment system (eg, essay tests, oral examinations, MCQs) should be explicit (and plausible);
- course designers should be able to defend how the content of an assessment procedure – the questions or items – has been arrived at: how has it been blueprinted?;
- examination procedures – due process – should be specified in detail;
- there should be explicit assessment criteria for test procedures which involve examiner judgement;
- examiners should receive training on assessment generally, detailed information about the procedures in which they are to be involved, and receive feedback on their performance;
- assessment procedures should be routinely quality assessed, including measures of reliability.

'Contemporary good practice' in assessment would specifically additionally recommend:

- the use of multiple assessment methods to counter possible bias associated with individual methods;
- explicit justification for any use of choice-of-question in tests, and description of how equating is achieved;
- ensuring that the issue of differential examiner marking tendencies is addressed.

As in other areas of endeavour in higher education, it seems that the future will involve more bureaucracy (and work) to achieve the worthy goal of assured high quality.

FINDING OUT MORE

Universities will provide staff development sessions on examinations and assessment which will help flesh out some of the issues raised by this chapter and enable discussion of problems or ideas which may be relevant to particular disciplines. Such sessions should be helpful to new staff. But some subject areas – especially the professions, most particularly medicine – have considerable assessment industries related to them, with journals devoted to the business, huge international conferences and the like.

Access to a library and the Internet should provide a university teacher with all the further reading and reference materials that they could reasonably need. Some leads into the literature and Internet sources of information are given at the end of this chapter.

OVERVIEW

What then are the most important principles of assessment? First, the function or purpose of any assessment procedure needs to be clear, eg formative or summative, and clearly related to (best, integrated with) the course teaching and learning. Second, the approach needs to be valid and appropriate to that purpose – this is a largely qualitative judgement. Third, it needs to be reliable or consistent in its application. Fourth, to achieve these ends, assessment procedures need to be discussed and themselves examined. Using these four principles as questions with which to evaluate any part of the assessment system with which they are involved, could enable university teachers to start involving themselves in what, with likely increasing consumerism in higher education and associated legal challenges, seems likely to be a hot academic topic for the millennium.

REFERENCES

Brown, G, Bull, J, and Pendlebury, M (1997) *Assessing Student Learning in Higher Education*, Routledge, London

Case, SM and Swanson, DB (1998) *Constructing Written Test Questions for the Basic and Clinical Sciences*, National Board of Medical Examiners, Philadelphia (available only electronically, but gratis, from: http://www.nbme.org)

Downing, SM and Haladyna, TM (1997) Test item development: validity evidence from quality assurance procedures, *Applied Measurement in Education*, **10** (1), pp 61–82.

Evans, GR (1999) *Calling Academia to Account*, Society for Research into Higher Education and the Open University Press, Buckingham

Gibbs, G, Habeshaw, S and Habeshaw, T (1988) 53 *Interesting Ways of Assessing your Students*, Technical and Educational Services, Bristol

Harden, RM and Gleeson, F (1979) Assessment of clinical competence using an objective structured clinical examination, *Medical Education*, **13**, pp 51–54.

McManus, IC (1998) Personal communication

Mehrens, WA and Popham, WJ (1992) How to evaluate the defensibility of high stakes tests, *Applied Measurement in Education*, **5** (3), pp 265–83

(QAA) Quality Assurance Agency for Higher Education (1997) *Subject Review Handbook* (QAA 1/97) Quality Assurance Agency, Bristol

Wakeford, R, Southgate, L and Wass, V (1995) Improving oral examinations: selecting, training and monitoring examiners for the MRCGP, *British Medical Journal*, **311**, pp 9331–35

Wood, R (1991) *Assessment and Testing: A Survey of Research*, Cambridge University Press, Cambridge

FURTHER READING

Books are a prime source of theory and evidence in assessment. My favourite is the classic by Heywood (see below), but three good general up-to-date books are:

Brown, G, Bull, J, and Pendlebury, M (1997) *Assessing Student Learning in Higher Education*, Routledge, London (particularly recommended).

Brown, S, and Knight, P (1994) *Assessing Learners in Higher Education*, Kogan Page, London

Brown, S, and Glasner, S (eds) (1999) *Assessment Matters in Higher Education*, Society for Research into Higher Education and the Open University Press, Buckingham

Heywood, J (1977) *Assessment in Higher Education*, Wiley, Chichester (older, thoughtful, challenging but [technically] out of date).

Wood, R (1991) *Assessment and Testing: A Survey of Research*, Cambridge University Press, Cambridge (a good reference source on assessment based upon a more general review of assessment – ie beyond higher education).

Case, SM and Swanson, DB (1998) See above (the best guide in the world on writing objective test items).

Streiner, DL and Norman, GR (1995) *Health Measurement Scales: A Practical Guide to their Development and Use*, 2nd edn, Oxford University Press, Oxford (the science behind objective testing: sampling, reliability, etc).

THE INTERNET

The Internet is increasingly the prime source of information on experiments and developments in education, generally, and assessment, specifically. But as many sites, links and references have only a short lifetime, it is inappropriate in a book to list many. But one of the most useful UK higher education sites is 'DeLiberations' at London Guildhall University (http://www.lgu.ac.uk/deliberations/home.html) a website specifically for academics and educational developers and where assessment is a permanent discussion issue.

6 Encouraging Student Motivation

Stephen E Newstead and Sherria Hoskins

INTRODUCTION

A few years ago one of us was involved in a programme of research on student cheating in higher education. The research team had a strong suspicion that incidents of cheating were related to student motivation and wanted to test out this hypothesis. We were thus faced with the problem of how to measure student motivation. We were struck by how little research had been done in this area, by how few measures of student motivation there were, and in particular by how difficult it was to obtain a quick and readily usable indication of what students' motives were in studying at university. This led us to consider how we could identify, first, what motivates students, and second, differences between **intrinsic** and **extrinsic motivation**.

To this end, we devised a very quick and simple (but totally unvalidated) measure: we simply asked students to indicate what was the single main reason why they were studying at university. The responses were, of course, many and varied, but we were able to categorize the great majority of them into three main categories, which we called 'stop gap', 'means to an end' and 'personal development' (Newstead, Franklyn-Stokes and Armstead, 1996). These categories are summarized in Table 6.1. The percentage figures give the proportion of students who were placed into each category out of a university sample of 844 students whose responses could be categorized.

Table 6.1 Reasons for studying

	Percentage of students
Stop gap	10%
– avoiding work	
– laziness	
– allowing time out to decide on career	
– social life	
– fun and enjoyment	
Means to an end	66%
– improving standard of living	
– improving chance of getting a job	
– developing career	
– getting a good qualification	
– getting worthwhile job	
Personal development	24%
– improving life skills	
– reaching personal potential	
– gaining knowledge for its own sake	
– furthering academic interest	
– gaining control of own life	

Those classified as stop gap students (10 per cent) were studying because they could think of nothing else to do, wanted to defer taking a decision, or simply wanted to enjoy themselves for three years. Those classed as means to an end students wanted to achieve something through their degree, whether this was a better paid or more interesting job, or simply qualifications to put after their names. This was much the most common category, with two-thirds of our sample being classified in this way. Personal development students (nearly a quarter of our sample) were ones who were interested in the subject itself or wanted to use their degree to realize their own potential or to develop their personal skills.

While the classification was largely *post hoc*, and was carried out with incomplete knowledge of existing educational theories of motivation, it is striking how similar our classification is to those arrived at by other researchers. For example, a key distinction is often made between intrinsic and extrinsic motivation. Intrinsically motivated students enjoy a challenge, want to master the subject, are curious and want to learn; while extrinsically motivated students are concerned with the grades they get, external rewards and whether they will gain approval from others (Harter, 1981). While the fit is not perfect, the parallels with our own classification system are clear, with **intrinsic motivation** corresponding closely to personal development and **extrinsic motivation** corresponding to means to an end.

Other major distinctions that have been made in the literature also map closely onto our categorization. Dweck and her colleague (Dweck and Elliott, 1983) have drawn the highly influential distinction between performance goals and learning goals. Students with performance goals are motivated primarily by obtaining good marks, while learning oriented students wish to actually learn something from their studies. Performance goals are linked to means to an end (and **extrinsic motivation**), while learning goals are linked with personal development (and **intrinsic motivation**). Other distinctions in the literature related to Dweck's are those between ability and mastery goals (Nicholls, 1984) and between ego involvement and task involvement (Ames, 1984). There are, of course, important differences in emphasis in all these approaches, but there is enough similarity between them, and enough overlap with the distinctions made in our own characterization, to conclude that the concepts underlying them are reasonably consistent and widespread.

Interrogating Practice

What do you know about the motivation of the students you teach? If they are training for a specific career, does this affect their motivation in a particular way?

Amotivation and achievement motivation

Stop gap motivation was not especially common in our student sample, but it did occur. While this has not been extensively discussed in the literature, the related concept of **amotivation** has received some attention. Deci and Ryan (1985) describe amotivated students as ones who do not really know why they are at university, think themselves incompetent and feel that they have little control over what happens to them. In a real sense, then, these students show an absence of motivation.

This highlights another aspect of motivation: that it has strength as well as direction. Thus far we have looked at motivational goals, in other words what students' aims are. But even students with identical goals may have very differing strengths of that motivation. A simple example would be two students, both of whom were studying to get a better job, for one of whom it was their lifelong and heartfelt ambition, and for the other of whom it was little more than a passing interest. Although their motives would be the same, the different strengths of these motives might be expected to lead to very different behavioural outcomes, for example in their ability to persevere in adversity.

Many educational writers discuss **achievement motivation** as one of the principal factors influencing outcomes in higher education (Entwistle and Ramsden, 1983). A student who is high in achievement motivation can be seen as lying at the opposite end of the scale from an amotivated student. Such a student is concerned primarily with achieving a successful outcome at the end of his or her studies. This cuts across many of the dimensions discussed earlier, in that both extrinsically and intrinsically motivated students can be high or low in achievement motivation. In other words, achievement motivation is largely a measure of the strength of motivation, rather than of its direction.

It is a gross oversimplification, but nevertheless it seems reasonable to suggest that our own research and the existing literature have identified three main types of motivation: intrinsic, extrinsic and achievement motivation (with amotivation simply being the opposite end of the continuum to achievement motivation). Clearly, however, it is of little use knowing what students' motives are unless the impact of these on how students behave is known.

Motives and behaviour

There is surprisingly little evidence as to the behaviour associated with different motives. Some fairly simplistic predictions can be made. For example, one might expect that students high in **achievement motivation** will actually achieve higher grades. Furthermore, given that **intrinsic motivation** seems so central to higher education, one would surely expect that students with this motivation should perform better academically than those with **extrinsic motivation**. One might also predict that the study strategies would be different in different groups of students; for example, intrinsically motivated students might be expected to develop a deeper understanding of the material than extrinsically motivated ones, and perhaps also to be more resistant to discouragement in the light of a poor mark. There is, surprisingly, little clear cut evidence on any of these predictions.

One line of evidence concerning the relationship between motives and behaviour derives from the work on students' approaches to studying (eg Entwistle and Ramsden, 1983). Research into these approaches, using the **Approaches to Studying Inventory**, is arguably the most extensively researched area in higher education in recent years. The main focus of this research has been on the distinction between **deep** and **surface** approaches to studying. A deep approach is concerned with conceptual understanding of the material, and incorporating this into one's existing knowledge; whereas a surface approach is characterized by rote learning of material, with the intention of reproducing this in another context (eg, an examination). Each of these approaches is linked to a certain type of motivation, with deep approaches being associated with **intrinsic motivation** and surface approaches with **extrinsic motivation**.

Crucially from the present perspective, these associations were derived empirically, through the use of factor analysis. What this means is that specific types of motivation and specific approaches to studying tended to be associated with each other in the responses given by students to questionnaire items. Subsequent research has shown the main factors to be remarkably robust. However, the link between motives and strategies may not be as neat as it seems at first sight. Pintrich and Garcia (1991) found that intrinsically motivated students did indeed use strategies designed to develop a conceptual understanding of material, but that extrinsically motivated students did not, as would have been predicted, use more rehearsal strategies.

In addition to deep and surface approaches, another approach consistently emerges in the analysis of responses to the Approaches to Studying Inventory. This is usually termed the **strategic approach**, and it is closely related to **achievement motivation**. Strategic students vary their approach depending on the circumstances; if they judge that a surface approach is necessary in one situation, they will use it, but in others they might use a deep approach. Their main aim is to secure high marks and they will adapt their strategy in whatever way they see fit to try to achieve this aim.

Australian research by Biggs has also identified achieving orientation as a major factor in students' approaches to learning. Biggs (1987) characterizes the achieving motivation as a desire to obtain high grades even when the task to be completed does not inspire interest. Biggs states that this motive is facilitated by competition which provides students with the opportunity to increase their self-esteem.

In the same way as Entwistle and Ramsden (1983), Biggs associates this type of motivation with a specific learning strategy, which he terms the achieving strategy but which is very similar to the strategic approach.

The relationship between motivation and academic success has been investigated by Pintrich and Garcia (1991), and the picture that emerges is not a simple one. Overall, there was no direct relationship between intrinsic motivation and academic success, but instead an interaction between motivation and the strategy adopted. In essence, students who lack intrinsic motivation can still perform well, providing they adopt appropriate study strategies to compensate for this. Research into students' approaches to studying has produced mixed results. While some authors have reported a correlation between deep approaches and academic success (eg Entwistle and Ramsden, 1983) this is not always found to be the case (eg Clarke, 1986). Hence there is little evidence to support the claim that intrinsic motivation leads to academic success. As we shall see, one possible reason for this is that intrinsic motivation, while valued by lecturers, is not necessarily rewarded in the assessments they give students.

Interrogating Practice

Reflect on the correlation between motivation and academic achievement as demonstrated by students you teach. How well do your intrinsically motivated students perform?

Measuring student motivation

In addition to the measures of achievement motivation contained within the instruments developed by Entwistle and Ramsden (1983) and Biggs (1987), a small number of other motivation measures has been developed specifically for use with students in higher education. The two most important of these are the Academic Motivation Scale developed by Vallerand *et al* (1992) and the Motivated Strategies for Learning Questionnaire developed by Pintrich *et al* (1993).

The Academic Motivation Scale consists of 28 items which are designed to assess three types of intrinsic motivation, three types of extrinsic motivation, and amotivation. It would appear to have reasonable reliability and validity (Vallerand *et al* 1992), and its short length means that it can realistically be used in educational research.

The Motivated Strategies for Learning is a much longer scale, containing 81 items, and has rather more sub-scales. It is also American in orientation, and thus far seems to have not been used in this country. Although the scale has good reliability and validity, it is rather too long to be of great use in educational research, at least outside the United States.

The development of motivation

We have seen the kinds of things that motivate students, leading us to consider their motivation through the years of a degree course.

Interrogating Practice

In your experience, do students come with high motivation? What happens to their motivation during their stay at university? Does your department inspire them to ever higher levels of motivation? If so, how?

One measure of students' motivations on arriving at university is Entwistle's (1998) Approaches to Study Skills Inventory for Students (ASSIST). Part of this involves questions about reasons for entering higher education. In a study carried out at the University of Plymouth, this inventory was administered to some 600 first-year students, with the results as given in Table 6.2 (taken from Sharpe *et al*, in submission).

Table 6.2 Percentage of students agreeing strongly or fairly strongly with questions on the ASSIST scale (Sharpe *et al*, in submission)

The qualification at the end of this course would enable me to get a good job when I finish	92%
The course will help me develop knowledge and skills which will be useful later on	89%
I wanted a chance to develop as a person, broaden my horizons and face new challenges	63%
The opportunities for an active social life and/or sport attracted me	63%
I would be able to study subjects in depth, and take interesting and stimulating courses	61%
I basically wanted to try and prove to myself that I could really do it	46%

Having done well at school, it seemed to be the natural thing to go on to higher education	39%
It would give me another three or four years to decide what I really wanted to do later on	37%
I suppose it was a mixture of other people's expectations and no obvious alternative	9%
I rather drifted into higher education without deciding it was what I really wanted to do	7%

These results are broadly consistent with the findings obtained using a very different method (and on students already in higher education) by Newstead *et al* (1996). The main reasons for entering higher education were to get a good job and to develop useful skills (ie means to an end). Next most frequent were reasons relating to personal development, such as to study subjects in depth and develop as a person. Less frequent were the stop gap reasons, such as to delay taking a decision or simply drifting into higher education. The only slight mismatch is in the high ranking given in the Sharpe study to an active social and sporting life. This is probably because the reason is indeed an important one for many people, but is seldom the single most important reason (the Newstead study asked simply for the single main reason for studying).

The similarity of the findings in these two studies might suggest that students' motives do not change a great deal over the course of their degrees. There is direct support for this contention in the research of Fazey and Fazey (1998). They used Vallerand's Academic Motivation Scale to carry out a longitudinal investigation of students' motivation over the first two years of their degree courses at the University of Bangor. Their results indicated that students were high on both intrinsic and extrinsic motivation on entry to university but much lower on amotivation. From the present perspective, the interesting finding was that the levels of these three types of motivation showed virtually no change over the first two years at university. In a sense this is a disappointing finding since one might have hoped that higher education would have led to students becoming more intrinsically motivated by their subject. It is of course possible that this does happen to some students but is offset by an equal number who become less intrinsically motivated.

Encouraging student motivation

Lecturers frequently bemoan the lack of student motivation and ask what they can do to improve this. Hopefully, the foregoing overview will have at least hinted that there is no quick fix. Indeed, before even addressing this issue it is necessary to ascertain what aspect of student motivation needs to be addressed. Most lecturers would agree that a complete lack of motivation of any kind – amotivation – is highly undesirable. Further, most lecturers would claim that intrinsic motivation is more desirable than extrinsic. Hence these are the two principal questions that will be addressed in this section.

First, then, how can we avoid students becoming amotivated? For some students, this will be next to impossible, since they may have entered higher education with the sole aim of enjoying the social life. But there is also evidence that what we do to students at university can lead to their becoming amotivated. Hoskins (1999) has recently completed a research programme investigating students' approaches to essay writing, and has discovered through a combination of focus groups and questionnaires that certain factors of this process lead to students losing motivation. Of particular importance is the feedback given, both in terms of the mark awarded and the written feedback provided.

One group of students approached essay writing with an understanding motivation, in that they enjoyed writing, had an intrinsic interest in the essay and tended to read extensively. Because of the amount of reading they did, they often had problems focusing their essay and adhering to the word limit. As a result they tended to receive poor marks but had difficulty in understanding where they had gone wrong or what skills they needed to overcome the problems. These students felt that marking was often inconsistent and contained insufficient detail to be helpful. In consequence, they avoided using an understanding motivation on the grounds that they felt it unlikely to lead to a good mark.

One of the most prominent themes in the focus group data collected by Hoskins was the almost unanimous perception of essay marks as unsatisfactory. Students often felt that there was no relationship between the amount of effort they put into an essay and the mark they were awarded, and that it took a disproportionate amount of effort to achieve small percentage increases. They were highly critical of what they regarded as a 'glass ceiling' – an unwritten rule which seems to prevent them getting marks higher than an upper second. Since they found it relatively easy to produce an essay which got a high lower second or low upper second mark, there was little incentive to do any extra work given the existence of this glass ceiling. The belief that the range of marks awarded for essays is too limited given the potential range available was also a constantly recurring theme.

It is only part of the answer to this problem, but it would appear that one way of avoiding amotivation is to make sure that students are given full and appropriate feedback; and, if it is clear that they have put in extra work and not received a particularly high mark, then feedback on why this has occurred needs to be given. When terms such as 'developing an argument' are used, there needs to be some explanation of what this means. One way of achieving this might be by setting up a database of examples which could act as an essay feedback bank that staff could draw on. This would enable them to demonstrate what aspects of an essay are likely to attract good marks. The use of marking schemes also has the potential to improve the quality of the feedback, though there is the danger here of 'downsliding' (Collins and Gentner, 1980), where students (and perhaps staff also) focus on low level activities such as correcting spelling mistakes at the expense of more complicated revisions such as trying to develop an argument.

Of course, lecturers will argue that they have insufficient time to do all this, and there is undoubtedly truth in this. What may be required is an overhaul of assessment systems so that lecturers are able to give appropriate feedback. If the assessment process is so overwhelming that proper feedback cannot be given, then there is surely something wrong with the system.

Interrogating Practice

How is the provision of constructive feedback addressed in your department? Can you think of some other ways of providing constructive feedback to students further to the suggestions offered above?

The second issue is that of how to encourage intrinsic rather than extrinsic motivation. There is much evidence to suggest that the majority of students tend to adopt surface approaches (of which extrinsic motivation is a part) at university (Ramsden, 1992). The evidence presented in Table 6.1 also indicated the extent to which means to an end motivation was prevalent in one group of students.

Again there is no easy or guaranteed solution to this, and some authors are rather pessimistic as to what can be achieved by individual lecturers or even groups of lecturers. Biggs (1993) points out that university education is part of a system, and that most systems are resistant to change, instead tending to return to the state of balance that has developed within them. What this means is that students' approaches to study and their motives are determined by a number of aspects of the higher education system, including their perception of the department and university they are in, and even of the university system in general. Trying to change students' motives by changing the way one module or group of modules is taught is unlikely to be effective, since all the other aspects will be working against this change. Similar rather disappointing conclusions come from attempts to train students to approach their studies in different ways. Norton and Crowley (1995) found that the training programme they devised had little effect on how students studied. Purdie and Hattie (1995) found that their training programme led to a temporary improvement in approaches to studying but that these rapidly reverted after the training came to an end.

However, there is one aspect of higher education which does seem to be crucially important in students' motivation, and that is the assessment system (see Chapter 5). Entwistle and Entwistle (1991) describe how final year students start with good intentions, are intrinsically motivated and attempt to adopt deep approaches to their studies; however, as examination time approaches they become increasingly extrinsically motivated and adopt surface, rote learning approaches. Similar findings have emerged in research by Newstead and Findlay (1997). One way of changing this might be if the assessment system were to be one which encouraged conceptual understanding as opposed to rote learning. It would appear that the standard three-hour essay-based examination does tend to produce surface approaches, despite the best intentions of lecturers. This might be altered through the increased use of problem solving, case studies and the like, where knowledge has to be used rather than just learned. What is more, such assessments could take place under formal examination conditions, thus avoiding some of the problems associated with continuous assessment (such as student cheating, which is where this chapter began).

Finally, it may be possible to guide students to help themselves by encouraging them to adopt strategies which will keep up their motivation. A recent study by Wolters (1998) investigated the kinds of strategies that students used to regulate their own motivation, and found that these varied between students and as a function of the task in question. Among the most common strategies were reminding themselves of the extrinsic rewards (usually the need to do well in an exam), cognitional strategies such as reading through notes and preparing new notes, and changing the environment in which studying was taking place (eg, taking breaks or moving to a quieter room). It is not known which of these strategies were the most effective and it is probably the case that they will not be equally effective for all students, but informing students of the self-regulatory strategies available might conceivably be of some help.

OVERVIEW

The current chapter has provided a brief insight into some of the research findings regarding student motivation. In simple terms, students can be motivated or amotivated, reflecting the extent to which they want to succeed. In addition, they can be intrinsically motivated and/or extrinsically motivated. Intrinsically motivated students want to learn for learning's sake, while extrinsically motivated students study for external rewards.

However, these factors are not easy to measure, and as a result there are few measures of motivation in higher education and relatively little research in this field. One might expect that motivation would correlate with both student behaviour and with academic achievement but research has produced inconsistent results. In addition, one might expect students to become more highly motivated and more intrinsically motivated during their time in higher education; once again, however, results are inconclusive.

In this chapter we hope to have highlighted the importance of ascertaining how motivated students are by the specific tasks set, and also of determining the kind of motivation that these tasks elicit. We have no ready panacea for solving the problems of student motivation, but it seems reasonable to suggest that the provision of high quality feedback and the adoption of appropriate assessment systems are at least part of the answer.

REFERENCES

Ames, C (1984) Competitive, co-operative, and individualistic goal structures: a cognitive-motivational analysis, in *Research on Motivation in Education: Volume 1 student motivation*, eds R Ames and C Ames, pp 177–207, Academic Press, San Diego

Biggs, J (1987) *Student Approaches to Learning and Studying*, Australian Council for Educational Research, Victoria

Biggs, J (1993) What do inventories of students' learning processes really measure? A theoretical review and clarification, *British Journal of Educational Psychology*, **63**, pp 3–19

Clarke, RM (1986) Students' approaches to learning in an innovative medical school: A cross-sectional study, *British Journal of Educational Psychology*, **56**, pp 309–21

Collins, A and Gentner (1980) A framework for a cognitive theory of writing, in *Cognitive Processes in Writing*, eds W Gregg and ER Steinberg, Lawrence Erlbaum Associates, New Jersey

Deci, E and Ryan, RM (1985) *Intrinsic Motivation and Self-determination in Human Behavior*, Plenum, New York

Dweck, CS and Elliott, ES (1983) Achievement motivation, in *Handbook of Child Psychology: Socialization, personality and social development*, ed EM Hetherington, **4**, pp 643–91, Wiley, New York

Entwistle, NJ (1998) Motivation and approaches to learning: motivating and conceptions of teaching, in *Motivating students*, eds S Brown, S Armstrong and G Thompson, pp 15–23, Kogan Page, London

Entwistle, NJ and Entwistle, A (1991) Contrasting forms of understanding for degree examination: the student experience and its implications, *Higher Education*, **22**, pp 205–27

Entwistle, NJ and Ramsden, P (1983) *Understanding Student Learning*, Croom Helm, London

Fazey, D and Fazey, J (1998) Perspectives on motivation: The implications for effective learning in higher education, in *Motivating Students*, eds S Brown, S Armstrong and G Thompson, pp 59–72, Kogan Page, London

Harter, S (1981) A new self-report scale of intrinsic versus extrinsic motivation in the classroom: motivational and informational components, *Developmental Psychology*, **17**, pp 302–12

Hoskins, S (1999) The development of undergraduates' approaches to studying and essay writing in higher education, PhD thesis, University of Plymouth

Newstead, SE and Findlay, K (1997) Some problems in using examination performance as a measure of student ability, *Psychology Teaching Review*, **6**, pp 14–21

Newstead, SE, Franklyn-Stokes, A and Armstead, P (1996) Individual differences in student cheating, *Journal of Educational Psychology*, **88**, pp 229–41

Nicholls, JG (1984) Achievement motivation: conceptions of ability, experience, task choice and performance, *Psychological Review*, **91**, pp 328–46

Norton, LS and Crowley, CM (1995) Can students be helped to learn how to learn? An evaluation of an approaches to learning programme for first year degree students, *Higher Education*, **29**, pp 307–28

Pintrich, PR and Garcia, T (1991) Student goal orientation and self-regulation in the classroom, in *Advances in Motivation and Achievement*, ed M Maehr and PR Pintrich, **7**, pp 371–402, JAI Press, Greenwich, USA

Pintrich, PR *et al* (1993), Reliability and predictive validity of the motivated strategies for learning questionnaire (MSLQ), *Educational and Psychological Measurement*, **53**, pp 801–13.

Purdie, NM and Hattie, JA (1995) The effect of motivation training on approaches to learning and self concept, *British Journal of Educational Psychology*, **65**, pp 227–35

Ramsden, P (1992) *Learning to Teach in Higher Education*, Routledge, London

Sharpe, R *et al* (in submission), Attitudes and approaches to studying in entry level undergraduate students (article submitted for publication)

Vallerand, RJ *et al* (1992) The academic motivation scale: a measure of intrinsic, extrinsic and amotivation in education, *Educational and Psychological Measurement*, **52**, 1003–17

Wolters, C (1998) Self-regulated learning and college students' regulation of motivation, *Journal of Educational Psychology*, **90**, 224–35

FURTHER READING

Brown, S, Armstrong, S and Thompson, G (eds) (1998), *Motivating Students*, Kogan Page, London. This is an edited book stemming from a Staff and Educational Development Association (SEDA) conference on Encouraging Student Motivation, offering some interesting and useful contributions.

Hartley, J (ed) (1998) *Learning and Studying: A Research Perspective*, Routledge, London. A well written book covering a range of wider issues relevant to student motivation. It draws on up-to-date research, providing useful examples. It provides good insight into how psychologists investigate learning to include their findings.

<table>
<tr><td>

7

</td></tr>
</table>

Lecturing for Learning

Jennifer Horgan

INTRODUCTION

The growth in participation in higher education during the 1990s and measures to widen access are bringing into the university system students from a broad spectrum of ability and from diverse backgrounds. These factors present an enormous challenge to university lecturers who are expected to 'combine the talents of scholar, writer, producer, comedian, showman and teacher in ways that contribute to student learning' (McKeachie, 1994).

This chapter looks at the lecture method as a means of promoting student learning and considers ways of making lectures more effective. The case studies illustrate how a number of university teachers have adapted their approach to lecturing by making students take a more active part in class. The reasons for adopting this approach are discussed, and students' views of good teaching are explored and compared with those expressed by practitioners.

This chapter does not consider the lecture from a performance perspective. In lecturing, the importance of aspects, such as using your voice effectively, reinforcing your message and building a rapport with your audience, should not be under-estimated. One way in which lecturers can gain feedback on all the different elements of their craft is by exposing their teaching to observation by a peer or other professional observer. This is now recognized as an important means of improving practice and it is discussed fully in Chapter 17.

REASONS FOR LECTURING

The demise of the lecture method has long been predicted, yet it still remains the most widely used teaching method in higher education. It is not hard to see why lectures are popular with those charged with organizing university education as they provide a cost-effective means of teaching large groups of students. However, university teachers in many disciplines also argue that a lecture approach is an absolutely essential component of any **course** and they cite compelling pedagogic reasons for choosing this method of teaching. Primarily, lectures are seen as necessary for providing background information and ideas, basic concepts, and methods required by students before they can learn much on their own and become effective participants in classroom discussion.

Interrogating Practice

Why are lectures important in your discipline? How do your reasons for using the lecture method match up with those given below? Have you any other reasons to add to the list?

Cashin (1985) lists the following reasons for using the lecture method:

- lectures can provide new information, based on original research and generally not found in textbooks or other printed sources;
- lectures can be used to highlight similarities and differences between key concepts;
- lectures can help communicate the enthusiasm of teachers for their subjects;
- lectures can model how a particular discipline deals with questions of evidence, critical analysis, problem solving and the like;
- lectures can organize subject matter in a way that is best suited to a particular class and course objectives;
- lectures can dramatize important concepts and share personal insights.

COMPARISON OF THE LECTURE METHOD WITH OTHER TEACHING METHODS

Many research studies have compared the effectiveness of the lecture method with other methods of teaching. McKeachie *et al* (1990) concluded that the lecture method is only as efficient as other methods of teaching as a means of transmitting knowledge. Teaching methods where active discussion is used are found to be more effective when the following are measured:

- retention of knowledge after the end of a course;
- transfer of knowledge to new situations;
- problem solving and thinking;
- attitude change.

Bligh (1998), in a very comprehensive review of the literature, also concluded that the lecture is as effective as other methods as a means of transmitting information, but not more so. It is less effective than other methods for promoting thought and changing students' attitudes.

In spite of these findings, it seems likely that the lecture will retain its place as the most widely used teaching method for some time to come. If limitations of the lecture method are recognized, what strategies can be used to improve the quality of student learning?

MAKING LECTURES MORE EFFECTIVE

The traditional lecture

Common sense and our own experience tell us that people learn better if they think about what they are learning and have an opportunity to engage with the material, rather than simply get the chance to see it and hear about it. Research into learning supports this common sense view and is discussed in more detail in Chapter 3. As Ramsden (1994) points out, 'Active engagement, imaginative inquiry and the finding of a suitable level are all much more likely to occur if teaching methods that necessitate student activity, student problem-solving and question-asking, and co-operative learning are employed'. However, in the traditional lecture the student takes a largely **passive** role and there is little opportunity for **active learning** such that the learner can engage with the subject matter being presented. Many lecturers feel that the traditional lecture is the most effective way of 'covering the material' but this approach is rarely satisfactory from the learner's point of view. It has been said that most of us are so busy 'covering the material' in a lecture that we miss the chance to 'uncover it'. In fact, Ramsden (1992) argues that the use of the traditional lecture may actually be detrimental to the quality of student learning, in that it leads students to expect learning to be a passive experience and does not provide them with opportunities to engage in **deep** processing of the subject matter. Initially students may object to lecturers who choose a more active approach, but as they get used to the approach they respond well, a point borne out by evaluation comments outlined in Case Study 2 (see page 91).

Ramsden (1994) suggests that many new lecturers see teaching as the efficient transmission of knowledge from the teacher to the learner and rarely think of the impact of this approach on students' learning. The initial focus for the new lecturer is, quite naturally, on the quality of the presentation and the skills involved in classroom management. It is only later when confidence has built up that many new lecturers feel able to turn their attention to the needs of the student as learner.

Attention levels during lectures

Various studies on attention levels during a 50-minute lecture reveal that during the first 10 minutes attention levels are high, but as the lecture proceeds attention levels drop and continue to do so if students are not actively involved in some way. Research studies on memory and retention of material show that students frequently forget, or never learn, much of the material presented to them during a typical 50-minute traditional lecture. Learning of material can be consolidated if students are given an opportunity to use it within a short time of its initial presentation.

Bligh (1998) refers to research carried out on factors that cause students to forget and concludes that facts presented during the middle of a lecture are not remembered as well as those at the beginning or the end. He suggests that lecturers need to take this into account by introducing novel points and/or contrasting approaches during the middle of a lecture. The material is recalled more effectively if key points are flagged up in advance, using what Brown (Brown and Atkins, 1988) refers to as 'advance organizers'.

Note-taking is used by students as a means of maintaining attention during a lecture, as an aid to memory and as the basis for revision of the material covered. Bligh (1998) uses the terms 'encoding' to describe the use of notes to aid memory and finds that there is overwhelming evidence to support the view that note-taking during a lecture aids memory of the lecture. He also cites studies that support the view 'that students who have notes to revise from, will do better in examinations than students who do not'.

The need for a structured approach

Students will learn and remember much more if their learning is organized and many would argue that the main role of the lecture is to enable students to find a framework in which to fit new facts and ideas. McKeachie (1994) suggests that in order to be effective 'the lecturer needs to build a bridge between what is in the students' minds and the structures in the subject matter'. This is one of the main themes in Bruner's theoretical framework, discussed under constructivism in Chapter 3. He describes learning as an active process in which we construct new ideas or concepts based on our current/past knowledge. If this is the case, the role of the teacher is to translate the information to be learned into a format that fits into the learner's current state of understanding.

However, it is important to give students opportunities to develop their own way of structuring new material rather than imposing a rigid framework on them, and McKeachie (1994) argues that some students do not learn well if the lecturer is too highly organized. We need to encourage students to take more responsibility for their own learning, 'our teaching should consist of guiding rather than governing student learning'. This point needs to be to kept in mind.

Interrogating Practice

What approaches have you experienced or used in lectures that you believe encourage student learning? How can bridges be built between structures in the subject matter and students' understanding? How can we help students make new meaning of the material presented to them?

PUTTING IDEAS INTO PRACTICE

How can this information on attention levels, active learning and structure help us to improve our lecturing technique? In other words, how can we make the lecturing less like a lecture (passive, rigid, routine knowledge transmission) and more like active communication between teacher and students?

Case Study 1: Active Learning in First Year Lectures in Computer Science

University of Wales, Aberystwyth

Mark Ratcliffe uses an interactive approach in all his lectures as a means of promoting active learning. With first-year undergraduates taking the module Introduction to Programming, he lectures on Java programming, and punctuates his lecture with questions to the whole class. At the beginning of the academic year when students do not know each other, or he them, he divides the lecture theatre in areas and takes answers from each couple of rows in turn. Care is taken to prevent students feeling overwhelmed by answering in such an arena. After week five of the course when students have been away on a team-skills weekend, he can target questions at named students. He then finds enthusiastic students wave their arms in the air before he has even posed the question. Students are encouraged to ask questions during the lecture. Mark punctuates his lecture with questions at roughly 10-minute intervals and the whole class is expected to work on the answer to ensure they are all actively thinking about the material. This approach keeps interest high throughout the class and ensures that everyone is involved in the topic being presented. Students learn well in this demanding classroom environment.

Mark cautions those who have not used this approach before by saying that it is important to have a clear structure so that student questions feed into the lecture and take it on step by step, as it is easy to be side-tracked. Student evaluation reports show a high level of satisfaction with this approach.

General points

The literature abounds with ideas for making lectures more effective, especially when dealing with large numbers of students (eg Gibbs, 1992). The main points to consider are listed below, although some of these will not necessarily be relevant or applicable to all disciplines:

- Structure the lecture carefully; so that you provide a solid framework into which students can fit new knowledge (see page 87). Show students an outline of this framework.
- Ensure that you provide students with clear signals to help them appreciate direction, links and points of separation between parts of the content. These are

called **signposts**. Make sure that they can 'see the wood as well as the trees'. Make links between the present lecture and past or future lectures.

- Make some statement of educational intent at the outset. Ideally state your **aims**, **objectives/learning outcomes** (Chapter 4) so that students will know what you wish them to achieve.

- Make sure that your lecture is not overloaded with content. For example Russell, Hendricson and Herbert (1984) have shown that students learn more when information density is not too high. You may not cover as much as you wish, but if the material is understood and can be applied, your time has been well spent.

- Organize your lecture so that you change the demands made on students every 10 to 15 minutes. This should ensure that attention levels are kept high.

- Make your lectures more participatory, and adopt this approach right from the start of the course when norms and expectations are being established. A good example is shown in Case Study 1.

- As the lecture proceeds, continue to show students the lecture outline on an overhead transparency so that they can chart their way through and note the significant elements.

- Provide a summary of the main points as you complete each section and an overall summary at the end of the session (this can be used profitably at the beginning of the next lecture to remind students of what has already been covered).

- Give students an opportunity to interact as soon as possible with the new material being presented so that they are able to make links between the new material and what they have learned in the past. You may wish students to work individually or in a **buzz group** for short periods during the lecture, or you may give them follow-up work to be completed outside class.

- Help students to take good lecture notes – concept maps, spray diagrams and mind maps are alternative ways of taking notes that students may wish to explore with your help. Many lecturers now publish full lecture notes on their web sites. You may wish to pause occasionally and allow students to check their notes against those of the person sitting next to them.

- Make good use of handouts – these may be gapped handouts where you leave space for students to add their own notes. You may wish to provide students with diagrams, references or articles for further reading.

Interrogating Practice

Thinking about the list above, which of these practices have you used in your lectures? Are there any others you could use?

Structuring a lecture

Brown and Atkins (1988) suggest the following checklist of questions for use after a lecture has been prepared.

1. What are the central questions of the lecture?
2. What do you expect students to learn or understand from your lecture?
3. What lecture methods will you use?
4. Will the opening be clear and interesting?
5. Are the sections of the lecture clearly organized and clearly linked?
6. Are the main key points clear, accurate and linked?
7. Are your examples and illustrations apt?
8. Will any reservations and qualifications you plan to make be clear and apt?
9. Will your section summaries and final summary be clear and coherent?
10. What activities will students have to carry out during the lecture?
11. What possible weaknesses are there likely to be in the presentation?
12. How do you plan to combat these possible weaknesses?
13. Are any audio-visual resources you might need going to be available?
14. How will you **evaluate** (Chapter 13) the effectiveness of your lecture?

Ways of varying student activity in lectures

The following suggestions are offered as means of engaging students with the subject matter being presented. Several of these devices are illustrated in the Case Studies.

- Give students a question or problem to be tackled individually and then ask students to share their ideas in small groups, commonly called buzz groups.
- Show a video clip with instructions on what to look for.
- Present material live from the Internet with instructions on what to look for, what data to collect, as illustrated in Case Study 3 (see page 93).
- Demonstrate a task or device and include instructions on what to look for.
- Set a brief multiple-choice question (**MCQ**) test (if you are able to ask a colleague to help with administering this it can be a very effective way of providing almost instant feedback on students' understanding of the topic being discussed).
- Solve a problem collectively.
- Ask students to discuss briefly, in groups of two or three, a research design or interpretation of a set of findings.
- Ask students to frame questions in relation to data or to make estimates (eg percentages of various crimes, range of accuracy of instruments). Students can compare their ideas in small groups. You can then show them the correct figures.

- Ask students to invent examples and compare them with those of another student.
- Ask students to consider briefly likely advantages and disadvantages, or strengths and weaknesses of a procedure or theory. Then outline the advantages and disadvantages so that they can compare these with their views.
- Turn a part of your lecture into a question and answer session – this needs courage and you may lack confidence to do this with a large group in the early stages of your career. It is possible to get round this by providing students with a 'question box' so that you have prior notice of questions and an opportunity to think about the answers. It may be advisable to pump-prime the box with some good questions!

(Adapted from Brown and Atkins, 1988.)

Case Study 2: Improving Learning in Geography Lectures

University of Derby

Irene Brightmer teaches a course on the Geography of Health and Disease to a class of over 60 second-year students at the University of Derby. The timetable slot involves three hours of teaching time, so Irene uses a variety of strategies to keep students actively involved.

She often uses video footage to illustrate points and emphasizes the need to help students use video as a learning resource, rather than as a source of entertainment. She gives students suggestions about how they should take notes from the video and provides a list of points that they should look out for. The subject matter presented on overhead transparencies during the lecture often requires students to look at tables of data collected from a number of different countries. Her strategy here is to break students into pairs and ask each pair to look for trends and contrasts between years, etc. By using this approach students are able to learn from each other and are not able to take a passive role. Whenever possible, Irene starts a topic by asking students to volunteer information based on their own experience, for example, by asking 'Think of the number of people you know who have died from degenerative diseases or infectious diseases, etc'. She warns that this approach is more risky as you are not entirely in control of the situation, but she is convinced that students learn more by being actively involved. She mentions that students comment adversely on the fact that they have to work too hard in lectures.

STUDENT VIEWS OF 'GOOD' LECTURING

Having looked at the research evidence on how to improve the quality of learning in lectures, and in the case studies seen how some experienced university lecturers have developed their teaching to incorporate good practice, let us now turn to students' views of 'good lecturing'.

A study carried out at the University of Lancaster looked at student perceptions of good teaching (Ramsden, 1992). The most frequent descriptions of good lecturing commented on the lecturer's ability to pitch material at the right level, to provide a clear structure and to maintain an appropriate pace. The most striking aspect of comments from students related to the effect of a lecturer's on a student's approach to learning enthusiasm and his or her ability to provide good explanations.

Parallels can be drawn with a more recent survey carried out at the University of Virginia, where a cross-section of undergraduate students were asked to give their opinions about lecture methods and about the qualities that they found most appealing in a lecturer (Lacoss and Chylack, 1998). They were also asked to comment on which aspects of lecture style, format and environment they found most conducive to learning and retention of material.

Students consistently praised those professors who introduced variety, interaction, structure and intensity into their lectures. No one style of lecture was singled out as being more effective than any other and, in fact, students appreciated variety in lecturing style. The ability of the lecturer to make use of examples, demonstrations and changes of tone ('to break the trance') was thought to be more important than the style used.

Particularly appreciated were lecturers who incorporated responses from students, by soliciting questions during lectures, made themselves available afterwards or who collected feedback from a bulletin board on the Web. The comments made by students about lecturers attempts to 'connect with them', were particularly interesting. They welcomed attempts to jolt them out of the passive role in lectures and agreed that such interactive advances were 'well worth the initial awkwardness they felt'. This approach was said by the group to promote better student preparation and result in greater respect and enthusiasm. Lecture techniques identified by students as particularly helpful were:

- use of outlines and lists;
- delivery paced to allow note-taking;
- pauses to allow clarification;
- short intermissions for review of material/personal reactions/questions;
- repetition of the main points;
- final recap of the key points.

Finally, students saw the lecturer as providing an active example of learning and processing information that, in turn, helped them to digest the material on their own'.

Case Study 3: Lecturing With the Aid of the Internet

Welsh Institute of Rural Studies at the University of Wales, Aberystwyth

Dave Powell teaches courses on Countryside Organizations to HND and degree students at level 1, and on Human Impact on the Environment to degree students at level 2. He makes use of the Internet in teaching both these courses and has integrated its use with PowerPoint presentations. After the lecture he also mounts the PowerPoint presentation onto the Internet so that students are able to reinforce their learning very effectively.

With the level 1 course Dave accesses the Web pages of the Countryside Organizations as he speaks, and finds that students respond well to the attractive forms of presentation used by these organizations. With the course on Human Impact on the Environment, use of the NASA Web site enables him to obtain up-to-the-minute data on ozone destruction. Data on regional pollution and low level ozone levels are available for use in the same way. He is able to introduce an immediacy to the lecture that would not be possible were he to use any other technique. Dave does warn of the need to have fallback data available to allow for technical hitches.

OVERVIEW

Effective lectures need to be structured, well-planned learning experiences that shake students out of the passive, stenographic role and provide a challenging learning environment. The experienced practitioners whose approaches have been examined in the case study material in this chapter have reached the same conclusions about what constitutes good lecturing in higher education. No one pretends that this approach is easy and many experienced lecturers will feel cautious about such change and feel uneasy about teaching in a less controlled environment. The best advice that can be given to anyone contemplating a change, from a traditional lecture to a more interactive approach, is to suggest that step-by-step change works best for both students and the lecturer. If your first attempt does not work as you had planned, do not abandon the idea, but rather reflect on why this was so and try again.

REFERENCES

Bligh, D (1998) *What's the Use of Lectures?* Intellect, Exeter

Brown, G and Atkins, M (1988) *Effective Teaching in Higher Education*, Methuen, London

Cashin, WE (1985) *Improving Lectures*, idea paper no 14, Manhattan, Center for Faculty Evaluation and Development, Kansas State University

Gibbs, G (1992) *Lecturing to More Students: Teaching more students, part 2*, Polytechnic and Colleges Funding Council, Oxonian Rewley Press, Oxford

Lacoss, J and Chylack, J (1999) *In Their Words: Students' Ideas about Teaching*, http://www.virginia.edu/ trc/lacoss.htm

McKeachie, WJ (1994) *Teaching Tips: Strategies, research and theory for college and university teachers*, Heath and Co, Lexington

McKeachie, WJ, Pintich, PR, Lin, Y-G, Smith, DAF and Sharma, R (1990) *Teaching and Learning in the College Classroom: A review of the research literature*, 2nd edn, MI: NCRIPTAL, University of Michigan, Ann Arbor

Ramsden, P (1992) *Learning to Teach in Higher Education*, Routledge, London

Ramsden, P (1994) Current challenges to quality in higher education, *Innovative Higher Education*, **18** (3), pp 177–87

Russell, IJ, Hendricson, WD and Herbert, RJ (1984) Effects of lecture information density on medical student achievement, *Journal of Medical Education*, 59 (1), pp 881–89.

FURTHER READING

Bligh, D (1998). See above. Second edition of this classic in the field which comprehensively reviews the literature on lecturing.

Gibbs, G (1992). See above. A quick and easy practical guide to lecturing, concentrating on approaches with large classes, by an influential figure in higher education.

8 Teaching and Learning in Small Groups

Sandra Griffiths

BACKGROUND AND DEFINITION

In Britain there have been numerous attempts to define precisely what is meant by **small group teaching** in higher education (Abercrombie, 1970; Bligh, 1986). From a historical perspective, some of these attempts were linked to the fact that small group teaching often took place in association with the lecture method. Many of the aims and practices of small group teaching reflected this link. This led to the view that the method existed only insofar as it supported the proper business of teaching; the formal lecture (see Chapter 7).

Attempts to define the concept using the words '**seminar**' and '**tutorial**' were problematic. These names were often used interchangeably and carelessly. This led some writers to abandon the use of seminar or tutorial in favour of the term 'group discussion'. The use of group discussion was congruent with a major objective of the activity, that is to teach students to think and to engage with their own and others' learning through the articulation of views (Stenhouse, 1972; Bligh, 1986). However, preoccupation with a precise definition can be limiting.

In this chapter, consideration is given to the enormous and unique potential of the small group to promote learning. It is viewed as an exciting, challenging and dynamic method open to use in a variety of forms and to serve a range of purposes appropriate to different disciplines. Therefore terms will be explored in their most diverse and flexible forms. The process is identified not as a didactic one but rather as a participative experience, in which students are encouraged to take responsibility, along with tutors, for their own learning.

A HIGHLY SKILLED ACTIVITY

Many writers (Bligh, 1986; Griffiths and Partington, 1992) argue that small group teaching is among the most difficult and highly skilled of teaching techniques. In addition to the primary objective of teaching students to think, the tutor must have a number of subsidiary objectives if the small group is to function. Writers generally agree that the method requires a wide knowledge of subject matter and ability to attend to detail while keeping an eye on the overall picture. Appreciation of how groups function, openness of spirit, accommodation of different views, receptivity to new ideas and maturity to manage a group of students without dominating them, are all necessary for effective small group teaching. These attributes are best thought of as skills to be developed over a period of time.

Not only do tutors have to learn how to teach using small group methods but also students have to learn how to work in small groups. Here, it is assumed that it is the tutor's job to assist students to learn, to equip them with self-confidence and facilitate group cohesion. Therefore, a tutor using these methods is much more than a subject matter expert.

In recognizing that small group teaching is a difficult and highly skilled teaching technique, it is important to know that it is also one of the most potentially rewarding teaching and learning methods for tutors and students alike.

GROUP SIZE

On the question of group size, broadly speaking, it is any teaching and learning occasion which brings together between 2 and 20 participants. The participants may be students and their tutors, or students working on their own. Because of the relatively small numbers of students involved, the financial cost of the method can be high.

CONTEXT

In recent years the experience of small group teaching and learning has come under threat. With the expansion of student numbers in higher education, class sizes have increased dramatically; tutored small group teaching is expensive when compared with the lecture. A resulting re-examination has had a profound impact on small group teaching and learning. It has led many tutors to re-evaluate critically the nature of the method and to maximize its potential to the full with some quite interesting and innovative results. **Peer tutoring**, **peer assessment**, peer learning and **peer support** have become more common, (for example Griffiths, Houston and Lazenbatt, 1996). In defence of the method, it has been necessary for assurances to be made that time devoted to teaching in this format is well orga-nized and well spent.

This re-examination has also coincided with other changes in the external envi-ronment. The move towards the **accreditation** of university teachers in higher edu-cation is resulting in a considerable culture shift. Part of this shift involves a growing recognition by lecturers that they are responsible not only for what is taught but also, in part, for how students learn.

LEARNING IN SMALL GROUPS

The interpersonal and interactive nature of small groups make them a challenging and appropriate vehicle for engaging students in their own learning. Students are engaged in small groups, both as learners and as collaborators in their own intellec-tual, personal and professional development. Furthermore, there is strong evi-dence from students themselves that they benefit from, and enjoy, the experience in a whole range of different ways (Rudduck, 1978; Luker, 1989; Griffiths, Houston and Lazenbatt, 1996). These might best be summed up as both cognitive and affec-tive in nature. Alongside understanding and knowledge benefits, students suggest that participation, belonging and being involved are all important dimensions of the experience. The implications of these findings are that the process of building and managing groups, and assisting with the development of relationships, is of paramount importance.

In the light of the **Dearing Report** (NCIHE, 1997), the question of the development of **key skills** in higher education has once again come to the fore (see Chapter 10).

The small group is viewed as a critical mechanism for exploring the develop-ment of a range of key skills. It is within the small group that self-confidence can be improved, and teamwork and interpersonal communication developed. Develop-ment of these group work and other skills are reported by students (Griffiths, Houston and Lazenbatt, 1996) to foster conditions whereby they can observe their own **learning styles**, change these styles to suit different tasks and engage more deeply with the content of their subject. These latter attributes are often cited as prerequisites for a **deep approach** to learning. This revitalized interest in key skills has succeeded in according group work a new status.

Despite moves towards mass participation and larger classes in higher educa-tion, the quality of the learning experience, the need to deliver key skills and the potential for innovation, have contributed to the retention and enhancement of the small group method. Small groups are used extensively, and in many different ways, eg in **problem-based learning** approaches (see Chapter 24).

PLANNING

Successful small group teaching and learning does not happen by chance. Planning for effective small group teaching is as important as planning any other teaching activity. This point sometimes goes unrecognized because the actual activity of learning in small groups can at first glance appear unstructured. Some lecturers are put off by the seemingly informal, loose or open-ended nature of small group learning. Others fear this informality will be a recipe for chaos or that the group will develop into a therapy session. All types of teaching must be planned as part of a coherent package, with appropriate use of different methods within each component.

This appearance of informality is deceptive. Behind the facade of the informal group lies a backdrop in which all the learners are playing within a known set of rules which are spoken or unspoken. The approach might better be described as a kind of structured spontaneity. In other words, the creative flow of ideas is possible precisely because the lecturer or leader has a clear framework, deliberately planned to meet the **objectives** of the session. Within this framework, students feel safe to develop their ideas. Equally important, staff feel safe to try out and practise the skills of small group teaching.

Planning for small group teaching may take many forms. It will have much in common with features of planning for any learning occasion. Typically the teacher might consider the intended **learning outcomes**, selection of suitable type of small group teaching method and learner activity.

Beyond these general features the session plan will be dependent upon the requirements of specific disciplines, the culture of the institution, the overall context of the programme or module and the particular learning needs and prior knowledge of the students.

Whatever form the plan takes, it is critical that precise intentions for small group work are outlined. It is salutary to ask often whether what is being aimed at, and undertaken in small groups, is qualitatively different from that which is being carried out in other delivery modes. The gains for the students should justify the extra costs incurred. In short, the aims and content of the teaching session should dictate and justify the means.

Interrogating Practice

Using your own experience as a learner in small groups, identify strengths and weaknesses of different approaches used in your discipline.

PREPARING LEARNERS

In a study into peer tutoring in higher education (Griffiths, Houston and Lazenbatt, 1996) staff indicated that they had recognized the need for student preparation on the 'knowledge of subject' side but had not recognized, prior to their action research, the extent to which students would need training, and ongoing facilitation, to work in the new ways. These new ways refer to working within learner groups. This finding concurs with evidence from other quarters (Griffiths and Partington, 1996), where students offering advice to lecturers say that lecturers too often assume that they, the students, know how to work in groups. It is just as important to prepare students to work in groups as it is to prepare yourself.

Interrogating Practice

How do you assist learners to organize small group sessions where you are not present? How could you improve on your current practice?

Preparing students to work in small groups can mean providing specific training for students on how groups work. Such training will develop an understanding that all groups go through a number of stages. Hence, when conflict arises in the group, for example, it can be understood and dealt with as a natural feature to be resolved, rather than perceived as a descent into chaos. Preparation can also mean affording structured opportunities at strategic points within the teaching programme to examine how the group is functioning, what problems exist and how resolution can be achieved. Some lecturers achieve this by providing guidelines (ground rules) at the beginning of a small group session or at the beginning of a series of seminars or workshops. Some lecturers go further, believing that students (either individually or as a group) can themselves effectively be involved in establishing and negotiating ground rules and intended outcomes. Such activities may constitute a **learning contract**.

Such a learning contract is an important way of effecting a safe and supportive learning environment. Establishing the contract may involve tutors and students in jointly:

- setting, agreeing and understanding objectives;
- agreeing assessment procedures and criteria (if appropriate);

- allocating tasks to all participants, tutors and students;
- developing ground rules for behaviour within the group.

The staff/student contract provides a mechanism for continuing review. It is recommended that time be set aside every third or fourth meeting to evaluate the progress and process of the group's working against the original contract.

PHASES OF GROUP DEVELOPMENT

Social group theorists describe the initial phases in the life of a group using a variety of terms such as inclusion, forming and approach-avoid ambivalence (eg Adair, 1996; and Tuckmann, 1965). These works discuss the behaviour of individuals working in groups. What is also recognized is the conflicting tendency to avoid the situation of joining groups because of the demands, the frustration and even the pain it may bring about. This 'moving towards, pulling away' behaviour can easily create tension in the early stages of a group if it is not handled sensitively. Certain behaviours may be a natural part of the initial joining stages rather than a conscious act of defiance or withdrawal by a student. Understanding how students are likely to behave can assist the tutor to provide a framework that fosters confidence and allows trust to develop.

The ending of the group often brings to the surface many issues to do with termination. How intervention is handled at this stage will have a bearing on helping the members to move on. The tutor needs to be aware of appropriate ways of ending different types of group activity. For discussion and guidance on managing behaviour in groups see Jacques (1991).

Interrogating Practice

Consider small group teaching sessions you have facilitated. Think about the different types of individual and group behaviour you have witnessed. What were the possible causes?

SIGNIFICANCE OF THE SETTING

Few tutors in higher education work in an ideal setting with tailor-designed group workrooms. A great deal can be done, however, in setting up the room to encourage participation and interaction. The research into the influence of environmental factors on interaction has been fairly extensive and shows that physical arrangements have a powerful effect. For example, Korda (1976) documents the effect on encounters when one person is seated and the other is not.

It is well known that communication increases if the differences in social level or status are small. Therefore, part of the tutor's task is to play down the differences in roles and, in particular, play down his or her own authority. This will facilitate the free flow of discussion. It is not a straightforward matter since the tutor must relinquish authority while all the time remaining in control. This knowledge about the need to minimize social status differences has an impact on where the tutor actually sits within the group.

In fact, it is possible to arrange a room so that certain desired effects are achieved. Three situations (Griffiths and Partington, 1992) serve as examples of this point.

1. Nervous students can be encouraged to participate more readily if their place in the group is opposite (ie in direct eye-contact) to either a sympathetic tutor or an encouraging, more voluble student peer.
2. A dominating, vociferous student can be quietened by being seated immediately next to the tutor.
3. The level of student participation and of student-student interaction can be affected by the choice of room itself. Is the tutor's own room with all his or her paraphernalia of authority likely to be more or less conducive to student participation? What is an unadorned, stark seminar room with a rectangular table and a special high-backed lecturer's chair at one end likely to dictate for the processes of the group?

Interrogating Practice

Visualize yourself in a room where you teach small groups. Where should you sit to maximize your interaction with the group? Where might a student sit to avoid interaction with the tutor or with other students? Where might a student sit if he or she wishes to persuade others of a point of view?

TYPES OF SMALL GROUP TEACHING

A specific method selected for small group teaching will derive from the objectives set. There are many different methods of small group teaching; some methods are more suited to certain disciplines than others. However, few methods are peculiar to one subject alone. A large number of methods can be adapted for use in any subject. It is important to remain flexible and open to try out a variety of methods drawn from a wide repertoire. It may be necessary to overcome a tendency to find one method that works well and use this method frequently. The effect on learners of over-exposure to one method of teaching is worth considering.

Below is a brief description of various ways of working with small groups. It is not intended to be comprehensive, nor are all types mutually exclusive. Some methods are described in terms of a special setting that encourages the application of principles or techniques; for example, brainstorming is a structured setting for the use of lateral thinking. Other methods are described in terms of their size or purpose.

- *Brainstorming* – generation of ideas from group to foster lateral thinking. No criticism, until all ideas logged.
- *Buzz group* – two or three people asked to discuss an issue for a few minutes. Usually then shared with larger group.
- *Cross-over groups* – brief discussions then transfers between groups.
- *Fishbowl* – small groups within large, observation group then discussion and reversal.
- *Free discussion* – topic and direction from group; tutor or leader observes.
- *Open-ended enquiries* – students determine structure as well as reporting back on outcomes.
- *Peer tutoring* – students learning from one another and teaching one another.
- *Problem-based tutorial group* – small groups using problem-based learning.
- *Role-play* – allocated or self-created roles. Important to facilitate students to enter and come out of role.
- *Self-help group* – run by and for students, tutor may be a resource.
- *Seminar* – group discussion of a paper presented by a student (note term often used in different ways).
- *Simulation/game* – structured experience in real/imaginary roles. Guidelines on process important and feedback critical.
- *Snowballing* – pairs becoming small groups becoming larger groups.
- *Step-by-step discussion* – planned sequence of issues/questions led by student or tutor.
- *Structured enquiries* – tutor provides lightly structured experiments and guidance.
- *Syndicate* – mini-project work, followed by reporting to full class.
- *Tutorial* –meeting with very small group, often based on feedback to an essay or assignment (note term often used in different ways).

- *Tutorless group* – group appoints leader and may report back; may focus on discussion or completion of some other type of set task.

> *(Adapted from several sources, but owing much to Habeshaw, Habeshaw and Gibbs, 1988)*

There are several approaches not mentioned above that can be used in small or large groups. The main determining factor is the amount of interaction that is desirable. Apart from that it is necessary to ensure that in a larger group all members can see, hear, and so on. Case studies, **problem classes** and demonstrations fall into this category.

Interrogating Practice

Study the list, noting methods you are familiar with and methods you have employed. Select one or two methods you have not used before and work out how you can try them out in the near future.

Case Study 1: The Use of Small Groups in Teaching and Learning on an Undergraduate Music Degree at the University of Ulster

Course: BMus (Hons)
Year of study: 2
Module: Renaissance Studies
Delivery: lectures/classes, seminars and workshops
Class size: 20–25 students

Seminar programme

For this part of the **module** the class is divided into five groups. The tutor, ensuring a mix of personalities, determines the formation of the groups. Each group delivers two presentations to the whole class. The higher of the two marks awarded contributes towards the module assessment. The assessment criteria are negotiated with the class. Each group is asked to maintain a diary, recording meetings and discussion and their management of particular tasks.

Structure of each one-hour seminar:

1. Group presentation (15–20 minutes).
2. Listening groups consider presentation and agree questions (10 minutes).
3. Questions and discussion (15 minutes).
4. Reports completed (10 minutes).

As the presentation is a group endeavour, groups are encouraged to involve each member, not only in the presentation and delivery of the presentation but also in the response to questions during the seminar. Students are reminded to think of interesting ways in which the presentation might be delivered to engage the attention of their audience. The 'presentation' might take the form of a panel discussion or a debate; it might be modelled on a gameshow programme. Each presenting group is required to submit a one-page summary one week prior to the seminar. This is copied to the other groups to familiarize them with the treatment of the topic.

At the end of the seminar each of the listening groups completes a report which invites comments on the effectiveness of the presenting group's management of the situation and their knowledge of the topic, including their response to questions. The tutor monitors the proceedings and completes a separate report. The marks awarded by the students and the tutor are equally weighted in the final assessment.

(Dr Desmond Hunter, Module Tutor)

SKILLS FOR EFFECTIVE SMALL GROUP TEACHING

Among important skills for teachers, those of listening, asking questions and responding are paramount in small groups settings. Listening and responding, often overlooked and undervalued, are concentrated on here. Many general teaching texts deal with the skill of questioning, for example Brown and Atkins (1988).

Interrogating Practice

Consider how much time you spend listening to students and encouraging students to listen to one another. Check out your perceptions of your real talk time/listening time by asking students for feedback.

Listening

The mental process of listening is an active one that calls into play a number of thinking functions including analysis, comprehension, synthesis and evaluation. Genuine listening also has an emotional dimension since it requires an ability to share another person's feelings, understand their situation and quite possibly their feelings.

Intellectual and emotional meanings are communicated by the listener and speaker in both verbal and non-verbal forms. So how you listen will be observable through gestures and body language. Your listening skills may be developed by thinking about all the levels of a student's comment, in this way:

- what is said: the content;
- how it is said: tone and feelings;
- when it is said: time and priority;
- where it is said: place and environment.

Listening attentively to individual students in the group and to the group's mood will heighten your ability to respond. This may require a new approach, one which demands practising silence, but if you persevere you will find this an attainable skill, through which remarkable insights can be gained.

Responding

Listening in silence by paying undivided attention to the speaker is an active process, engaging and heightening awareness and observation. The other aspect of positive listening is of course to intervene in a variety of ways for a variety of purposes. The more intense our listening is, the more likely it is that we will know how to respond, when to respond and in what ways.

Interrogating Practice

Jot down some of the reasons for making tutor responses in groups.

There are many ways of responding and many reasons for responding in a certain way. Appropriate responses are usually made when the tutor has considered not only the cognitive aims of the session but also the interpersonal needs of the group and the individual learner's level of confidence and knowledge. Different responses will have different consequences for the individual student and for the behaviour of the group as a whole. Therefore, an appropriate response can only be deemed appropriate in the context of the particular small group teaching session.

Interrogating Practice

Along with a small group of colleagues, determine what skills you might usefully develop to increase effectiveness as a facilitator of groups.

OVERVIEW

This chapter has considered a selection of appropriate group methods; mentioned a range of group formats; referred to individual and group behaviour and offered an opportunity for teachers to consider how they might develop and enhance their practice, including by offering suggestions for further reading.

REFERENCES

Abercrombie, M (1970) *Aims and Techniques of Group Teaching*, SRHE, London
Adair, J (1996) *Effective Motivation*, Pan, London
Bligh, D (ed) (1986) *Teaching Thinking by Discussion*, SRHE and NFER Nelson, Guildford
Brown, G and Atkins M (1988) *Effective Teaching in Higher Education*, Routledge, London
Griffiths, S, and Partington P (1992) *Enabling Active Learning in Small Groups: Module 5 in Effective Learning and Teaching in Higher Education*, UCoSDA/CVCP, Sheffield

Griffiths, S, Houston K and Lazenbatt, A (1996) *Enhancing Student Learning through Peer Tutoring in Higher Education*, University of Ulster, Coleraine

Habeshaw, S, Habeshaw, T and Gibbs, G (1988) *5   nteresting Things to do in your Seminars and Tutorials*, 3rd edn, Technical and Educational Services Ltd, Bristol

Jacques, D (1991) *Learning in Groups*, Croom Helm, London

Korda, M (1976) *Power in the Office*, Weidenfeld and Nicolson, London

Luker, P (1989) Academic staff development in universities with special reference to small group teaching (unpublished PhD thesis), University of Nottingham

NCIHE (1997) (Dearing Report) *Higher Education in the Learning Society*, National Committee of Inquiry into Higher Education, HMSO, London

Rudduck, J (1978) *Learning Through Small Group Discussion*, SRHE, University of Surrey

Stenhouse, L (1972) Teaching through small group discussion: formality, rules and authority, *Cambridge ournal of Education*, **2** (1), pp 18–24

Tuckmann, B (1965) Developmental sequences in small groups, *Psychological Bulletin*, **63** (6), pp 384–99

FURTHER READING

Griffiths and Partington (1992). See above. An in-depth look at the topic. Useful interactive exercises and video to highlight skills.

Habeshaw, Habeshaw, and Gibbs (1988). See above. Very useful for practical advice and activities.

Supervising Projects and Dissertations

Stephanie Marshall

'The waiter analogy is useful [when considering what constitutes good project and dissertation supervision]: a good waiter in a good restaurant is around enough to help you when you need things but leaves you alone enough to enjoy yourself.' (Murray, 1998)

Readers undoubtedly will agree with the sentiments expressed above, as would students reflecting on their desired role for their supervisors in the supervision of projects and dissertations. But how is such a fine balance achieved, and is it really possible for a supervisor to attain the ideal of knowing when to be 'hands on' and when to be 'hands off'? This chapter seeks to explore this question, first, by providing a background to the use of projects and dissertations in undergraduate teaching, moving on to consider a working definition; and second, by mapping out the terrain – that is, the key issues supervisors need to think through and be clear about prior to introducing such a strategy for promoting learning; and, finally, summarizing the key management and interpersonal skills required of the supervisor in order to promote efficient and effective supervision of projects and dissertations.

WHY PROJECTS AND DISSERTATIONS?

Over the past decade, the use of projects and dissertations in university curricula has been seen as increasingly important for a number of reasons. Projects and dissertations have always been viewed as an effective means of research training and of encouraging a discovery approach to learning, through the generation and analysis of primary data. Such an approach is aimed at the development of higher level cognitive skills such as analysis, synthesis and evaluation. Alongside this obvious rationale, projects and dissertations are also seen as an effective means, first, of diversifying assessment; second, addressing concern to promote transferable skills and skills for employability (Chapter 10); third, empowering the learner; and, finally, providing student motivation. Projects and dissertations have come to be seen as an important component of degree programmes across the disciplines, due to such a rationale as above, and the clear emphasis they place on the learner taking responsibility for their own learning (Chapter 11).

DEFINITIONS

Projects and dissertations are often discussed as one in the educational development literature (Day, Grant and Hounsell, 1998; Wilkins, 1995). It is worth considering both distinctions and similarities prior to offering a working definition.

A project as distinct from a dissertation is generally defined as aimed at generating primary data (Williams and Horobin, 1992). Dissertations, on the other hand, are categorized as generating secondary data, often in the form of a long essay or report (Parsons and Knight, 1998).

Henry (1994) researched extensively the use of projects in teaching on behalf of the Open University. She offers a six-point definition of a 'project' which I would suggest is not dissimilar to a dissertation, stating that: 'The student (usually) selects the project topic; locates his or her own source material; presents an end product (usually a report and often for assessment); conducts an independent piece of work (though there are also group projects). The project lasts over an extended period and the teacher assumes the role of adviser' (p12).

The similarities between projects and dissertations are obvious, in that both require project management skills: scheduling, action planning, time management, and monitoring and evaluation. Over recent years the term 'dissertation' in the context of undergraduate work has come to be employed less, and use of the term 'project', incorporating the notion of project management, employed more. Case Study 1, drawing on the University of York 1998 prospectus, exemplifies this trend.

Case Study 1: Definitions of Projects as Offered in the University of York Undergraduate Prospectus

Electronics

'The individual final year project is usually chosen from a range of suggestions from staff, although many others are suggested by students...The essence of the project is to provide open-ended and flexible opportunities for students to explore those subject areas where they most want to specialize at advanced level, and for them to be able to show initiative, originality and project management skills over a prolonged period of time.'

History

'In a few courses on collaborative project work, students work together; they have a tutor for consultation and guidance, but are themselves primarily responsible for shaping and producing the project they have been set...students quickly find that there is very little "spoon feeding". Self-reliance is strongly encouraged. Our task is to help students learn how to find things out for themselves, to organize their work independently and to develop their own interest in historical scholarship.'

Music

'At the heart of the course is a series of projects which offer opportunities for you to work at your own pace and to contribute to the group-study of a topic...You will have considerable freedom in your choice and timing of projects...The organization varies from one to another, but all have the same general pattern...'

All three explanations of project work offered in Case Study 1 emphasize project management skills on the part of the student. Such a definition suggests both projects and dissertations are a piece of project management with an emphasis on the student determining the parameters within which they will operate to deliver a time-bound externally described output – a project or dissertation of a certain length and format. Within this specified time framework, students determine the parameters of their own work and are offered the potential to pursue their own interests within a given discipline area. The role of the supervisor thus moves away from that of teacher providing the format within which students will be expected to perform to that of **facilitator**. It is this definition that offers the distinction between the supervision of projects and dissertations and routine supervision of students, by teaching staff, ie a time-bound, managed activity that requires project management skills on the part of both supervisor and supervisee. This is the definition of a project and dissertation which informs discussion in this chapter.

Projects and dissertations clearly offer a teaching and learning strategy which passes the onus for learning onto the student, thus requiring the supervisor to reposition themselves away from the role of teacher, moving vertically up the axis to that of facilitator, as illustrated in Figure 9.1.

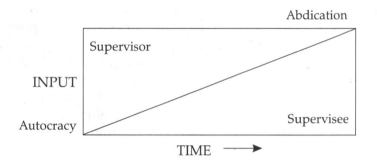

Figure 9.1

The implications of this shift in role offer the greatest potential for student learning at the same time as offering the greatest potential for role conflict on the part of the supervisor. As Day, Grant and Hounsell (1998: 51) suggest, 'avoiding the twin traps of over- or under-supervising is never easy'.

Establishing and agreeing the appropriate working relationship between supervisor and supervisee offers the key to maximizing the learning potential of projects and dissertations. How to achieve such a working relationship is explored in detail in the next section.

MAPPING THE TERRAIN

Prior to embarking on the introduction of projects or dissertations, supervisors should review their own project management skills. There would appear to be four key questions that the supervisor needs to address: first, their own motivation in choosing a project or dissertation as a learning strategy; second, whether to opt for a structured or unstructured project or dissertation; third, their own role as supervisor; and, finally, ways of broadening support for supervisees.

The aims and objectives of the learning strategy

In planning any project or dissertation, supervisors must be clear as to why they are choosing such a method of teaching and learning to promote the aims of the learning programme. The labour intensity and potential for undue pressure on the supervisor further to pursuit of the project method have been discussed elsewhere (Henry, 1994). All **Quality Assessment Overview Reports** (NISS, 1997) suggest that projects and dissertations form an important place among any departmental repertoire of teaching and learning strategies. Furthermore, projects and dissertations do appear to feature as distinct evidence of a significant piece of student-centred learning in course programmes which might otherwise appear rather traditional. There is general agreement that projects and dissertations are best left until the latter part of the degree programme (Jacques, 1989; Thorley and Gregory, 1994), and, indeed, 'for most students, the single most significant piece of work carried out is the final-year research project or dissertation. Not only can it assist with the integration of subject material, but it provides an introduction to research techniques and methods' (QO 10/95). It is this unique feature of projects and dissertations – ie the shift in control from supervisor to supervisee – which can offer the greatest challenge to both student and supervisor. This shift is explored further in section three.

Interrogating Practice

Reflect on projects or dissertations you have supervised or, indeed, have recently completed. How was this learning strategy used to promote the aims of the curriculum?

Structured versus unstructured projects and dissertations

There has been much written both in favour of structured and in favour of unstructured projects and dissertations. At one end of the spectrum, it is agreed that providing students with a structure reduces the risk of failure at the same time as making the supervisory role easier in the sense that the supervisor will be able to monitor student progress through clearly prescribed stages (Race and Brown, 1998). The main critique of such a method is that projects and dissertations can appear insufficiently open-ended, thus presenting a number of students with little real challenge (QO 2/95). At the other end of the spectrum, it is agreed that providing students with extended project and dissertation work allows them to collect a range of evidence, proceeding on to test a range of theories and explanations. The result should be a demonstration and familiarity with key theories, and an awareness of the importance of using sufficient evidence (QO 8/96). However, the main critique of adopting the unstructured approach is that students, in being given too much choice, may flounder. Alongside student **autonomy**, academic staff will be forced to supervise too great a range of projects. Both these factors can result in a compromise of quality (QO 10/95).

Interrogating Practice

Reflect on the parameters offered for projects and dissertations within your department. Would you classify these as structured or unstructured? What are the strengths and weaknesses of the approach adopted by your department?

The role of project and dissertation supervisor

Determining how to supervise projects and dissertations offers a great challenge. As with any project, 'front loading' (putting the most time in at the beginning) at the planning stage – both initially on one's own and then with the supervisee(s) – is essential. Stone (1994) refers to the 'walk-through' approach as offering an essential planning tool. By this he means that the supervisor should mentally walk through every step of the project, considering such issues as phasing and likely time allocation. It would seem most appropriate to pursue this method to promote dialogue with supervisees. There are four key features of the supervisory framework which will require planning for and sharing with the supervisee(s). First, determine and agree educational objectives; second, determine and agree specific objectives to include formative deadlines; third, agree set targets; and, finally, review and ensure understanding of the assessment criteria. Within this framework, time allocation for supervision needs to be made clear to avoid any possible future confusion. Most departments offer details of supervisors' office hours (NISS, 1997). Within these dedicated supervisory hours, the supervisor needs to ensure equity of quality time for supervisees, and thus should spend some time going through a few simple calculations.

Interrogating Practice

Reflect on how much time, to include planning, delivery, supervision, and review, you would normally spend on a taught course which equates in credit value to the project or dissertation you are or will be supervising. What does this mean in terms of hours a week you should make available for project or dissertation supervision? What does this mean in terms of time allocation for each of your supervisees?

Once a framework for supervision has been determined as above, legal (eg health and safety regulations), ethical (eg issues of confidentiality) and financial (eg restricted budgets for science experiments) constraints should be addressed. Such issues undoubtedly will be addressed in departmental guidelines for project and dissertation completion, and can be reviewed elsewhere (Williams and Horobin, 1992). As more additional guidance data to inform the execution of projects and dissertations is gathered, it ultimately will save the supervisor much time in the long run by establishing and codifying their own clear guidelines and criteria, offering these to supervisees as either a hand-out or a Web page, or both.

Supervising unstructured or semi-structured projects and dissertations implies assisting students in formulating research questions; second, choosing methods; and finally, scoping the means of data collection. As the end product should be the supervisees' intellectual property, the supervisor must be sensitive to the supervisees' ability to determine these for themselves. There is a fine line between guiding and telling, and much will depend on the ability and vision of the student, combined with the sensitivity of the supervisor.

Interrogating Practice

Reflect on your role. At which stage(s) of the project or dissertation will you take on a 'teaching' role, and at which stage(s) a facilitatory role? Consider the skills required at both ends of the spectrum.

Focusing on the facilitatory role should prompt a response which includes: asking the supervisee open-ended questions, reflecting questions back and encouraging the supervisee to explore strategies to take their work forward. Facilitation skills have been written about extensively, as they do not necessarily require the supervisor to demonstrate their own technical skills but rather interpersonal skills, which can prove far more difficult to learn (Williams and Horobin, 1992). Furthermore, with the increase in student numbers, it is highly likely that supervisors will be required to supervise a group of students working outside what the supervisor might perceive to be their own area of expertise.

Interrogating Practice

Reflect on your own departmental practices. How do students choose their supervisor, or are students allocated to a supervisor? Will you be expected to supervise students outside your area of expertise?

Further to supervisory responsibility being determined, the supervisor and supervisee should establish an agreed, appropriate working relationship. At the first meeting, the supervisor and supervisee should discuss expectations in terms of apportioning responsibility. The most recognized formalized approach to agreeing a working relationship is that of a **learning contract**, or what Williams and Horobin (1992: 43) refer to as creating a 'we culture'. Ryan (1994) offers a template for a supervisor checklist and student contract which itemises the range of responsibilities to which both parties agree: eg timetabled regular meetings, writing up supervisory meeting notes, ethical issues, submission of progress reports, and involvement in peer group support.

Ways of broadening support

With the massification of higher education, and the recognition of the value of teamwork, peer support has increasingly been viewed as a learning strategy that should be promoted within the curriculum (Thorley and Gregory, 1994) for a range of reasons. For example, working in project teams provides moral support at the same time as promoting teamwork skills. Such an approach is becoming more widespread, eg problem-based medical education (see Chapter 24). The group often has a greater range of total experience and skills than any one individual. It is particularly beneficial to be able to draw on a range of students' skills such as an exceptionally IT literate student, a student capable of sophisticated statistical analysis, or a student capable of maintaining morale when the going gets tough. It could be a requirement of the department that peer support teams meet at prescribed times to provide feedback.

Jacques (1989: 30) advocates this method, suggesting that

> 'Many of the issues to do with the progress of a project can be just as well dealt with by students themselves, provided they have a reasonably clear structure to work with. In the case of individual projects, students can report and be quizzed in turn by the rest of a peer group at regular meetings on matters like:…What are you proposing to do?…How can you break that down into manageable steps?…What or who else could help you?…'

He advocates using a similar set of guidance questions towards the end of the project, moving on to suggest ways of engaging these peer groups in summative evaluation, prior to formal submission of the project. Clark (1992: 7), writing about the supervision of group work projects in the History Department at the University of York, advocates the supervisor being close on hand to offer interventions if requested by students, noting that when he dropped in on his first ever project group to offer advice on writing-up, he was told with much amusement, 'Go away, we don't need you'.

Other ways of broadening support are explored in Chapter 12 and include the setting up of a **Web site poster board** with guidance notes (eg format, word length) and frequently asked questions (**FAQs**), and encouraging students to post up queries (Web sites such as WebCT, COSE, MERLIN). However, the supervisor will need to monitor the poster board to make appropriate interventions, ensuring accurate resolution of problems takes place. Finally, there are an increasing number of books on the market targeted at the student population, providing additional guidance and 'how to' tips (eg Parsons and Knight, 1998).

MANAGING SCHEDULING

The pressure of time will be felt by both supervisors and supervisees when working to deadline. In order to keep projects and dissertations on track, a range of documentation can prove useful. The use of guideline criteria and learning contracts as initial documentation was referred to in the previous section. Schedules, action plans and checklists similarly are useful tools. Some useful examples are provided by Day, Grant and Hounsell (1998) and a simplistic version of a checklist offering a 'walk-through' approach to supervision is illustrated in Case Study 2. Checklists and documentation are most useful to avoid memory overload, but also to provide a written record of the meeting to include agreed action points. Such written records are invaluable in cases of student appeals.

Case Study 2: Checklist for Preparation for Project and Dissertation Supervisory Meetings

The checklist which follows results from brainstorming sessions with academics enrolled on staff development workshops aimed at promoting professional supervision of dissertations and projects.

Planning for the supervision – how will you:
- discuss current strengths and weaknesses;
- encourage the student to plan for taking the work forward;
- set a short-term objective (to include contingency planning) within an action plan;
- set a more detailed time and action framework?

What will your agenda be?
- agree action plan and/or:
- review progress against action plan;
- feedback on performance;
- troubleshoot, problem solve;
- revisit assessment criteria;
- revisit and redefine action plan and timescale.

What information will you need to refer to?
- supervisee's written progress reports;
- supervisee's draft material;
- departmental project regulations and assessment criteria.

Arrangements for the supervision meeting
- ensure 'quality time' free from interruptions;
- ensure the venue is conducive to open discussion.

The supervision meeting
structured and well organized:
- **opening** – clarify purpose and agree agenda;
- **middle** – facilitate discussion of ideas, discuss specific issues, monitor progress, give constructive feedback, question effectively, set and agree objectives leading to the next supervision meeting;
- **end** – record action plan, to include short-term objectives; end on a positive note.

By adopting such methods as offered in Case Study 2 and checklists presented elsewhere (Day, Grant and Hounsell, 1998; Wilkins, 1995), both supervisor and supervisee will share a sense of purpose and progress. This will result in the supervision meeting being viewed as a constructive means of monitoring the milestones on the route to successful project and dissertation completion.

OVERVIEW

This chapter examined the greater use made of projects and dissertations across disciplines and endeavoured to provide a working definition. Projects and dissertations were described as offering a unique learning opportunity in that, first, they are sufficiently time-bound to afford the student the opportunity to demonstrate their project management skills and, second, they are clearly a student-centred learning experience which requires the supervisor to take on the role of facilitator. It was argued that for supervisors to offer effective and efficient supervision of projects and dissertations, they would have to examine and refine their own management and interpersonal skills. In the case of the former, a range of planning tools were offered. In the case of the latter, it was suggested that the supervisor should broaden support for the student, so that the supervisor could take on the role of facilitator, prompting and encouraging the student to seek out his or her own solutions and strategies for moving forward. It is this combination of unique features which makes the use of projects and dissertations such a powerful learning tool.

REFERENCES

Clark, C (1992) Group projects in the department of history, Staff Development and Training Newsletter, Staff Development Office, York

Day, K, Grant, R and Hounsell, D (1998) Chapter Seven, in *Reviewing Your Teaching*, Edinburgh: CTLA & UCoSDA

Henry, J (1994) *Teaching Through Projects*, Kogan Page, London

Jacques, D(1989) *Independent Learning and Project Work*, Open Learning, Oxford

Murray, R (1998) *Research Supervision*, Centre for Academic Practice, Strathclyde

NISS (1997) Quality Assessment Overview Reports, http://www.niss.ac.uk/education/hefce/qar/overview.html

QO 2/95 'Subject Overview Report – Chemistry' in NISS (1997) Quality Assessment Overview Reports, http://www.niss.ac.uk/education/hefce/qar/overview.html

QO 8/96 'Subject Overview Report – Sociology' in NISS (1997) Quality Assessment Overview Reports, http://www.niss.ac.uk/education/hefce/qar/overview.html

QO 10/95 'Subject Overview Report – Environmental Studies' in NISS (1997) Quality Assessment Overview Reports, http://www.niss.ac.uk/education/hefce/qar/overview.html

Parsons, T and Knight, P (1998) *How to do your Dissertation in Geography and Related Disciplines*, Chapman & Hall, London

Race, P and Brown, S (1998) *The Lecturer's Toolkit*, Kogan Page, London

Ryan, Y (1994) Contracts and checklists: practical propositions for postgraduate supervision, in *Quality in Postgraduate Education*, eds O Zuber-Skerritt and Y Ryan, Kogan Page, London

Stone, B (1994) The academic management of group projects, in *Using Group-Based Learning in Higher Education*, eds L Thorley and R Gregory, Kogan Page, London

Thorley, L and Gregory, R (1994) *Using Group-Based Learning in Higher Education*, Kogan Page, London

Wilkins, M (1995) *Learning to Teach in Higher Education*, Coventry Printers, Warwick

Williams, M and Horobin, R (1992) *Active Learning in Fieldwork and Project Work*, CVCP USDTU, Sheffield

FURTHER READING

Day, K, Grant, R and Hounsell, D (1998) See above. Chapter Seven deals specifically with supervising projects and dissertations, and has some examples of useful pro-forma.

Habeshaw, S, Habeshaw, T and Gibbs (1989) *53 Interesting Ways of Helping Your Students to Study*, Technical and Educational Services Ltd, Bristol

Henry, J (1994) *Teaching Through Projects*, Kogan Page, London. A comprehensive and thorough examination of the use of project work to inform extension of this practice by the Open University.

Rudestam, K and Newton, R (1992) *Surviving Your Dissertation*, Sage, London

Zuber-Skerritt, O and Ryan, Y (1994) *Quality in Postgraduate Education*, Kogan Page, London

Williams, M and Horobin, R (1992) See above. As with all the contributions to this extensive volume of aspects of active learning, useful to dip into, particularly to examine the changed role of the supervisor in projects and dissertations

C&IT learning environments to assist in promoting peer support and monitoring of projects and dissertations.

Internet addresses

WebCT (http://www.webct.com/)

COSE (http://www.staffs.ac.uk/COSE)

MERLIN (http://www.hull.ac.uk/merlin/welcome.html)

10 Teaching and Learning for Employability

Margaret Noble

INTRODUCTION

The development and place of skills and capabilities in the curriculum have been major aspects of the higher education agenda for more than 10 years. During this time developments and shifts of emphasis have occurred, influenced by debates at both national and institutional level. There has been an increasing emphasis on student experience in higher education, focusing not only on the development of academic and intellectual capabilities and subject knowledge, but also on the development of skills to equip students for employability.

Throughout the 1980s there was 'growing awareness that study and learning skills were not only vital for effective functioning during a student's education but also had many similarities to the skills students would need in the world of work: communication skills, information skills, record keeping and time and task management' (Gibbs *et al*, 1994). By the early 1990s it was quite widely accepted that students often were not adequately prepared with these skills during their experience in higher education. This view appeared to be endorsed by government, and resulted in a range of skills development and work experience projects funded by the Department for Education and Employment (DfEE) under its Higher Education Quality and Employability division. The Quality Assurance Agency (QAA) has also placed priority on the development of employability skills, evident in the **programme specification** templates that programmes are likely to be required to produce.

A report from the Committee of Vice-Chancellors and Principals (CVCP) in 1996 stated that 'it is one of higher education's purposes to prepare students well for working life'. It argued that through higher education, students should be able to develop attributes useful for success in employment and their future life. Two years later the Employment Skills Overview Group (ESOG) outlined the considerable developments that had taken place. It concluded that 'in most institutions a consensus is developing that it is part of the job to enable students to develop the personal and intellectual attributes that will help them succeed at work and in life generally' (CVCP, 1998a).

Why should 'employability skills' form a central part of the curriculum? Two main arguments have been put forward. First, developing graduate skills will lead to improved competitiveness of the UK economy and, second, that making graduates more attractive to employers will meet some of the frequently made criticisms of graduates (CVCP, 1998b). However, it is also evident that many students select first degree programmes not on the basis of securing employment, but due to their intrinsic interest in a particular subject or discipline (Purcell and Pitcher, 1996, cited in CVCP, DfEE 1998c). Furthermore, students' needs are diverse and the needs of the increasing number of mature students, many of whom may already have considerable work experience, may require a different approach.

DEFINING EMPLOYABILITY

Abilities and attributes connected with employability have been variously termed core skills, **key skills**, transferable skills and career management skills. Debate on their definition and on how students best acquire them continues. Many universities and colleges now include preparation for work within the curriculum, with course aims frequently encompassing an implicit focus on developing employability. Skill development is also an integral part of many university mission statements and some students have logs of skill profiles as well as academic transcripts.

There has been much debate about what these employability attributes should be, although there is recognition that they include general, personal and intellectual abilities 'that go beyond those traditionally made explicit within an academic or vocational discipline' (CVCP, 1996). It is also generally accepted that developing students' learning skills is central. The **Dearing Report** (NCIHE, 1997) placed emphasis on the importance of learning to learn in the list of four key skills it identified.

Interrogating Practice

In your subject, do you consider preparing students for employment to be your responsibility? Has your institution/department been involved in a development project or programme for key skills? What were the goals and outcomes of the work?

There has been considerable debate on what is meant by employability and what key skills are. Key skills are often considered to be: communication; application of number; information technology; improving own learning and performance; working with others; and problem solving. Others have seen employability as synonymous with career management, being 'the ability to understand oneself, to manage complex and multiple life choices and to handle transitions' (DfEE, 1997b). The Association of Graduate Careers Advisory Services (AGCAS) currently supports such a definition, but notes that it is ever changing, and that any definition needs to include not only skills and **competences**, but also attributes and attitudes (AGCAS, 1999). Another influential report suggests that employability skills cover four main elements: traditional intellectual skills such as critical evaluation and the transfer of theory to practice; the new core or key skills; personal attributes such as flexibility and self-reliance; and knowledge about how organizations work (CVCP, 1998b).

It is evident that many of the 'skills' identified for employability are not in fact skills, but are rather attributes and attitudes of mind. This raises a number of issues. Can these be taught? Is employability really about developing skills to bring about the effective transfer of personal skills to other settings?

Many academics would argue that employability skills have long been an implicit aspect of course design and that there is little need for change. However, there is evidence to suggest that many students remain unaware of the development of these attributes and that if, as a first step, students could identify them and where they acquired them, this would be significant progress in developing employability. One of the challenges for higher education has been how to combine these generic competences with the **learning outcomes** and academic processes that form part of most courses. One area of synergy has been the increasing emphasis on independent self-managed learning; self-reliance skills are increasingly recognized as being of major importance for success at work.

TEACHING AND LEARNING STRATEGIES

Teaching and learning strategies adopted to develop student employability have been wide-ranging. Developing employability skills can be time-consuming. Many initiatives during the 1990s would not have taken place without considerable development monies from government at national, regional and local levels. Within the curriculum various strategies have been adopted, focusing either on whole-institution or subject-based approaches and operating at different levels. Examples of initiatives at all levels, undergraduate and postgraduate, can be found (DfEE, 1993; 1997b).

Some institutions have argued that it is most appropriate to introduce employability skills, in the shape of skills for independent learning, at the start of higher education programmes. Others have chosen to introduce dedicated **modules** covering areas such as personal effectiveness, study skills, career management, etc at **levels** two and three, arguing that by this stage students are beginning to make choices about future career options.

Initiatives have ranged from free-standing personal and professional development awards, to career management modules, employability programmes, the provision of greater student guidance and increased opportunities for work and work-related experience through placement activities, involvement in live projects and student job shops.

Of note has been the increasing involvement of career services. Between 1996 and 1998 the DfEE funded a number of projects to explore ways of embedding the skills of career management into the curriculum through guidance modules. The reports published as part of this theme present a useful series of case studies on ways of integrating career management into the curriculum. They cover institution-wide and discipline-based approaches involving a range of activities including **open** and **distance learning**, computer-based learning materials, involvement of employers in curriculum delivery and the development of career management modules (see Further Reading). A major problem facing institutions is, however, one of resources to support this kind of development work.

Approaches to teaching and learning for employability are extremely diverse and there is no one accepted way in which this has been adopted. Indeed it would be inappropriate for a single model to be adopted given the diversity of student background and the varying culture of institutions. In his review of learner **autonomy**, McNair (DfEE, 1997a) identifies four models to providing student guidance: student-centred, tutorial, discipline-based and professional, each supported by a range of materials and having particular resource demands.

Skills development and its place in the curriculum can be viewed as a continuum, from acknowledgement of importance but little explicit assessment at one end, to dual accreditation with vocational qualifications at the other. Discussion has taken place in several institutions on where employability skills provision should be positioned, with a range of contrasting models adopted. Some universities have run pilots of dual accreditation with vocational qualifications, as in the University of Exeter Career Management Skills project; others have developed separate skills programmes.

Gibbs *et al* (1994) argue that it is not sufficient to tack skills onto conventional academic curricula but that it is necessary to bring elements of the world of work into the classroom, thus confronting students with real world problems (see Chapter 11). They argue that 'the curricula themselves have to be transformed if skills development is to be worthwhile' (Gibbs *et al*, 1994: 5). At Oxford Brookes University, where skill development programmes first began in the 1970s, all course proposals and course reviews are required to outline the way in which the development of transferable skills is built into course design, delivery and assessment. Furthermore, all students leave the university with a profile of transferable skills achieved.

Technological solutions have taken an increasingly prominent role in recent years. At the University of Central Lancashire interactive CD ROMs have been developed, encouraging students to explore career choices. Initiatives such as these usually generate dialogue around a range of issues, including how far initiatives in this area should be credit-bearing, whether skills programmes should be compulsory or optional and whether the skills should be made explicit or implicit.

Free-standing or integrated?

An area of considerable debate has been whether to develop separate employability skills modules or to integrate and embed them within subject teaching. Three advantages of embedding are often identified:

- it gives employability skills the same status as subject knowledge;
- it identifies the importance of skills to academic success;
- it obliges all lecturers to develop a subject context for employability skills (CVCP, 1997b).

Discipline-based approaches involve embedding the required, or identified, employability skills as part of a module or group of modules either through linking the process of skill acquisition to existing course components or through redesign of the curriculum. Integrated approaches can, however, pose difficulties. A common problem is that skills can become so embedded that they are lost or they are 'tagged on' the end of a module and are accorded little value by students. In contrast, the advantages of the stand-alone, or bolt-on, approach are that it ensures skills are covered. It involves relatively low costs as it does not require a redesign of whole curricula and it opens up the possibility of modules targeted at supporting the needs of particular students. Such programme modules can either be generic and capable of being adopted by many departments or customized to meet the specific needs of particular courses. However, running them as bolt-on modules can be problematic, not least because some students will see little relationship between the module and their main programme of studies. Either mode can put pressure on curriculum time.

In reality there is a continuum between these two approaches; some skills are generic and common across disciplines, others are clearly distinctive to individual subjects and may be an integral part of the subject. It is for departments and institutions to decide how far to move along the continuum and which approach to adopt.

Whether institutions have adopted integrated or stand-alone programmes, there has been debate as to whether such modules should be a compulsory part of the curriculum. Academic staff often resist giving up 'valuable curriculum time' to skills-based modules. However, experience has shown that when modules are optional or voluntary, students in need are the least likely to attend.

An alternative approach adopted by some universities and colleges has been to see extra-curricular and off-campus activity through, for example, part-time employment, student union activities and a range of work placement and work experience opportunities, as a means of developing employability. Students are sometimes given the opportunity to gain an additional qualification as part of this work. This approach has the advantage of minimal disruption of the curriculum while also placing an emphasis on the significance of work experience in developing employability skills. The University of York, for example, has recently introduced the York Award and at De Montfort University students can opt to work towards a Certificate in Professional Development.

Despite the increased focus on developing employability, many students are still leaving university without such skills (Harvey, Moon and Geall, 1997). The response of several higher education providers has been to offer graduate skills programmes, often combining a short programme on management and business skills with a period of work placement. The Business Bridge programme run in Liverpool and the Graduate Enterprise Link programme developed by the University College of Ripon and York St John are notable examples.

Interrogating Practice

Do the students you teach undertake free-standing key skills development modules or sessions, or do they have similar developments built into their subject programme of study? What skills are included? Who does the teaching?

Ownership and location

Many employability modules have been developed by central teams based in educational development or similar units. This raises the issue of whether such units should have ownership of skill programmes, not least because of their role in championing such developments. This may mean, however, that those delivering skills programmes are not tied into subject departments and therefore lack understanding of the context in which skill programmes should be developed. Furthermore, subject staff may be concerned about curriculum time accorded to such programmes. Review of a range of models suggests that skill programmes are best delivered by subject departments drawing on central resources for specialist support.

AGCAS argues that career services have an important role to play but that insufficient resources are normally allocated to this role. The range of activities that career services have been involved in are diverse, including running projects on career management skills, providing access to part-time employment, graduate skills projects and records of achievement. The potential role of careers services is highlighted in the range of DfEE-funded career management projects (eg Manchester Metropolitan University/NICEC, 1998).

Assessment

The assessment of employability skills is a problematic area. Some would argue that such skills should not be explicitly assessed and there are obvious problems in how to measure success in this area. It is clear, however, that assessment plays a major role in learning, not least because many students tend towards **strategic learning** (see Chapter 3). Learning logs, portfolios and action plans typically form a major part of assessment strategies of skills for employability. Assessment raises the whole issue of grading. It can be argued that, in common with the approach in vocational qualifications, a pass/fail or competent/not yet competent approach is most appropriate. However, if a module is being offered at level 2 or 3 there is often strong pressure for marks or grades to be awarded. This raises issues of how to identify assessment criteria comparable to other areas of the curriculum and how to apply traditional marking schemes to this type of learning. Typical questions include: how easy is it to assess self-awareness and personal values? Are younger students disadvantaged when compared to mature undergraduates? It is clear, however, that to ensure the credibility of this area of work, **credit** and assessment are both required.

> ## Case Study 1: Developing Employability Skills Through an Institution-wide Skills and Capabilities Curriculum at the University of Lincolnshire and Humberside

Evolution

The university's mission, 'to provide our students world-wide with the best employment prospects and to equip them to become lifelong learners' made an emphasis on skill and capability development essential.

Early work was funded through Enterprise in Higher Education/DfEE and a range of possible models for skills development were trialled, including work-based initiatives and programmes offering dual academic and vocational accreditation. Much debate focused on whether such skills should be integrated within modules, taught as a separately designed unit or as an additional, or extra, element to a student's main programme of study. The university's Learning Development Unit was active in stimulating debate on the development of a new learning environment. The unit developed a level 1 programme in 'learning to learn', focusing on developing students' learning and research skills through the use of an interactive technology-based learning system. Within this programme there was strong emphasis on **learning style** profiling, assessment of the skills needed for the different elements of a student's programme and for future study and career.

The model finally adopted was a university-wide programme (the University Skills and Capabilities Curriculum, USCC) of skill development involving explicit assessment of 'employability' skills and occupying one-fifth of each level of all undergraduate degree programmes (see Figure 10.1).

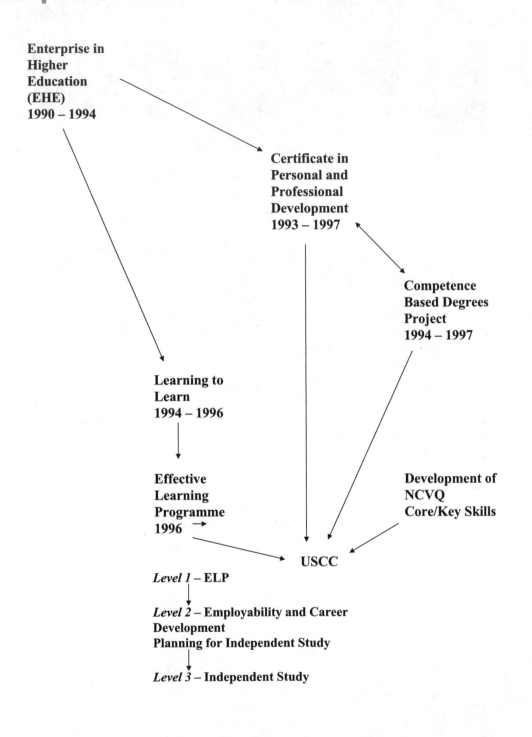

Figure 10.1 The development of a university-wide approach

The USCC incorporates employability skills identified as being central to students' progress, both at university and later. At level 1 the Learning to Learn programme was renamed the Effective Learning Programme (ELP). The level 2 units had a greater emphasis on skills needed for employment and careers. The Semester A unit is Employability and Career Development and Semester B, Independent Study Preparation and Planning. The following example of learning outcomes from the Employability and Career Development unit indicates the scope of one USCC module.

On completion of the module students will be able to:

- outline major labour market trends and explain their relevance to careers choices;
- identify the range of capabilities required by employers and explain why they are valued in employment;
- explore a range of career options appropriate for graduates in a particular subject area (or areas) and research one or more of these in depth;
- develop one or more capabilities likely to be needed post-graduation;
- develop an action plan appropriate to their career aspirations;
- demonstrate effective job search strategies;
- prepare background material needed for recruitment and selection processes, including a personal profile, targeted curriculum vitae, and other appropriate material (eg an accompanying letter, completed application forms);
- develop strategies for participating in recruitment and selection processes, including interviews and tests.

Level 3 was the culmination of independent learning through the completion of an individual study. This offers students an opportunity to experience research and to develop further and consolidate independent learning skills (notably self-organization and management). The role of the skills team in the Independent Study is to provide supportive materials and seminars on project planning, information retrieval, report writing, and advanced oral presentations.

The entire programme is assessed. Student and tutor materials and guides, in paper and electronic formats, support each unit. Electronic learning systems and the facility for staff to establish local Web sites and on-line discussion groups to support the learning process have become increasingly important.

The USCC programme was influenced by national developments, although students taking it do not work towards dual accreditation of skills (vocational and academic). As part of a DfEE project, a recording and profiling tool for key skills for staff and students has been developed. Students profile their key skills development through a range of settings, including work experience and placement, extra-curricular activities and curriculum-based activities. Staff map the curriculum to key skill frameworks and work with students on assessing progress in achieving targets through curriculum-based activities. Both tools can be accessed through the Web site (http://home.ulh.ac.uk/cfll/keyskill.html).

Issues

An essential element in developing the programme was ownership by schools and subject departments. The team developing the programme was drawn from across the university and had representatives from a wide range of subjects and central units, including careers, learning support and educational development units. Each USCC unit was developed as a free-standing 'off-the-shelf' unit that could be selectively adapted by teaching staff. This has staff development implications, including ensuring that appropriate staff are deployed to support and develop the learning process.

Evaluation

Initial reaction to the programme was somewhat sceptical. However, as it has developed it has been generously received, and surprisingly, most subjects are working very closely to the 'off-the-shelf' model. Providing staff with the option to use the programme in a flexible way was clearly important in gaining its acceptance. The sense of ownership has been of central importance; for students the close alignment to subject study has developed a direct relationship with career aspirations and study options. Evaluation shows students believe that key skills are an important element of achieving a degree and gaining employment and are of clear relevance to effective learning. Students have also expressed a preference for employability skills to be developed as part of their subject study and to be awarded credit.

To gain university-wide acceptance of a common skills-based curriculum has been a significant achievement, although the programme has not been without its critics. There remains scepticism in certain quarters, and what has been introduced is more 'measured' than might be the case if the enthusiastic group of staff behind this represented the whole body of staff.

A central aim of the USCC has been to ensure achievement of the university mission and in particular the enhancement of student employability. The institutional support provided by the Vice-Chancellor's Office was of major significance in ensuring effective implementation, as was the wide consultation and involvement of staff across all departments.

Continual re-evaluation of the curriculum is important. Evaluation carried out to date indicates that level 2 has perhaps been more widely accepted than level 1, which several students have seen as often not stretching enough. Work is currently taking place with local sixth form and further education colleges to understand more clearly the skills that students bring with them and to ensure that the university curriculum builds on these. Interestingly, some part-time students have been critical of USCC. Their comments have fed into suggestions to modify the curriculum. Accreditation of Prior (Experiential) Learning **(AP(E)L)** has been one option; however, it is evident that many students enter part-time study seeking career re-direction and with the clear intention of developing their employability. As many have few formal learning skills, a skills and capabilities curriculum clearly has an important part to play in their studies.

Close monitoring and evaluation will be essential over several years both to assess feedback on the model and to assess the impact on post-university career development.

Interrogating Practice

What lessons about developing employability skills in your department do you draw from the case study? How far should responsibility for the development of employability skills lie with the individual lecturer, the programme, the department, the educational development unit (or similar), the school or the university?

OVERVIEW

There is growing pressure for employability skills to be developed as part of the higher education experience. Due to a range of external factors and agencies it is an agenda that institutions will come under increasing pressure to be explicit about. Other factors such as the emphasis on records of achievement and **progress files,** and the need for higher education to address the professional development needs of graduates, will also play a part in encouraging greater consideration of employability skills.

There are, however, factors that work to inhibit emphasis on employability skills. These factors include the dominance of the research agenda, the increasing proportions of mature students who may require a different emphasis, the needs of professional bodies, over-loaded curricula, resource implications of changing the curriculum and the diffuse nature of power and accountability in many institutions. Within institutions the agenda has clear strategic implications and requires support.

It is evident that a single approach to developing employability skills is inappropriate and it is for each institution to determine the way forward in line with the culture and ethos of its provision. However, review of skill development programmes suggests that on top of the key requirement of **active learning**, skills provision will only be successful if it is:

- timetabled – an optional, drop-in session will be perceived by students as being of fringe interest;
- credit rated – if skill and capability development is to be taken seriously by both students and academics it must be assigned academic credit;
- relevant – the skills tutor must be familiar with the course syllabus and the nature of their assignments;
- realistic – employability skills should be developed through realistic assignments/exercises related to the students' own interests;
- integrated – into the curriculum either through specifically designed units or through clear understanding of the ways in which employability skills can be achieved through subject units;
- assessed – since students will be better motivated when assessed and will recognize the significance attached to achievement of skills;
- graded – this encourages students to strive for excellence;
- interesting – through, for example, the use of dynamic and innovative teaching methods;
- supported – by academic and learning support staff;
- goal-driven – based on clear objectives;
- flexible – continually evaluated and modified to suit students' needs.

In summary, development of employability skills presents a major challenge to 'make more explicit the development of attributes that have long been implicit and to help students appreciate the importance of such attributes and better articulate them, especially to employers' (CVCP, 1998a: 6). Such development is not necessarily best achieved by individual lecturers working alone. There are clear benefits in team-based approaches.

REFERENCES

AGCAS (1999) Higher Education Careers Services and the Development of Employability, Skills Briefing Paper 99/01, Association of Graduate Careers Advisory Services, Manchester

CVCP, CIHE, CBI (1996) *Helping Students towards Success at Work*, Council for Industry in Higher Education, London

CVCP, CIHE, and CBI (1998a) *Helping Students towards Success at Work: an Intent Being Fulfilled*, Committee of Vice-Chancellors and Principals, London

CVCP, DfEE (1998b) *Skills Development in Higher Education Short Report*, Committee of Vice-Chancellors and Principals, London

CVCP, DfEE (1998c) *Skills Development in Higher Education Long Report*, Committee of Vice-Chancellors and Principals, London

DfEE (1993) *Catalogue of Higher Education Regional Development (HERD) Projects*, Department for Education and Employment, Sheffield

DfEE (1997a) *Getting the Most out of HE: Supporting Learner Autonomy Higher Education and Employment*, Department for Education and Employment, Sheffield

DfEE (1997b) Network News: Career Management Skills Newsletter Edition One

Gibbs, G, Rust, C, Jenkins, A, Jacques, D (1994) *Developing Students' Transferable Skills*, Oxford Centre for Staff Development, Oxford Brookes University

Harvey, I, Moon, S and Geall, V (1997) *Graduates' Work: Organisational Change and Students' Attributes*, Centre for Research into Quality, University of Central England, Birmingham

Manchester Metropolitan University and The National Institute for Careers Education and Counselling (1998) *Career Management Skills: Final Evaluation Report*, Manchester

NCIHE (1997) (Dearing Report) *Higher Education in the Learning Society*, National Committee of Inquiry into Higher Education, HMSO, London

Purcell and Pitcher (1996) *Great Expectations: The New Diversity of Graduate Skills and Aspirations*, Institute of Employment Research, University of Warwick, Coventry.

FURTHER READING

All recommendations are useful reports, often of 'what was done and how to do it'.

Careers Advisory Service (1998) *Career Management Skills for Postgraduates: Final Project Report*

Cheltenham and Gloucester College of Higher Education (1998) *Advanced Career Management and the Curriculum Link: Final Report*

College of Ripon and York St John (1998) *Researching Pathways: the Final Report*, York

Harvey et al (1997) See above.

Lewis, D and Tomlinson, S (1998) *Key Skills Evaluation* (Report produced as part of the HERD project for the Humber sub region), University of Lincolnshire and Humberside

Little, B (1998) *Developing Key Skills through Work Placement*, Council for Industry in Higher Education/Quality Support Centre (Open University), London

University of Exeter (1998) *Career Management Skills; Final Report*, Exeter

Supporting Learning From Experience

Liz Beaty

INTRODUCTION

The value of practical experience within higher education programmes has a long history. Laboratory classes and experiments are used in science and engineering, simulations and games have been a feature of management and social science courses, while many art and design courses develop technical skills alongside knowledge and aesthetic appreciation. Projects are a feature of many final year degree programmes and are an essential ingredient of most Master's programmes. Beyond these methods are 'sandwich' courses, which use placements to give students experience in the workplace as part of their academic studies. Health professionals have integrated programmes where they undertake academic study alongside supervised practice in hospitals. Such approaches are based on the premise that **experiential learning** should be an important part of a degree programme, especially those which have a professional or applied orientation.

Many vocational courses plan for experiential learning to take place outside of the university as **work-based learning**. This chapter will focus on learning from experience in both the university environment and natural settings where the experience is the stimulus for learning.

Employability is a key issue for graduates from higher education (see Chapter 10). The importance of the experiential base of a degree has been increasingly acknowledged. In teacher training, for example, there has been a move to increase the importance of classroom practice with mentoring from practising teachers. In nursing, however, the growing importance of the knowledge base has resulted in a move in the opposite direction.

Degree programmes assess and award credit for learning based on experience gained inside the university. Increasingly, credit is also being awarded for learning gained from experience on **placements** outside of the university. This will become more important as degree programmes become more flexible and with more use of systems of credit accumulation and transfer including assessment of prior (experiential) learning (AP(E)L).

The challenge is to bring experiential learning into courses so that students leave the university able to transfer their learning into their future life and work. This development requires more than simply putting theory into practice. Acting professionally as a doctor, producing saleable art work or designing a robust bridge requires a complex interweaving of knowledge, technical skills and application of professional ethics. This requires something akin to wisdom, which is usually attributed to learning over a long period of time through worldly experience and thoughtful contemplation. Experiential learning is holistic; it acknowledges the student as a person. Championing experiential learning is fundamentally about nurturing people in order to enhance their life and the society within which they live.

This chapter describes different models for using experiential learning in higher education and offers suggestions for course design which can successfully integrate theory with practice. It goes on to describe the skills needed by teachers in supporting students in experiential learning through supervision, mentoring, tutoring and facilitation of action learning.

Interrogating Practice

Before you read on, write down aspects of the courses that you teach which are based on learning from experience.

ACADEMIC LEARNING AND EXPERIENTIAL LEARNING

There is a difference between learning in the natural world and learning in the constructed world of higher education. Learning from everyday experience is serendipitous, what we learn and how we learn is situated and context dependent. In an academic environment, learning is intentional; what is to be learned is prescribed and how it is to be learnt is carefully structured: '...Academics want more to be learned than that which is already available from experiencing the world. The whole point about articulated knowledge is that being articulated it is known through exposition, argument, interpretation; it is known through reflection on experience and represents therefore a second order experience of the world'. (Laurillard, 1993: 25)

If learning in the academic context is to affect positively how individuals approach the world, ie their future actions, academic learning must be perceived as relevant, and be learned in a way which promotes transfer. The learner must understand enough to know when and how to transfer this knowledge to their future activity. As well as understanding the ideas, the student must understand the significance of the ideas. Teachers, therefore, need to use examples, case studies and practical experiments, running alongside theoretical ideas, to set them in a context and to make them relevant. If the relevance is directly experienced by the students, themselves, then the learning will be reinforced.

Experience does not always lead to learning and theories of experiential learning have focused on the importance of reflection. The most well-known model is based on Kolb's **learning cycle** (1984) (see Chapter 3) which suggests that in order to learn effectively from experience, there must be a movement through reflection on experience where observations on the features of and issues in the context are brought to conscious attention. There follows a focus on generalizing from these experiences and understanding them. This part of the cycle is where theories and ideas are brought to bear on the experience. In the third part of the cycle there is an attempt to evaluate the experience and to plan for change through experimentation. The following step takes us back into experience, but this time the experience is informed by the learning cycle so that the result is different due to learning that has taken place through the cycle.

If experience in the natural environment is to result in learning which promotes enquiry, critical thinking and understanding, the experience must be interrogated and reflected on in the light of theory. This means that experience is not, on its own, enough to support learning. Rather, deliberate and conscious reflection is a requirement for effective experiential learning to take place. Teachers, therefore, need to work alongside students in supporting this reflection and critical appraisal of experience in order that students learn from it.

The learning cycle takes place over a period of time and is a *post hoc*, deliberate approach to learning from experience. This large reflective cycle involves reflection on action. In giving students opportunities to learn from experience we are also helping them to become conscious of the relationship between ideas and action. In experiential learning, the process of learning takes precedence over the content.

BRINGING EXPERIENTIAL LEARNING INTO COURSES

There are two basic ways of making experiential learning an integral part of course design. The first is to provide opportunities for experience in the form of structured and pre-planned practical work which will develop skills and technique within the controlled environment of the university. The second way is to give students the opportunity to learn from experience within a naturalistic environment in a work placement. In both cases, the key to effective learning is the support given to the student to draw out learning from the experience and in linking **critical incidents** in the experience to ideas and theories which shed light on them.

Practical exercises and project work will lead to little learning if they do not actively help students to integrate their studies. Similarly, work-based learning will be sterile if not adequately supported through a cycle of action and reflection and underpinned by a critically addressed knowledge base.

Interrogating Practice

List two or three learning objectives or learning outcomes from a course that you teach which require students to engage in experiential learning. What teaching and learning methods are used to achieve these outcomes?

USING EXPERIENCE INSIDE THE UNIVERSITY

Methods which promote experiential learning inside the university include:

- laboratory experiments (Chapter 20);
- simulations;
- case studies, including problem-based learning (**PBL**);
- micro teaching;
- projects (Chapter 9).

Each of these examples uses mainly teacher designed experiences within the course to allow practice of technical or interpersonal skills and to promote understanding of the relevance of the course to the 'real world'.

Laboratory experiments

Laboratory experiments require the student to undertake a series of tasks in order to observe the results. These can be individual or team-based experiments. The methods are usually prescribed and the expected results known. The point of undertaking the experiment is not 'real science' but practice of technique, skill of observation and recording, while demonstrating the relevance of theory to outcomes. Such a method, particularly when students are working in teams, offers much scope for **deep learning** in that it derives from a critical reflection of the experience and deliberate focus on the significance of observations.

Simulations

Simulations are attempts to create a realistic experience in a controlled environment. They can be very simple and require only the participation of the students within a described scenario or they can be elaborate rule-governed games which demonstrate complex relationships. Simulations have been created using computer technology to show how altering variables affects complex machinery. Other types of simulations involve case scenarios of interpersonal relationships to demonstrate how certain behaviours produce different reactions. These latter types are used extensively in areas like management and social work education, and often involve role play. The advantage of simulation is that the experiences are real but there is no lasting effect on the external world. So the simulation can involve making mistakes, say, in bridge building or controlling nuclear power plants, operating on a patient or managing a redundancy programme, without a real disaster. They create powerful learning opportunities but they also require a great deal of careful planning and construction. A good simulation can take many months of development but, once developed, it can be used again and again. Two important considerations for teachers in using simulations are, first, to make sure that the learning which comes from undertaking the simulation is linked back to the objectives of the course, otherwise the students may learn that effects take place without critically analysing why and how. Second, in role play simulations, although the context is simulated, the feelings of people within the simulation are real. It is important to debrief properly these events both in terms of how people reacted to the case and their role within it, as well as in terms of the learning objective.

Case studies

Case studies are complex examples which give an insight into the context of the example as well as illustrating the main point. These are used extensively in vocational degrees where an understanding of complex relationships is important.

Case studies can be either real or imaginary. If they are based on reality, source material may come from newspapers, journals or non-published reports (where permission will be needed for use within the course). Imaginary cases may take a good deal of preparation from the teacher. The aim is to build up a picture of an issue or problem through a case study and then give the students exercises and tasks to complete in relation to the case. The exercises will require the student first to understand the nature of the case and then to analyse the appropriate features of it in order to complete the task. This can make a rich learning experience. Again case studies lend themselves to teamwork where multiple perspectives on a case can support critical appraisal and broader understanding. Extensive use of case studies can support a complete course design. Problem-based learning uses teams working on a series of case studies as the primary focus of learning (see Chapter 24). Concepts and theories from discipline areas are studied as they arise through the case.

Micro teaching

Micro teaching involves intensive practice of a skill under observation. Usually the practice is videotaped and then reviewed with a mentor giving feedback. The practice can be in a real situation or more usually in an artificial practice room. This is used extensively in training: for example, presentation and interview skills. The recording allows feedback to be given in relation to specific behaviours and the student is able to see what the mentor sees, also making the teaching session more focused on individual characteristics. Feedback on micro teaching is usually given in a one to one tutorial.

Projects

Projects are used where teachers want to give students scope to study a topic in depth. Projects can give students experience of research, analysis and recording as well as valuable practice in writing reports. In the example which follows, experiential learning is brought to a course through intensive group projects which are carefully structured by the tutors to support integration.

Case Study 1: Integrating Team Project, Civil Engineering, University of Brighton

Context

Integrative projects (IPs) are used at various times throughout the degree programme in civil engineering. Their purpose is to integrate aspects of academic studies such as separate subjects or writing skills with technical skills and also to create an experience which integrates human aspects by forcing students to work to a sharp deadline with other people. In this way the projects simulate work experience within a real environment but under the control and structure provided by the teacher.

Short intensive projects usually last for one week. Students work in groups of four or five, selected by the tutor. The specific aims of the project differ throughout the three years of the course. For example, one is based on integration of design skills, another on the skills involved in undertaking a feasibility study.

The projects begin with a briefing and students are given documentation which describes the project and gives a schedule for the week. The schedule includes site visits, client interviews, discussion sessions and formative assessment tasks. This documentation also details health and safety procedures and rules for the work plan. The week is scheduled with times for various events and visits, allowing sufficient freedom for teams to organize their time and to cooperate and undertake different tasks within the project. Tutors are available for consultation throughout the week.

The assessment of the project involves a final report, a group presentation, and interview with a panel of tutors.

(Beaty, France and Gardiner, 1996)

Interrogating Practice

Consider how you could apply these methods to a unit of your teaching.

USING EXPERIENCE IN A NATURAL SETTING

Methods which promote experiential learning outside of the university are:

- field trips;
- placements;
- work-based learning projects.

Field trips

Field trips combine work in university and work in a naturalistic setting. For example, geography students may be taken to a particular landscape to do tests and collect samples, taking their observations and collections back to the university for further analysis. Field trips may also allow questions to local people, collection or copying of documentation, etc. The advantage of field trips is that the visual and physical impact of the surroundings bring the theory to life. Field trips allow many secondary, learning objectives to be met. As in the example of the integrative project above, the effect of going away as a group and being together in one place for an extended time can offer opportunities for team-building and cooperation. It is important for the success of the field trip that planning is thorough and briefing is carefully handled. The purpose and scheduling of the trip must be transparent to both tutor and student.

Placements

Placements give the student experience of a working environment over a period of time. Placements usually give students a role within the organization, which is supervised and chosen to allow them to participate in a meaningful way. The organization offering the work placement needs to be able to rely on getting a suitable and adequately prepared student able to undertake the assigned role. The university needs to be sure that the organization will fulfil its agreement in helping the student gain appropriate work experience along with necessary mentorship. Articulating and agreeing expectations are therefore crucial.

Placements can be affected greatly by the attitudes of the various parties to the agreement. Students need to get involved, be reasonably flexible and willing to learn from their experienced colleagues. Similarly, the balance of helpfulness and constructive criticism from colleagues in the workplace will support learning. A good relationship between the university tutors and managers in the workplace is essential to ensure that the placement offers the right degree of challenge and support to the student.

Work-based learning projects

Work-based learning projects create a client relationship between the student and the organization. For undergraduate degrees, the students undertake projects for a client organization but without being employees. The role of the university is to ensure that learning is generated from the experience of project work regardless of the success of the project itself. The role of the university in the relationship with the client organization varies considerably. In some cases the student is totally in control of the relationship, while in other cases the teacher carefully controls and documents any agreements made. Clients are sometimes involved in the assessment of work-based learning through attending presentations or reporting on aspects of the project outcomes. As with placements, the control is shared three ways and the clarity of roles and responsibilities is a key to the successful outcome. In work-based projects there is a danger that work on the project dominates, with learning from experience of doing the project taking second place. The role of the teacher is to focus student attention on the learning potential throughout the life of the project and to inform the process with relevant academic content.

ACTION LEARNING AS A SUPPORT FOR WORK-BASED PROJECTS

Using action learning as a group process to support students' learning from their experience can be highly supportive of the individual and the project because the emphasis is on learning and on action.

Action learning is based on the relationship between reflection and action. It involves regular meetings in groups (known as sets) where the focus is on the issues and problems that individuals bring and planning future action with the structured attention and support of the group. Put simply, it is about solving problems and getting things done.

McGill and Beaty (1995) define action learning as:'…a continuous process of learning and reflection, supported by colleagues, with an intention of getting things done. Through action learning individuals learn with and from each other by working on real problems and reflecting on their own experiences. The process helps us to take an active stance towards life and helps to overcome the tendency (merely) to think, feel and be passive towards the pressures of life'.

In the action learning set, students can learn through reflection on their progress and in many ways they learn about themselves as well as about the project they are undertaking. Because it is a group method, they also learn a great deal by listening to other group members discussing their projects.

The key components of action learning are:

- Individuals meet together in a set. For ease of working, about five to seven people make up the set.
- Each individual brings a real issue or project to the set that they wish to work on.
- The whole set works on progressing each project one at a time, sharing the time evenly between them.

- The aim is for each student to be able to take action on their project and to learn from their reflection on experience.
- Regular meetings three to four hours every four to six weeks for a cycle of meetings over an agreed period (for example six, nine or 12 months).
- The set will create explicit ground rules to ensure effective working.

Action learning is thus based on the idea that effective learning and development come from working through real life problems with other people. As a support for experiential learning it stresses the dual importance of understanding and action.

Case Study 2: Example of a Work-based Learning Project Based on an Action Learning MA in Work-based Learning, Coventry Business School

The Coventry Business School Master's course in work-based learning offers valuable lessons that are transferable to undergraduate programmes of study. This programme was designed to give managers the opportunity to study as they undertake a project at work. The course is run over one year and is based on project work supported by action learning and tutored workshops. A module on work-based learning is taken during the first term and followed by two terms' work on the project. Participants work in action learning sets which support their learning throughout the programme. Each participant chooses a project which they have authority to undertake and which could be expected to yield outcomes within one year. Examples include 'introduction of performance measures, managing absence in an organization, introduction of an appraisal system, recruitment and retention of volunteer persons' (Johnson, 1998). Participants meet in their sets for half a day on a four-weekly cycle. In these sets they discuss progress and blockages with their projects and take away a number of action points to be dealt with by their next meeting. In the set meetings there are opportunities to identify any knowledge or skills that they need which could be provided by the university, the employers or other participants on the course. The sets are facilitated by an experienced member of the course team whose role is to link each set with the course, but the lead is taken by the students themselves. The focus of the course is on the learning rather than the project. The course is popular with industry and public sector employers as it gives value to the organization at the same time as providing professional development for individual managers.

THE TEACHER'S ROLE

This section describes the roles of the teacher in supporting learning from experience. As experiential learning is essentially about student activity, the teacher's role will be in the form of structuring that experience and facilitating learning through appropriate interventions. Roles for the teacher in supporting experiential learning range from tutor, coach, trainer, mentor, supervisor, facilitator. These roles are often combined, with one teacher taking on multiple roles.

Tutoring

In this role the teacher is concerned with the structure of the learning experience. The process of the learning has been pre-specified at least in terms of what is to be covered (in work placements the timing of when things are covered will not necessarily be under tutor or student control) and the tutor's job is to make sure the experience is as useful as possible. The tutor is seen by the student as being in charge of the learning environment and particularly as a guide to the assessment of learning.

Coach or trainer

The role of coach is often to promote practical skills, where the student is taken through the steps of learning how to do some action, and skill is developed mainly through practice. It is the role of the coach to notice where the student is going wrong or being ineffective and where intervention would be helpful. The coach will call 'time out' of an activity to demonstrate good practice and to go carefully and slowly through steps where mistakes could easily be made. This type of teaching is very important in areas of professional practice where the development of technical skills goes hand in hand with understanding the context.

Mentor

The mentor is often a more experienced version of the student, an older or more knowledgeable peer. Mentorship therefore often involves observation both by the mentor and of the mentor. Feedback is supplemented by discussion and debate with a feeling of more comradeship and less hierarchy than is evident with the other roles. Mentorship is a growing function with many professional areas requiring mentors for induction and for people taking on new responsibilities. As with many of the roles that support experiential learning, it succeeds or fails on the basis of the relationship that is established between the mentor and mentee.

Supervision

Supervisors require many of the same skills as the mentor, but while mentors act as guides, working alongside the student, supervisors are more remote and act as monitors of progress. Supervision requires a clarity about the nature of the learning that is required and supervisors are usually experts carrying responsibility for the working area and for students' progress. The issue for supervisors is often about when to intervene and when to allow students to learn through discovery. Individuals attack problems in different ways and have different **learning styles**. Supervisors, therefore, must be sensitive to the way in which the student is tackling the problem and not impose their own approach inappropriately.

Facilitation

In experiential learning the word facilitator is often used in preference to the word teacher. Facilitation implies that the activity is one of support rather than initiating. The experience belongs to the student and the facilitator helps the student to get most out of the experience by providing appropriate resources and intervening in support of the learning. There are different models of facilitation where at one extreme the student is an autonomous learner, in total control of content and process, with the facilitator supporting.

In most courses in higher education the facilitator will have control of the process. This allows students to follow up their interests by choosing the topic of a project, but the timing, the rules for undertaking it and the assessment of the project are in the control of the teacher.

In general, experiential learning requires more facilitation and less direct teaching than academic learning. The process of learning comes to the foreground and the content emerges from the experience.

Interrogating Practice

Think about the experiential learning that you wish to promote and consider the role you will take. Now define that role and its functions.

OVERVIEW

Academic courses which do nothing to link theory into practice through situated cognition and harnessing learning from experience will be sterile.

Experiential learning can take place in departments in the form of projects, experiments, working with case studies, or it can be external to the department as work-based learning, field work and practice placements.

To be effective, experiential learning within a naturalistic environment involves an intentional cycle of action and reflection. Experiential learning which is based on deliberate teaching events such as laboratory experiments and simulations must be carefully linked to theoretical study within the course.

The challenge for modern higher education is not simply to train the next generation of academics, it is rather to tie learning from experience inextricably to academic study and vice versa in a strong lifelong process of learning which develops the person and society. That is why attention to supporting experiential learning within course design is crucial.

REFERENCES

Beaty, E, France, L and Gardiner, P (1996) Consultancy style action research: a constructive triangle, *International Journal for Academic Development*, **2**, (2)

Johnson, D (1998) Workbased learning qualifications at Master's level: academically valid or the emperor's new clothes?, MA dissertation, Coventry University

Kolb, D (1984) *Experiential Learning*, Prentice-Hall, Englewood Cliffs, New Jersey

Laurillard, D (1993) *Rethinking University Teaching*, Routledge, London

McGill, I and Beaty, L (1995) *Action Learning: A guide for professional, management and educational development*, 2nd edn, Kogan Page, London

FURTHER READING

Jarvis, P, Holland, J and Griffin, C (1998) *The Theory and Practice of Learning*, Kogan Page, London

Schon, D (1987) *Educating the Reflective Practitioner*, Jossey-Bass, San Francisco

Staff and Educational Development Association (1996) *Induction Pack for Teachers in Higher Education*, SEDA, Birmingham

Sutherland, P (ed) (1997) *Adult Learning*, Kogan Page, London

Weil, SW and McGill, I (eds) (1989) *Making Sense of Experiential Learning*, Society for Research into Higher Education/Open University Press, Milton Keynes

12 Using Information Technology for Teaching and Learning

Su White

INTRODUCTION

The prospect of using information technology (IT) for teaching and learning may seem daunting to the new academic. The need to acquire additional skills as part of the teaching repertoire may put extra strains on an already heavy workload, while associated administrative tasks such as organizing student access to computers may seem onerous. In addition, the job of coordinating and integrating the IT-based activities into the rest of the teaching programme will require additional planning, reflection and understanding with no clear certainty of the benefit of such effort. However, approached in a systematic and structured way, the potential rewards can be significant, and beneficial for both the learner and the academic practitioner. It is an area of activity brought into focus in the United Kingdom by the **Dearing Report** (NCIHE, 1997) which extended the agenda to include communications and information technologies – commonly referred to as **C&IT**.

This chapter is not concerned with the minutiae of how to create and develop IT resources for teaching and learning. It is beyond its scope to consider how to create pages for the **World Wide Web** (WWW), write a piece of tutorial courseware, or set up a moderated discussion list or **video conference**. This chapter is concerned with the analysis of IT tools, and the consideration of their effective use and potential gain.

Using IT for teaching and learning is not a new activity; it started out as **computer-assisted learning** (CAL) which became a significant minority activity in the 1960s. At that time the underlying educational philosophy was based on behaviourist models designed to generate programmed learning. This was the era of mainframe computing and the usage was largely initiated by military training applications, with some academic research backed by central budgets. Those who created the learning programmes used specialized programming languages, and it was not an activity that could easily be undertaken by teachers or academics. However, by the 1970s, there had been a growth in experimental use of computers for teaching, although the underlying technologies still restricted applications to experimentation within a text-based environment. As such, the applications were isolated activities, conceived in their own right. Creation of resources had become a little less difficult, but it still required technical specialists to produce materials.

By the 1980s, applications were broadening out in range and variety, a change which again reflected the underlying change in technology away from centralized mainframe computers; 1981 was the year in which the personal computer was launched. The ways in which applications could be created were becoming more accessible to non-specialists, through the use of specialized but accessible programming using authoring languages. However, the creation and use of computer-based materials in learning and teaching was still restricted to a small specialist group of enthusiastic academics.

An important aspect of effective use and integration of technology is the way in which it effectively reflects and articulates a given learning model. At the same time as technology has moved forward, the dominant models of learning have changed from behaviourist, through objectivist, to **constructivist**. In the objectivist model, knowledge is located outside the learner, and exists separately from the learning context. In the constructivist model the learner, in acts of understanding, constructs knowledge (Chapter 3). It is debatable whether as yet the use of technology for learning has managed to effectively integrate and reflect the current model (Jackson, 1998).

The approach taken in this chapter is to view the role of IT in teaching as providing an additional learning resource that must be integrated into the total learning experience, in the same way that lectures, fieldwork or course notes are all learning resources. If each individual resource is viewed as being mediated in a different way, then using IT in teaching may be regarded as a means of enabling **computer-mediated learning** to take place. This is very much in line with the conversational model of learning proposed by Laurillard (1993).

From this viewpoint it is constructive to consider the use of IT in terms of the way it can affect conventional teaching situations. For example:

- How will it enable the learners to manage their own learning?
- How can it supplement or complement the lecture programme?
- How can it support working with large groups, support disparate ability levels, enable cost-effective **small group teaching**, or assist in acquiring **key skills**?

GETTING STARTED

A key consideration in achieving the effective use of IT for teaching and learning is the understanding that IT is a tool waiting to be harnessed. All of the lessons learnt in the development of practice (understanding student learning, organizing teaching, **assessment**, motivation and **evaluation** – see respective chapters) can be drawn on, and it is essential that practitioners build their use of IT upon the foundation of good teaching methods which have already been established.

Many new academics will have basic familiarity with IT, but this will vary according to discipline. If the range of skills is not great, then it will be worthwhile spending a small amount of time acquiring those IT skills that seem most relevant. An overview of the set of skills required can be obtained by reading this chapter. Familiarity will provide a confident starting point from which it is possible to imagine potential gains, such as ways in which using IT in teaching could make the learning better for the students, or could enable more effective use of time. It is also useful to find out what other uses academics are making of technology, and what benefits and problems they have identified through their practice.

Interrogating Practice

Make an inventory of your own IT skills. Find out if other academics in your department are using IT in teaching and learning. What are they doing and what do they and their students perceive to be its strengths and weaknesses?

WHAT ARE WE TALKING ABOUT?

It is possible to use IT in teaching and learning in a whole range of ways:

- accessing **electronic journals**;
- computer-generated presentations to accompany lectures;

- electronic publication of lecture notes;
- research using the Web or CD ROM;
- running electronic discussion groups with your learners;
- setting computer-based bibliographic searches;
- setting worked examples making use of tools such as spreadsheets or databases;
- using computer-based learning programmes;
- using e-mail communications for class management;
- using real current databases to retrieve information;
- video conferencing with other students overseas;
- word-processed lecture notes.

Rather than providing an exhaustive list, this chapter will try to place the use of IT in a conceptual framework to identify which type of approach would be most appropriate for a particular set of circumstances.

TECHNOLOGY FOR THE LEARNER

Using technology within the learning process offers the opportunity to structure the learner's interactions and pace their progress through the curriculum. It may be useful to consider ways in which learning resources may be tailored to accommodate differing teaching methods and **learning styles** (see Chapters 13 and 16), and readers are advised to integrate the key points of relevant chapters into their approach to IT.

One particularly useful way to view the learner's experience of technology is from the perspective of the levels of interactivity that it enables. Rich, technology-based learning resources will have a variety of components that will vary the pace and tone of the learning experience. This is effective in the same way that lectures may be enhanced by varying the pitch and timbre of the voice; raising or slowing the pace; involving the audience more or less.

Irrespective of the underlying pedagogic model, it may be useful to consider for any particular computer-based activity, or part of that activity, where on a gradient of interactivity, between passive and active, it can be located. The learner's experience can move through increasing levels of interactivity towards those that are significantly active and predominantly concerned with process, as in Figure 12.1.

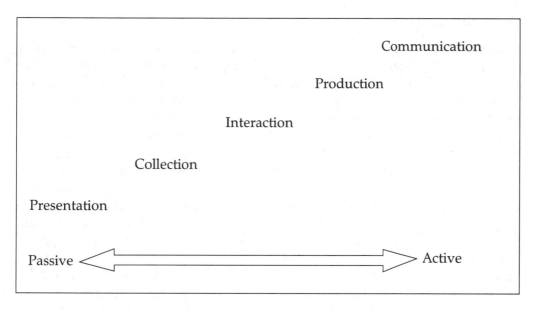

Figure 12.1 Comparing passive content with active process

Passive to active

In the description which follows under 'Presentation', activities are categorized in discrete areas, whereas in fact the categories represent steps in a continuum. It is useful when reviewing the role of technology to consider where the bulk of activity for the learner lies in terms of the steps outlined.

Presentation

At the level of passive use, IT may be concerned solely with content (presenting information in text or graphics). Such uses are often the first things that are generated by technology, for example, word-processed lecture notes, producing computer-generated slides and presentations, creating reference materials which are accessible via the Web or from CD ROM. These types of uses have advantages such as being easy to maintain and update from year to year, and may not add significantly to the ordinary workload and are by now relatively commonplace. But they are concerned with content rather than process, and are not sufficient on their own. This is not to say that they are not valuable; significant parts of university learning materials are content-focused – bibliographies, course descriptions, examination regulations, seminar schedules, and so on. It is important to realize that such resources alone are unlikely to produce a rich learning experience.

Collection and interaction

Introducing the collection of information from the learner is an example of the way in which the first stage of additional activity can be introduced, adding **formative** self-assessment questions and providing some feedback on the learner's knowledge, understanding, and recall. The information gained may also be used to suggest the next step for the learner.

This works in the same way that text may be made more active by requiring some learner intervention while accessing that text. Common techniques in paper-based learning texts include self-assessment questions, reflections, or related activities. For example, self-assessment questions can be presented and marked by the computer providing the learner with feedback, as enabled within the Software Teaching of Modular Physics (**SToMP**) teaching programme (Bacon and Swithenby, 1996). Students can also be instructed to reflect on their learning, perhaps recording their conclusions either on paper, or on a computer-based word processor, notebook or text editor. The information may be augmented by worksheets that may or may not be part of the computer environment.

In addition to integrating some of the activities common in paper-based text, it is possible to combine further use of technology at this stage. Thus, in addition to reading through the presented information, we might require the learner to manipulate a real tool (perform some kind of on-line search, or database query, or some spreadsheet calculations) in order to obtain related information. In such an instance the teacher is able to define the knowledge domain (with more or less accuracy) but is dependent upon the learner using and developing additional skills to provide access to the knowledge.

Constructed interactions are a key component of classic computer-assisted learning that provides a learning environment which offers the learner structured introductions and interactions as a means of explaining and enabling understanding of particular sets of knowledge and the underlying concepts. Such an environment may include the features described above, but will use some kind of authoring package or programming to determine the order of presentation, and transitions through the programme. It should be noted that producing such applications to high quality is time consuming and expensive.

A more sophisticated and complex world-view is provided for the learner when information is presented and accessed via a mathematical or graphical modelling programme, **simulations** or **role play**. This may involve the lecturer making use of a ready-made programme, with which they will have to be familiar before introducing it into teaching. Ready-made programmes have an advantage in that they are less prone to crashing. Small-scale simulations are sometimes integrated into CAL programmes or tutorials that guide learners through a set of learning pathways and offer a more constrained version of such interactions.

In either case the necessary groundwork can be time-consuming. Usage may require the preparation of additional notes or worksheets for the learners, and perhaps some kind of induction or training sessions to familiarize the learners with the operation of the programme and the objectives of the role play or simulation. The computers and their network must be powerful enough to let the programmes run satisfactorily, and they may require on hand technical support, or demonstrators to assist learners if they encounter problems while using the programmes.

Production

Programmes that enable learners to produce new resources by using computer-based tools can provide the next layer of interactivity. If we are to facilitate **deep learning**, an objective must be to provide opportunities for the learner to engage with the learning. As well as enabling learners to acquire key skills, use of real-world programmes, as tools used in the context of academic study, has proved highly effective in enabling such engagement to take place.

Simple examples include learners working individually to produce their own hypertext for the World Wide Web. For example, music students at the University of Southampton have produced pages which describe and discuss the products of their research into composers (Hall, Park Woolf and White, 1999). Groups of students may work together to produce electronic slide shows which they use as visual aids during a group presentation.

In such instances, the programme acts as an integrator, providing the framework within which to assemble, organize and reflect upon content knowledge through the use of real-world IT skills.

Communication

Probably the highest level of interactivity is achieved by incorporating dialogue into the learning process. In face-to-face formats this is often in the form of tutorial or seminar discussions. With a computer as a facilitator the dialogue can be introduced in a number of different ways. At its most closed form this is as feedback or pre-programmed discussion of an interactive tutorial system. Such programmes require considerable skills to assemble, and require a large number of development hours for a very small number of teaching hours. However, the more recent alternative, and less development-intense form of interactivity, has been achieved through the use of computer-mediated communications. Here the learner communicates with the tutor, or other learners, either via some form of e-mail, structured bulletin board discussion, or through a live 'chat room' style discussion. Such applications are sometimes introduced to keep in contact with learners who are on placement, or work experience, but are also relevant in traditional university teaching, offering an additional means of achieving small group teaching. Tutors who work in an on-line environment may need to acquire moderating skills (the art of managing electronic discussions) if they are to make the best use of this resource.

Another automated closed style of discussion is enabled by electronic access to frequently asked questions (FAQs) in the style of an 'Answer Garden' (Ackerman and Malone, 1990). Answers are planted to be picked as needed, and new answers are added to the garden as they are needed to grow organizational knowledge. This type of system is less open than the use of external teacher-directed participation into a closed, peer (**Intranet**) electronic discussion group. A closed discussion is again less open than unconstrained participation in a wider (Internet) electronic discussion group. However, all are predominantly at the highly interactive end of the gradient, providing the learner with the opportunity to process, reflect upon, and interact with information rather than try to simply 'learn' presented knowledge. Examples of the various types of software that can realize the different levels of interactivity are shown in Figure 12.2.

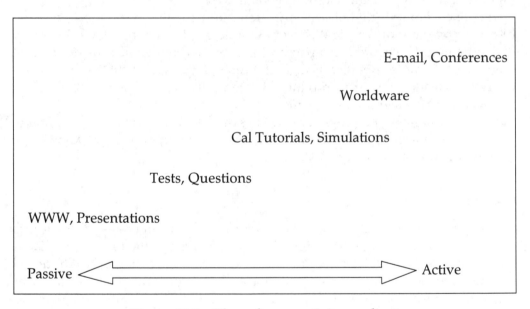

Figure 12.2 The software activity gradient

Most commonly, the examples integrate a range of styles of interactivity around a core style.

This gradation has similarities to the classifications of primary, secondary and tertiary courseware identified by Mayes (1995). In this model, primary courseware provides computer-based access to subject-matter content. In the constructivist model, exposure to content alone is not enough, so the technology is adapted to support learners in tasks involving the selection of appropriate content, linking this together in new ways, and thus building new constructs. This produces what is termed secondary courseware. There is, however, still a missing ingredient of dialogue. If courseware can integrate dialogues that involve discourse between learner and teacher, between peers, and these dialogues can be integrated in some re-useable way, then we would produce tertiary courseware.

Case Study 1: University of Southampton Interactive Learning Centre

A Learner's experience of technology

All the examples which follow are based on current practice in UK higher education. The list is by no means exhaustive, and you may know of more examples yourself. It is unlikely that any one student would experience all of these learning methods during a single undergraduate course, but they are provided to give examples for academics thinking of remodelling courses.

Presentation

- Attend a lecture prepared using a presentation package.
- Collect word-processed lecture notes.
- Access lecture notes via the Web.
- Read or print course notes from a CD ROM or the Web.
- Check assessment framework published on the Web.
- Follow course outline published on the Web.
- Read answers to FAQs on the Web.
- Select final year options after research on Web.

Collection

- Answer multi-choice questions (**MCQs**) for marking by optical mark reader (**OMR**).
- Complete self-assessment questions within computer-presented tutorial.
- Sit part of the end of semester examinations using computer-assisted assessment (CAA).
- Complete course questionnaire on the Web.
- Complete electronic evaluation questionnaire.

Interaction

- Use electronic tools (eg spreadsheet, statistical package) in conjunction with electronic notes.

- Research using bibliographic database (via NISS, see Other Resources, page 160).
- Learn about the Internet using **Tonic**, an interactive course run by the Netskills project (see Other Resources, page 160)
- Use computer-based multi-choice questions to self-test during learning and revision.
- Use computer-based simulation of animal experiment.
- Use 3D graphics package to view and manipulate molecular structures.
- Practise accounts procedures using Teaching and Learning Technology Programme (**TLTP**) computer package (Byzantium).
- Learn facts and revise for exams using Web-based notes.

Production

- Design questionnaire and write in HTML to collect data via the Web.
- Plan and present art exhibition using Virtual Curator programme, supported by advice from the **CTI Centre** for Art and Design.
- Use research datasets to extract data and become familiar with statistical procedures.
- Research and co-author some Web pages.
- Perform statistical analysis using a spreadsheet.
- Make **modelling calculations** using an industry standard simulation package.
- Prepare written assignment integrating the use of a number of standard office software packages.
- Present dissertation in both word-processed format and as hypermedia.
- Use word processor to produce curriculum vitae.
- Use computer-aided design programme to produce engineering drawings.
- Submit coursework summary using a presentation package.

Communication

- Engage in *ad hoc* electronic discussions.
- Participate in a live electronic discussion using a MUD object orientated (**MOO**) (MUD stands for multi-user dimension or 'multi-user domain').
- Submit assignments for peer marking using e-mail.
- Locate a foreign language mentor via the Web, and make contact using e-mail.
- Participate in moderated group e-mail discussions as part of course assignments.
- Locate a foreign language mentor via the Web, and make contact using e-mail.
- Participate in moderated group e-mail discussions as part of course assignments.

Interrogating Practice

Compare each of the items mentioned in the 'Learner's Experience' list with the learning needs of your students. Would your students benefit from the introduction of the items? Could their introduction be defended in terms of efficiency and effectiveness?

EVALUATING YOUR INNOVATIONS

A detailed discussion of the evaluation of IT in teaching and learning is beyond the scope of this chapter, but some of the suggestions in Further Reading (page 159) may prove useful. However, before embarking on teaching innovations that make use of technology, it may be worth reviewing plans in the light of a number of considerations. One consideration is how far all learners will have reasonable access. An approach to the use of technology for learning and teaching can be to consider the issue in terms of the four building blocks of the ideal learning environment identified by Collins, Brown and Newman (1989) in their exploration of the cognitive apprenticeship. Their evaluative framework can be used to identify a set of questions or considerations that are illustrated under the four categories which follow.

1. Content
Can computers be used to deliver materials in a way that may be of special benefit to the teacher? For example, electronic notes may be preferred because they allow boring material to be presented without demanding teacher intervention. The use of electronic collections means that the resources are always available and cannot have been borrowed or lost. Is access via an electronic proxy the only means that enables the learner almost first-hand experience of a resource? Access might otherwise be impossible because of factors such as geography, security, or the rare and fragile nature of the primary source.

2. Method
Does the method of a particular programme enhance the quality of learning? Electronic presentation of the course materials may be useful to the learner, providing them an opportunity to study independently in their own time, space, or pace. Electronic publication may increase the ability of an institution to exert quality control on the production or delivery of materials. Does the choice of a particular method of delivery overcome technical problems? One of the drivers which has

moved many users away from traditional computer-based training programmes towards the different style of delivery possible via the Web has been the ability of the Web to be accessed from many and different sorts of computers. Does the use of technology offer the learner an opportunity to enrich their methods of learning? Using a resource-based system enables the learner to cut and paste between presented material and their own course work.

3. Sequence

Does using technology enable the learner to have better control of the sequence of access to information? Does the use of electronic delivery enable complementary materials to be presented side-by-side? An advantage of **hypermedia** systems is that they can be used to integrate different activities alongside the presentation of material, so that the learner is presented with knowledge and process in context, rather than separately. The use of hypermedia may also add the ability to search across the resource collection in a manner not possible in paper-based or non-integrated materials.

4. Sociology

Does the use of technology alter the organizational aspects of learning? Using computer course materials may enable the consolidation of a range of courses, which it might otherwise not be practical or cost-effective to run individually. Using the Web as a medium for the publication of simple course management information is becoming relatively widespread since it offers gains to the learners (easy access to essential administrative information) and the educators (single publication of routine information).

OVERVIEW

Pointers towards the types of IT material used in teaching and learning in higher education have been given. The issues of training and of the time needed to generate some materials have been raised. The need to evaluate the impact of IT interventions has been emphasized, as has the importance of creating/using materials that will promote deep learning. IT in teaching and learning is most valuable when it is integrated with other approaches and when it is used to mediate learning.

REFERENCES

Ackerman, MS, and Malone, TW (1990) *Answer Garden: A Tool for Growing Organizational Memory*, ACM Conference on Office Information Systems 1990, pp 31–39, ACM Press

Bacon, RA and Swithenby, SJ (1996) A strategy for the integration of IT-led methods into physics: the SToMP approach, *Computers and Education*, **26**, pp 135–41

Collins, A, Brown, JS and Newman, S (1989) Cognitive apprenticeship: teaching the craft of reading, writing and mathematics, in *Knowing, Learning and Instruction: Essays in honor of Robert Goaser*, ed L Resnick, pp 453–94, Erlbaum, Hilldale, New Jersey

Hall, W, Park Woolf, B and White, S (1999) Interactive systems for learning and teaching, in *Handbook of Internet and Multimedia Systems and Applications*, Furht, B (ed), in press, University of Southampton

Jackson, B (1998) Evaluation of learning technology implementation, in *Evaluation Studies*, ed N Mogey, pp 22–25, Learning Technology Dissemination Initiative, Edinburgh

Laurillard, D (1993) *Rethinking University Teaching: A framework for the effective use of educational technology*, Routledge, London

Mayes, JT (1995) Learning technology and groundhog day, in *Proceedings of Hypermedia at Work: Practice and theory in higher education*, eds W Strang, V Simpson and D Slater, University of Kent at Canterbury

NCIHE (1997) (Dearing Report) *Higher Education in the Learning Society*, National Committee of Inquiry into Higher Education, HMSO, London

FURTHER READING

Barnett, L, Brunner, D, Maier, P and Warren, A (1996) *Technology in Teaching and Learning: a guide for academics*, University of Southampton. This readable two-book guide with video contains a wide range of useful examples, and sets the use of technology in the context of ongoing change in the higher education system (http://www.tsms.soton.ac.uk/ilc)

Harvey, J (1997) *Brite Ideas*, Learning Technology Dissemination Initiative, Scottish Higher Education Funding Council. A small, straightforward reference guide with practical advice on using technology in teaching and learning. Based on the experience of the Scottish Learning Technologies Dissemination Initiative (http://www.icbl.hw.ac.uk/ltdi/)

Harvey, J (1998) *Evaluation Cookbook*, Learning Technology Dissemination Initiative, Scottish Higher Education Funding Council (http://www.icbl.hw.ac.uk/ltdi/cookbook.htm)

OTHER RESOURCES

Mailbase

There are a variety of electronic discussion groups covering the whole range of CAL, virtual universities, evaluation, and computer assisted assessment. (http://www.mailbase.ac.uk)

Netskills

This is a specialist project covering skills associated with the area of online learning and the Web. (http://www.netskills.ac.uk)

NISS

NISS (National Information Services and Systems) operates within the UK education sector and provides on-line information services for the education and research community. Probably the best place to start looking for links to current teaching and learning initiatives. (http://www.niss.ac.uk/education/other-he.html) Turpin, S, White, S (1998), Introducing Learning Technology in Higher Education, Teaching and Learning Technology Programme. This short video brings together interviews with a range of academics to provide an overview of some of the uses of learning technology, plus a discussion of associated issues. Support material is also available from (http://www.tsms.soton.ac.uk/tl)

Virtual library

The virtual library on educational technologies has pointers to many sources of relevant information both UK and world-wide. (http://agora.unige.ch/tecfa/edutech/welcome_frame.html)

13 The Evaluation of Teaching

Dai Hounsell

INTRODUCTION

It is nearly three decades since the first books on the **evaluation** of university and college teaching began to appear in Britain, and initially, there seems little doubt, the topic was highly controversial. It dumbfounded many academics while leaving some aghast at what they saw as an affront to their academic autonomy and an unwarranted deference to student opinion. Nowadays evaluation raises very few eyebrows. It has come to be seen not only as a necessary adjunct to accountability, but also as an integral part of good professional practice. And from this contemporary standpoint, expertise in teaching is viewed not simply as the product of experience: it also depends on the regular monitoring of teaching performance to pinpoint achievements and strengths, and to identify areas where there is scope for improvement.

Alongside this gradual acceptance of the indispensability of evaluation has come a greater methodological sophistication. In its infancy, evaluation in British universities was strongly influenced by American practice, in which the use of standardized and centrally administered student ratings questionnaires had been the predominant approach (eg Flood Page, 1974). Yet it was not widely understood by many who imported such questionnaires that they had been designed principally for **summative** purposes: that is, to yield quantitative data which could be used to compare the teaching performance of different individuals, and thus provide an ostensibly more objective basis for decisions about staffing contracts, tenure and promotion. They could not therefore be as readily adopted in systems of higher education such those in Britain or Australia, where teaching was commonly collaborative (Falk and Dow, 1971). Here the foremost concern was with the use of evaluation for developmental rather than judgemental purposes, and thus with contextualization rather than standardization (Hounsell and Day, 1991). It was therefore necessary to develop more broadly based approaches to the collection and analysis of feedback (eg Gibbs, Habeshaw and Habeshaw, 1988; O'Neil and Pennington, 1992; Hounsell, Tait and Day, 1997; Day, Grant and Hounsell, 1998; Harvey, 1998) and which are surveyed in the present chapter.

Interrogating Practice

What recommendations or guidelines do you have in your institution or department on collection and analysis of feedback from students?

CONTEXTS AND FOCUS

There are many reasons for wishing to evaluate the impact and effectiveness of teaching. New lecturers are usually keen to find out whether they are 'doing OK', what their strengths and weaknesses are as novice teachers, and how their teaching compares with that of other colleagues. More experienced lecturers may want to find out how well a newly-introduced course/module is running, and a programme coordinator that a fresh intake of first-year undergraduates is settling in reasonably well. To some extent, obtaining feedback can also have a cathartic function – an opportunity for the students to 'let off some steam' and 'to tell us what they really think about the course'. But the motives for seeking feedback to evaluate teaching may be extrinsic as well as intrinsic. The advent of **quality assurance**, for example, has brought with it the routine expectation that academic departments and faculties will regularly make use of feedback to investigate whether their curricula are succeeding in their **aims** and achieving appropriate **standards**. Similarly, providing documentary evidence to show that feedback has been sought (and has been constructively responded to) is emerging as an almost universal requirement in accredited professional development programmes for university teachers, while also being increasingly adopted as a basis for demonstrating teaching expertise in promotion procedures.

These differences in purposes are likely in turn to influence the nature of the feedback sought. The kinds of feedback evidence appropriate to a claim for promotion to a senior post (where excellence will need to be demonstrated) will be markedly different to those applying to someone approaching the end of their probationary period, where the prime concern will be to demonstrate competence at or above a given threshold (Elton, 1996; Hounsell, 1996). Such evidence may well be presented by means of a **teaching portfolio** (Chapter 18). Generally speaking, feedback which is collected for extrinsic purposes has to fulfil a set of formal requirements, whereas someone collecting feedback for their own individual purposes usually has much greater scope over what kinds of feedback they collect and in what form. In either case careful consideration has to be given to what would be the most appropriate focus for feedback in any given instance. If, for example, the intention is to capture as full and rounded a picture as possible of teaching in its various guises, then the equivalent of a wide-angle lens will be needed. This can encompass questions of course design and structure, teaching-learning strategies, academic guidance and support, and approaches to assessment, together with interrelationships between these. But there may also be occasions when the overriding concern is with a specific aspect of teaching such as **computer-based learning** or the quantity and quality of comments on students' assignments, and where only a close-up will capture the kind of fine-grained information being sought.

These considerations will be influential in determining not only how and from whom feedback is to be sought (as will be apparent below) but also when it is to be elicited – a dimension of evaluation that is often overlooked. There is a widespread practice, for example, of waiting until the end of a course before canvassing student opinion, usually on the grounds that the students need to have experienced the whole course before they can effectively comment on it. But one consequence is that students often find it difficult to recall with much precision a series of practical classes, say, or a coursework assignment that took place several months previously. Another is that none of the issues or concerns that students raise will be addressed in time for them to derive any benefit – a situation which is not conducive to good teaching and likely to undermine students' interest in providing worthwhile feedback.

Interrogating Practice

At what points in your teaching do you gather feedback from students? Does this give you time to respond to issues they raise?

SOURCES OF FEEDBACK

In contemporary practice in higher education, there are three principal sources of feedback which are widely recognized. These are:

- feedback from students (by far the commonest source of feedback);
- feedback from teaching colleagues and professional peers (Chapter 17);
- self-generated feedback (the aim of which is not to enable university teachers to act as judge and jury in their own cause, but rather to cultivate **reflection** and promote self-scrutiny).

If it is to be considered appropriately systematic and robust, any feedback strategy is likely to make use of at least two – and preferably all three – of these sources, since each has its own distinctive advantages and limitations. Feedback from students, for instance, offers direct access to the 'learners' eye-view', and students are uniquely qualified to comment on matters such as clarity of presentation, pacing of material, access to computing or library facilities, 'bunching' of assignment deadlines and helpfulness of tutors' feedback on written work. There are some issues where departmental teaching colleagues may be better-equipped to comment: for instance, on the appropriateness of course aims, content and structure; on the design of resource materials; or on alternatives in devising and marking assignments, tests and examinations. And third, self-generated feedback, which is grounded in the day-to-day teaching experiences, perceptions and reflections of the individuals concerned, opens up valuable opportunities to 'capitalize on the good things' and to 'repair mistakes quickly before they get out of hand' (Ramsden and Dodds, 1989: 54).

Over and above these three main sources of feedback, there is a fourth which, though readily available, is often under-exploited or goes unnoticed: the 'incidental feedback' which is to be found in the everyday routines of university teaching and course administration and therefore does not call for the use of specific survey techniques. It includes readily available information such as attendance levels; pass, fail, transfer and dropout rates; patterns of distribution of marks or grades; the nature of the choices which students make in choosing between assignment topics or test and examination questions; and the reports of external examiners or subject reviewers. It can also encompass the kinds of unobtrusive observations which can be made in a teaching-learning situation, such as a lecture: how alert and responsive the students are; whether many of them seem tired, distracted or uninvolved; to what extent they react to what is said by looking at the teacher or avoiding his or her gaze (Bligh, 1998; Brown, 1978).

Interrogating Practice

How do you make use of incidental feedback? Is it used in your own reflective practice?

METHODS OF FEEDBACK

The question of the source from which feedback is to be obtained is closely related to the question of how it is to be sought (Figure 13.1). Indeed, any such overview of sources and methods in combination helps to underscore the great wealth of possibilities that are currently available to university teachers in seeking and making use of feedback.

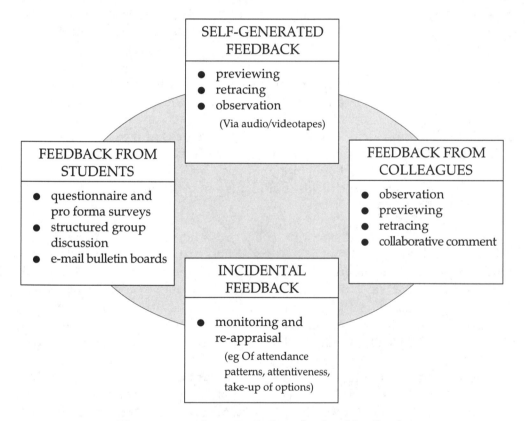

Figure 13.1 Sources and methods of feedback

As far as methods of obtaining feedback from students are concerned, questionnaires remain extremely popular (see Case Study 1) – largely, one suspects, on two grounds. First, there is the widespread availability of off-the-shelf questionnaires, which (though of widely varying quality) are to be found in abundance in the many books on teaching and learning in higher education (eg Hounsell, Tait and Day, 1997), as well as being regularly bartered and cannibalized by course teams and individuals alike. And second, there are the signal attractions of a method which offers every student the chance to respond while at the same time generating data which are quantifiable. However, these easy virtues can trap the unwary. Over-intensive and indiscriminate use in some institutions has led to 'questionnaire fatigue' on the part of students, while among staff there has been a growing awareness of the drawbacks of the questionnaire method. Concerns have been expressed about the considerable resources of time and expertise that are necessary both in designing questionnaires which are salient and to-the-point, and in systematically processing and analysing the resulting data. Happily, there is a growing range of alternative approaches to the canvassing of student opinion, including:

- 'instant' and 'one-minute' questionnaires together with a variety of pro formas, the majority of which aim to side-step questionnaire fatigue by combining brevity with more ample opportunities for student comment;
- structured group discussion, student panels and **focus groups**, which offer less formal and relatively open-ended ways in which groups of students can constructively exchange and pool thoughts and reactions;
- electronic bulletin boards, to which students e-mail their comments and queries for open display.

Methods of obtaining feedback from colleagues and peers are equally diverse. Probably the best-known method is direct observation, where a colleague is invited to 'sit in' on a lecture, seminar or practical and subsequently offer comments as a knowledgeable third-party (Chapter 17). But there are likely to be situations – especially in small classes and in one-to-one tutorials or supervisory meetings – where the presence of a colleague would be obtrusive and inhibiting. It is here that the techniques of previewing and retracing come to the fore (Day, Grant and Hounsell, 1998: 8–9). Previewing involves looking ahead to a forthcoming class and trying to anticipate potential problem areas and explore how they might best be tackled. Retracing, on the other hand, is retrospective and is intended to review a specific teaching session, while it is still fresh in the mind, in order to pinpoint successes and areas of difficulty. Both techniques entail the use of a colleague as an interlocutor and critical friend, prompting reflection and the exploration of alternatives. Colleagues can also adopt a similar role in the critical scrutiny of course documentation and teaching materials or in collaborative marking and commenting on students' written work.

Case Study 1: A Questionnaire about Practical Classes

The University of Edinburgh

Many examples of end-of-course/module questionnaires are readily available. Here is an example of a questionnaire used to collect feedback from practical/laboratory class teaching.

A questionnaire about practicals

Please put a tick in the appropriate box to indicate your response to each of the following statements about the practicals you attended as part of the course.

The practicals	Strongly agree	agree	unsure	disagree	strongly disagree
● covered key areas and ideas	☐	☐	☐	☐	☐
● were well-linked to lectures	☐	☐	☐	☐	☐
● helped relate theory to practice	☐	☐	☐	☐	☐
● were well-planned and structured	☐	☐	☐	☐	☐
● were lively and stimulating	☐	☐	☐	☐	☐

The demonstrator

● made clear what was expected of students	☐	☐	☐	☐	☐
● helped students with any difficulties they encountered	☐	☐	☐	☐	☐
● was interested in students and their progress	☐	☐	☐	☐	☐

As a student

- I looked forward
  to practicals ☐ ☐ ☐ ☐ ☐
- I enjoyed being in
  practicals ☐ ☐ ☐ ☐ ☐
- I learned a lot
  from the
  practicals ☐ ☐ ☐ ☐ ☐

Please add below any comments about what would have made the practicals better for you:

Inevitably, the services of hard-pressed colleagues and peers can only be drawn on occasionally and judiciously, but many of the same techniques can also be adapted for use in compiling self-generated feedback. Video and audio recordings make it possible to observe one's own teaching, albeit indirectly, while previewing and retracing are equally feasible options for an individual, especially if good use is made of an appropriate checklist or pro forma to provide a systematic focus for reflection and self-evaluation. Case Study 2 gives an example of a pro forma which can be used in retracing a fieldwork exercise. Checklists can help to underpin previewing, retracing, or direct or indirect observation, and aspects for consideration are reviewed in Chapter 17.

Case Study 2: A Pro Forma that can be Used for Retracing Fieldwork

The University of Edinburgh

Fieldwork is a typical case where feedback from direct observation of teaching is not usually feasible. Here the most appropriate way to obtain feedback is by retracing. This method readily lends itself to other teaching situations, eg pro formas can be adapted for one-to-one sessions in creative arts that may run for several hours in which a one-hour sample observation would not yield useful feedback.

A pro forma for retracing fieldwork

Record by ticking in the appropriate column the comments which come closest to your opinion

How well did I...?	Well	Satisfactory	Not very well
make sure that students had the necessary materials, instructions, equipment, etc			
get the fieldwork underway promptly			
try to ensure that all the set tasks were completed in the time available			
keep track of progress across the whole class			
handle students' questions and queries			
provide help when students encountered difficulties			
respond to students as individuals			
help sustain students' interest			
bring things to a close and indicate follow-up tasks			

ANALYSING AND INTERPRETING FEEDBACK

Any technique for obtaining feedback is going to yield data that need to be processed, analysed and interpreted. Some techniques (for instance, structured group discussion) can generate feedback in a form which is already categorized and prioritized, while questionnaires can be designed in a format which allows the data to be captured by an **optical mark reader** or, in some institutions, processed by a central support service. Yet while possibilities such as these do save time and effort, there are little or no short-cuts to analysis and interpretation, for these are not processes which can readily be delegated to others. There is a body of thought, as Donald Bligh has noted, which contends that the actions of a lecturer and the students' response to that lecturer (as represented in the feedback they provide), are not accessible to an outside observer or independent evaluator, but can only be properly understood 'in the light of their intentions, perceptions and the whole background of their knowledge and assumptions' (Bligh, 1998: 166). It is not necessary to endorse this view unreservedly. Put in uncompromising terms, no one is better placed than the teacher most directly concerned to make sense of feedback and to weigh its significance against a knowledge of the subject matter in question, the teaching aims and objectives, and the interests, aspirations and capabilities of the students who provided the feedback.

Equally crucially, it does not seem unreasonable to concede that there are occasions when involving others in the challenge of analysing and interpreting feedback has very particular and distinctive benefits. First, a sometimes uncertain path has to be steered between the twin snares of, on the one hand, dismissing unwelcome feedback too readily and, on the other, dwelling on less favourable comment to the neglect of those features of one's teaching which have attracted praise and commendation. In circumstances such as these, calling on the 'second opinion' of a seasoned teaching colleague makes good sense. Second, specialist help may often be required in analysing and interpreting findings – and especially so when a standardized student questionnaire has been used and results for different individuals are being compared. Recent studies at the London School of Economics (Husbands, 1996; 1998) draw attention to the complexity of the issues raised. Third, the interrelationship of information and action is far from unproblematic. Good feedback does not in itself result in better teaching, as American experience has suggested (McKeachie, 1987). Improvements in teaching were found to be much more likely when university teachers not only received feedback but could draw on expert help in exploring how they might best capitalize upon strengths and address weaknesses.

Interrogating Practice

In your department, what happens to feedback data from student questionnaires? Is it made public to the students involved? How do staff analyse, review and act upon the findings from this source? How are students informed about changes made in response to their views?

ACTING ON FEEDBACK

This last point is a crucial one, especially given that many university teachers will not have easy access to a teaching-learning centre or educational development unit offering specialist guidance and support. It is therefore important to acknowledge that acting on feedback constructively entails a recognition of its practical limitations. Sometimes feedback produces unclear results which only further investigation might help to resolve, or it may be necessary to explore a variety of possible ways both of interpreting and responding to a given issue or difficulty.

Two examples may help to illustrate this. In the first of these, feedback on a series of lectures has indicated that many students experienced difficulties with audibility. But where exactly might the problem lie? Was it attributable to poor acoustics in the lecture theatre, or because many of the students were reluctant to sit in the front rows, or because the lecturer spoke too softly or too rapidly? And what would be the most appropriate response: installing a microphone and speakers, encouraging the students to sit nearer the front, better voice projection and clearer diction by the lecturer, or greater use of handouts and audio-visual aids, so that students were less reliant on the spoken voice?

The second example is one in which pressures on resources have led to larger tutorial groups, and feedback has revealed that students are dissatisfied with the limited opportunities they have to contribute actively to the discussion. One way forward might be to halve the size of tutorial groups by scheduling tutorials at fortnightly rather than weekly intervals. Another might be to experiment with new strategies to maximize tutorial interaction and debate. And a third might be to reconfigure teaching-learning strategies, enabling fuller opportunities for tutorial interaction through greater reliance on self-study materials.

As these two examples make clear, in many teaching-learning situations there is no one obvious or ideal response to feedback, but rather an array of options from which a choice has to be made which is appropriate and feasible. Some options may have resource implications; some may necessitate consulting with colleagues; and some (the second example above is a case in point) may best be resolved by giving the students concerned an opportunity to express their views on the various options under consideration.

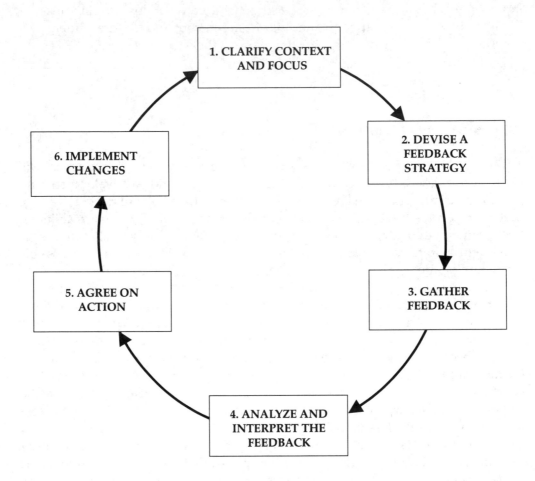

Figure 13.2 The evaluation cycle

OVERVIEW

This chapter has looked at the principal factors to be considered in evaluating teaching. The sequence followed was not fortuitous, as Figure 13.2 suggests, for the processes involved, when viewed collectively, can be seen as a series of interlocking steps which together comprise a cycle of evaluation. Overlooking any one of these steps is likely to be dysfunctional. Neglecting to clarify focus and purposes, for example, may result in feedback which is unhelpful or of marginal relevance, while failing to respond to issues which have arisen by not implementing agreed changes risks alienating those who have taken the trouble to provide feedback.

It would be misleading, nonetheless, to see this cyclical perspective on evaluation as a counsel of perfection. No university teacher can realistically subject every aspect of his or her day-to-day practice to constant review, nor can workable evaluation strategies be devised in isolation from careful consideration of the resources of time, effort and expertise which would be called for. Effective evaluation may be less a matter of technique than of the exercise of personal and professional judgement.

REFERENCES

Bligh, D (1998) *What's the Use of Lectures?*, 5th edn, Intellect, Exeter

Brown, G (1978) *Lecturing and Explaining*, Methuen, London

Day, K, Grant, R and Hounsell, D (1998) *Reviewing your Teaching*, Edinburgh and Sheffield: University of Edinburgh, TLA Centre/CVCP Universities' and Colleges' Staff Development Agency

Elton, L (1996) Criteria for teaching competence and teaching excellence in higher education, in *Evaluating Teacher Quality in Higher Education*, eds R Aylett and K Gregory, Falmer, London

Falk, B and Dow, KL (1971) *The Assessment of University Teaching*, Society for Research into Higher Education, London

Flood Page, C (1974) *Student Evaluation of Teaching: The American experience*, Society for Research into Higher Education, London

Gibbs, G, Habeshaw, S and Habeshaw, T (1988) *53 Interesting Ways to Appraise your Teaching*, Technical and Educational Services, Bristol

Harvey, J (ed) (1998) *Evaluation Cookbook*, Learning Technology Dissemination Initiative, Heriot-Watt University, Edinburgh

Hounsell, D (1996) Documenting and assessing teaching excellence, in *Evaluating Teacher Quality in Higher Education*, eds R Aylett and K Gregory, Falmer, London

Hounsell, D and Day, K (1991) Feedback, evaluation and quality in teaching in higher education, in *Managing the Higher Education Environment*, ed M Wright, Napier Polytechnic/ EAIR, Edinburgh (proceedings of the 13th International Forum of the European Association for Institutional Research, Edinburgh, 1–4 September 1991)

Hounsell, D, Tait, H and Day, K (1997) *Feedback on Courses and Programmes of Study*, University of Edinburgh, TLA Centre/Universities' and Colleges' Staff Development Agency/Institute for Higher Education Development in South Africa, Edinburgh, Sheffield and Johannesburg

Husbands, CT (1996) Variations in students' evaluations of teachers' lecturing and small-group teaching: a study at the London School of Economics, *Studies in Higher Education*, 21 (2) pp 187–206.

Husbands, CT (1998) Implications for the assessment of the teaching competence of staff in higher education of some correlates of students' evaluations of different teaching styles, *Assessment and Evaluation in Higher Education*, **23** (2) pp 117–39

McKeachie, WJ (1987) Instructional evaluation: current issues and possible improvements, *Journal of Higher Education*, **58** (3), pp 344–50

O'Neil, M and Pennington, RC (1992) *Evaluating Teaching and Courses from an Active Learning Perspective*, Universities' and Colleges' Staff Development Agency, Sheffield

Ramsden, P and Dodds, A (1989) *Improving Teaching and Courses: A guide to evaluation*, 2nd edn, University of Melbourne, Melbourne

FURTHER READING

The following are practical guides, each approaching evaluation in a distinctive and contrasting way.

Day, K, Grant, R and Hounsell, D (1998) See above. (http://www.tla.ed.ac.uk/ryt.html)

Gibbs, G, Habeshaw, S and Habeshaw, T (1988) See above. These two handbooks mentioned above provide a range of practical examples of checklists, questions and pro formas.

Harvey, J (ed) (1998) See above. (http://www.icbl.hw.ac.uk/ltdi) Of particular interest to anyone wishing to evaluate the use of C&IT in university teaching.

14 Supporting and Guiding Students

Jenni Wallace

INTRODUCTION

This chapter explores how a university can support a student through the journey of achieving a degree, further to the recent changes in higher education which have impacted on both the institution and curriculum. Guidance and flexible support infrastructures are fundamental in any serious attempt to support learners.

DEFINITION

Guidance has a central role in enabling individuals to take control of their lives: as learners, workers and citizens. In different contexts it includes tutoring, advising, counselling, and mentoring, and together these enable individuals to find the best options for their particular needs, giving them the skills to reflect on their personal, academic and vocational objectives, to set goals, adopt appropriate learning strategies, cope with crises and, finally, to review and manage their progress in and beyond formal education (DfEE, 1996).

BACKGROUND

After the expansion of higher education in the early 1990s, it became apparent that an increasing number of students were not completing their programmes of study. The Higher Education Funding Council for England (HEFCE) (1997) research project on undergraduate non-completion in higher education describes the social process between student and institution, in which the main elements may be characterized as *student preparedness* and *student-institution compatibility*.

For example:

- incompatibility between students and their course or institution (further to students often having insufficient information, leading to the reality differing from their expectations);
- lack of preparation for the higher education experience (students not having the self-management skills);
- lack of commitment to the programme of study (peer and parental pressure being the main reason the student applies to the university);
- financial hardship;
- poor academic progress.

It follows that those students who are better prepared – that is, who know how to ask for help and use the support opportunities – are more likely to complete their courses. However, the diverse groups that now make up the student population have very different requirements, and institutions need to look further at the learning experience, pastoral care and support services they provide and consider whether they meet the students' needs.

Focusing on retention of students is essential, as is the development of proactive strategies that put the support in the right places at appropriate times.

Interrogating Practice

We can all remember those times when we experienced being new to a situation: first day at school, first day of a new job, and more poignantly, first week of taking up a new post at a university. Take a moment to reflect, and ask yourself how it actually felt to be a new member of staff. How do you think students are experiencing being new to your university?

RESEARCH

There have been two major works that have focused on student support and guidance. The first was HEQC's *Guidance and Counselling* (1994). The Charters for Higher Education and the national systems for quality assessment and audit were the driving forces for this work, which had as its aim: '…to assist higher education institutions in their response to changes in the student population by the development of co-ordinated guidance provision for both students and potential students, including a staff development function and the development of feedback mechanisms' (page vi).

HEQC (1994) emphasized the fact that guidance starts when the student first approaches the institution, carries on during the stages, and continues at exit and often beyond. The quality of this guidance relates strongly to the quality of the learning experience. The outcomes highlighted the importance for the whole institutional approach, in which there are policies, nominated staff roles with clear lines of responsibility, effective information systems, good organizational communication, and developed guidance networks with provision for peer-supported learning opportunities for students.

Some examples of the sort of provision that HEQC (1994) highlighted as good practice include:

- starting a mature students society;
- developing an access forum;
- running guidance conventions and open days;
- holding workshops for new staff and students;
- developing better networks;
- generating better guidance materials;
- providing staff handbooks;
- developing AP(E)L materials;
- running a range of staff development activities.

This project suggested that to promote sustained development and to foster a guidance culture, further essential activities would need to be defined, for example:

- a whole institutional policy, explaining the rationale for guidance, outlining the specific provision, explaining the explicit standards, explaining the mechanisms for appeal or complaint, or, in other words, defining the entitlement;
- a whole institution systems approach with an emphasis on organizational structures and clarifying staff roles in recruitment and guidance, to ensure impartiality of guidance as far as possible of those involved;
- guidance networks;
- curriculum developments;
- focus on accessibility and the student experience;
- increase participation rates;
- encourage peer support;
- improve communication, between academic and non-academic staff members, between all staff and students, especially on modular courses where there is no core teaching group;
- monitor and evaluate the guidance systems.

The second major work that focused on student support and guidance was the DfEE Guidance and Learner Autonomy Project (GALA), carried out during 1994–96. This project was based on some common assumptions:

- the development of autonomous individuals is a key objective of all higher education, which guidance helps to achieve;
- guidance is primarily a learning, rather than a helping, process;
- it is normal and proper for all learners in higher education (both students and staff) to require guidance from time to time, to explore ways of learning to meet the challenge of change;
- the fundamental ethic of guidance is based on the interest and autonomy of the individual learner;
- guidance is not the exclusive role of specialist staff.

GUIDANCE

Guidance is central to the learning process, so it is obvious that a good quality system should aim to develop mechanisms that recognize the needs of individual learners, as each student will differ in their:

- level of motivation and expectation;
- levels of retention of knowledge, and their long and short-term memories;
- levels of knowledge, skills and practical experiences;
- time they have available to study;
- powers of problem solving;
- confidence levels and capacity for learning new things.

Guidance for all students should support ways of accessing knowledge and developing critical thinking, which will enable the advancement of the individual. The role should be shared by all those who come in contact with the student body, including administrators, technical staff, learning support staff, and academics. The skills required are those of listening, advising, informing, assessing, counselling, advocating, tutoring and enabling. This should be followed by knowing and understanding the mechanisms in place to collect relevant information (except confidential information) which needs to be fed back through appropriate channels to inform progress. This can be visualized as a feedback loop, with student and staff views being regularly recorded so that current recruitment strategies and new curriculum developments can be better informed by student need and experience.

SKILLS TO SUPPORT AND GUIDE

Tutorial method

One method of helping students to become autonomous can be achieved by assisting them in the development of critical thinking. The role is to promote a reflective process which examines past values, day-to-day ideas and behaviours, all of which can be quite daunting when contemplating new perspectives and actions. The skill of listening empathetically as the student explores this unknown territory is essential. The tutor becomes a sounding board reacting to the students' experiences, and helping them make connections between occurrences. The tutor can encourage the identification of assumptions underlying student behaviours, choices and decisions, and help them gain some understanding that aspects of their situation are of their own making, and open to change, helping students to realize 'that while actions are shaped by context, context can be altered to be more congruent with people's desires' (Brookfield, 1987: 10).

Critical thinking is difficult, as it requires the suspension of previously held beliefs. However, most students enter the higher education system expecting some change, and as they strive for clarity in understanding, the opportunity to discuss these activities is enormously helpful. Guidance and support should therefore provide opportunities for reflection and analysis, that allow students to articulate and understand assumptions underpinning their day-to-day actions. Guidance is then a learning process for all, the students gaining a better understanding of themselves and the tutor learning more about students' learning needs.

Clarifying the language

It is helpful to define a common language before assigning roles and responsibilities. Six types of guidance are referred to in the literature:

1. Academic guidance: embracing subject specific guidance, advice and information on students' overall academic programmes; feedback on assessment; academic development; learning skills and development; recognition and reflection upon learning and key skills profiling.
2. Guidance on professional development: furthers academic guidance to include profiling and careers guidance.
3. Programme guidance: embraces structural and regulatory requirements; programme planning; assessment requirements.
4. Learning support: embraces learning skills and strategies to include targeted additional learning support; library and IT induction; specialist support for disabled students, open learning materials.

5. Personal guidance: includes welfare issues; financial and other personal issues.
6. Administrative guidance: includes information and advice on all aspects of the administrative system to which students will relate: pre-entry, entry, on-programme, and post-programme.

Interrogating Practice

The headings which follow are developed from work at the University of North London. They demonstrate a range of activities and procedures necessary to give students support and guidance needed to access their university course successfully.

Use this as a checklist to: (a) consider the same or similar provision in your own institution; (b) find out who is responsible within your university for this provision, and add their name and contact number.

Guidance pre-entry provided through responsibility

All the information which follows will be provided on the Web:

1. General information on the university and its provision: eg, prospectus, subject information, student accommodation, marketing materials.
2. Information on the curriculum: eg, prospectus, subject information.
3. Information for international students: eg, international prospectus.
4. Information on CATS, AP(E)L: eg, learning choices supported by open days, interview process, admissions documentation.
5. Information on student exchange, study abroad and placements: eg, opportunities, prospectus, subject information, marketing materials.
6. Information and guidance for students with special needs: eg, admissions procedures.
7. Information on student support services: eg, careers advice, learning support, counselling service.

On-programme guidance provided through responsibility

Personal

1. Student support services: provide written information and guides on how to access support, operate open access and appointments systems, support for students with disabilities.
2. International office: provides advice specifically related to international students, works with faculties and departments to offer advice and support sessions.

Academic

1. Subject-specific and programme information: eg, faculty and interfaculty programme planning procedures.
2. Placements, work-based learning, sandwich year, year abroad: eg, integrated guidance in programme/scheme, integrated career development sessions, profiling.
3. Assessment: eg, according to an agreed procedure.
4. Learning support: eg, learning support programmes for referred students, learning resources.
5. Student representation: eg, boards of study, student representative training programme, student feedback.

Administrative

1. Student handbook: eg, regulations and procedures, open access, surgery hours, individual appointments.
2. Guidance on academic structures: programme planning rules and schemes, supported by access to trained administrative staff (and Web module).
3. General advice on student administration: fees, term dates, assessment in written format.

Post-programme provided through responsibility

1. Transcripts and references: eg, systematic procedure for their placement on file.
2. Careers and post-completion activities: eg, first destination survey, careers information.
3. Alumni: eg, continued contact, network involvement of graduates on university activities.

> ### Case Study 1: Supplemental Instruction: Peer Support

(UK programme used at over 20 universities, developed from an American model)

Supplemental instruction (SI) is a programme designed to assist any student wishing to improve his or her academic performance. It provides proactive intervention early on in a non-remedial format which has benefits for all students, regardless of their current level of academic competence. SI is group-based, and has traditionally been attached to specific high-risk or historically difficult courses. An SI supervisor is responsible for identifying targeted courses, gaining support from the department or faculty and from the individual staff. The supervisor selects and trains the SI leaders (students) and monitors and evaluates the programme. SI is offered where the tutor invites and supports the programme. The tutor and the supervisor screen the SI leaders for content competence, and approve selection. SI leaders, usually second-year students, are trained in active learning and study strategies. They also are trained in interpersonal, team and group handling skills and a range of activities which enable them to improve their own management of group study sessions. SI leaders prepare for their sessions based on the needs of the group, liaise with the tutor, attend weekly supervision sessions with the supervisor and their peers, and conduct one-hour sessions with their group. The SI leader is a 'model' student and a facilitator who helps students integrate course content and learning strategies. The SI group session takes place at a regular time, with a student leader taking full responsibility for the publicity of the session. The student leaders facilitate the group and do not re-teach material. They ask and encourage the group to solve its own difficulties from the group resource. The leaders prompt the group members to explore how they learn as much as what they learn.

This case study looks at an academic assistance programme based on SI that uses the notions of encouraging autonomy in learning, while developing the skills of academic enquiry and critical thinking. This is managed usually by second-year students for the benefit of first years. This is an example of peer support, and plays an important role in highlighting the fact that students can be guided and supported by each other. The programme is known as supplemental instruction, originally developed in the United States at the University of Missouri, Kansas City. Universities in the United Kingdom have developed the model to meet the needs of their individual academic cultures. It is known at University College

London and Kingston University as PAL (peer assisted learning) and at the University of Manchester it is known as PASS (peer assisted study support). It is based on the premise that all learning is student-centred, and an active process fully involving the learner, with close collaboration with those who support the learner – a true partnership that supports all involved.

Purpose of the development

The traditional way of supporting learners having difficulties with their taught courses has often been very resource intensive (one-to-one) and there seems to be no conclusive evidence that the approach of separating study skills support away from course content is in any way successful (Wallace, 1996). A similar position is taken by the supporters of critical thinking, who affirm that general critical thinking skills cannot be developed in isolation from a specific context (Brookfield, 1997). It was felt that a programme was needed to integrate learning strategies into course content.

The second major concern was a high attrition rate of first-year students, and the university needed to look at ways of bringing students back into their studies. An initiative was needed to combat attrition and define a range of retention strategies.

Key concept

It is acknowledged that historically there have always been difficult courses, eg ones that deal with ideas and others such as law and medicine where facts have to be memorized or, for example, any courses with a mathematical basis, which may be defined as high risk and capable of resulting in student failure. With this as the first premise, it takes the focus away from the student, and puts the responsibility firmly with lecturers to identify difficulties, making sure the resources and the curriculum are responsive to the needs of all students. Such a proactive approach requires careful planning so that difficulties can be anticipated and addressed, thus minimizing the potential for failure.

The model

The key purposes are as follows:

- to focus on 'preparation for learning' to equip students with the necessary skills and strategies of academic enquiry, critical thinking, ownership of learning and the building of self-confidence;
- to encourage the empowerment of learners to become autonomous in their learning in a managed environment without direct staff input;

- to recognize that problems are often inherent in the courses themselves rather than in the students, as it targets courses and not students. It strives to reduce failure rates, as well as helping students to improve performance across the board;
- to facilitate active student involvement which provides an environment for creating effective learning;
- to develop a methodology that allows for the feedback of learning to move between the learners and the teachers, so that both understand the learning needs of the students and the expectations set by the academic staff;
- to embed learning strategy and study skills into course content and not to encourage the learning of the subject in isolation. This is achieved by processes of collaboration and cooperation among learners and course tutors who invite the programme into their curriculum area. This is accomplished by training second-year students to act as group facilitators, and to give feedback on the learning needs of the first-year student;
- to provide a supportive environment in which students discuss and process course material, openly admitting to their difficulties.

Four areas of benefit:
- individual students build up confidence and self-esteem which leads to the ability to master course concepts and dramatically develops study and cognitive skills;
- student leaders develop a range of skills including group, team leadership and communication skills, that they are able to apply in other situations. They also gain a deeper understanding of their own subject area;
- academic staff involved in SI receive regular feedback on how course content is being received by the learner;
- the institution is able to respond to student requests to provide other ways of offering support and benefiting from a more effective learning community.

The goals of SI sessions are to help students become more independent learners and more critical thinkers. Though guided and supported by second-year students, the learning task is the responsibility of the first-year students themselves.

QUALITY ISSUES

Assurance

Guidance can improve the student experience by ensuring that students are placed on programmes as close to their interests, commitments and abilities as possible. Second, it encourages students to take control of their own learning careers. Successful educational guidance can end feelings of isolation and marginalization, and students can come to understand that they do have some control over decisions which appear to affect them (HEQC, 1994).

The Quality Assurance Agency (QAA) has made the student learning experience central to the current round of assessment visits. The questions that they pose are:

- Is there an appropriate strategy or system in place that supports and guides?
- Is it consistent with the aims and objectives of the curriculum?
- Does it match with the profile of the incoming students?
- What written materials are available, eg the student handbook?
- What is written in the course literature, eg modular handbook?
- What evidence has been gathered of the students' satisfaction with the course? Do you use more than questionnaires?
- Admissions and induction set the tone: what arrangements have been made?
- Are there clear messages about the availability and purpose of any support, eg academic guidance?
- Is it matched to the curriculum and student learning needs, and is it matched to the assessment methods? Can you relate student achievement to academic advice given?
- What welfare/pastoral support is there? Is it understood by all concerned?
- Does this occur in/out of the university, eg placements, year abroad, clinical placements.
- What support is there between the academic staff and the support services?
- Careers guidance, final destination: how does this link to the curriculum, is it an add-on or part of the curriculum offer? (QAA, 1998: 27)

Policy

Policies and statements that define the rights and responsibilities for learners have an important role in developing a culture that is then able to deliver a high standard of support while students study for a degree.

OVERVIEW

The development of institutional policy can be informed by the following principles:

- an emphasis on student autonomy and self-reliance, that students should be equipped to access information, advice and guidance as required and that guidance systems should support this approach;
- a clear identification of roles and responsibilities for information, advice and guidance;
- the provision of clear information to students on all aspects of their experience at the university;
- clear statements on how each responsibility area will provide the main information, advice and guidance within its remit;
- that aspects of advice and guidance are located with the relevant professional areas – ie, academic tutors will concentrate on academic issues and refer students on if they are seeking information and advice on administrative or personal issues.

Institutions should develop transparent flexible systems that enable both students and staff to access information and support when the need arises, thus encouraging choice and individual responsibility. Any university that can adopt this approach should enable its students to move towards becoming autonomous learners

REFERENCES

Brookfield, SD (1987) *Developing Critical Thinking*, Open University Press, Milton Keynes

DfEE (1996) *Living with Diversity*, An Executive Summary of Issues from the Guidance and Learner Autonomy Project

HEFCC (1994) *Choosing to Change, Extending Access, Choice and Mobility in HE*, Higher Education Funding Council for England, Bristol

HEFCE (1997) *Undergraduate Non-Completion in Higher Education*, Higher Education Funding Council for England, Bristol

HEQE (1994) *Guidance and Counselling in Higher Education*, Higher Education Quality Council, London

QAA (1998) *Subject Review Handbook: October 1998–September 2000*, Quality Assurance Agency, Bristol

Wallace, J (1996) Peer tutoring, in *Opening Doors*, eds S Wolfendale and J Corbett, Cassell, London

FURTHER READING

Allan, D (ed) (1996) *In at the Deep End*, Innovation in Higher Education Series
Written accounts from new university teachers.
Race, P and Brown, S (1998) *The Lecture's Toolkit*, Kogan Page, London. A useful section on making the most of your academic tutorials.

15 Quality and Standards

Robin Middlehurst

INTRODUCTION

Achieving high standards of **academic practice** is part of the professional responsibility of each academic. Providing a high quality learning experience for students and facilitating high standards in student attainment are also collective responsibilities for each department, unit or faculty and each higher education institution. However, what counts as a 'high standard' and what elements are included in the achievement of a 'high quality learning experience' is both complex and dynamic. At any one period of time, different interpretations and expectations may exist, and over time, shifts in direction and emphasis will occur. Such changes reflect evolving relationships between universities, the state and the wider society as well as changes in knowledge, technology and the nature of academic disciplines. It is important, therefore, for each academic to keep abreast of current debates about **quality** and **standard**s and to relate these to their own practice.

DEFINITIONS

The meaning of 'quality' and 'standards' in higher education has been subject to considerable debate over the past decade in both the United Kindgom and elsewhere (Green, 1994; Middlehurst, 1996; Brennan, de Vries and Williams, 1997). This debate reflects different and sometimes conflicting expectations of what higher education should provide and deliver. For example, the expectations of employers and professional bodies about the focus of higher education programmes and the achievements of graduates, government pressures to identify value-for-money, the influence of long-standing academic cultures and practices and the individual interests of students are not necessarily in harmony (Harvey, Burrows and Green, 1992). Determining the nature of 'high quality education' and 'appropriate standards of performance' depends on the aims and purposes of that education, the experience of it and the uses to which it will be put.

In many countries, the terms 'quality and standards' are used interchangeably. However, in the UK higher education system, these terms have different, but overlapping, focuses. 'Quality' is used in a generic sense to refer to all those elements that relate to teaching and learning processes, particularly as they impact on students' experiences of higher education and the conditions that support student learning. 'Standards' refer more narrowly to student attainment in terms of expected and actual levels of attainment (HEQC, 1996). Expected levels of attainment will be embedded in qualification and credit frameworks, and in curriculum design and assessment methods (for example, the 'standard' of an honours degree programme in history or a module in **key skills**). Actual levels of attainment are represented in the products and processes of students' learning and in the grading of their performance (for example, this student has achieved a first-class degree in history or is competent in a set of key skills at a specified level).

A word of caution is needed. Technical definitions of standards and quality exist side-by-side with the way these terms are used in every-day language where their meanings are wider and looser. For example, academics may refer to 'the quality of this year's intake' meaning the standard of students' performance or grades at entry to university and their potential for high academic attainment while at university. People also talk about 'standards of teaching' when referring at one and the same time to teacher performance and the wider context for student learning.

Individuals and institutions need not only to be aware of and to reflect on the context that gives rise to different definitions and meanings, but also to develop their own understanding of quality and standards. Developing personal and collective definitions provides a framework for academic practice and an aid to reflection on and measurement of student (and staff) performance.

Interrogating Practice

1. How do you define quality in relation to your own teaching? How do your students understand quality in their learning and your teaching? Do your definitions and their views match?
2. What do you understand by academic standards? Do your colleagues in the course or pathway team share your perspectives?
3. How do you help students to understand the academic standard they need to attain for success in their programme?

CONCEPTS AND TERMINOLOGY

Being clear about definitions of quality and standards is important since such definitions are used to guide the design, assessment and review of educational provision and educational achievements. However, definitions by themselves may not be enough to explain everything that you, your department and institution need to pay attention to in relation to quality and standards. This section looks in more detail at some underlying concepts and at the 'quality terminology' that is used in higher education.

In both a technical and a popular sense, achieving high quality and high standards depends on many components. Together these components create a *system*; and the system can be sub-divided into inputs, processes and outputs/outcomes, as in Table 15.1. Particular components are relevant at different stages of the educational process, for example, when designing programmes, assessing students, or reviewing the work of a department. Looking carefully at the interrelationships between components helps one to form judgements about the standards and quality of the education offered to students.

Table 15.1   An example of a systemic approach to quality and standards

Inputs	Processes	Outputs
Qualifications of staff	Curriculum design	Qualified graduates
Educational experience of students	Learning support	Number/type of awards
Range of learning resources	Student assessment	Students' work
		Graduates' knowledge, skills

Interrogating Practice

If you were designing a system for producing high quality learning in your subject, what would you regard as the key inputs, processes and outputs? Try asking the same question of a group of undergraduate or postgraduate students; how do your conclusions and theirs compare?

Over the past 20 years, in all sectors (and much earlier in some sectors: Drummond, 1992; Juran, 1995) notions of quality and standards have become central to the way things are done, managerially and professionally. The main shift has been from a tacit and implicit approach to an explicit, systematic approach. Underlying this shift has been the recognition, first, that achieving high quality and high standards depends on the interaction of various elements as described above. These elements include both quantitative factors (such as the amount of available resources) and qualitative factors (such as staff and student attitudes and management approach). Second, attaining the desired goal of high quality, high standards requires deliberate organization and sustained effort over time.

Moving from tacit and implicit approaches to systematic and explicit approaches implies the development of a shared language and shared understandings. A technical language has therefore evolved. The most common terms are '**quality specification**', '**quality control**', '**quality assurance**' and '**quality enhancement**'.

Each of these terms refers to a different, though often overlapping, activity and a different set of responsibilities. These responsibilities tend to be carried out in different ways at different levels inside and outside the institution (see Table 15.2).

Table 15.2 Terms and responsibilities for quality

Term	Responsibility			
	National	Institutional	Unit	Individual
Quality specification				
Quality control				
Quality assurance				
Quality enhancement				

If each of these activities is integrated, then a virtuous circle of 'continuous improvement' can be achieved.

QUALITY AND STANDARDS IN CONTEXT

Just as definitions have changed over time, so have arrangements and responsibilities for specifying and assuring quality and standards. A full analysis of changes over time is beyond the scope of this chapter. Interested readers should refer to the legal and constitutional framework for higher education (most recently, the Further and Higher Education (FHE) Act 1992), to the work and reports of agencies that have had formal responsibilities for quality and standards and to the literature on these subjects (see References, page 202).

Table 15.3 National agencies with responsibilities for quality and standards

Agencies	Dates
Council for National Academic Awards (CNAA) (new universities)	1967–92
Committee of Vice-Chancellors and Principals (CVCP) (old universities): (Academic Audit Unit)	1980–92
Higher Education Quality Council (HEQC) (all HE)	1992–97
Funding Councils' Quality Assessment Divisions (all HE)	1992–97
Quality Assurance Agency for Higher Education (all HE)	1997 →

Responsibility for quality and standards, as Table 15.2 indicates, extends from the individual academic to the national level, with various key organizing points in between – at course team or pathway level, at department or faculty level and at institutional level. Institutions are likely to adopt different ways of describing and structuring the roles and tasks that flow from these responsibilities, although the underlying principles are likely to be the same (HEQC, 1996). It is through this interlocking chain of responsibilities that academics and their institutions demonstrate their accountability for the public, personal or business funds invested in higher education.

The illustration of an integrated system for quality and standards appears tidy and coherent; reality is somewhat messier, not least because higher education and the national quality frameworks are constantly evolving.

National arrangements

The United Kingdom's regulatory and constitutional framework for the specification and assurance of quality and standards differs in certain important respects from other European countries (NCIHE, 1997a) and shares many features with Commonwealth or North American countries (Brennan, de Vries and Williams,

1997). However, across the world, academics do share common understandings of quality and standards (as evident, for example in the system of internationally refereed journals) and there are common patterns evident in international arrangements for the assurance of quality and standards (Commission of the European Communities, 1993; Brennan, de Vries and Williams, 1997).

At national level in the United Kingdom, a new **Quality Assurance Agency (QAA)** for Higher Education was set up in 1997 as a private company limited by guarantee and a registered charity. It has a board of directors drawn from the funding and representative bodies in higher education and independent members representing employers, professional bodies and industry. The Funding Councils have a statutory responsibility under the terms of the 1992 Further and Higher Education (FHE) Act to secure the assessment of the quality of education in publicly-funded institutions and they contract with the QAA to undertake this function on their behalf.

The QAA was set up in the same year (1997) that the recent National Inquiry into Higher Education reported on its findings and recommendations – the **Dearing Report** (NCIHE, 1997b). Many of the tasks and responsibilities that the QAA is now taking forward were outlined in this report, although the report itself leaned heavily on work that was in progress under the auspices of predecessor organizations. The main elements of the QAA's work are listed in Table 15.4. These elements are separated between 'specification' and 'assurance' activities.

Table 15.4   Quality Assurance Agency: tasks as at 1999

	Standards	Quality
Specification	Qualification and credit frameworks	Codes of practice Progress files
	Benchmark standards for subjects	
	Programme specifications	
Assurance	Academic Review Institutional Review	

The underlying rationale behind the QAA's work is to create a new framework for the specification and assurance of quality and standards in higher education that is appropriate for a mass, modern higher education system. Before this system is fully in place, current systems of external review will continue, gradually migrating to new forms. The current systems that academics are likely to encounter include **Subject Review** and Continuation **Audit**, both undertaken by the QAA.

Institutional arrangements

Higher education institutions have formal responsibilities for academic standards and, specifically, for the standards of their awards if they have been granted degree-awarding powers through charter or statute. The institutions, through their representative bodies, contract with the QAA for the external review of their academic standards and their awards.

Institutions can be divided, broadly, into those that have degree-awarding powers (for research and/or taught degrees) and those that do not. Those that have such powers will have committees that regulate the degree-awarding process (ultimate responsibility lies with senates and academic boards), while others will operate through the committees and processes of a validating university. All institutions, however, are likely to have formally constituted committees that define, monitor and review policy in relation to quality and standards and institutional officers who support policy development and implementation in these areas. Institutions are also likely to have organization-wide arrangements and procedures relating to **external examining**.

The Funding Councils expect each institution to have a strategy for teaching and learning and the QAA expects a parallel strategy for assuring quality and standards. Institutions will differ in how these strategies are produced (perhaps by a pro vice-chancellor and central committees, perhaps by each faculty, then coordinated centrally). Ultimately, these central policies and strategies should provide a framework for quality and standards in teaching and learning, acting as a guide for what is done at all levels of the institution. Subsequently, institutional reviews, whether conducted by the QAA or by internal agents, will check the application of policy and the operation of committees against the strategic framework established by the institution.

Interrogating Practice

Check that you know which committees have responsibility for monitoring quality and standards in your institution and find out what the relevant institutional strategies are.

During the 1990s, many institutions were 'quality audited' (see Table 15.3). The audit process conducted by the HEQC asked a series of questions about institutional management of quality and standards. Although the audit process is changing (towards 'Institutional Review') many of the questions remain relevant and answering them will help individuals to understand what accountability for quality and standards means in practical terms. The questions (see list which follows) also offer useful prompts for the development of policy and strategy and for monitoring implementation. In order to undertake the necessary monitoring, institutional managers will need evidence from other levels (faculty or course board minutes, for example) that policies are being implemented and strategies are succeeding.

Quality audit questions

- What are you trying to do?
- Why are you doing it?
- How are you doing it?
- Why are you doing it that way?
- Why do you think that is the best way?
- How do you know it works?
- How might it be done better?

In addition to these basic questions, the QAA is developing codes of practice to assist institutions in their task of assuring quality and standards, some based on earlier guidelines which remain useful sources of information. HEQC's Guidelines (1996), for example, cover the following areas of institutional responsibility:

- a framework for quality;
- entry to higher education;
- programme design, approval and review;
- teaching and learning;
- student development and support;
- student communication and representation;
- student assessment;
- external examiners;
- staffing;
- research degree students;
- collaborative provision.

An institution is usually a large and complex organization. Attaining and maintaining high quality and high standards across all its academic (and non-academic) activities therefore requires effective leadership and careful planning, management and review. It also requires strong values that underpin a culture of collective responsibility and commitment. In several countries, in Europe and elsewhere, institutional heads have acknowledged that a 'mature, self-critical academic community' – the key to attaining high quality and high standards – can be recognized in quite simple terms as a community that is:

- committed to learning and development;
- capable of self-evaluation against accessible and verifiable standards;
- actively seeking input to and feedback about its activities from key stakeholders;
- regularly using external comparators;
- striving for consistency and equity in its processes and systems;
- a place where quality is everyone's business.

Faculty/school or department level

At the 'middle' of the institution there exists an important level that acts as mediator between institutional strategies and policies and local interpretation and implementation of the strategic framework. Different institutions have different structures and arrangements, but the principle operates in most cases. One of the most comprehensive frameworks for quality management at this level (in this case, the department) has been published by the Engineering Professors' Council (EPC, 1996). Some of the main elements of the framework are listed in Case Study 1 as a possible checklist for academics and administrators and a guide to the link between responsibilities at different levels.

Case Study 1: Possible Framework for Managing Quality at Department Level

1. Departmental management
- Policy and objectives: stating the values, policy and objectives of the department for maintaining and improving the quality of education and research training in the department.
- Organizing for quality: clear definitions of the responsibility, authority and interrelation of all staff dealing with quality matters.
- Quality assurance system and documentation: including a manual of quality procedures.
- Quality improvement: for example, regular review processes and rapid response mechanisms to resolve shortcomings as they arise.

- Integration and externality: the department has to be linked vertically to senior management and to professional peer networks outside the discipline, and horizontally to other support services in the institution.
- Academic standards: statements that address how academic standards are constructed and applied in the department, eg using clear definitions of **level of award**, having clearly identified aims and **learning outcomes**, communicating expectations and responsibilities to students and staff.

2. *Quality management of the educational process*

- Design of programmes of study.
- Admissions and entry standards.
- Delivery and management of programmes of study: management structures such as course teams and personal tutors; preparation of syllabuses.
- Student guidance and support: statements of student entitlement, induction procedures for new students.
- Service support for programmes of study: service teaching, central administration, library and computing facilities.
- Staff-student communication.
- Problem reporting and corrective action.
- Assessment and academic standards: eg, how the **validity** and **reliability** of assessment arrangements are achieved and marking maintained.
- Research supervision: including admissions criteria and processes, selection of supervisors, induction and research training.
- Review of quality and standards: programme elements and whole programmes.
- Collaborative arrangements: eg, validation and approval of programmes, link tutors.

3. *Staffing*

- Recruitment, induction and probation.
- Staff appraisal and development.

4. *Control of the quality management framework*

- Document control: marking each document and revision with names of authors and dates, maintenance of a master list.
- Records and evidence: systems for the identification, collection, indexing, filing, storage and maintenance of the records.
- Review of the framework: a check or audit to determine whether the actual quality management activities comply with requirements and expectations.

(adapted from EPC, 1996: 3–11)

At departmental level, you may encounter two external review processes. One is undertaken by professional and statutory bodies (PSBs) if such bodies accredit the course you run. The purpose of such reviews is to ensure that educational provision is of a standard and quality appropriate for the training of practitioners in the relevant profession. The other form of external review, subject review, is undertaken by QAA on behalf of the funding councils. While the latter is changing, some of the key elements may still be worth noting:

- the writing and submission of a self-assessment document by the subject provider;
- a visit to the department by external assessors (mainly academic staff from other institutions);
- judgements being made by the assessors on the quality of education in the subject by means of evidence drawn from observation of teaching and learning, scrutiny of students' work and discussions with staff and students;
- the publication of a report including graded judgements on the quality of education delivered by the subject provider.

Course and pathway leaders/teams

While the intermediate level (faculty, school or department) has responsibility for establishing and maintaining the quality management framework, much of the operational activity is undertaken by course or pathway teams. Wisker (1996) has outlined some of the responsibilities at this level. These include, academic leadership, management of other staff, pastoral care of students, quality assurance and advocacy in relation to the course or pathway.

The course team lies at the heart of the teaching and learning process. This group of people, both academic and administrative, is directly and continuously involved in delivering 'high quality, high standards'. It is their ideas, their commitment, their professionalism and attention to detail that ensures that students have the best educational experience and that the standards of the awards offered by the institution are maintained and improved. It is important, therefore, that a culture of quality is developed within the team. Some of the main ingredients of this culture include:

- a student or client-centred focus for teaching and learning;
- close working relationships and interdependence for the design and delivery of programmes and modules;
- effective leadership, management and administration and mutual respect for varied expertise and different kinds of competence;

- clearly articulated and well-understood educational purposes, levels and assessment/grading criteria for students' work;
- regular and effective channels of communication between team members (academic and administrative), between staff and students and between the team, other teams and other levels of the institution;
- continued professional development appropriate to the needs of individuals and the team/unit as a whole;
- systematic reflection (both formal and informal) on the work and output of the team – with fresh ideas being sought and incorporated from outside sources;
- adequate and appropriately deployed resources.

Developing a quality culture depends on the contribution of each team member and does not happen without considerable effort and commitment. It is important to recognize that some of the necessary ingredients involve procedural and administrative systems and the systematic collection of data (as outlined above) while others involve behaviours, attitudes, values, styles of working and patterns of relationships. For the team to achieve internally and externally recognized quality and standards, both sets of ingredients are needed.

Interrogating Practice

Reflect on your role and responsibilities in a formal or informal course team of which you are a member. How do you contribute to the creation of a 'culture of quality'?

Individual teachers, scholars and 'managers of learning'

We have now come, full circle, to where this chapter began – with the professional responsibilities of each academic. While there are layers of responsibility for quality and standards at all levels of the higher education system, individuals make the difference between an effective, vibrant, dynamic system and an ineffective, bureaucratic or static system. Individual commitment, care, consideration, competence and imagination affect what students experience within higher education and what they achieve (Barnett, 1992). Teaching can be delivered in numerous ways, but in all cases individual competence and imagination are called for. While teaching is increasingly shifting from an individually planned and executed activity to a group activity, quality and standards are still dependent on the contributions of each individual member of a team or group.

As a professional and scholarly activity, university teaching requires a high level of knowledge and competence. Individual teachers need to exhibit and help students to acquire the values of curiosity, integrity and critical appraisal, a commitment to lifelong learning, to personal and professional growth through **reflection** and self-evaluation (see Part 2), to accountability for their own professional activities and to undertake responsible and ethical practice. Competence in teaching requires knowledge and understanding of teaching and assessment methods and the principles that underlie effective learning. University teachers, as scholars, also need to contribute to the development of their discipline and (at least) to keep in touch with current research and scholarship, integrating this into their teaching.

Quality in teaching is dependent on both its fitness *for* purpose and its fitness *of* purpose. In terms of the former, learning activities and aims need to be matched with relevant disciplines and specialisms, with students' needs and interests and with particular contexts such as **work-based learning**, clinical teaching or **distance** education. In terms of the latter, teaching and learning need to be targeted at the level and standards agreed for the programme: undergraduate or postgraduate. Collectively, academic staff have the responsibility of ensuring that the design, management and teaching of their programmes facilitates effective learning by their students. The ultimate test of success, as Barnett (1992: 211) argues, lies in whether students have, through the teaching and learning processes, increased their capacity for critical and creative thought and action and their independence as autonomous learners, thinkers and actors.

Individual academics as well as course teams need to make clear to students, and to others, what kind of skills and attributes are being sought in higher education and those which contribute to the achievement of academic awards at different levels. To a large extent, this will involve individual teachers making explicit their tacit understandings of academic standards. The work sponsored by the QAA on benchmark standards at subject level and on national qualifications and **credit frameworks** is designed to provide guidance to individuals and institutions in this task. Already, however, in relation to the award of credit at different levels, a number of regional and national credit consortia have been active in producing **level** descriptors to guide curriculum design and student assessment.

Interrogating Practice

How do you structure progression into your programmes and modules/units?

Decisions about the relative weighting of particular skills and attributes at different levels of study, the range of their application as set out in formal and informal curricula and the form and style of their presentation in student assignments (in terms of, for example, accuracy, depth, insight, scope, sensitivity, rigour) are further ingredients in determining and articulating academic standards. Individual teachers will need to give attention to all of these elements. The Dearing Report (NCIHE, 1997b) proposed that **programme specifications** should be prepared as a means of setting out the particular requirements and weightings of skills in each programme; in modular degree schemes, mapping tools may help to identify where skills are to be acquired and assessed within particular modules and pathways.

Interrogating Practice

How do you ensure that students acquire the intellectual skills and attributes associated with 'a higher education'? Which skills, attributes and qualities are most important in your discipline/programme? How do you seek to test the acquisition of such skills and attributes? What criteria are you using to make judgements about attainment?

OVERVIEW AND CONCLUSION

This chapter has outlined the layered tapestry of quality and standards in higher education. Insofar as learning is an individual activity where students have chosen to follow a particular programme, each individual will have a set of expectations about what they wish to or may expect to achieve. Higher education is also an activity in which public and private funds are invested, and this leads to further sets of expectations and requirements. The structures and cultures of institutions and departments and the development of disciplines also produce sets of expectations about aims, methods and outcomes of teaching and learning. Identifying, articulating and achieving high quality and standards is thus a complex process, dependent on many layers of thought and action as well as systematic effort to integrate activities, judgements and decisions at vertical and horizontal levels of the higher education system. Achieving high quality and standards in a mass higher education system does not happen by chance. It happens through the exercise of professional and managerial knowledge and competence as well as a strong commitment to the aspirations and needs of all who benefit from higher education.

REFERENCES

Barnett, R (1992) *Improving Higher Education: Total quality care*, SRHE/Open University Press, Buckingham

Brennan, J, de Vries, P and Williams, R (1997) *Standards and Quality in Higher Education*, Higher Education Policy Series 37, Jessica Kingsley, London

Commission of the European Communities (1993) Quality Management and Quality Assurance in European Higher Education: Methods and Mechanisms, *Studies*, **1**

Drummond, H (1992) *The Quality Movement*, Kogan Page, London

Green, D (ed) (1994) *What is Quality in Higher Education?*, SRHE/Open University Press, Buckingham

Engineering Professors' Council (EPC) (1996) *Specification for a Quality Management Framework at Departmental Level*, Occasional Paper No 9, University College, London,

Harvey L, Burrows, A and Green, D (1992) *Criteria of Quality*, summary report, University of Central England, Quality in Higher Education

Higher Education Quality Council (1996) *Guidelines on Quality Assurance*, HEQC, London

Juran, J (ed) (1995) *A History of Managing for Quality*, ASQC Quality Press, Milwaukee, Wisconsin

Middlehurst, R (1996) Degree standards and quality assurance: a discussion, in *Changing Conceptions of Academic Standards*, eds J Brennan *et al*, pp 71–96, Quality Support Centre, Open University, London

NCIHE (1997a) The development of a framework of qualifications: relationships with continental Europe, report 11, National Committee of Inquiry into Higher Education/97/860

NCIHE (1997b) (Dearing Report) *Higher Education in the Learning Society*, National Committee of Inquiry into Higher Education, HMSO, London

Wisker, G (1996) *Leading Academic Programmes and Courses*, Staff and Educational Development Association, SEDA Paper 97, Birmingham

RECOMMENDED READING

Brennan, J, de Vries, P and Williams, R (1997) See above. Gives a rounded picture if you are seeking an overview of how different countries approach the regulation of quality and standards in higher education.

In order to keep up to date with changes at national level, read the regular bulletins issued by the QAA. You should also keep up to date with the regulations issued by your own institution and be aware of the debates and activities on quality and standards in your subject/academic field.

Part 2
Development of the Academic for Teaching and Learning

16 Reflective Practice

Margot Brown, Heather Fry and
Stephanie Marshall

INTRODUCTION

We are frequently exhorted to encourage our students to be **reflective** and to adopt reflective practices. These concepts are as relevant to ourselves in relation to our progress as teachers as to our students. This chapter focuses on how (new) academics can develop reflective practice in respect of their teaching.

REFLECTION

Reflection is a valuable but much abused concept. It has a central part to play in transforming and integrating new experiences and understanding with previous/existing knowledge (see Chapters 3 and 11). It has gained most currency as a key part of learning from experience (Kolb, 1984). However, it is often viewed as a very passive and overly 'naval-gazing' activity. In reality, it is something which works best with engagement and proactivity on the part of the learner. As teachers, we seek to build situations for our students in which they will be forced to reflect. We do this through strategies such as asking them questions, encouraging self-assessment (Boud, 1995), encouraging them to write diaries (Boud, Keogh and Walker, 1985), using **critical incident analysis**, and asking them to analyse and critique ideas and practice in less structured ways. By so doing we are seeking to bring about learning by changing previous knowledge, and to inculcate habits which will build reflection into learning, thus ensuring that learning will not end the minute the student graduates from university. Reflection can be used in the context of cognitive, psychomotor, affective and interpersonal domains. It can be used to help learners construct new schemata in relation to theories and concepts and in relation to practice (see Chapters 3 and 11). As teachers we should be seeking to become reflective practitioners.

NOVICE TO EXPERT

There have been many studies in the professions tracing the development of practitioners from **novice** to **expert** (for an overview, see Eraut, 1994). Professions in which such work has taken place include the police, nursing, and school teaching. One of the original classifications of the stages of progression is that of the Dreyfus brothers (1986). Level 1, the novice stage, is characterized by adherence to taught rules and little discretionary judgement; level 2, the advanced beginner, takes more account of the global characteristics of situations but tends to treat all aspects and attributes as having equal importance. At level 3 the practitioner is considered competent and is beginning to see actions as part of longer-term goals, and is able to undertake conscious and deliberate planning and perform standardized or routine procedures. At level 4, that of proficiency, situations are seen more holistically, important aspects are more readily recognized, decision making is less laboured and guiding axioms can be interpreted differently according to situation. The expert, the level 5 practitioner, no longer relies on rules and guidelines and has an intuitive grasp of situations based on deep understanding, knows what is possible, and only uses analytic approaches in novel situations or when new problems occur. Thus the expert stage is characterized by implicit and unconscious practice. For the experienced teacher in higher education, much practice will be at the expert level. For the new lecturer (and every occasion on which a lecturer tries out a new technique) practice will not have reached this implicit and almost instinctive state. Reflection is something which helps us to continuously examine practice and move it on to higher levels; it facilitates maintenance and improvement of practice.

BECOMING A REFLECTIVE PRACTITIONER

The notion of 'becoming a reflective practitioner' is one referred to regularly in induction programmes for new academic staff. However, the various components of such practice are rarely unpacked, either in general terms or in relation to specific activities.

When we are expert practitioners, if we wish our practice to continuously move on, we will have become 'unconscious reflectors', the state all teachers in higher education are in with respect to their discipline; specific knowledge where they constantly meet, challenge, innovate, create and incorporate new knowledge and understanding.

How can teachers become more self-aware of how they teach, the implications this has for learning, how this links to appropriate assessment and how one can be discriminating in the choice of method (within time and resource constraints) which will be most appropriate in any given situation? The rest of this chapter attempts to indicate some approaches which may help the practitioner to progress along this road.

When looking at the range of activities that a teacher in higher education might be involved in, it is appropriate to consider reflective practice as an activity which will take place continuously, but noticeably, first, on or during an individual teaching and learning activity; second, on completion of a course module; and third, on completion of a programme of study. To assist the 'novice' to become an 'expert', reflective practice must be linked to action (Kolb, 1984; Freire, 1985). Such a concept is explored below.

An individual teaching and learning activity

Using the classification of novice to expert referred to earlier, the individual teaching and learning activity would appear to be the logical starting point for developing the skills of reflective practice for practitioners new to teaching or engaged in a new area of teaching. For example, further to the delivery of a lecture, consideration of the success or otherwise of the activity could lead the teacher to focus on one or two areas about which they have concern: eg pacing of delivery and gauging student engagement. Reaching a conclusion – in this case, 'the pacing was too fast' – further to such 'contemplation' (Jarvis, Holford and Griffin, 1998), is what distinguishes reflective practice from the process of thinking. Repeated practice, and focusing on different aspects of delivery of the lecture, will assist the practitioner to move along the continuum beyond level 1 – or novice, towards level 5 – or expert. Furthermore, such an approach will assist the practitioner in moving from reflection-on-practice at one end of the continuum to reflection-in-practice at the other end (Schon, 1987).

Completion of a course module

There are a range of opportunities for reflective practice at the completion of a course module, which include weighing up feedback from individual learning activities. Continued reflective practice should assist the process of offering a balanced and meaningful analysis of student feedback questionnaires, module assessment, feedback via staff-student committees or board of study student representation. For example, are student feedback questionnaires to be considered solely on their numerical analysis – contrary to all the best advice (see Chapter 13), or are other factors, such as diverse learning needs and styles, to be taken into account? Is module assessment reflected on purely in terms of degree classification, or is a more diagnostic approach adopted whereby the teacher is asked to reflect on points at which students may have been better assisted in their learning? Brown and McCartney (1999) assert that reflection aids the transformation of experience into knowledge, and, in the examples just provided, it would follow that not only will reflective practice benefit the individual practitioner, but all involved in the department's teaching and learning activities, assisting teachers to move along the novice-expert continuum.

Completion of programme of study

Further to teaching, learning and assessment across all aspects of a study programme, the practitioner will have reflected on a range of different activities. Through an iterative process, the skills of reflecting 'on', and reflecting 'for' action, should lead to the ability to reflect 'in' action. This ability to reflect while in action, adapting and changing one's behaviour further to this reflection, is what distinguishes the expert from the novice. It is what Schon (1983) suggests is the mark of a professional, in that professionals are capable of thinking on their feet, responding to unique situations, and producing new skills.

Recording and utilizing reflective practice

As with students' recording of reflection, the most commonly accepted means of recording reflective practice is to retain a 'learning log' or diary. Clearly from the above it follows that mere recording is not sufficient, for without reflection informing future behaviour or action, in this context, it is meaningless. Thus on conclusion of a teaching and learning activity, one might make notes such as 'next time I will…'. This diary will serve as a useful *aide-mémoire* in planning teaching activities, allowing the teacher the benefit of recorded hindsight and points of detail to which they should pay attention to improve subsequent teaching activities.

CONCEPTIONS OF TEACHING

Ramsden (1992) draws together the work of several researchers (notably Margaret Balla, Gloria Dall'Alba, Elaine Martin and John Biggs) to develop a typology of 'Higher education teachers' theories of teaching' (1992: 111–19). Other similar typologies exist (see Chapter 22). Three broad theories were identified (it is not suggested that all aspects of one practitioner's teaching will only fall within one of the theories; they are 'ideal' types). Theory one centres on the notion of teaching as telling or transmission, theory two typifies teaching as organizing student activity, while theory three centres on teaching being an activity which makes learning possible.

Interrogating Practice

List up to five statements which describe what you consider teaching in your discipline to be about. For each statement decide into which of the three conceptions of teaching it fits. Does your overall conception of teaching (as represented by your statements) fall mainly into one of the three groups?

Teaching and learning styles

As suggested, the more experienced reflective practitioners will be able to adapt their approach to assist the bringing about of successful outcomes in their students. Unpacking of the factors contributing to successful learning requires an awareness of one's own conception of, and style of, teaching.

There have been several attempts to classify particular styles or types of teaching by linking a number of teaching practices or behaviours into sets (eg Butler, 1987; Entwistle, 1988.) This work is useful to practitioners who may wish to identify their favoured approaches; however, it is not suggested that teachers only ever exhibit behaviour from one set or style of teaching.

Table 16.1 Four postulated styles of teaching and their suggested behaviours (adapted from Entwistle, 1988)

Style 1: Do I...	Style 2: Do I...
challenge students to move beyond existing knowledge;	emphasize practical learning;
value students' originality;	provide structured tasks with detailed directions;
foster creativity by introducing new resources and activities;	encourage concise, ordered formats and outcomes;
provide a 'stimulus rich' environment;	foster creativity through phototypes and replicas;
work with big ideas with no standard structure or format;	cover content in detail;
set open ended tasks?	set clear tasks;
	finish on time?

Style 3: Do I...	**Style 4: Do I...**
encourage students' personal expression and imagination;	emphasize ideas, concepts, theories;
give praise generously;	analyse and evaluate ideas;
enjoy change and variety;	want students to have a bank of knowledge;
promote cooperative tasks;	have consistent and reliable rules and procedures;
create an unstructured, friendly environment;	dislike distraction;
develop content through a variety of media including artistic, aesthetic or literary?	rely on logical reasoning; need time to think through ideas and organize programmes?

The more aware teachers are of the characteristics of different styles, the more effective they will be in supporting effective learning for students. We all have to undertake a range of tasks, for example, the request to return marked scripts by a particular time on a particular day (style 2); keeping a steady line of positive communication between personal supervisor, module tutors, examination boards, pastoral or counselling services, students (style 3); ensuring students are prepared for assignments and examinations (style 4); developing a variety of teaching strategies to meet the different learning needs in student groups (style 1). The more flexible teachers are in respect of tasks which require different approaches, the more effective they will be. This same flexibility of approach is required of students.

Interrogating Practice

What different strategies for teaching have you used over the past month (eg, role play, small group work, teaching a skill through demonstration, lecture)? Which did you feel most comfortable with? Do the method(s) you felt most comfortable with map onto your conceptions of teaching and/or any one of the four teaching styles?

As teachers, one way we can reflect on practice is to consider the implications and effects of our actions on different learners. A way of doing this is in relation to learning styles. Butler (1995) has shown that failure of a student to learn can be attributed not only to matters such as motivation and prior learning, but also to a mismatch between the lecturer's teaching style and the students' learning style.

Learning styles

An understanding of learning styles and their characteristics is part of a teacher's 'tool box' of analytical and reflective skills. Observing and analysing learning characteristics has led to definitions of learning style (see also Chapter 3), which includes the axiom that the way in which an individual typically approaches a learning situation derives from a mix between their cognitive process and personality. It can be argued that there are basic differences in personality which affect styles or approaches to learning and the way thinking is organized (Briggs Myers, 1987).

Although learning style theorists have developed different terminology to describe learning characteristics, there is broad agreement that in any group of learners there will be at least four bands of learning styles represented, though not in equal proportion. The characteristics of these styles have been identified to include those listed in Table 16.2.

Table 16.2   Four postulated styles of learning and their characteristics
(adapted from Butler, 1995)

Style A	Style B
works well alone;	organizes material well;
plans work effectively;	enjoys problem solving;
good at meeting deadlines;	works things out well on paper;
reads instructions carefully;	precise and thorough;
is wary of open ended tasks;	sees links between ideas;
takes good notes;	may want too much information before beginning work;
is impatient of other ways of working;	may be overcautious;
can be preoccupied by detail – misses the 'big picture';	not necessarily a creative thinker;
not always able to work well with others.	learns well through formal lectures.

Style C	Style D
can come up with creative solutions;	works well with others;
can see the whole picture – but may ignore detail;	willing to try new ideas;
	is intuitive – can't always explain 'why';
will often pinpoint new questions;	enjoys variety and change;
can be uncritical of ideas;	prefers skim reading;
finds categorizing difficult;	does not tend to plan in advance;
may work in bursts of energy;	may leave things until the last minute;
easily distracted;	does not always attend to detail;
responds to varied stimuli – video, music, etc, which generate responses.	may have problems organizing time;
	divergent thinker.

No learning (or teaching) style is judged better or worse than another. Each style is valid for that learner. Many learners will share characteristics from more than one group but will feel most comfortable when taught in ways that correspond to their 'dominant' style. Learners who are more strongly 'C' in their learning style, for example, will respond well in situations where a variety of teaching strategies are the norm but will be less responsive to an undiluted diet of didactic approaches. However, while each style may be valid for the individual learner, inevitably that learner will encounter situations, individuals or tasks which do not match their preferred learning style. Some of these tasks will prove more challenging and extra support from the tutor will be required. For example, if a task requires reading for attention to detail, then those who more naturally skim read may need guidance to unlock the text – for example, structured questions based on small sections.

Avoiding pitfalls

Learning style deals with only a limited, though important, number of variables which affect the learning process. Students bring with them a wide variety of other characteristics which influence their learning experiences. These include existing content knowledge, abilities and skills; personal background including socio-economic status, gender, ethnicity and language; and motivation to learn (see Chapters 6 and 14). It would not be helpful to use an understanding of learning style to identify or 'label' students, to ignore the other variables – temporary or permanent – which influence learning, or to use them as a self-fulfilling prophecy.

Learning styles can help teachers understand more comprehensively problems which students may encounter, and identify appropriate teaching strategies to provide support. Teachers can plan to address different learning styles in two main ways. One is to structure contact time with students to encompass a variety of styles. This approach is outlined in Case Study 1, taken from a BEd programme for primary school teaching. Another way is to ensure that all styles are addressed over a course, as outlined in the second case study.

Case Study 1: College of Ripon & York

A Module Contributing to a Four-year BEd, Leading to Qualified Teacher Status

This case study considers the planning of a year two module consisting of three three-hour sessions on primary geography. The group size varies between 48 and 60. The final session of three hours explored 'the reaching of distant places' and included the numerous teaching strategies (indicated in brackets).

Teaching/learning activity undertaken	Learning style addressed
● Why teach young children about distant places? Uses a structured cue sheet. (Paired discussion and feedback by pairs forming sixes and general points recorded.)	C, D
● What links do young children have in their daily lives which link them to the wider world? (whole group – question/answer)	C, A
● Exploring definitions of 'Third World' to provide context for teaching (mini lecture)	B, A

- Which distant locality should be chosen as   C, D
  focus of study?
  (ranking activity using different
  criteria to prioritize selection, groups of 4–6.)

- Children's perceptions of distant places   B, A
  (resume of recent research, mini-lecture)

- Using story to understand settlement   C, A, D
  patterns
  (whole group and breaking into
   small groups)

- Analysis of selected teaching resources   B, A, D, C
  (identifying key knowledge already held by
  learners; presenting new information
  visually or orally; working in groups with
  individual tasks delegated within the group
  to be brought together for presentation)

All students also completed a 2000-word assignment selected from one of the four curriculum areas making up the module. The assignment sought evidence of reading from the required list and incorporated planning a unit of work for the classroom.

Case Study 2: Undergraduate Module: Education for a Culturally Diverse Society, University of York

This module, offered to first and second-year undergraduates in the Department of Educational Studies, comprised nine two-hour sessions. The group size ranged from 10–16.

Due to the shorter length of time for each session, breaking up the two hours into activities which respond to four learning styles is less effective. Additionally, the focus of the course is less practice-based as the students are not planning to be practising teachers. This does not mean that the spread of learning styles will be any different in the group nor the need to address them any less.

Over the nine weeks, learning styles were addressed in different ways.

Teaching/learning activity undertaken	Learning style addressed
Seminar preparation – involved working individually, using library resources and set reading	A, B
Lecture	A, B
Requiring students to be out of their seats and moving around the room	D, C
Identifying analysis of key theories in selected texts	B, A
Using personal testimony through video, poetry, literature, autobiography	C, D, A
Preparation of presentation on topic of choice related to course	A, B, C, D
Analysing incidents as reported (as part of problem-solving task) using cue sheets and role cards to show perspectives	D, C, B
Reviewing National Curriculum documentation in light of theories of cultural pluralism	B, A
Working in small group setting on task set with focus on cooperation and communicating results to whole group	A, B, C
Using photographs, text and video, develop questions to highlight analysis	C, D, A

Students also write an extended essay, 5000 words, on a topic of their choice which requires analysis, evidence of wide reading and linking of ideas and theories.

To promote effective teaching and learning requires a range of teaching strategies, some of which may be uncomfortable to individual teachers. However, reflecting on practice and revisiting the concept of teaching and learning styles can assist the practitioner in devising a range of teaching strategies which, with practice, will become part of the repertoire in the varied delivery of a course module.

> ### Interrogating Practice
>
> Examine a teaching occasion which did not go as well as expected. List unexpected factors and try to account for them. How could you change your practice? (You may wish to seek help from a teacher more experienced with these methods or students to help you identify what worked less well than expected and why.)

OVERVIEW

This chapter has considered factors which could assist teachers to become effective and reflective practitioners. An effective practitioner is likely to be one who reflects on their teaching, updates their skills and thinks of teaching from the perspective of its impact on learners rather than from the perspective of 'covering content'. Ramsden identified six key principles of effective teaching in higher education (1992: 96–102). Subsequent formulations have not substantively changed the items he identified:

- making the teaching session interesting and giving clear explanations;
- concern and respect for students and student learning;
- appropriate assessment and feedback;
- clear goals and intellectual challenge;
- independence, control and active engagement of learner;
- learning from students.

All these are clearly important considerations to the reflective practitioner, but added to this should be included the need for confronting one's own conceptions of teaching. Through a focus on teaching and learning styles, it is hoped that practitioners will have gained some additional tools which will assist in the deconstruction of their own conceptions of teaching, leading to reflection on the most appropriate and effective teaching and learning strategies for both teacher and student.

REFERENCES

Boud, D (1995) *Enhancing Learning through Self Assessment*, Kogan Page, London

Boud, D, Keogh, R and Walker, D (eds) (1985) *Reflection: Turning experience into learning*, Kogan Page, London

Briggs Myers, I (1987) Introduction to Type: *A description of the theory and application of the Myers-Briggs Type Indicator*, Consulting Psychologists Press, Palo Alto

Brown, R, and McCartney, S (1999) in *Developing the Capable Practitioner*, eds D O'Reilly, L Cunningham and S Lester, Kogan Page, London

Butler, K (1987) *Learning and Teaching Style in Theory and Practice*, The Learner's Dimension, Columbia, CT

Dreyfus, H and Dreyfus, S (1986) *Mind over Machine: The power of human intuition and expertise in the era of the computer*, Basil Blackwell, Oxford

Entwistle, N (1988) *Styles of Learning and Teaching*, David Fulton Publishers, London

Eraut, M (1994) *Developing Professional Knowledge and Competence*, Falmer, London

Freire, P (1985) *The Politics of Education*, Macmillan, London

Jarvis, P, Holford, J, and Griffin, C (1998) *The Theory and Practice of Learning*, Kogan Page, London

Kolb, D (1984) *Experiential Learning*, Prentice-Hall, Englewood Cliffs, New Jersey

Ramsden (1992) *Learning to Teach in Higher Education*, Routledge, London

Schon, D (1983) *The Reflective Practitioner*, Jossey-Bass Publishers, San Francisco

Schon, D (1987) *Educating the Reflective Practitioner*, Jossey-Bass Publishers, San Francisco

FURTHER READING

Brookfield, S (1995) *Becoming a Critically Reflective Teacher*, Jossey-Bass Publishers, San Francisco. Written specifically for teachers in higher education. Guides readers through many processes for becoming critically reflective about teaching.

Eraut, M (1994) See above. Most useful in exploring the nature of professional knowledge and theories of professional expertise.

O'Reilly, D, Cunningham, L, and Lester, S (1999) *Developing the Capable Practitioner*, Kogan Page, London. The focus of this book is on developing the capable practitioner, with one of its five sections devoted to 'The reflective practitioner'.

Schon, D (1987) See above. A must for any professional taking reflective practice seriously. Focuses particularly on reflection-in-action.

17 Observation of Teaching

Hazel Fullerton

INTRODUCTION

Observation of teaching, as a means of enhancing the quality of teaching and learning, is now commonplace in the British higher education sector. However, until the early 1990s there was little observation of teaching taking place, except as part of the training of teachers for the school sector. The practice has since increased steadily as many universities and colleges have come to recognize the value of observation schemes. For others, the impetus to adopt direct observation has been driven by the development of the Teaching Quality Assessment methodology (now the **QAA Subject Review**). Many staff now see direct observation as an integral part of their own professional development as teachers and see value from the process, both in engaging as the observer and the one being observed. This gradual acceptance of direct observation has helped to break down some of the 'no-go' areas associated with colleagues observing each other's teaching, and frequently these are being replaced by an open door policy at departmental level. Many have been supported by the first publication (Brown, Jones and Rawnsley, 1993) to bring together a collection of papers outlining a range of approaches and models of observing teaching.

Teaching observation is an essential part of development programmes for new lecturers and for established staff, and it has become increasingly common among departmental peers. It aims to develop and enhance effective practice and provide a springboard for further development through shared reflection.

RATIONALE

It is axiomatic that every lecturer strives to be competent in all facets of their duties, but how to achieve this in all aspects of teaching is not always obvious. Many will have had the related experience of delivering research papers and there may be considerable temptation to revert to that style. However, that approach may mean that the lecture is almost certainly pitched too fast, too high and too impersonally. Previous experience also comes into play, with new lecturers frequently relying upon a style in which they were taught. Most can remember inspirational lecturers who made learning exciting and meaningful and whom they would like to emulate. In reality, it is unlikely that many watched in a sufficiently analytical way to be able to identify the elements that constituted the real magic.

Interrogating Practice

Take 10 minutes to note down the key aspects of teaching by a good teacher or lecturer that you would wish to emulate.

BENEFITS

The observation process benefits both the observer and the observed. It is also a rare opportunity for an observer to see and analyse what students are actually doing. Participants on courses for new lecturers consistently rate feedback from teaching observations as the most valuable aspect of their learning and development of practice. For them it is an opportunity to validate what is working well, to exchange practical ideas, problem solve and to explore and align practice with a developing understanding of theory, as well as to learn from the practice of others.

Observation offers:

- insight into what helps learners to learn and what happens in effective teaching sessions;
- feedback on individual teaching skills and style;
- discussion, collaboration and exchange of ideas;
- mutual support between colleagues;
- earmarked 'quality time' to talk about learning and teaching;
- feedback on piloting a new idea, method or solution to a problem;

- triangulation with other evaluative procedures, eg student perception questionnaires, module and programme evaluations;
- focused reflection on teaching sessions;
- the opportunity to see exemplary practitioners at work.

Interrogating Practice

Who is regarded as a good teacher in your department? Ask if you can come and observe. (If you explain why, he or she will be flattered.)

WHEN AND WITH WHOM

The right time to start having one's teaching observed is now. At any stage of a career there are things to be learnt, but this is especially true for the new lecturer who needs feedback, reassurance, hints and help. No one expects a new lecturer at the start of a career to be proficient immediately. New lecturers may find that as part of their probation, there is a requirement for them to have a number of teaching sessions observed and that systems are set up for observation by a **mentor**, staff/educational developer or course tutor from a training programme. It is also beneficial to set up a reciprocal arrangement for mutual observation with another new lecturer to share experience of teaching and learning in a less formal way. Observers should be selected to include those who can discuss and offer expertise in teaching the discipline, as well as comment on the communication with and engagement of the learners.

Interrogating Practice

You may wish to check the requirements for direct observation of teaching in your own department and, if you are on probation, as part of any initial training programme run by your college or university.

WHAT TO OBSERVE

What to observe is as open and varied as is the role of lecturers. It may include lectures, tutorials, seminars, laboratory classes, fieldwork, creative workshops and teaching with patients. Commonly it is lectures that are observed, as they are likely to conform to a fairly standard format and much store is set on making them effective, especially as the size of lecture groups has increased. They offer a relatively short, contained, learning experience with specific **objectives**, requiring a clear structure as well as clear communication and explanation.

ASPECTS FOR OBSERVATION

The features for an observation will vary according to the type of session and for the discipline concerned. For a typical lecture session (see Chapter 7), observers will note:

- the appropriateness and achievement of objectives;
- communication of objectives to learners and links to prior knowledge;
- structure of the session, eg an introduction, organization into sections and a summary;
- delivery – including pace, audibility, visibility;
- communication with students – including interaction, questioning and activities;
- the engagement of students in the learning process.

For most types of small group teaching activities, such as tutorials and seminars (see Chapter 8) an observer might note:

- the relationship of the session to the articulated objectives;
- interaction of students with the tutor and each other;
- facilitation skills of the tutor, including managing the group activity, questioning, listening and responding;
- involvement of all members of the group;
- encouragement of students;
- use of the teaching space;
- the quality of formative feedback to students;
- provision for summing up and consolidating what has been learned;
- making students aware of their developing skills.

> ### Interrogating Practice
>
> When you next engage in an observation of a teaching activity in your discipline, either as the observed or the observer, what features of teaching that do not appear in the above lists would you want to discuss?

PROCESS

Observation can be considered as a four-stage process consisting of an initial discussion, the observation itself, a follow-up discussion meeting, production of a written record that may include a reflective response from the observed. This is the case at the University of Plymouth. Practice will vary across the sector and institutional guidelines may place different emphasis on the stages, often combining the final two. A three-stage scheme operates at the University of Bradford (Martin and Double, 1998).

Stage 1: initial discussion
The discussion in advance of the session, which can be in person, by phone or even e-mail, can provide the observer with:

- an understanding of the context of the session;
- information on the background of the students;
- the purpose and objectives of the session and how it relates to the rest of the student learning experience;
- any aspects on which the observed wants specific feedback;
- any relevant documents for the session, such as handout or case study material.

New lecturers often say they want feedback on 'anything and everything'. With experience they become more specific.

Stage 2: observation
When undertaking an observation, the observer will normally arrive early and place themselves unobtrusively in the room, not becoming involved in the session. Unless it is a very large group, the observer's presence should be explained to the group. The observer will probably make notes, either chronologically or related to specific agreed criteria, or using departmental or institutional pro forma (checklist) for the purpose (some examples are given in Brown, Jones and Rawnsley, 1993).

Many institutions have developed their own pro formas for observation based upon the framework used in the **QAA Subject Review** (Quality Assurance Agency for Higher Education, 1997). An observational pro forma from the University of Plymouth is given in the appendix to this chapter.

It is helpful if the observer records some actual phrases or actions which can demonstrate what affected the learning or interaction in the session. The observer will watch both what the students do as well as what the lecturer does. It is sometimes claimed that the presence of the observer influences the behaviour of the group. In the author's own institution, students have never reacted by playing up as is sometimes feared. On the contrary, groups may behave too well and not respond in as lively and interactive a way as might normally be expected.

Stage 3: follow-up discussion

The observer may require up to one hour, ideally immediately after the session (if not, within 24 hours), for the follow-up discussion. This is probably the most valuable part of the process for both the observed and the observer. Almost regardless of their experience, the sharing of beliefs, values, approaches, interpretations, ideas, and experiences creates a rich and creative dialogue. However, if not handled with sensitivity, it can be counter-productive, as will be discussed later.

Stage 4: record of the observation

A written record of the observation is usually given to the observed as a summary of the main points arising from the session, and might also include action points from the feedback discussion. The departmental or institutional pro forma may commonly form the basis of this record. Observers should produce this record of the observation as soon as possible while their recall is still clear. The report writer should make specific notes of strengths so that the lecturer will continue to embody them, but also indicate what development needs would be worth focusing on next. At the University of Plymouth, the observed is then usually expected to make a written response to the observer's record, to comment on what they will do as a result and note any implications for their own continuing professional development. An alternative practice is to have the observed write their own summary record and development plan.

Confidentiality of records of observation can be a contentious issue and, in general, the record should be kept confidential to the observed and the observer. The observed may wish to include the record in his or her teaching portfolio (see Chapter 18). In some institutions, heads of departments may want to see records of their staffs' teaching observations, or at least an assurance that it has taken place. Also such records may become part of the agenda for **appraisal** discussions.

> ### Interrogating Practice
>
> A great deal can be learnt from watching a selection of teaching sessions on video. Make observational notes for yourself using an approved pro forma or checklist from your department or institution. If you can, borrow the Universities' and Colleges' Staff Development Agency (UCoSDA) pack 'Making the Grade' (from your staff or educational development unit) which also contains observational notes by observers using the Teaching Quality Assessment (now QAA Subject Review) pro forma.

FEEDBACK

It is good practice to give the feedback as soon as possible after the observation. The observed is usually asked to comment on the session, to identify what went well and why, and reflect upon what went less well and why. It is as important that the observer also ensures that the things that worked effectively are raised.

There is always an element of nervousness about the giving and receiving of feedback. No matter how experienced one is, the feelings associated with feedback cannot be ignored. They become less of a concern when the purpose is clearly recognized as contributing to the development of both participants. There should be a shared intent and an awareness that it may also be a creative process leading to personal development by both sides, thereby enhancing the quality of teaching and learning. Embarrassment when working with colleagues can be reduced by agreeing ground-rules for giving feedback and by the use of standard pro formas for observational schedules.

Guidelines for giving feedback

Giving feedback to colleagues is a skill needed throughout an academic's professional life:

- Having got the observed to reflect first, the observer should start with the positive points, and there are always positive elements. End on a positive note too.
- Focus on the behaviour that can be changed rather than the person.
- Tailor the amount of feedback to what the observed can make use of at that time.

- Less effective aspects can be dealt with by factual objective comments, eg 'When you turned to write on the board, I couldn't hear you at the back'. Alternatively, aspects could be posed as problems to solve, eg 'There is a problem when you realize that time is running out and there are still things you wanted to cover. Have you any thoughts about how to deal with that?'
- Be constructive by making positive suggestions for improvement: there is no point giving feedback on something the observed can do nothing about, eg to say, ' If you were to spend less time behind the lectern, it would be easier for the students to relate to you', is preferable to,'You're too short and no one can see you'.
- Avoid making value judgements, eg reporting that, 'After the first 20 minutes of your main section, the students seemed to drift and become restless', is going to lead to more useful discussion than saying, 'You were really rather boring and went on in the same way for too long'.
- Use questions to guide the discussion where possible and encourage the observed to reflect on practice and help develop an action plan, eg 'What effect did you feel it had when you said that?', 'How do you think you could have involved them more in this?', 'How do you know if they achieved this objective?', 'What were you trying to achieve at this particular point?', 'How did you feel about this part?', 'How can you address this concern?'

Guidelines for receiving feedback

Receiving feedback is never easy:

- Clarify what kind of feedback is going to be helpful to you.
- Be prepared to accept honest and constructive criticism.
- Explore ways to address any areas of less effective practice identified.
- Ask for examples or ideas for other approaches.
- Good feedback will lead naturally on to the development of an action plan which may include observing another practitioner with known expertise in a particular area of teaching, further reading or a staff development session.

OTHER MODELS AND INNOVATIONS

This chapter has so far concentrated on observation as it will affect new lecturers who may be involved in some initial formal training. However, in the case of established staff, 'peer observation' of teaching has become more prevalent across the sector with self-selecting colleagues undertaking one or more observations on each other per year. Observation in pairs is the most common form, although staff may also work in triads, in which A observes B, who observes C, who observes A.

Alternatively, two members may observe a third, or one may observe the two others **team-teaching**. Jarzabkowski and Bone (1998) give some useful guidelines and checklists for peer observation. At Anglia Polytechnic University, a form has been specially developed to help the observer reap the full self-development potential from peer observation (Cosh, 1998). Clusters involve groups of four or five, each undertaking observations of at least one other member of the group. Smith (1998) describes a system whereby peer clusters come together to share and identify issues which have resulted in significant curricular change.

Many academic staff find video recording a means of obtaining the ultimate objective record of a teaching session. Despite fears that this may be intrusive in teaching, lecturers usually forget about the presence of a video camera in a teaching session within 10 minutes. It can be used as a self-appraisal process or shared with others in teaching process recall (Claydon and McDowell, 1993). Using this approach, the observed is very much in control of the replay initially, choosing the parts to show and seek comment on. With time and confidence, the lecturer invites more comprehensive feedback. This scheme is illustrated and demonstrated in a video pack produced by the University of Northumbria at Newcastle (Claydon and Edwards, 1995).

Case Study 1: Routine Observation of Teaching with a New Lecturer

With a Probationary Lecturer in the School of Electronic and Electrical Communications Engineering, University of Plymouth

Context

The mentor was undertaking this third observation using a standard pro forma (see Appendix, page 230). The lecturer was specifically incorporating aspects arising from previous observations, ie to specify learning objectives at the start and to incorporate an in-class exercise. He had also requested feedback on interaction with students and use of the exercise.

From observer's comments:

- Good 'route map' to the session but be careful with assumptions about how much the students actually know.
- You could be more positive in your responses to students. If you compliment them when they raise a good point or question, you will maintain good interaction.

- Your strengths include a clear voice (no need to shout), and a good sense of humour. The group activities worked very well, reinforcing the learning process. Don't be afraid to move around the group, checking their understanding and how they're getting on. The screen in this room is not good, so your overhead transparencies have to be very clear.

From the observed's reflective notes:

- I was pleased that aims, objectives and 'route-map' came over as sensible and I was glad to get positive feedback on the handouts and exercise. I hadn't been at all sure it would work with a group of 50. I'll try to remember to compliment students for asking their own questions as well as for answering mine. I hadn't realized the problem with the screen; it's good to be made aware of it. I'll watch the time more carefully to allow for questions at the end.
- There were a lot of suggestions on general factors that will help my overall performance, as opposed to simply enhancing the future delivery of this particular lecture.

OVERVIEW

The use of observation of teaching has become an established part of practice in teaching and learning in higher education. Observation is common in initial training programmes for new lecturers and those who have been trained in this way see it as a natural and highly valued part of their own continuing professional development. It is also becoming embedded into institutional systems for quality assurance, for example as an integral part of internal quality review processes, and for many staff it is a standard item for discussion on their appraisal agenda. Observation of teaching is more acceptable and useful when it is used for formative development rather than in summative assessment.

As observation becomes more widely established, a greater range of models and means of recording practice is emerging. The more common the practice becomes, the less self-conscious staff will feel about observation of their teaching and the sooner all parties will benefit from the dialogue, reflection and enhanced practice generated. For the new lecturer, observing and being observed offers a fast track to confidence and enhanced performance through insight into teaching and learning.

REFERENCES

Brown, S, Jones, G and Rawnsley, S (1993) *Observing Teaching* (SEDA Paper 79), Staff and Educational Development Association, Birmingham

Claydon, T and McDowell, L (1993) *Watching Yourself Teach and Learning from it.* Paper in *Observing Teaching*, (SEDA Paper 79), Staff and Educational Development Association, Birmingham

Cosh, J, (1998) Peer observation in higher education: a reflective approach, *Innovations in Education and Training International*, **35**, 171–76

Jarzabkowski, P and Bone, Z (1998) A 'how–to' guide and checklist for peer appraisal of teaching, *Innovations in Education and Training International*, **35**, 177–82

Martin, GA and Double, JM (1998) Developing higher education teaching skills through peer observation and collaborative reflection, *Innovations in Education and Training International*, **35**, 161–70.

Quality Assurance Agency (1997) *Subject Review Handbook, October 1998 to September 2000*, Quality Assurance Agency for Higher Education, Gloucester

Smith, B (1998) Adopting a strategic approach to managing change in learning and teaching, in *To Improve the Academy*, ed M Kaplan, New Forum Press and the Professional and Organizational Development Network in Higher Education, Stillwater, OK

FURTHER READING AND VIEWING

Brown, S, Jones, G and Rawnsley, S (1993). See above. A particularly good source of advice on setting up the process; establishing ground rules and examples of different pro formas and checklists, including self assessment forms.

UCoSDA (1996) *Making the Grade: Achieving high quality assessment profiles, video and use guidebook*, Universities' and Colleges' Staff Development Agency, Sheffield. This very useful package includes two videotapes containing 10 recorded examples of teaching in a range of disciplines. The accompanying book includes examples of forms formerly used in teaching quality assessment for observation and comments by assessors.

Claydon, A and Edwards, A (1995) *Teaching Process Recall: A user's guide*, Educational Development Service, University of Northumbria at Newcastle. An illustrative video with a booklet explaining the TPR procedure. This would be useful for a small group of new lecturers working together on observing practice.

APPENDIX: OBSERVATION FORM FROM THE UNIVERSITY OF PLYMOUTH

This form is designed primarily for working with new lecturers. The person to be observed completes the front sheet, the observer completes the middle two sheets after the follow up discussion and the lecturer completes the final page, after reflection.

Observation of Teaching and Learning
Please complete this side before the session commences

Name	**Date**
Observer	**Venue**
Group	**Start time**
Number of Students	**Length of observation**
Type of session	**Time of feedback**

Aim
*In terms of **your** aims and relationship to module descriptor.*

Objectives
*What are the specific learning objectives planned for the **students** (eg knowledge and understanding, key skills, cognitive skills, and subject-specific, including practical/professional skills)?*

Outcomes
*How **students** will benefit in the longer term from this and the related learning experiences.*

Any particular factors/problems taken into account when planning the session?

Any aspects of this session which are new to you?

How have you incorporated suggestions made previously (if applicable) from any recent development?

Are there any particular aspects you would like feedback on?

Observer's Comments

The breakdown of each category (in italics) is a guide to the observer as to aspects for comment and discussion. They are not intended to be comprehensive or that each has to be covered every time. Different disciplines will have additional aspects to consider.

Teaching Characteristics - Comments

1. **Planning and start of session**

   Appropriateness of aims, objectives and outcomes. Communication of these to students. Orientation eg aims, objectives, "route map". Continuity with other sessions and students' prior knowledge.

2. **Presentation**

   Structure. Relevance and organisation of content. Attitude to subject matter. Clarity of presentation. Emphasis of key points. Pace of session. Summary, (end and/or interim). Student follow up work etc.

3. **Student Participation**

   Question and answer technique. Exercises/activities. Class management. Instructions to students. General class atmosphere. Level of participation and interaction between students. Attention and interest. Attitude to students. Awareness of individual needs. Evaluative procedures. Student - teacher rapport.

Observer's Comments (continued)

Teaching Characteristics - Comments

4. Methods and approaches
Choice/variety of teaching/learning methods. Use of OHP and/or other technologies, board, handouts, real examples and other linked materials etc. Use of appropriate reinforcement. Examples and analogies. Emphasis of key points. References and links to research.

5. General
Were the objectives achieved? Appropriateness of teaching/learning methods. Was effective communication achieved? Awareness of needs of learners and differences in approach? Any accommodation problems?

6. Future areas of focus

7. Strengths

Course Member's Notes about Observation

Name: ....

Please complete and return this page to your observer after your post-session discussion

What have you found helpful about the observation process?

In the light of comments are you likely to adapt any approaches? What further reading or formal or informal staff development would help?

Any further comments about the session and observation?

18 Teaching Portfolios

Heather Fry and Steve Ketteridge

DEFINITION

A teaching **portfolio** is a personal record of achievement and professional development as a university teacher. It is a carefully selected collection of material gathered from the mass of materials that teachers generate. But it is more than this because it is structured, has been purposefully collected over a period of time and normally includes specially prepared commentary. A portfolio can demonstrate a level of attainment, progression, professional development and/or achievement. The portfolio will commonly be used to help make decisions on probation, expertise and promotion, and is essential in obtaining membership of the **Institute for Learning and Teaching** (ILT) (Chapter 2).

BACKGROUND

Teaching portfolios are nothing new. One of the pioneers of the teaching portfolio was Queen's University, Canada, where they were introduced in the 1970s (Kappa, 1995). Since then their use has spread across North America, where it has been estimated that by the mid 1990s some 500 colleges and universities were experimenting with the use of teaching portfolios or 'dossiers' (Seldin, Annis and Zubizarreta, 1995). Their usage has extended to other English speaking countries, notably Australia (Weeks, 1996). In Britain it is the work of Graham Gibbs, while at Oxford Brookes University, that has particularly focused attention on the value of portfolios (Gibbs, 1988).

The teaching portfolio provides a means of illustrating the experience and expertise of a university teacher. It is comparable with the types of portfolio that are produced by many professions, for example the professional development records assembled by those seeking membership of the Institution of Electrical Engineers or Royal Institution of Chartered Surveyors. We are all familiar with the concept of demonstrating achievement in research, typically successful grant applications and publications, coupled with subsequent listing in the curriculum vitae. The portfolio provides a comparable means of documenting teaching activity that can also be subjected to feedback and review by colleagues.

The teaching portfolio has come to prominence in Britain in recent years with, first, universities seeking ways in which individuals can demonstrate their expertise in teaching and, second, as it is a requirement for membership of the ILT. Many institutions view portfolios as an appropriate means of assessing the individual, whether for passing the probationary hurdle or setting out a case for promotion on the basis of excellence in teaching. It should not to be forgotten that the teaching portfolio is not a confidential document, but that it is open to scrutiny by panels and assessors. In some cases (eg, health sciences) this might influence the nature of some of the supporting material presented.

PORTFOLIO CONTENTS

Institutions generally provide guidelines on the precise structure and contents of a teaching portfolio. There may be requirements to submit materials in different categories in order to ensure spread, comprehensiveness and comparability. Typically a portfolio will have three components:

1. an index or map of the material included;
2. collection of selected material and/or evidence;
3. self-evaluative commentary.

The balance between the three elements may vary considerably depending upon the purpose of the portfolio and/or institutional mission, and may reflect the nature and concerns of different disciplines. Typically the contents of components 2 and 3 are organized into categories, according to the purpose of the portfolio. The requirements for passing probation, achieving success on an ILT accredited programme (including through **AP(E)L** routes) and for promotion (for example, to a higher lecturer grade) are likely to involve different portfolio structures.

The ILT has indicated that it will require a separation of components 2 and 3, calling the former 'Evidence' and the latter 'The portfolio'. In this chapter we will continue to use 'portfolio' as a general term to describe both these parts together.

Types of evidence that might be collected

- courses, modules and units taught;
- information about the context of your teaching;
- self-authored documents and/or study guides;

- module descriptions including aims and objectives;
- curriculum development work;
- problem-based learning cases;
- AV materials;
- teaching strategies;
- student handouts or workbooks;
- documentation to support practical teaching;
- instruments for assessment of student learning;
- analysis of examination results;
- student evaluation instruments, views and results;
- quality assurance reports;
- external examiners' reports;
- examples of student work;
- video, audio and photographic material;
- computing and IT materials;
- written commentary from observed teaching sessions;
- details of courses and workshops attended on teaching and learning;
- educational publications.

Interrogating Practice

Choose any five examples from the list above and think of the specific pieces of evidence you would present for each one.

The self-evaluative aspect of a portfolio may take many forms. Often authors will be seeking to demonstrate that they understand the reasons for adopting a particular approach or technique, and have taken appropriate steps to enhance their teaching practice after due reflection. It is important to show response to feedback from students and peers and consideration of the impact of one's teaching on student learning. The self-evaluative aspect is intended to show how the author has developed practice through a consideration of actions taken and implementation of improvements. Additionally, authors should demonstrate that practice has been informed by educational theory. Lyons (1998) surveys some experiences of staff developing as reflective practitioners – an aspect of portfolio construction that many new staff find the most difficult.

Possible types of self-evaluative commentary

- critical incident analysis;
- reflective report on development of practice (Chapter 16);
- reflection on feedback from observed teaching (Chapter 17);
- short exposition on development of a lecture or module to take account of evaluation comments;
- reflective teaching log or diary;
- forms designed for self-assessment and development of teaching (Day, Grant and Hounsell, 1998);
- reports of **action research** conducted;
- analysis of personal development needs.

Interrogating Practice

As a start towards getting into a reflective frame, think about the last piece of teaching you did. List: (i) the aspects that seemed to go well; (ii) the things that didn't seem to work quite as well as expected; and (iii) how you might change the latter and why.

Portfolios for some purposes will need not only a list of recent development activities, but also a clear plan setting out your **continuing professional development** (CPD) needs, arising from an analysis of your own strengths and weaknesses. For example, this feature will be essential in portfolios being used for ILT membership.

Case Study 1: Reflections Upon the Writing of a Teaching Portfolio

This case study sets out the reflections of lecturer in law on her experience of having created a portfolio as part of a postgraduate certificate in teaching at South Bank University.

A portfolio is a rare form of assessment in that the product is a genuine illustration of the learning process achieved. I found myself experiencing satisfaction in being able to see what I had learned about teaching and learning while I was preparing the portfolio. Now it is one of the few pieces of work upon which I have been assessed and enjoy reading again.

For me, one of the most difficult points was in not knowing how to start the portfolio. The other was deciding when the work was ended.

So, how to begin? Some words of advice that I had been given rang impatiently in my ears: 'Don't leave your portfolio until the last minute!' The hunt for some positive ideas as to how to begin led me to consider writing a reflective diary. This would be my personal record of the main events occurring in each week's teaching and learning, and my reflections upon them.

Shunning technology for once, I requisitioned a large exercise book from the stationery cupboard and started writing, adding to the diary every week or so. At the end of the first semester, I searched through the diary for proof that I had achieved each of the learning outcomes for the unit before writing up my thoughts for the assessors. This part of the process was not so much one of writing (although there was plenty of that) but of thinking about what it was important to write.

I did not know when the task was finished, but I soon realized that a portfolio is never completed as long as you are developing as a teacher, so that any ending must be self-imposed. I stopped writing the portfolio in time for the deadline for its submission.

(Penny White)

THE PORTFOLIO AT THE PROBATIONARY STAGE

Even though in most universities new lecturers are under pressure to establish their research, it is also important to start collecting information and evidence about teaching and the promotion of student learning. In managing the numerous demands on your time, it is important to start work on a portfolio as soon as possible:

- be clear about the criteria pertaining in your institution and/or for the ILT;
- check the deadlines for submission;
- start collecting representative documents from your first day as a university teacher;

- look at existing portfolio examples where they are available;
- treat the task seriously and participate in any preparatory workshops your institution may offer;
- discuss your portfolio with your mentor/adviser/tutor;
- think through what types of reflective and evaluative commentary you will offer and what you will need to do to prepare them;
- acknowledge any joint contributions;
- be discriminating in final selection – the issue is quality, not quantity;
- be prepared to produce further evidence to show that the materials were used/are genuine;
- present the portfolio and its contents professionally.

Universities provide varying amounts of support for staff preparing portfolios. For example, Nottingham Trent University (1998) has developed a resource pack to assist lecturers in preparing portfolios. The pack resembles a workbook in which lecturers may respond to prompts to help them tease out information and engage in self-evaluation. It is designed around the six aspects of provision used in **QAA Subject Review** and includes a needs analysis for CPD. The Open University similarly helps participants on its accredited programmes for those who teach in higher education. It provides a portfolio guide intended to support the collection and analysis of evidence of teaching ability in a highly structured manner.

Two different examples of institutional frameworks for teaching portfolios are shown in the following case studies. The Queen Mary and Westfield College study is an example of a well-established, general-purpose portfolio framework, used for a variety of functions, including promotion. The second study, from the University of Nottingham, is part of their certificated programme and exemplifies a model that has more emphasis on specially prepared items. Institutional frameworks will be subject to considerable review in the light of the adoption of the ILT guidelines.

Case Study 1: Framework for a Teaching Portfolio, Queen Mary and Westfield College, University of London

The framework sets out five broad categories under which evidence should be presented and gives some representative examples.

1. Teaching performance and effectiveness

Versatility, volume and level of teaching
Statement on range of subject matter and levels taught. Evidence of scope (range of subject matter) of undergraduate teaching: number and size of classes/groups, supervision of project students, also taught Master's courses. Graduate students.

Styles of teaching
Statement on range: lecturing, small groups, seminar, practical teaching, workshops, fieldwork, teaching with patients, etc.

Quality of delivery
Evidence from course questionnaires (or other method), giving details of quantitative ratings (if available). Evidence from direct observation of teaching by senior colleague, head of department or other appropriate reviewer. Evidence of excellence in postgraduate supervision (if applicable). Examination results/assessment profiles from modules singly or jointly taught.

2. Planning and preparation

Teaching and learning methods
(a) Specific examples stating subject matter and level, and commenting on appropriateness and effectiveness of techniques. (b) Examples of innovation, such as computer-assisted learning, methods to promote independent learning, active learning in classes.

Teaching materials
(c) Examples of course materials, learning materials, course guides, handbooks, manuals, software. Innovation in curriculum development. (d) Statement on contribution in course design, teaching objectives and programme development.

3. Assessment and examination of student learning

Assessment strategies
(a) Statement on the range of methods used, examples and explanation of articulation with teaching and learning strategies. (b) Mechanisms for giving students prompt feedback on their progress, having regard to numbers on courses, to include evidence from students.

Innovation

(c) Development of new assessment methods.

4. Professional development as a teacher

Professional qualifications in teaching or higher education. Professional updating workshops and courses attended. Contribution to continuing education programmes or staff development workshops. Membership of professional groups. Educational or teaching groups within professional bodies and societies.

5. Other relevant information

For example:

- invitations to teach elsewhere (as a guest lecturer);
- publications in pedagogic journals;
- publication of student textbooks or teaching software;
- leadership in team teaching, contribution to the development of teaching in the college or elsewhere;
- professional service to other universities (as an external/visiting examiner or subject adviser/consultant);
- teaching appointments, such as visiting professorships;
- promoting your subject through schools or popular lectures;
- membership of validation panels.

Case Study 2: The University of Nottingham Portfolio

The reflective portfolio is the assessed product for one 20-credit module that is a third of the postgraduate certificate in academic practice at Nottingham. Participants are required to provide reflective commentaries and appropriate illustrative evidence on three specific aspects of their work. Each commentary is limited to 1500 words. The three aspects are:

1. The review and improvement of student learning.
2. Team working and academic administration.
3. A personal development plan.

During the module participants are asked to work with a small group of colleagues on the course in a 'base group' to provide an opportunity for learning and reflection. They are individually required to carry out an investigation into a student learning issue and present this action research project orally to their peers in the base group. The peers will assess the project presentation and give feedback to the presenter using assessment procedures and criteria agreed by the group. Aspect 2 is an analytical account of the functioning of the base group, while aspect 3 identifies needs, establishes priorities and sets targets for CPD.

The main purpose of the illustrative evidence is to supplement the analysis in commentaries and to avoid the necessity for too much descriptive material. The emphasis is on the quality of the analysis and reflection, not on the provision of very detailed evidence. Evidence supplied conforms to three criteria:

- Validity: evidence helps to develop the analysis in the commentary and is mapped onto the module requirements.
- Authenticity: the evidence belongs to the person submitting the portfolio.
- Currency: the evidence is up to date and not more than five years old.

(Kate Exley and Richard Blackwell, 1998)

ILT PORTFOLIOS

Published guidelines (ILT Planning Group, 1999) set out the likely requirements for securing membership and associate membership of ILT by new and experienced teachers in higher education. They indicate the submission of: (a) 'file of evidence' consisting of work samples that demonstrate achievement of specified outcomes; (b) a 'portfolio' consisting of an introduction, summary of evidence, reflection on the evidence, and a continuing professional development plan.

The 'file' should contain evidence corresponding to the five specified groups of outcomes:

1. Design and plan a course (module or unit).
2. Teach and support learning in the subject. Achievements.
3. Assess students' learning achievements
4. Contribute to the maintenance of student support systems.
5. Evaluate and improve the teaching process.

The two categories of membership will require submissions demonstrating fulfilment of different numbers of outcomes. Your staff or educational development unit will provide you will full details of the latest requirements of the ILT.

ASSESSING PORTFOLIOS

Portfolio assessment is a contentious issue. Portfolios generally have reasonably high **validity**; however, because they are so individual and may only be examined by two or three assessors, they generally have poor **reliability**. The provision of clear and open criteria for assessment and a specified structure both help to make portfolios a fairer method of assessment. Criteria may include requirements for minimum and maximum lengths or word counts relating to specific sections. The number of peer-observed teaching sessions and a time limit on items valid for inclusion are also often specified. There are very few public statements of assessment criteria. Generally, universities have yet to get to grips with portfolio assessment procedures that would be entirely defensible. Some of the tensions and unresolved issues associated with portfolio assessment have been reviewed elsewhere (Fry and Ketteridge, 1999).

However, as with all assessment decisions, there is an element of balance to be struck between the form of the assessment, its purpose and how it will be judged. With the university teaching portfolio, the **formative** educational value of producing a portfolio, its relative feasibility and the validity of its content currently overshadow issues of reliability. One difficulty is that they are now being used for **summative** purposes. Owing to these factors many institutions, at present, when making summative decisions, will opt for a threshold judgement of either satisfactory completion or referral, rather than attempt finer grades of judgement. This is also the initial approach taken by the ILT.

The practical difficulties of portfolio assessment are confirmed in an analysis of the process of reviewing teaching portfolios by colleagues working in the field of biochemistry at Cornell University. Quinlan (1999) has noted (albeit in a study with a small sample, n=7) that assessors were likely to compare teachers' portfolios to their own experiences, that of their colleagues, and to a vision of what is typical, the norm or traditional practice. This reinforces the need for clear assessment criteria. Further analysis showed that readers of portfolios justified their final decisions on the appropriateness and achievement of educational goals. What is also interesting in this study is that when examining what assessors paid most attention to in the portfolio, and indeed spent most of their time on, they rated the teachers' reflective commentary as the second most important piece of evidence in the portfolio.

OVERVIEW

Teaching portfolios are becoming commonplace, as they represent a tangible means of demonstrating competence and professionalism. Producing a portfolio will become as normal an activity as writing a curriculum vitae. The most difficult aspects are likely to be the reflective commentary and being discriminating in selection of appropriate evidence. Experience gained in producing a portfolio early in one's career will be good preparation for later usage in connection with applications for promotion, or to present to prospective employers to demonstrate evidence of one's teaching expertise, or to remain in good standing with ILT. Various frameworks exist to help staff develop their portfolios for different purposes at different stages in their careers. Those seeking membership of the ILT will be guided by the latest guidelines.

REFERENCES

Day, K, Grant, R and Hounsell, D (1998) *Reviewing Your Teaching*, Centre for Teaching Learning and Assessment, The University of Edinburgh/Universities' and Colleges' Staff Development Agency

Fry, H and Ketteridge, SW (1999) Developing teaching in undergraduate medical and dental schools: introduction of teaching portfolios in the context of a national requirement programme, in Selected Proceedings, 8th Ottawa Conference on Medical Education, Philadelphia

Gibbs, G (1988) *Creating a Teaching Portfolio*, Technical and Educational Services Ltd, Bristol

Lyons, N (1998) Portfolios and their consequences: developing as a reflective practitioner, in *With Portfolio in Hand: Validating the new teacher professionalism*, ed N Lyons, pp 247–64, Teachers College Press, Columbia University, New York

Nottingham Trent University, Centre for Learning and Teaching (1998) *Teaching Portfolio: A staff resource pack*, The Nottingham Trent University

Kappa, C (1995) The origins of teaching portfolios, *Journal of Excellence in College Teaching*, **6** (1), pp 5–56

Quinlan, KM (1999) *Inside the Peer Review Process: How Academics Review a Colleague's Teaching Portfolio*

Seldin, P, Annis, l, Zubizarreta, J (1995) Answers to common questions about the teaching portfolio, *Journal of Excellence in College Teaching*, **6** (1), pp 57–64

Weeks, P (1996) The teaching portfolio: A professional development tool, *International Journal for Academic Development*, **1** (1), pp 70–74

FURTHER READING

Newble, D and Cannon, R (1994) *A Handbook for Medical Teachers*, Kluwer Publishers, London. Contains a useful appendix on constructing a portfolio that can easily be used in many disciplines.

Seldin, P (1997) *The Teaching Portfolio*, Anker Publishing Company Inc, Bolton, MA. Contains many examples of portfolio material from different disciplines, but embedded in the American system.

ILT, National Framework for Higher Education Teaching. Consult your staff or educational development unit for the latest guidance.

19 | Continuing Professional Development

Patricia Partington

DEFINITIONS

Higher education in the 1990s is providing more than ever before for the **continuing professional development** (CPD) needs of diverse UK organizations and their staff; but how comprehensively and effectively does it provide for the CPD of its own personnel? This chapter explores the past and current state of CPD for higher education staff themselves and ends with suggestions of how the current provision might be improved. The emphasis is on academic staff and their own responsibilities for their career-long professional development, although the role of leaders and managers in encouraging and enabling the CPD of their staff will be addressed.

First, for clarification, we need to define what we mean by CPD in the context of staff in higher education. The term and concept has currency now across a wide range of UK organizations, including institutions of higher education. In colleges and universities the term is increasingly used with reference to all categories of staff and, in many cases, in relationship with cyclical staff **appraisal** schemes and associated training and development plans, ideally systematically linked to departmental and institutional planning and goals. The last section of this chapter will emphasize the importance of the integration of individual CPD planning with departmental and institutional strategies. To define the term more closely we will consider each element.

The word 'development' is a broader concept than, for example, 'training' and implies a longer-term approach and one which has benefits for the individual as

well as the institution. 'Training' has a more task-specific focus and, for some people, an unfortunate connotation of remedial activity, ie bringing someone up to a
particular level of **competence** rather than support them in going beyond that.

The term 'professional' is more complex and sensitive, especially in respect of
academic staff and their work. The arguments for and against the notion of an academic as a 'professional' have been well rehearsed over the past decade (Warren
Piper, 1994; Kogan, Moses and El-Khawas, 1994). It has been argued that academic
practice involves up to three areas of professionalism:

1. One's professionalism in the subject – law, engineering, surveying,
    medicine, nursing etc, which implies scholarship and research in keeping
    subject knowledge up to date and requires formal evidence of CPD. This
    evidence may be quantified through a points scheme and/or accumulation of
    portfolio documentation.
2. The professionalism of the teacher in communicating the subject.
3. The professionalism of the manager in activities such as module and course
    leadership and other management tasks in support of academic practice.

Implicit in the term 'professional' is more than the nature of the activities engaged
in, but also the manner in which those are carried out, ie 'professionally'.

Finally, the notion of 'continuing' is of significance particularly in the current climate of change and its implications for developments in the practitioner's role in
higher education. 'Continuing' carries with it the idea of career-long or lifelong
development and the existence of CPD programmes implies that staff are recruited
not only for the knowledge, skills and attitudes they have on appointment, but also
on account of their capacities to be flexible, adaptable, creative and amenable to
change. In other words, they are appointed with the expectation and the capability
of learning continuously throughout their careers. Moreover, to attract and retain
such individuals, institutions and their departments need to develop into 'learning
organizations', in which a culture is created of fostering and providing adequate
resources for continuing learning and development for all groups of staff. Further
features of 'learning organizations' can be found in Lessem (1991) and Marquardt
and Reynolds (1994).

It can be seen from the preceding definitions that systematic and embedded
schemes of CPD require considerable commitment from both the individual and
the organization, in respect of understanding and valuing its role and potential, as
well as the investment of time and resources. We move on now to an exploration of
that commitment – past, present and future – within higher education.

THE BACKGROUND

CPD is a relatively new concept for most staff in colleges and universities; they recognize more readily the terms 'staff development' and 'staff training', the former being commonly applied to activities for academic and related staff groups and the latter used predominantly for support staff programmes. Both these terms, however, lack a sense of continuity and career-long renewal. Institutions of higher education have, from their very beginnings, had at the heart of their activities the continuing development of knowledge; knowledge creation, extension and dissemination are, after all, their primary goals. Academic staff have always felt and exercised their obligation to keep themselves at the forefront of their subject through scholarship and research. 'Managing oneself and CPD' in this respect has been perceived as an integral part of the role, and stems from an individual's own intrinsic interest in the subject and its development.

Subject knowledge development is now recognized as being only part – although the crucial part – of the continuing development needs of an academic. From the 1970s onwards, emphasis has been growing on the need for the development of professional skills of staff to carry out their roles. Factors which have contributed to this increasing emphasis have included:

- increasing student numbers and greater diversity of educational needs;
- developments in modes of learning and teaching;
- requirements to be accountable for our practices;
- more intense external scrutiny of academic research and teaching.

These factors and others have focused attention on teaching skills and on administration and management abilities, in addition to research and scholarship.

The mainspring of the focus of attention on teaching developments was the work of a number of central committees of inquiry in the 1960s. These were: the Hale Committee (on university teaching methods) (HMSO, 1964), the Brynmor Jones Committee (on audio-visual aids to teaching and learning) (HMSO, 1965), and the Robbins Committee (on higher education expansion) (HMSO, 1963). In response to their recommendations, the 1970s saw sporadic developments in academic and support staff training in individual universities and colleges. These were paralleled by national developments led by the Committee of Vice-Chancellors and Principals (CVCP), including the establishment of two national coordinating committees and two part-time coordinating officers for the training of university teachers and university administrators. The Committee of Scottish Higher Education Principals (COSHEP) was also at this stage active in encouraging stronger interest and more activity in the development of teaching and learning skills. There were simultaneous developments in training programmes for technical staff in universities, in which the technician staff trades union (then ASTMS) played a significant part, as did the Association of University Teachers in the movement towards enhanced provision of academic staff development.

During the 1980s there was consolidation of these UK-wide and institutional projects leading to the establishment, by the end of the decade, in most higher education institutions of a facility for the promotion and provision of programmes of development in learning and teaching. The activities of the CVCP's Academic Staff Development Committee and Co-ordinator were influential in two major ways at this time. First, the publication of a *Code of Practice on Academic Staff Development* (Brown, 1986) established for the universities a baseline of involvement by academic staff in training and development. Second, by lobbying the University Grants Committee (UGC), the funding body at that time, a central unit was established in 1989 – with membership of all universities – to provide a UK-wide resource for the enhanced support of professional development for all staff: The Universities' Staff Development and Training Unit.

A second strand of activity during the 1980s focused on efficient and effective leadership and management of higher education and further strengthened the emphasis on the need for continuing development for all staff: senior leaders – both academic and administrative, as well as academic and support staff. The Jarratt Committee (CVCP, 1985) reported its findings in 1985, which included detailed recommendations on staff management and their development. Among them were suggested actions which, although contentious, would have significance for the shift from *ad hoc* programmes of staff development to more sustained and strategic CPD. The recommendation by the Jarratt Committee that staff should undertake regular and systematic staff appraisal linked to provision of better resourced and more comprehensive staff development represented the beginnings of a more strategic, continuing and professional approach to developmental activities. This was the positive aspect of the proposal. There were difficulties, however, which were associated with this recommendation and with the developments in teaching training driven by the Vice-Chancellors and Principals, in that the proposals were seen by staff as politically motivated and they were perceived as a potentially damaging incursion into the rightful autonomy of institutions to manage their own affairs.

Some recommendations were, therefore, contended by individual staff, their leaders and their professional associations. Action on recommendations, such as the introduction of obligatory staff appraisal, was taken against resistance and through compulsion attached to pay settlement. All this led to the perception by academics of the early schemes of CPD in teaching and management skills as politically and managerially enforced.

By the early 1990s, the result was that, unlike CPD for research and scholarship, 'managing oneself and CPD' in the other two areas of professionalism – teaching and management – was not 'owned' by academics but was seen to be imposed rather than integral to the role. This view, which militated against acceptance and uptake of comprehensive CPD, was to be further intensified during the 1990s by the superimposition of additional centrally and politically driven systems.

Interrogating Practice

What is your university's policy on appraisal for academic staff, and how is it linked with the identification of your development and training needs? Who is responsible for assisting you in following up identified CPD? Your mentor? Head of department? Someone else?

CURRENT PRACTICES

Current practices in academic staff CPD remain varied and largely unsystematic, yet more extensive and better funded than at any former stage, and comprise variable provision of teaching and management support alongside continuing and enhanced support for the development of research activity. The impetus provided by the three rounds of the Research Assessment Exercise (RAE) and the comparatively rich sources of funding associated with these have strengthened efforts right across all institutions of higher education to position their staff as favourably as possible to succeed. This has led to the continuation of the primary investment of finance and time into research development activity. Other innovations in the area of quality have forced review and development of teaching and management practices. **Academic audit** of institutional quality assurance procedures (now Institutional Review), introduced in 1990, and Quality Assessment of higher educational provision at subject level (now **Subject Review**) have both had some measure of influence on improvements in CPD. The issue remains that the recognition and the rewards for investment of time in research activity, including associated CPD, far exceed those rewards – both material and in esteem – related to performance and development in teaching. If an academic reviews the costs to them, their department, institution and the whole sector of the combined Quality Audit and Assessment exercises, they can clearly see that the continuing costs of carrying out these systems far outweigh any related enhancement funds put back into the sector, eg the Higher Education Funding Council for England's (**HEFCE**) Fund for the Development of Teaching and Learning (FDTL) and similar initiatives in Scotland and Wales. Precisely the opposite is true for research, where the costs to the sector of the RAE are relatively modest when compared with either the costs and burden of organizing the educational quality systems or indeed the associated rewards and recognition.

The most damaging factor in this dilemma is not so much the disparity in investment, recognition and reward across the two key functions of academic practice, but rather the polarization of two essentially symbiotic academic pursuits. It is my view that, however great the emphasis we put on professionalism in processes of teaching and learning, we need always to recognize the critical importance of the content – the knowledge, understanding, applications and skills – which those processes are designed to support. There is no more trenchant a criticism a student can give of the learning experience than that the tutor is not in command of the body of knowledge being taught. The complex, challenging and potentially intensely rewarding relationships between tutor, student and process revolve more crucially around a deep and ever deepening understanding of the subject knowledge than at any other stage of education. This is the reason why the co-location and interrelationship of research, scholarship, learning and teaching is so important to be preserved and why the current quality and management trends which lead to their polarization are so absurd and potentially so damaging.

Interrogating Practice

What provision is available in your university for CPD? Who will help you in the development of your research and research supervision, teaching and learning, academic and self-management? Do you have a personal development plan?

Some universities have well-established centres or units designed specifically to support the professional development of the academic. Case Study 1 outlines the support offered by the Centre for Academic Practice at the University of Strathclyde, the work of which is highly regarded throughout the sector.

Case Study 1: The Centre for Academic Practice

University of Strathclyde

The Centre for Academic Practice (CAP) was established in 1987 to promote and support good practice in teaching, learning and higher education management. CAP supports the university's aim to be 'a place of useful learning'. To this end CAP supports staff and students, establishing productive links between the two roles. Development needs are identified through the appraisal system, and institution, faculty and department plans and priorities.

To address these needs, the CAP strategy is to offer a range of development activities: a postgraduate certificate/diploma in Advanced Academic Studies, consultancy with departmental or faculty groups, a three-day course for new lecturers, extended (six months) programmes, guest seminars, a workshop programme, research and materials development.

The value of this approach is that the diverse needs of academic are met:

- new lecturers receive training;
- new supervisors are trained;
- research staff have dedicated training programmes;
- heads of departments and research managers are trained;
- partnerships between CAP, senior officers and administrators produce relevant targeted training;
- CAP influences policy, through links with university committees, including the articulation of the University's Staff Development Policy and Strategy, and working to sustain Investors in People standards.

The effect of the CAP approach on the development of academics is to meet their professional development needs at different stages in their careers. Partnerships allow CAP to influence policy and bring the subject of staff development to policy discussions.

(Dr Rowena Murray)

This central significance of subject content should influence the ways in which we conceive of and plan for academic staff CPD in comprehensive and integrative ways, bringing together development of all aspects of academic practice. Regrettably, the various forms of external scrutiny have had the opposite effect, with the result that the following features characterize current practice in CPD.

- CPD in support of research and scholarship, eg regular and continuing attendance at and participation in research conferences and other activities, continues to be supported and seen as important, integral to effective academic practice and a significant contributor to career progression.
- CPD in support of the range of management functions of academics has been marginalized, and any remaining provision is largely *ad hoc* and confined to staff at the level of head of department and above.
- CPD for teaching and learning is now largely related to 'passing the quality review', which on the one hand means that it is now addressed at subject level as well as at institutional and individual levels and there is therefore more activity. On the other hand, the nature and quality of the provision of CPD are restricted and driven by the perceived parameters of the review process.
- On a positive note, those who have participated as reviewers or auditors (by now approximately 3500 academic staff in total) have gained considerably by a rich, varied and concentrated period of CPD in teaching and learning over two or three years.
- For the majority of staff, however, the relating of CPD to Quality Review results largely in short-term planning and in achieving the perceived minimum required to 'pass the test'.
- The 'passing the test' syndrome leads to a superficial approach to training in teaching and learning, for example (a) focusing on what a tutor should do – or rather avoid doing – in the 'snapshot' observation sessions; (b) temporarily reviving already extinct appraisal systems; (c) instituting a limited period of peer observation; and (d) providing lists of courses attended and names of those staff involved.
- Paradoxically, these review-oriented approaches can do the role of CPD a disservice and diminish its value in the eyes of academics, who understandably recognize their superficiality. To those who recognize the infinite complexity and challenge of the learner/tutor/subject relationship, the 'tips for the trade' approaches advocated to help surmount an imminent hurdle represent a temporary but essentially trivial prop, which will soon outlive its value. There is no real evidence yet of sustained CPD in teaching and learning for longer periods beyond review cycles.

In summary, what we see now at the end of the 1990s is certainly more provision of forms of academic staff training and development, but little which could truly be described as strategic, coordinated and systematic continuing professional development. The tension between the two main areas of the academic role continues and has, if anything, been intensified. The time required to prepare for the range of external reviews – of research, subject provision, institutional quality procedures, professional or statutory accreditation – has itself played a part in eroding the time available for the embedding of systems of staff appraisal linked to individual and departmental goals, personal development planning and the provision of genuine CPD. Moreover, the responsibility has been taken away from individuals, many of whom now feel coerced into participation in trivial activities, designed to help their departments achieve the odd additional 'brownie point', but which serve little purpose beyond that.

We approach the millennium with progress having been made in respect of the quantity of academic staff development provision, but with scepticism first about its credibility and long-term value and, second, about any claim that we have yet, across higher education, achieved the establishment of CPD in academic practice. Ironically, the results of Institutional Audit (HEQC, 1994, 1996) and Quality Assessment (QAA Subject Overview Reports – 1996–98) demonstrate this. The former HEQC reports indicate inadequacies in staff development provision, and from the latter it is evident that the lowest graded aspect overall of the six aspects of provision within the QAA's methodology is 'Quality Assurance and Enhancement' (now Quality Management and Enhancement), within which falls their assessment of staff development. The question remains, therefore, of how we might achieve the targets set as long ago as 1986 in the previously mentioned CVCP's Code of Practice, and do so in a way in which training and development extend in diverse but integrated forms across the whole range of academic practice.

Interrogating Practice

What training and development activities does your institution offer in support of academic practice? Is there an institutional policy which requires all staff who teach to be involved in training and development? Is there provision for part-time tutors and demonstrators?

THE WAYS FORWARD

Two new developments might support our achievement of sustained and integrated CPD: the findings of the Dearing Committee (NCIHE, 1997), which focused its recommendations on the significance of lifelong learning for students in higher education and extended these also to the providers of that learning; and the consequent establishment of the Institute for Learning and Teaching (ILT), the body which will confer professional status on members of the academic profession in respect of their teaching responsibilities.

The requirements of the ILT, which has been formally launched in 1999 following a recommendation of the Dearing Committee, will lead to the identification and application of criteria of professionalism in one part of the academic role. A positive effect of this could be that it might lead to the development of criteria of professionalism across the other areas of academic practice; whereas the negative result might be further polarization of teaching and research and institutionalized divisions between those who research and those who teach.

However, it must ultimately be recognized that no external body or review procedure can effect the changes required to embed CPD for academic and other staff within higher education. Such changes will depend on individuals, departments and the institution as a whole working in partnership in recognizing the potential of CPD, not only for the external organizations for whom they provide it, but also for themselves, and then taking joint responsibility for its planning and provision. The following suggestions are now offered in support of shared ownership of CPD and with the intention of encouraging the realization of its potential for the learners and the practitioners in higher education.

1. First and foremost, individual staff members need to be persuaded that investment of their time in CPD will be recognized and rewarded. This means that departments and institutions need to review their rewards and promotions structures to base career progression on success across the full range of academic practice, including recognition for CPD undertaken in all areas.

2. More than the review and re-shaping of procedures and their results, this implies some interim staff training in the presentation of the information on which progression and promotion depends. Procedures in institutions and departments should encourage from career start the continuing writing of 'academic practice and development portfolios'. There are current useful examples of preparation of '**teaching portfolios**' (see Chapter 18), but if we are to assimilate properly the wider concept and practice of CPD, then these should be reviewed and extended to include a continuing record of practice and development in all aspects of the academic role. The models of 'teaching portfolio' given in this volume could be adapted to incorporate the other dimensions. Since the majority of staff still regard the interrelationship of teaching, scholarship and research as one of the most distinctive features of higher education, they would be at least as likely to respond as favourably to this as to the narrower teaching-focused version.

3. Leaders and managers, and heads of departments, need to find means of encouraging individual staff to take responsibility for 'managing themselves and their own CPD'. Furthermore, those taking on a role in academic management, at whatever level, will need to take time out to consider their own CPD. This issue is taken up in Case Study 2. Since the preceding sections of this

chapter have identified the limitations of external, political, internal and managerial attempts to foster enhanced training and development, it is clear that the onus of responsibility needs now to be put where it rightfully belongs – with the individual staff themselves. They are closest to the learning experience of students and are most likely to know how that might best be enhanced through their own CPD focused on teaching and learning.

Case Study 2: Preparing for Academic Management

Academics, by virtue of the profession, are often self-sufficient: used to working in isolation, using their own initiative, and managing their own resources. In many universities academic staff are ill-prepared when it comes to accepting responsibility for management at any level. Academic management involves different functions and requires a different set of skills that may need to be developed. This case study highlights the key management functions, their associated skills, and approaches by which the aspiring academic can develop and enhance these skills. It is based on the knowledge and perceptions gained by an independent management and organizational development consultant who has been working in higher education and the public sector for many years.

What is meant by management?

Management is all about deploying human and physical resources to meet the goals of the project, department and the organization. While on the surface this may appear to be a relatively simple task, in practice the process is a complex one requiring the manager to demonstrate specific skills within key functions.

The key functions are:

- strategic management;
- business planning;
- financial management;
- performance management.

In order to undertake these key managerial functions, a number of skills must be developed. These include:

- Visible leadership: the ability to formulate and communicate a vision to your staff. Visible leadership drives the business planning process.

- Motivating staff: managers need to demonstrate energy and enthusiasm in promoting the goals of the organization and to maintain staff morale.
- Communication: upwards, downwards, and crossing traditional boundaries; includes such activities as team briefing, focus groups, quality circles and problem solving.
- Delegation: empowering individuals with the authority to undertake projects. Using business plans and performance management techniques to steer the process. Knowing when to intervene and when to assist. Not to be confused with abdication.
- Feedback skills: giving clear and constructive feedback is crucial. This is where the greatest weakness often lies in academic (including research project) management. Of necessity incorporated into one-to-one staff review or appraisal schemes.

These skills can be conventionally addressed through management development programmes (sometimes to gain a formal qualification). Equally important are mentoring (academic managers are sometimes paired with managers operating elsewhere in the public sector or in industry), coaching (by more senior colleagues in the institution) and shadowing (in one's own institution or another).

(Lindsay Wright (e-mail:Lindsay.Wright@btinternet.com))

To be successful in encouraging individual staff, senior and departmental managers might consider the disbursement of internal teaching development funds not only to departments and groups of bidders, but also to individuals who submit proposals identifying developments, which are transferable to other disciplines.

Institutional centres for the support of CPD, which are present in universities and colleges in a variety of forms (Partington *et al*, 1994), need to be reviewed to ensure their capacity to provide a resource for staff across the full range of CPD, and their capability to work with credibility in close partnership with academic departments and individual staff within them. Case Study 3, taken from Nottingham Trent University, offers a useful model for institutions seeking a forward looking, strategic approach to assisting academics in the development of their practice.

Case Study 3: Institutional Support for CPD

Nottingham Trent University

This case study demonstrates how a two-year funded project on peer observation of teaching helped to develop CPD across a university by empowering individuals and course teams to reflect and modify teaching practices and programme outcomes. It also highlights a series of recommendations that help ensure the embedding of CPD and lifelong learning into the infrastructure of a university.

In 1996, Nottingham Trent University was successful in being awarded £250,000 over two years, from the Higher Education Funding Council for England, Fund for the Development of Teaching and Learning, to develop a system of peer observation of teaching across the university. The organizational structure of the project, which became known as Sharing Excellence, involved approximately 20–65 staff within each of nine faculties. Fourteen coordinators were appointed to work at the departmental level, with a project manager coordinating the activities of this group across the university. This model of faculty coordinators was extremely successful, as flexibility and ownership at the local subject level proved to be essential.

Staff organized themselves into small teams of about four to six staff. Within the groups, each member observed two other staff teaching and in turn were observed twice in each semester. Participants included junior and senior staff, full and part-time staff, and technical support staff. Good practice identified at the small group level was passed to department and faculty level. Faculty coordinators organized events to discuss themes resulting from observation and issues that needed to be addressed. Two very successful university good practice days on learning and teaching acted as a main focus for staff across the university to meet together and share experiences. Key aims of this approach were to encourage the enthusiasts and nurture the successes.

The outcomes of this action were the identification and dissemination of good practice. In addition, teamwork was strengthened, collaboration (across course teams, departments, and faculties) became more evident, and case studies of good practice were produced.

Ownership of CPD was encouraged by developing both top-down and bottom-up support. At the subject level, each faculty coordinator was responsible for between 20 and 65 staff. Coordinators organized the peer observation process (developed a scheduling system, and set up the small groups) and conducted workshops for staff in observing classes and giving each other feedback. To involve senior management in the project, a steering group was formed (chaired by the deputy vice-chancellor). It included deans, heads of department, project director, project manager, a selection of faculty coordinators, and an internal and external evaluator. The ongoing and active support of senior managers is paramount if staff are to take CPD seriously.

Evaluation, when used in a formative and summative way, enriches project development and increases efficiency and effectiveness. The team were keen to ensure that an evaluation strategy was developed early to enable formative feedback and reflection to occur. Just as we want students to become reflective learners, we too need to apply reflective principles to our work. Indeed, reflection and evaluation became standing items on the agenda for the steering group.

The programme also included a widespread system of student feedback. This key and very successful feature was developed by the student coordinator, the only external full-time person to be appointed. Her role included collecting feedback from students in a variety of ways and producing a staff resource pack on student feedback. The resource pack contained details about why student feedback should be gathered, what to gather it about, when and how to gather student feedback, as well as analyzing and responding to that feedback. The pack was also designed to help staff carry out an audit and evolve a strategy on student feedback practices.

Key learning
1. Plan CPD activities thoroughly.
2. Seek internal and external funding.
3. Ensure good project management.
4. Strong and active support from senior management is essential.
5. Reward excellence in learning and teaching.
6. Develop a strategic infrastructure, which incorporates CPD with high levels of awareness throughout the university.

Finally, an ongoing and continuing strategy for CPD needs embedding in university structures. This does not necessarily mean doing more of the same. What it does require, however, is an infrastructure to support ongoing and future developments. Two of the most successful outcomes of the project were a Centre for Learning and Teaching (CeLT), and the appointment (at senior level) of nine faculty learning and teaching coordinators (one person from each of the nine faculties). These faculty coordinators spend one day per week in CeLT and another day working with faculty staff. The support structure is therefore embedded both upwards, downwards and sideways.

(Brenda Smith)

OVERVIEW

This chapter traced the growing concern for the development of professionalism in higher education, and the external factors which have led to the increased commitment to address staff development and training issues. In proposing recommendations for institutions looking to achieve a strategic, coordinated, systematic and embedded scheme of CPD, it was noted that this could not be achieved without considerable commitment from both the individual and the organization. The case studies from Strathclyde and Nottingham Trent provided useful models of what could be achieved in real terms, both benefiting from considerable senior management support.

REFERENCES

Brown, GA (1986) *Code of Practice on Academic Staff Development in Universities*, CVCP, London

CVCP (1985) (Jarratt Report) *Report on Efficiency Studies in Universities*, London

HEQC (1994) *Learning from Audit*, London

HEQC (1996) *Guidelines on Quality Assurance: Staff Development*, London

HMSO (1963) (Robbins Report) *Report of the Committee on Higher Education*, London

HMSO (1964) (Hale Report) *Report of the Committee on University Teaching Methods*, London

HMSO (1965) (Brynmor Jones Report) *Report of the Committee on Audio-Visual Aids in Higher Scientific Education*, London

Kogan, M, Moses, I and El-Khawas, E (1994) *Staffing Higher Education: Meeting new challenges*, Jessica Kingsley Publishers, London and Bristol

Lessem, R (1991) *Total Quality Learning*, Blackwell, Oxford

Marquardt, M and Reynolds, A (1994) *The Global Learning Organisation*, Irwin Professional Publishing, New York

NCIHE (1997) (Dearing Report) *Higher Education in the Learning Society*, National Committee of Inquiry into Higher Education, HMSO, London

Partington, PA, *et al* (1994) *Continuing Professional Development for Staff in Higher Education*, UCoSDA, Sheffield

QAA (1999) *Subject Overview Reports for the Units of Provision Assessed between 1996 and 1998*, Quality Assurance Agency, Gloucester

Warren Piper, D (1994) *Are Professors Professional?*, Jessica Kingsley Publishers, London and Bristol

FURTHER READING

Brew, A (ed) (1995) *Directions in Staff Development*, Society for Research in Higher Education/Open University Press, Buckingham. Useful contributions from across the higher education sector, offering case studies about a range of issues to do with CPD.

Middlehurst, R (1993) *Leading Academics*, Society for Research in Higher Education/Open University Press, Buckingham. Useful book exploring notions of leadership, focusing down on the role of the academic institutional leader, departmental leader, and individual leader.

Warner, D and Palfreyman, D (eds) (1996) *Higher Education Management: The key elements*, Society for Research in Higher Education/Open University Press, Buckingham. Useful contributions on such issues as financial management, committee work and research organization.

Part 3
Working in
Discipline-specific
Areas

20 Key Aspects of Teaching and Learning in Science and Engineering

Kate Exley

AIMS AND INTRODUCTION

This chapter aims to examine some of the distinctive features of teaching, learning and assessment in science and engineering in higher education. It will focus on aspects of the curriculum that differ from those of other academic disciplines, supplementing the more generic discussions of previous chapters. It will include a discussion of teaching and learning in practical and laboratory classes, problem classes and field course work, and a review of special issues in assessment in science and engineering.

Staff working in the disciplines of chemistry, physics, the life sciences, biomedical sciences, and the full range of engineering specialities will find the chapter particularly useful.

It is clear that there are significant differences in the ways in which lecturers in different disciplines view and approach their teaching responsibilities. This has been discussed and documented by Becher (1989) in his book *Academic Tribes and Territories*. These considerations may have had a profound influence on the time lecturers spend preparing and undertaking their different teaching roles (Smeby,

1996) and the repertoire of teaching and learning activities that they feel should be included in the curriculum.

CONTEXT

Many of the widespread changes in higher education over the last 20 years have had a particularly strong impact on the specialized teaching components in science and engineering curricula. For example, the substantial increase in student numbers had a significant effect on teaching in the workshop, laboratory and on the field trip, long before difficulties were felt elsewhere in the lecture theatre (Jervis, 1999). Most science and engineering courses also suffer from curriculum overload. The rate at which new things are discovered and understood is rapid, new material is frequently added to the curriculum and much less frequently is material removed. This expansion has been systematically tackled in medicine, in particular, through radical curriculum review and development (Chapter 24). However, this has not generally been the approach taken in science and engineering, where instead lecturers may feel more inclined to find alternative ways of covering a comprehensive programme of material in an ever-expanding curriculum.

A fundamental feature of curricula in science and engineering disciplines is that they are often viewed as 'linear subjects' in that many are designed on the basis that students need to understand A before they go on to study B and then C. Issues around modularization, prerequisites and widening access have, therefore, exerted a strong impact on the ways in which teaching programmes are designed in these subjects.

Another feature of recent change has been the introduction of a broad range of modules or courses, resulting in an increased choice of learning routes that are currently being offered by universities. For example, many science courses now include provision or indeed a requirement for the development of **key** (transferable) **skills** or a language. This may include opportunities for United Kingdom or overseas study placements through schemes such as ERASMUS programmes. This broadening of the curriculum has been strongly encouraged by recent governments through initiatives such as Enterprise in Higher Education (ED20, 1991). These developments are, in part, recognition of the fact that a shrinking proportion of science graduates will seek purely science-based employment. Many graduates look to the general job market for future work rather than to academia and pure research. In engineering, it is no longer considered sufficient to have gained a thorough understanding of technical aspects in the degree, but graduates also need to understand something of the ways engineers work in the 'real world' and be more skilled in the areas of business, communication and information technology (Jennings and Ferguson, 1995). Indeed, in some disciplines like engineering or pharmacy, this broadening of the curriculum to include key skills for employability is often strongly encouraged by the professional bodies which accredit or validate their courses.

The ways in which the development of key skills are included in the curriculum vary greatly, particularly whether the approach is to develop generic or discipline-specific skills modules or to attempt to integrate skills development into the curriculum as a whole (Chapter 10). One model for free standing skills modules in life science is illustrated in Case Study 1.

Case Study 1: First Year Life Sciences Skills Teaching

University of East London

Problem

Life sciences undergraduates have a wide range of abilities and experience, with over 40 per cent mature students. Reflecting the local community, English may not be the first language for many students. Additionally, many students have little recent or formal education and enter via access, etc.

Solutions

Skills for life sciences 1 and 2

An extrinsic compulsory, first-semester skills unit was introduced during modularization. A second-semester unit has subsequently been added. The aim of these units is to introduce all students to basic subject-specific knowledge (biology, chemistry, statistics), study skills, IT, basic practical techniques. These units are integrated with the other more conventional first-year units with intrinsic skills teaching.

Diagnostic tests in English, maths and biology are applied during induction week to identify those students in need of compulsory remedial teaching. Assessment is split between subject-specific knowledge, that is assessed by computer-marked multiple choice examinations (45 per cent), and a collection of tasks and assignments which form the profile (55 per cent, of which 20 per cent is for laboratory techniques).

Delivery is by large-group lectures, which may include group activities, and tutorials. The skills lecture topics include: audit and development plans, learning styles, and identification of the key skills required by employers and reflection.

Tutorials held fortnightly provide profile assignments, formative feedback and pastoral support. Self-help tutorials are held in alternate weeks. IT workshops are held in the computer laboratories and cover the use of Word, Excel, the Internet and e-mail.

The Workbook (Sieber *et al*, in press) provides exercises, worked examples, and assignments along with administrative information. It provides the basis for interactive group work during large-group lectures and profile activities. Different coloured sections represent each topic (study skills, biology, chemistry, IT, practicals, profile). It is updated annually and it continues to provide reference material throughout the degree course.

Multimedia **computer-aided learning packages (CAL)** have been largely written in-house to provide additional material and assignments. The packages are available on open-access or for use at home. They cover topics such as time management, practicals, graphs, revision and examination techniques and have proved to be popular with students.

These units are complex, and increasingly tasks are tailored to meet individual needs. The mixture of large group lectures, workshops, CAL and tutorials allows students to have individual feedback and support while retaining a relatively efficient delivery. Students are continuously encouraged to reflect and critically evaluate their performance.

(Dr Vivien Sieber)

Laboratory and practical classes provide an ideal opportunity for science and engineering students to work together in teams on projects, a requirement, which is consistently quoted by employers as a key skill for the workplace (Association of Graduate Recruiters, 1995; CVCP, 1998). An example of a team-based approach to the teaching of practical work in chemistry is given in Case Study 2.

Case Study 2: A Team-Based Approach to Practical Work in Chemistry

UMIST

For the course (Whiting *et al*, 1998), the students were timetabled for three weekly, three-hour sessions. Initially the students were given lectures on oral and poster presentation skills, report and proposal writing skills, methodology available for searching the chemical literature, team skills and meetings skills. All students were required to give a five-minute presentation on any area of their choice which was peer assessed. They were also required to undertake several different team exercises, during the initial training phase, some academic and others non-academic, in which they were encouraged to assess how they had interacted as teams.

For the major practical team-based projects, the students were split into groups of four by drawing names from a hat. They were then presented with a number of possible chemical projects from which they could select only one as a team. Academic staff submitted several project outlines that ranged in content from newly researched to well-established areas of chemistry. All of the project outlines were brief (usually containing no more than two references) and challenged the students to formulate a team action plan in the form of a two-page proposal. This plan had to be realistic within the laboratory timescale, considered safe and had to be costed. All teams were given a virtual budget of £400 and plans had to include the costing of all activities including the characterization of any synthesized compounds and purchasing reagents, etc. The costing of these services was priced so that judicious choice of techniques had to be made to avoid overspends.

In the next two weeks the teams searched the literature to formulate their research projects, with some help from staff members, after which they were required to present their team's final research plan. The presentation format was that two of the team members would each give a five-minute talk. The first member set the scene using the background literature, while the second presented the research proposal, justifying costings, timescale and use of personnel. Both of these presentations were peer reviewed.

Longer practical sessions were then run in which more complex experiments could take place. After three weeks in the laboratory, the students again had to give a presentation. The remaining two members of the group presented in turn, first, the group's progress and, second, how their plans would have to be adapted to fit the limited timescale. Presentations were again peer reviewed.

Then it was back into the laboratory for the final three weeks of the course to complete group projects. Teams ultimately presented their results to the department at a poster session, to which all staff were invited, and produced a project report that included the minutes of the team's weekly meetings, full cost accounts and a fully scientific report of the project results in a primary chemical literature format. Finally, there was a complete de-briefing session in which both individuals and teams were given the opportunity to evaluate the overall course, and how they worked as a team.

(Dr Andy Whiting, Dr Peter Gardner, Dr Frank Mair and Dr Mike Watkinson, 1998)

Another recent feature of science and engineering teaching has been the introduction of the four-year degree designated MSci, MEng, MChem, etc. This degree format provides an additional fourth year, available only to the most able students, to develop further research and transferable skills and allow study of some of the more advanced and/or specialized topics in the discipline. Many departments have used this fourth year to extend their use of more innovative teaching methods, using group work, **problem-based learning** and possibly building in experience of **work-based learning** in industry.

The four-year sandwich degree is also a popular alternative design in which students spend a whole year 'out' in industry, usually after their second year at university. Students gain from the experience in many ways, broadening their understanding of how knowledge is applied in the workplace, teamwork in projects, working for an employer and making useful contacts for their own future employment. Lecturers repeatedly report that students gain in maturity during their placement year, they develop work skills, gain in confidence and often clarify their career goals. This method of study does have huge implications for staff who are responsible for setting up placement opportunities, and subsequently supporting students when they are away from the university, through site visits and co-supervising arrangements with employers.

Depending on the mission of the university and the particular discipline, students in science and engineering disciplines may be drawn from a diverse international pool or very much from the local community. It is also becoming increasingly common for students to take on additional paid work to support themselves while studying. Universities are increasingly responding by offering opportunities for evening and weekend study and making greater use of flexible and distance-learning resources.

COMPONENTS OF CURRICULA

Here the adaptation and use of traditional forms of teaching are considered with particular attention being given to the specialized forms of teaching which characterize undergraduate courses in science and engineering, including:

- the lecture;
- teaching in small groups;
- laboratory or practical class;
- problem/design classes;
- field course teaching;
- project work.

The lecture

The lecture is generally the primary means for delivery of the major part of the curriculum in science and engineering, especially in the early years of degree programmes. The key feature of the lecture is that it often involves large groups, particularly in the first year where numbers may often exceed 100 students and can be as high as 300 or 400 students. Lectures are commonly used to communicate large amounts of factual information that can be highly complex and technical. Many lecturers believe that the lecture is merely the starting point for further study and is an effective method for providing an overview of a topic (Isaacs, 1994). This view is supported by the research into effective teaching carried out by Noel Entwistle and his colleagues (1992) which shows that the lecture is a very good way of providing a map of the topic or subject. However, the same research warns against the use of the lecture as the primary educational vehicle for covering the syllabus and aiming to provide the level of detail required to pass the examination. This view can cause difficulties for the scientist and engineer – some of whom would argue that the lecture is the only affordable teaching method available to them in which they can give detailed explanations of difficult concepts or complicated material. In reality this can lead to many students copying down much detailed factual information while remaining extremely passive learners in lectures.

Interrogating Practice

What will be the purposes of your next lecture? Can you think of four? What are the benefits and limitations of this method of teaching?

Subject overview reports for individual subjects are freely available from the **Teaching Quality Assessments** undertaken by the Higher Education Funding Council for England (**HEFCE**). For example, in chemical engineering (HEFCE, 1995–96), reports indicate that 54 per cent of providers did not encourage interaction with, or full involvement of, students in teaching and learning sessions. A common criticism of the lecture in science and engineering departments has been the passivity of students and the lack of opportunities for interaction and **active learning**. There is a number of activities that a lecturer can introduce to stimulate a greater level of student participation and involvement during the lecture. For example:

- short tests (sometimes called 'mini-tests') or quizzes at the beginning, middle or end of the session;
- brief questions to trigger 'buzz' discussions between pairs of students or small group debates;
- student tasks such as summarizing a lecture or solving or setting a problem;
- use of incomplete handouts with gaps or spaces that the student must fill in during the lecture. This technique can be very effective if used in combination with diagrams, tabulated data, graphs, etc, thereby giving students an opportunity to interact with the material and encourage active learning (Andresen, 1994).

Such means of promoting interaction with students in lectures commonly feature in feedback discussions following observed teaching sessions.

Teaching in small groups

The tutorial or seminar provides a method of teaching in which the primary aim may be the development of thought and discussion. The distinction between tutorials and seminars is blurred but usually refers to the number of students participating. The Hale Report (HMSO, 1964) suggested that more than four students would constitute a seminar; however, in the intervening years this number has clearly risen in most institutions.

The tutorial can be purely academic or purely pastoral or a combination of the two. Academic tutorials are often used in support of a series of lectures providing opportunities for:

- further and more detailed discussion of a topic;
- clarification and remedial action;
- problems, questions and application of information;
- integration of theory and practice;
- student-led debate and student presentations;
- feedback on understanding to students and on progress to staff.

It is clear that an effective tutorial must have a clear purpose for which both staff and students are prepared and that the tutorial takes place in an environment (real or electronic) in which all participants can easily communicate in order to exchange ideas and views. The tutorial represents a key component in the curriculum where students can develop skills of cognate scientific enquiry, eg developing a hypothesis, solving design problems, or understanding how to tackle a problem as a professional engineer or scientist. These skills are usually further developed and applied in the practical class and in the project.

> ### Interrogating Practice
>
> What are the specific aims and objectives of your next tutorial? How will you know if you have achieved them? What learning tasks will you introduce for the students?

Pastoral tutorials ('advisor' tutorials) are used to monitor and support students throughout their course of study. Initially a tutor may help with induction and aspects of curriculum choice, especially in modular systems, and will often feedback information on assessment. A tutor is a point of contact for a student who experiences academic or personal difficulties and, towards the end of a student's time at university, the tutor is also likely to help the student with his or her future career decisions and plans.

Seminars are often larger in size than a tutorial (20 students or so) and they can be tutor or student-led. Pre-set reading or problems are often given as preparatory work for the class. Seminars may involve students in working as individuals or in groups. In science and engineering the seminar model is often used at postgraduate level too – providing an appropriate forum for students at which they can present their research findings to a constructively critical group of academics and peers (Jacques, 1991).

The laboratory or practical class

In the 1860s practical courses were first offered in Oxford and London (Shepherd, 1979; Phillips, 1981). Prior to that, science courses had relied upon the 'demonstration lecture' to give insight into experimental processes and procedures. Although under pressure because of the complexities of organization and resource implications, laboratory and practical classes remain the most characteristic feature of science and engineering courses.

Kirschner and Meester (1988) have reviewed the literature relating to science practical work and identified several problems that may be associated with this type of teaching and these include:

- inadequate supervision;
- isolated exercises bearing no resemblance to past or future work;
- lack of student involvement and excitement;
- lack of purpose in course design.

Many of these problems can be tackled by using a transparent method of session planning which clearly links objectives, content and assessment and by keeping open effective communication channels for all involved. It is convenient to consider issues relating to effective teaching in laboratory or practical classes in three stages: before the class, during the class, and after the class.

Before the class

According to Black and Ogborn (1979) the purposes of practical classes can be summarized under three headings: training in techniques; learning the ideas of the subject; and learning how to carry out experimental inquiries.

However, a more detailed definition of aims and objectives needs to be articulated for each practical session. Lists of the general aims of practical classes in science and engineering follow, although it is suggested that an individual practical session will usually only be able to address three or four different aims.

Aims of science laboratory courses
These aims are to:

- instil confidence in the subject;
- teach basic practical skills;
- familiarize students with important standard apparatus and measurement techniques;
- illustrate material taught in lectures;
- teach the principles and attitudes of doing experimental work in the subject;
- train students in observation;
- train students in making deductions from measurements and interpretation of experimental data;
- use experimental data to solve specific problems;
- train students in writing reports on experiments;
- train students in keeping a day-to-day laboratory diary;
- train students in simple aspects of experimental design;
- provide closer contacts between staff and students;
- stimulate and maintain interest in the subject;
- teach some 'theoretical' material not included in the lectures;
- foster 'critical awareness' (for example extraction of all information from data, avoiding systematic errors);
- develop skills in problem solving in the multi-solution situation;
- stimulate the conditions in research and development laboratories;
- provide a stimulant to independent thinking;
- show the use of 'practicals' as a process of discovery;

- familiarize students with the need to communicate technical concepts and solutions;
- provide motivation to acquire specific knowledge;
- help bridge the gap between theory and practice. (Boud *et al*, 1980)

Aims of engineering practical classes
These aims are to:

- develop experimental, design and problem-solving skills;
- develop interpretation and observational skills;
- develop data recording and analysis skills;
- familiarize students with engineering equipment, techniques and materials;
- develop practical skills;
- develop communication and interpersonal skills;
- develop technical judgement;
- develop a feel for engineering problems and judgements (professional attitudes);
- integrate theory and practice;
- experience in working together in teams on design, research and development projects;
- gain confidence in applying knowledge and techniques to 'real' problems;
- develop IT skills, eg the use and application of CAD and design software;
- record outcomes of practical work in an appropriate fashion, eg a costed report or proposal;
- motivate students.

One useful way of planning a practical session is to develop a planning matrix linking together learning objectives, content and assessment. This will help both to clarify purpose and design the structure of the session (see Table 20.1).

Table 20.1 Planning matrix for laboratory and practical work

Number	Learning Objective	Learning Activity	Assessment Strategy
1	To weigh accurately and use the right balance for the job	Use of different balances, weigh powders in boats, irregular solids on balance pan, etc	Correct entries in work book assessed by demonstrator

| 2 | To prepare given concentrations from a standard solution | Preparation of known solutions using pipettes, volumetric flasks, etc | Short answers in laboratory report |

Effective practical teaching involves careful planning and organization. Whereas other forms of teaching, such as a lecture or seminar, rely heavily on the prepared-ness of teacher (and student), the practical class usually involves the coordination of several sets of key players, technical support staff, tutors, demonstrators, secre-tarial support, lecturer and students. Ensuring that all parties understand their roles and are able to execute them is crucial for the success of the class. This may involve the lecturer in planning meetings with technicians, demonstrator briefings, training sessions, attention to health and safety issues and early consultation with secretarial staff, for example about room bookings, handout production. A further complexity for classes involving living materials is the problem of getting material at the right stage of development on time.

Practical courses need to be planned so that they have a logical sequence and internal coherence. However, they also need to relate closely to other parts of the curriculum so that the link between theory and practice does not become lost. In reality this can sometimes be difficult to arrange. If so, the lecturer may need to explain the relevance and make the appropriate linkages at the start and end of the class.

During the class

Laboratory classes can operate in a variety of ways depending on purpose (Carter and Lee, 1981). These can be described under three general headings: controlled exercises; experimental investigation; and mini-research projects.

The three vary in the degree to which the lecturer or the student exerts control over experimental direction and activity. A controlled exercise is defined solely by the lecturer and is completed within a set teaching period. It is suited to the devel-opment of techniques, skills and the illustration of theory in practice.

An experimental investigation normally runs over a longer period of time. It includes elements of student choice within a framework determined by the lec-turer. Such a strategy is best suited to developing scientific inquiry and the skills of investigation that can include the skills of experimental design and evaluation.

A mini-research project is a significant piece of work, which is predominantly determined by the student or group of students, in consultation with a supervisor and, where appropriate, external facilitators from academia, industry or business.

This approach can model real life research and in engineering is often used to develop the skills of design and project management.

The nature of the class will strongly influence the ways in which a supervisor and demonstrators will work together to support the students. With increasing class size, demonstrators, now more than ever before, are key personnel in the running of most laboratory or practical classes. As a minimum, the lecturer should hold a briefing meeting with the demonstrator team before the practical class and provide written notes on their role (with specific reference to the particular practical class). In addition many universities and /or departments now hold special training events for their demonstrators and evaluate their performance using student questionnaires (eg Day *et al*, 1998). Demonstrators are now considered to be an integral part of the teaching team and as such are treated accordingly by universities, with lecturers having high expectations of the quality of their contribution to student learning. Their performance in the class may well be noted in **QAA Subject Review**.

Interrogating Practice

What do you expect your demonstrators to do in your practical or laboratory classes? How much training or coaching does your university/department provide for demonstrators? How do you know if they are doing a good job?

After the class

The two main responsibilities after the practical class are to assess student work and to evaluate the teaching session. However, assessment may also commonly take place during the practical classes, eg the assessment of practical skills or skills of data recording as illustrated in Case Study 3.

Case Study 3: Student Self-assessment: Records of Practical Work in Biology

The University of Liverpool

In practical biology it is important to record information at the time of observation or experiment, otherwise details may be lost. Until recently, laboratory record books were collected in and assessed at the end of the course and allocated a mark with feedback comments. As the numbers of students taking the course has more than doubled, this is no longer possible and a method of student self-assessment has been introduced.

During the first practical class the purpose and importance of the record ·books is explained and the students are told that books will be collected for checking at the end of the course. Clear guidelines are also given to the students on the way in which each experiment should be presented (reports to include sections on introduction and aims; materials and methods; observations and results; discussion and evaluation and finally the conclusion).

For the students to judge the quality of work, they are provided with two sets of criteria. The first describes the honours degree classes and the second details the components which should normally be included in each section of the laboratory record book. The latter is given as a series of posed questions, as not every component is always appropriate in each piece of work, eg, are the aims clearly stated? Does the discussion consider each point, or data set, in a logical order? The students use the criteria and hand them in attached to their record books at appropriate places.

In the first years of running the practical assessment in this way, the tutor second-marked all the books to monitor the process but now he feels able to sample-assess, thus saving staff time. The students have also benefited in that they have a clearer view of their own level of achievement and have had the opportunity to develop their skills of evaluation and judgement.

(Dr James Chubb, Department of Environmental Biology)

Evaluation is an extremely important aspect of practical teaching and is discussed in general terms elsewhere (Chapter 13). When reviewing practical courses it is especially important to illicit the views of all the people involved in its operation, including demonstrators and technical staff as well as those of the students and the academic staff. Any changes should be made immediately to course documents, handouts, and particularly the planning schedule.

The problem class or design class

The problem or design class provides an opportunity for students, usually working in small groups of between two and eight, to practise some of the skills and apply knowledge that they have gained elsewhere in the course. Tutors and/or demonstrators are available at hand to help guide the students and to provide help.

In science courses, students often work through a sheet of set examples, problems or exercises in which they are required to use techniques (eg statistical tests), apply methods (eg mathematical equations and models) and interpret data to help solve problems. Being able to practise in a supported environment is a crucial element in the development of these intellectual skills.

In engineering courses the focus of these group activities is often a 'real' or simulated design brief. The students are required to produce a design to the specification provided to meet the needs of a third party (this might be a 'client'). In increasingly unitized courses, students often display a real difficulty when they are asked to bring together and integrate their understanding and abilities to tackle a whole design task. Therefore these classes are considered to be an important part of the curriculum (see Case Study 4).

Case Study 4: Integrated Design Projects with Industry

The University of Nottingham

Edited versions of real construction projects are used as design briefs with some direct input and supervision from the original professional team and other external practitioners to simulate a real working environment for the students.

The students work on the brief in teams of six to eight for two weeks in Semester 2. The teams produce a practical solution to the brief that requires them to merge disparate parts of the undergraduate course and develop their **key (transferable) skills**. The groups need to integrate their knowledge and understanding of engineering and financial and organizational issues while using up-to-date computing and information technology systems. The students are assessed both individually and collectively.

(Professor David Nethercot, School of Civil Engineering)

The field course

Fieldwork is an important part of the curriculum in several science subjects, particularly in the environmental and biological sciences. Similar work may also appear in engineering programmes, such as those in civil engineering and surveying. Fieldwork provides an opportunity for students to develop their skills of observation, deduction and interpretation along with a range of key (transferable) skills such as teamworking and problem solving during an intense working period. However, the cost of running residential field courses and the increase in student numbers has meant that many field courses have been lost entirely or replaced by alternative teaching and learning strategies. Most science departments have radically reviewed their field course teaching so that current provision is firmly directed towards specific cohorts of students, and it has very clear objectives.

The virtual field trip has been a recent interesting development. A range of products have been developed under the auspices of the Teaching and Learning Technology Programme (TLTP) consortia such as the Bio-Diversity Consortia's 'Sonoran Desert' field trip (Davies and Robinson, 1995) and 'Worlds of the Reef' (Davies, Seaton and Ridley, 1996). These computerized versions of field trips aim to give the student a virtual insight into the methods used to collect, analyse and interpret experimental data. However, they are likely to be much more limited in the range of skills they can help develop and the amount of social cohesion they can generate in a class.

Ways of maintaining the true field course are discussed by Jenkins (1994). He considers practical ways of doing fieldwork with large classes and with tight budgets. The Science Education Enhancement and Development programme (SEED) has also produced a series of working papers which look at the practicalities of running large, long-haul and residential field courses for undergraduate students (Ternan, Chalkley and Elmes, 1998).

On a field course students may commonly work together, in small groups of between four and eight, on a mini-project which they may have helped to devise from the outset. Staff act as advisers to help ensure that the students initially produce a satisfactory and robust experimental design and have access to appropriate equipment and resources. The students then have the opportunity to collect data in the field and to experience all the usual trials and tribulations this involves. They are also guided in their choice and use of appropriate techniques of data processing and analysis. A further feature of many field courses is the requirement that the student groups present their work to their peers (oral presentations or using posters), in addition to producing a written report for summative tutor assessment. The fieldwork presentations provide an opportunity for formative peer assessment and feedback as well as giving the students a more integrative perspective and appreciation of the range of work carried out.

The project

For many science and engineering students the single most enjoyable and influential part of their undergraduate experience is the final year project (Bliss 1990). The types of project offered in science and engineering have become more diverse in recent years. They range from the traditional experimental research project at one end of the spectrum to the investigative projects at the other end, which are based on literature reviews, computer searches, quite possibly with some original input through questionnaire survey, site visits, or interviews with experts outside the university. In between there exists a range of intermediate types of 'semi-structured' projects.

The aims of the project (adapted from Ryder and Leach, 1997) are to:

- help students develop a critical attitude when working with data and scientific models;
- give an insight into the process of research and what it is like to be a researcher;
- give students an opportunity to think for themselves and use their own initiative.

The project forms a significant component of most undergraduate programmes, typically between 20–40 per cent of the final year and often running over the whole year. The project normally involves original research and where possible benefits from being carried out in working research laboratories. Various issues in undergraduate project supervision are covered in Chapter 9.

Interrogating Practice

Think of three projects you can offer to final year students in your discipline. How well can you resource these projects with respect to your time, budget, research space and equipment? Does your department have criteria for assessing project work? Do they include provision for assessment of key (transferable) skills developed in the project?

ASSESSING STUDENT LEARNING IN SCIENCE AND ENGINEERING

The diversity of methods and types of teaching and learning sessions which make up science and engineering curricula give an indication of the potential complexity of any comprehensive assessment strategy. The requirement to assess knowledge, skills and their combined application to problem solving and design warrants a brief addition to the generic discussion of assessment in this book (Chapter 5).

Interrogating Practice

List the kinds of assessment that your students will undertake during their programme of study, indicating which methods are used for formative purposes and which for summative purposes.

The traditional unseen written examination at the end of the module or course remains a well used method for assessing the knowledge base of students. In addition several forms of continuous assessment are now commonplace, including:

- assessment of practical work and skills (Case Study 3);
- assessment of group project work (Case Study 5);
- assessment of individual projects or dissertations;
- computer-based assessment ranging from multiple-choice questions (MCQs) to computer-generated data analysis, questions and simulations.

Case Study 5: Group-based Laboratory Projects and Group-based Assessment

The Queen's University of Belfast

First-year students were assigned to mixed interest groups of four (130 students in the class). Each group had an academic tutor who would act as a consultant over the four-week period allocated to the project work. In addition, each group had a budget to complete the project on citric acid production. An intensive induction session was held in which the project management and assessment methods to be used were described to the students with supporting documentation.

Student assessment

It was considered to be important to assess both the learning process and the product of the learning task (50 per cent each). Students were asked to present their findings in the form of a scientific poster that was assessed by staff and four external consultants from commercial companies. Students presented their posters and were asked probing questions to assess their depth of knowledge and understanding. The assessment criteria used for the poster presentation (the product) were as follows:

- clarity of content;
- presentation of results;
- overall visual appeal;
- oral communication skills;
- knowledge and understanding of the topic.

Students were also involved in self and peer-assessment to assess each student's contribution to the group process (the process). Students were asked to assess themselves and their colleagues on a scale of 0–6 on the basis of the following criteria:

- reliability and punctuality;
- contribution to the experimental design;
- ability to perform allocated tasks;
- acceptance of their share of the workload;
- overall contribution to the project.

Each student was awarded the same mark for the poster contribution (product) and the moderation of marks was through the peer and self-assessment of contribution to the group work (process). The students completely accepted this method of assessment and were very fair in awarding marks (Stefani and Tariq, 1996).

(Dr Lorraine Stefani, School of Biology and Biochemistry)

No matter what form the assessment strategy takes, it must make allowance for both **formative** and **summative** aspects of **assessment**. When assessing practical work, the planning matrix in Table 20.1 can help to clarify the main aims of the assessment and help to determine which is the most appropriate method to use. The biggest problem for students and staff alike, especially in modular programmes, is assessment overload. The traditional way of assessing practical classes has been to take in and mark individual experimental write-ups or laboratory reports. The increase in student numbers has put unsustainable pressure onto the task of assessment and triggered some innovative changes in assessment methods (eg Brown, Rust and Gibbs, 1994).

The view that if students do work, the tutor must always assess it, is increasingly being challenged as being both unrealistic and unhelpful in fostering a dependency in the learner. The list which follows provides suggestions for a tutor to manage practical work assessment with larger classes.

Assessing practical work with large numbers

Small-scale suggestions:

- use a standard marking sheet to give feedback;
- use model answers with highlighted errors;
- use photocopied explanations to common problems;
- use class time to look at common misunderstandings.

Intermediate suggestions:

- provide an integrated experimental schedule or workbook with fill-in spaces for results and discussion;
- mark a random sample of reports submitted by any one student, eg two reports from eight submitted.

Large-scale suggestions:

- use simple posters during the class – mark and give feedback in class;
- use peer and/or self assessment;
- use a skills/competencies checklist to observe and assess laboratory skills;
- combine with group work so that one group is responsible for only one experiment in a round of four experiments running over a four-week period and that only produces a report for their experiment (Bratton and Mason, 1993).

Increasingly science and engineering lecturers are wanting to assess group work, activities and projects. There are a number of questions that need to be asked when embarking on this strategy, eg, do you need to assess an individual student's contribution to the group effort? Do you want to assess the product that the group produces (eg report, design, model, poster) or do you want to assess the process, that is, the way the group have worked together? Who do you want to involve in the assessment – lecturer, tutor, demonstrators, students?

A number of difficult assessment issues are revealed by these questions. How can you sensibly extract an individual student's contribution from an activity that was designed to engender collaboration and group effort? There are many reasons why this may be necessary or desirable, such as university regulations, validating body requirements, and to prevent 'free-riding' students doing well in assessment. There are several ways in which this can be achieved – many of which include the use of clear criteria to assess the different elements that make up an appropriate contribution. Others include the use of **peer assessment** within the group, with the outcomes then being used to weight a tutor's mark. Yet other approaches have provided a shared group mark for the group's product (eg a design model) but have included an element of individual assessment, either through a written report or an oral presentation, as a weighting mechanism (see Case Study 3.). The simplest approach seems to be to award a group mark for the product which is shared between the group members in a way that they think is fair. In the majority of cases, experience has shown that the groups will split the mark equally between members and only in exceptional cases will they feel strongly enough to distribute the marks in such a way as to penalize a member who has not made an appropriate contribution (Seabrook, 1993).

FUTURE DIRECTIONS

Many of the changes that we have witnessed in the last 20 years will no doubt continue to have an impact on the science and engineering lecturer, curriculum and student. Strategies for making the most of limited contact time will be increasingly explored. In recent times we have seen the HEFCE support initiatives like the Course Design for Resource Based Learning Project which sought to encourage greater use of paper-based (written) and similar low technology learning resources, such as audio-taped lectures (Exley and Gibbs, 1993).

The promotion and use of communication and information technology solutions to teaching problems is also being strongly backed by all the UK funding councils, under the Joint Information Systems Committee (JISC). Making better use of computer packages already developed, rather than encouraging staff to become developers themselves, is the supported approach under Phase 3 (Implementation) of the TLTP. The development of 24, discipline-based, Computers in Teaching Initiative Centres (CTI) has helped to give a focus to this rapidly changing area of educational development.

Interrogating Practice

If you do not already know where your discipline's CTI Centre is based, visit the CTI Web site at http://www.cti.ac.uk/

OVERVIEW

The increased and widened student participation in higher education has had a profound effect on the ways in which the science and the engineering curricula can be effectively delivered. Many of the traditional practices of teaching and learning in science and engineering have not been sustainable without adaptation and innovation. Some of the changes have felt negative, put in place as a way of coping with demand, while trying to maintain quality of teaching and learning. However, many of the developments have had a very beneficial impact on enhancing student learning and assessment practices. Furthermore, they have provided an opportunity for staff and students to think about the acquisition of a wide range of key (transferable) skills, in addition to gaining a thorough knowledge and understanding of their particular discipline.

REFERENCES

Andresen, LW (ed) (1994) Lecturing to Large Groups: A guide to doing it less ...but better, SEDA Paper 81, The Staff and Educational Development Association, Birmingham

Association of Graduate Recruiters (1995) Skills for Graduates in the 21st Century, Cambridge

Becher, T (1989) Academic Tribes and Territories: Intellectual enquiry and the culture of disciplines, Society for Research into Higher Education and Open University Press, Milton Keynes

Black, PJ and Ogborn, J (1979) Laboratory work in undergraduate teaching, in Learning Strategies in University Science, ed D McNally, University College Cardiff Press, Cardiff

Bliss, J (1990) Students' reactions to undergraduate science: laboratory and project work, in The Student Laboratory and the Science Curriculum, ed E Hegarty-Hazel, Routledge, London

Bratton, D and Mason, D (1993) Learning by teaching: an experiment in practical chemistry, in Innovations in Science Teaching, eds K Exley and I Moore, Standing Conference on Education Development Paper 74, SCED (now the Staff and Educational Development Association) Birmingham

Brown, S, Rust, C and Gibbs, G (1994) Strategies for Diversifying Assessment in Higher Education, The Oxford Centre for Staff Development, Oxford

Carter, G and Lee, LS (1981) A sample survey of departments of electrical engineering to ascertain the aims, objectives and methods of assessing first year undergraduate laboratory work in electronic and electrical engineering, *International Journal of Electrical Engineering Education*, 18, pp 113–20

CVCP (1998) *Skills Development in Higher Education*, Full Report, The Committee of Vice-Chancellors and Principals, London

Davies, P and Robinson, D (1995) *Sonoran Desert: A Multimedia Field Trip to the Cactus Desert of Arizona*, Ransom Publishing Ltd

Davies, P, Seaton, N and Ridley, J (1996) *Worlds of the Reef: A Multimedia Expedition to the Rainforests of the Sea*, Ransom Publishing Ltd

ED20 (1991) *Enterprise in Higher Education: Key features of enterprise in higher education 1990–91*, DFE, London

Entwistle, N, Thompson, S and Tait, H (1992) *Guidelines for Promoting Learning in Higher Education*, Centre for Research on Learning and Instruction, University of Edinburgh, Edinburgh

Exley, K and Gibbs, G (1993) *Course Design for Resource Based Learning: Science*, Oxford Centre for Staff Development, Oxford

HEFCE (1995–96) *Quality Assessment Reports, Chemical Engineering*, www.hefce/niss.ac.uk/education/hefce/qar/chemical_engineering.html

HMSO (1964) (The Hale Report) *Report of the Committee on University Teaching Methods*, Her Majesty's Stationery Office, London

Isaacs, G (1994) Lecturing practices and note-taking purposes, *Studies in Higher Education*, **19** (2), pp 203–16

Jacques, D (1991) *Learning in Groups*, 2nd edn, Kogan Page, London

Jenkins, A (1994) Thirteen ways of doing fieldwork with large classes/more students, *Journal of Geography in Higher Education*, 18, pp 143–54

Jennings, A and Ferguson, JD (1995) Focusing on communication skills in engineering education, *Studies in Higher Education*, **20** (3), 305–14

Jervis, L (1999) *Laboratory Work in Science Education*, Science Education Enhancement and Development (SEED), University of Plymouth

Kirschner, PA and Meester, MAM (1988) The laboratory in higher science education: problems, premises and objectives, *Higher Education*, 17 (1), pp 81–98

Phillips, M (1981) Early history of physics laboratories for students at the college level, *American Journal of Physics*, 49, pp 522–27

Ryder, J and Leach, J (1997) Research projects in the undergraduate science course: students learning about science through enculturation, proceedings of the 4th International Student Learning Symposium, ed G Gibbs, Oxford Centre for Staff and Learning Development, Oxford

Seabrook, MF (1993) Enterprise in rural business development, in *Innovations in Science Teaching*, eds K Exley and I Moore, Standing Conference on Educational Development, SCED Paper 74 (now the Staff and Educational Development Association), Birmingham

Shepherd, R (1979) *Individual Practical Work in the Teaching of Physics in England*, University of Leeds.

Sieber, VK *et al* (in press) The Workbook: an innovative approach to first level science teaching, in *Innovations in Science Teaching*, 2, eds K Exley and I Moore, the Staff and Educational Development Association, Birmingham

Smeby, JC (1996) Disciplinary differences in university teaching, *Studies in Higher Education*, **21**, (1), pp 69–79

Stefani, LAJ and Tariq, VN (1996) Running group practical projects for first year undergraduate students, *Journal of Biological Education*, 30 (1), pp 36–44

Ternan, BS, Chalkley, BS and Elmes, A (1998) *New Developments in Field Work*, Science Education Enhancement and Development (SEED), University of Plymouth

Whiting, A et al (1998) *A New Team-based Approach to Practical Work with Chemistry*, Snapshots of Innovation 1998, Enterprise Centre for Learning and Curriculum Development, University of Manchester and UMIST, Manchester

FURTHER READING

Boud, D et al (1986) *Teaching in Laboratories*, The Society for Research into Higher Education and Open University Press, Milton Keynes. A full and detailed overview.

Exley, K and Moore, I (1993) *Innovations in Science Teaching*, Standing Conference on Educational Development Paper 74, SCED (now the Staff and Educational Development Association), Birmingham. A collection of edited case studies, detailing a range of teaching, learning and assessment approaches. Volume 2 is currently in press.

Gibbs, G, Gregory, R and Moore, I (1997) *Labs and Practicals with More Students and Fewer Resources, Teaching More Students* [7]. The Oxford Centre for Staff Development, Oxford. Readable and practical book offering a range of tested hints and tips.

Moore, I and Exley, K (1994) *Alternative Approaches to Teaching Engineering* (Volumes 1 and 2), The Universities' and Colleges' Staff Development Agency (UCoSDA), in association with The Engineering Professors' Council, Sheffield. A collection of edited case studies from engineers who have introduced novel approaches into their teaching and assessment practices.

21

Key Aspects of Teaching and Learning in Arts and Humanities

Krista Cowman and Sue Grace

AIMS AND INTRODUCTION

This chapter focuses on the subject areas of the arts and humanities which use primarily traditional teaching methods, ie the lecture, seminar and tutorial. This includes such areas as archaeology, English, history, philosophy, theology and women's studies, and areas of geography, most notably human geography, but does not include the performing arts. The chapter builds on the earlier generic chapters, and aims to examine the distinctive aspects of teaching in the arts and humanities. It will thus focus on:

- designing teaching programmes;
- large group teaching;
- communication and information technology;
- assessment.

As the teaching of these disciplines assumes the student possesses the requisite skills to acquire factual knowledge, this chapter explores the various ways in which students can be encouraged to engage with the subject at deeper **cognitive** and **affective** levels, as well as with particular ideas or theoretical approaches.

DESIGNING TEACHING PROGRAMMES IN ARTS AND HUMANITIES

One key feature in the success of any teaching programme is adequate programme design. This is an area which not all new teachers will initially feel the need to consider because frequently new academics will inherit ready-designed **modules** or **seminar** programmes. Within such ready-made programmes, however, it is usually considered desirable for teaching staff to make modifications to programmes in order to exploit their own particular expertise and knowledge. However, it is essential to have clear **aims** and **learning objectives** prior to the modification of any teaching programme. Chapter 4 of this book describes an outcome-based model of course design. Part of the process will be identification of learning needs of students, of the requirements of the institution, of the prior level of understanding and knowledge of the students, and of the abilities and knowledge of the deliverer(s) of the programme.

Interrogating Practice

Reflect on planning a discursive session. How do you move from the general aims to the more specific learning objectives? How can one frame learning objectives which allow sufficient latitude for the development of creativity, imagination and personal meaning and insight? How does such an approach help to focus on both the cognitive and affective development of your students, as well as on the content you wish to explore?

Challenges to traditional organization

Perhaps even more so than for other disciplines, new underpinning ideologies in the arts and humanities have challenged traditional course models, including the ways in which they are designed, to include their rationale. For example, in history or English literature, post-structuralism and post-modernism have challenged traditional hierarchies and consequently had impact upon courses structured upon outmoded notions of privilege. Much of this has raised contentious debate about the theory and practice within the discipline (Jenkins, 1991). Process and content are often inextricably bound in arts and humanities courses. Other social and intellectual changes have sometimes challenged courses based upon traditional male-dominated historical chronologies or upon traditional Anglo-centred canons of literature. New kinds of course coherence and structure have had to be created to cope with these challenges. The 'tools of the trade' of many disciplines in arts and humanities have changed out of all recognition in the past 30 years, and have in turn altered the nature of the disciplines. Whether this is because of intellectual movements, such as deconstruction or technological advances, eg in archaeology, the impact of these movements and changes has to be reflected in both process and content of curricula.

In some departments and disciplines, matters such as these will have been completely responsible for shaping course aims. But it is essential that newly-created programmes should be able to provide a clear sense of cognitive development and progression for students of the course programme. Such intellectual development can be more difficult to identify in arts courses than in disciplines clearly dependent on developing skills where there is a more apparent linear progression. Furthermore, teachers have to allow for their own subjectivities when determining intellectual progression in areas strewn with value judgements.

The impact of modularity

For students on very flexible **modular** courses, it is important that the course teacher or leader has a clear notion of the overall learning experience of the student, for this can quickly become fragmented and patchy. For staff teaching large numbers of students this can be an extremely difficult task. A new lecturer must strive to be acquainted with appropriate **levels** of work for each year group and to provide increasing levels of intellectual sophistication for second and third-year courses. The Higher Education Funding Council for England (HEFCE) subject reviews, for example, found this was not the case in all the history teaching it encountered (NISS, 1997).

Equal opportunities: respecting diversity

Concern for equal opportunities has been evident in both curriculum design and in the process of delivering the curriculum. In the case of the former, the past 20 years have seen the rise of women's studies to a respected and, indeed, essential component of the arts and humanities curricula. Furthermore, more recently, it has been recognized that the many arts and humanities curricula could be viewed as exclusive, for example, due to their predominant Eurocentricity. This issue has been taken up by the different subject bodies and, indeed, is frequently under review by universities' equal opportunities committees.

When considering curriculum delivery, to what extent should teachers planning an arts and humanities course be aware of their students' backgrounds and prior experience? Most teachers would agree that they should at least be aware of the level of the students' prior academic knowledge and of their experience of the academic subject in question. The level of prior learning can be more difficult to ascertain in discursive fields of study than in subject areas where knowledge is acquired more sequentially. In the arts and humanities, the level of personal involvement between supervisor and supervisee may be an even more fraught and contentious one because, for example, of the potentially political or emotive nature of some content and responses to it. There are many areas of discussion touched on in arts and humanities that relate to the inner lives of students. Some discussion sessions are particularly likely to raise controversy. For example, the discussion of literary texts may call for a particularly careful consideration of issues of race, gender or disability, both in the text and among the learners. The latter may not always be obvious: for example, although text-based discussion sessions would prove particularly inaccessible to sight-impaired students, less apparent may be the needs of the slightly hearing-impaired student. Teachers must consider strategies for dealing with such situations if and when they occur. Language problems for international students can be particularly intense in discussions of abstract concepts. It is a difficult job to set the pace to include such students and yet to satisfy others who wish to move faster.

Many arts and humanities disciplines are strongly rooted in cultural assumptions. The most basic of these notions may need re-examining in an internationally mixed group and the teacher will need to decide how much time, and what level of priority, they are prepared to give to such activity. Such features may be less of a problem where seminars are task-orientated or skill-based, but in the arts and humanities this is not often the case. Case Study 1 is therefore offered as an interesting example of an English and drama module designed to analyse the changes in the status of Shakespeare as a cultural and educational icon in the last 20 years, incorporating skills development through **field work**.

Case Study 1: Shakespeare in the Classroom

Queen Mary and Westfield College, University of London

This is a single-semester course for second and third year undergraduates at Queen Mary and Westfield (QMW), but through them it also reaches the staff and upwards of 200 school children every year in the very deprived inner-London borough of Tower Hamlets. It has been running for five years with year six and year eight children in three different schools: a mixed comprehensive where 70 per cent of the children speak English as a second language; an all-boys comprehensive; and a mixed Roman Catholic primary school.

The course is a direct result of a campaign that I spearheaded at the time of the introduction of the National Curriculum, in order to change initial government plans for the teaching and examination of Shakespeare at Key Stage 3 (14 years). I examine the critical, cultural and political issues surrounding the transmission of Shakespeare in contemporary multicultural Britain, and choose plays that will encourage students to question the comfortable heritage approach. The most successful have been *King Lear*, and (in conjunction with a production that I directed at QMW) *Richard III*. Both of these are, of course, very violent, but both are concerned with relationships between children and adults; the children loved them on both counts.

After an initial five weeks in college – learning about the chosen play and about ways of teaching it – students go into school, working in groups of two or three to a class of 30 children. All children within the year-group are included. Seminars continue in college during the teaching practice and I also make regular school visits. The project culminates with an end-of-term presentation to the year-group in which each class performs extracts from the play and from their own creative writing. Each group of undergraduates is given a single mark for their classroom work (including lesson plans and teaching diary). Students then individually submit 4000-word critical essays on the theory behind the practice.

This course is no picnic. Many of the children have already had bad experiences of life and can be correspondingly difficult to deal with. My students have to reappraise their own beliefs: about the subject, about social issues and, not least, about themselves. Students regularly tell me that the experience has changed their lives, one describing it as 'without doubt, one of the most harrowing, soul-destroying and frustrating experiences of my life. It was also, because of, not in spite of, this, one of the most rewarding'.

The results achieved by both school pupils and undergraduates on the course over the last five years have vindicated my initial hopes for its efficacy as a teaching and learning method. The process demands considerable trust between school and university, and between teachers, students and pupils. The undergraduates require constant monitoring and support, but there is a strong sense that everyone involved, from the youngest child to the most experienced teacher, is contributing to the intellectual and personal development of everyone else, and likewise learning from that experience. The technique is eminently transferable to other subject areas.

(Ros King, School of English and Drama)

Achieving professional distance

The new teacher must decide what professional 'distance' means, not only in respect of the social boundaries but often, in arts and humanities, in relation to the academic content of a seminar. To what extent should the teacher engage their personal self in academic debate? For many teachers in the arts and humanities disciplines, the answer will be 'not at all' and yet these are disciplines where content and ethics, practice and belief, are likely to impinge upon each other. For some teachers, student expectations will thus challenge the notion of the distant academic. Women's studies' students, for example, frequently see the need for their staff to identify, in some demonstrable way, with feminist politics and practices. Whether such personal involvement is desirable, or whether or not it is necessary, such expectations can cause changing dynamics within seminars, and teachers in such fields must at least be aware of them (Parsons, 1993). Further to this, the teacher needs to ask whether his or her students should be expected to remain at the same emotional distance from the content of academic material as staff, or whether a different level of personal involvement will be expected from students. Such problems are not exclusive to the arts and humanities, but are more likely to play a part in seminars where social constructions, beliefs and practices underpin the academic content.

Interrogating Practice

What does professional distance mean in terms of your discipline? How could you deal with issues of professional distance in your teaching?

Updating courses

The need to update material may be less pressing for many arts and humanities teachers than, for example, those teaching law or medicine. Many arts teachers would wish to question the notion of change for change's sake, especially as the currency of information can be seen to operate in a different way to its operation in the science-based subjects or social sciences. And so it might, for example, be easier for a historian to adapt an out-of-date article on a reading list to demonstrate the historiography of the topic in question rather than discard it as totally irrelevant. Indeed, in some arts disciplines, a 30-year-old article may have as much to contribute to an academic argument as a recently written piece. Nonetheless, this does not mean that lecturers do not need to constantly re-visit their course aims to ensure they are up to date.

While innovation for its own sake is not necessary in terms of course material, the arts lecturer should not be tempted to slip into the traditionally used teaching methods because the content remains unchanged. Cultural change in higher education and the changing mission statements of institutions require arts and humanities lecturers to constantly review the aims and objectives of the programmes for which they have responsibility. Most teachers find that while a second run of a course can be an improvement upon the first and can consolidate their ideas and practice, it is helpful to include new material and/or new approaches to ensure freshness and vigour in the programme.

LARGE GROUP TEACHING WITHIN THE ARTS AND HUMANITIES

It is impossible, in a short chapter, to systematically examine the many varied teaching and learning strategies employed in the arts and humanities at British universities. This section will therefore focus upon one type of teaching activity that has become increasingly common in teaching in the arts and humanities in the light of increased student numbers – large seminar groups. Many of the issues will translate to other types of group teaching, but in large groups the hazards seem to be more overt to those who are new to teaching. Whereas, traditionally, much teaching in arts and humanities has been in large lectures or very small (and even one-to-one) **tutorials**, this is no longer an option for most institutions. Increasingly university teachers are likely to be asked to teach larger groups of students.

From the points about curriculum content above, it follows that the seminar forum, where pre-encountered ideas are discussed among students, remains at the heart of much arts and humanities teaching, where discussion and debate are essential to the testing out of ideas and the finding of meaning, ie to aspects associated with **deeper** approaches to learning. Yet academics will increasingly find themselves encountering teaching and learning situations which do not mirror their own undergraduate experiences. The recent expansion of higher education has led to an unprecedented increase in the size of seminar groups, with numbers often upwards of 25. This presents particular problems when dealing with courses which are more concerned with theoretical approaches than factual knowledge.

Interrogating Practice

Reflect on your seminar teaching skills. Referring back to Chapter 8, what other methods might you try? How might these approaches ensure that each student is engaging with the issues?

In such situations, specific strategies are required to ensure the delivery of high quality teaching. These can be divided into three main areas: pre-course, which includes many of the planning issues already discussed in this chapter and also entails planning for the physical environment; delivery, which includes events within the actual contact time of the module or programme; and the 'final stages', which raises issues of summative **feedback** and **assessment**.

Issues of preparation

Large seminar groups require particularly thorough preparation. Teachers have to take careful preparation of academic content but do not, at least to the same extent, have to prepare for interaction with students. However, they will need to be clear how far they have clear outcomes in mind which will govern the extent and directions of their control of the seminar. By contrast, in a small seminar, the teacher has much more time to get to know students within the seminar room. A module delivered to 12 students in two-hour time slots would allow a student a rough time allocation of 10 minutes per session for interaction (if required – and acknowledging that conversation does not, in practice, work to allocation).

One of the greatest dangers is that of the 'lost' student. At worst this individual can disappear from the teaching and learning process altogether. However, there are other ways in which a student can fail to receive high quality teaching simply by being part of a large group. The physical presence of a student in a seminar room is not always sufficient to guarantee their participation. Particular strategies can be employed by the teacher to help avoid non-participation. For example, one of the successful methods increasingly employed to ensure all students do participate, and do have the opportunity to engage further with the material under discussion, but at their own pace, is through use of **poster boards** or discussion groups on the Web. A number of disciplines now paste seminar papers on a departmental website, with the expectation that all students will be involved in following up reading and/or discussion. Another way of increasing student talk time is short, focused, sub-groups, of student-to-student discussion within the larger seminar.

Interrogating Practice

Much has been written about the role of the tutor within a seminar (to draw out; to question; to probe; to expose; to convey knowledge; to play devil's advocate; etc). Jot down six aspects as they relate to your discipline. How will you ensure that all students engage with set tasks and subsequent debriefing activities?

Getting to know the group

It is important to be familiar with as many of the group's names as possible prior to the first meeting. Faces can be matched to names by looking at departmental files. Learn the names as soon as possible. A large group becomes far less daunting to all when it is broken down into individuals and discussion is infinitely easier (and possibly more meaningful) when facilitated by the use of names. For example, 'icebreaking' exercises can be used to aid this process and students can be encouraged to use names rather then 'he' or 'she' (Brown and Race, 1997).

Physical environment

It is the responsibility of the tutor to ensure that there is sufficient space within the teaching room to accommodate all the students comfortably. If this is not the case, the group may have to be divided, with different activities organized for the two cohorts. The furniture should be arranged, before the students arrive, in such a way as to encourage easy communication between group members (see Chapter 8). Chairs should be positioned to avoid making individuals deliver contributions over the heads of other students. Staff must remember that it can be extremely intimidating for students to speak in front of large groups, and this is a **key skill** which undoubtedly will feature in the programme aims, thus necessitating the appropriate level of training.

Delivery

Delivery should be well planned for, and is the vehicle by which promotion of the learning outcomes occurs. Careful consideration of the different strategies to encourage such learning as can best take place in small groups has been rehearsed elsewhere (Chapter 8), and this is offered in practical terms in the case studies of this chapter. Supporting students in developing the key skills, such as presentational skills through the use of structured guidelines and presentation, is illustrated in Case Study 2.

Case Study 2: Population Geography II

Queen Mary and Westfield College, University of London

This is a third level course which attracts about 40 students. All have taken the prerequisite course, population geography, and so can be assumed to have a basic knowledge of the course material. The course is organized around four key themes and aims particularly to encourage reading in depth as well as develop a wider understanding of the interrelationship between the themes. The format is a combination of lectures and student presentations. Every student must make a presentation on an aspect of one of the four themes, which they then write up as a course paper of 2500 words.

Students are given detailed guidelines on making the presentation, which must include the use of at least two overheads, one of which must include the structure of the presentation. Presentations take up to 10 minutes and are followed by about 10 minutes of discussion. All students have to be prepared to ask relevant questions of the presenter and develop a wider discussion of the themes of the presentations.

This method ensures active learning. The students read in considerable depth about an aspect of the course in which they are particularly interested, and present the material both orally and as a course paper. It widens the material of the course for all the other students and, in particular, promotes discussion, not only in the weeks of the seminars but also during lectures, since students feel much more confident about talking in a fairly large group. For the course teacher, it brings out difficulties students may be having with the course material and develops a far more interactive mode of teaching.

(Dr Ray Hall, Department of Geography)

Case Study 3, which follows, provides a further example of the delivery of a seminar to a large group of history students, and is designed to ensure all members of the group are active participants.

> ## Case Study 3: Seminar on British Women in the First World War

This two-hour seminar formed part of a course on the history of the First World War. The focus of the course was on social and cultural approaches. This particular seminar was placed a few weeks into the course, so certain levels of background knowledge could be assumed. There were 35 students in the group.

Preparation

There were two main tasks for this session: discussion of a particular article, and consideration and discussion of primary source material. An article (a fairly complex theoretical piece that explores some of the radical changes which might be made to conventional historical narratives of war from women's experiences) by Joan Scott (1987) had been previously set as required reading. As well as having to read this, students were encouraged to prepare further by reading selections of their own choosing from a wider reading list. It was therefore expected that they would come to the seminar with both some general background knowledge about the activities of British women during the First World War and with some awareness of the theoretical implications of this knowledge.

Arrangement and organization: ensuring participation

Organization is of prime importance when dealing with large numbers. It is essential to ensure that everybody in a group has ample opportunity to undertake adequate preparation. A summary sheet was handed out at the very first seminar with the required reading for each session, and the point made, verbally and in writing, that absence one week was no excuse for not having the reading for the next session.

As usual, the room was pre-arranged to facilitate small groups of no more than seven. When students entered, they were given activity sheets with some very open-ended questions regarding their preparatory reading, and allocated some time to discuss these questions in their small groups. This technique encourages participation in three particular ways:

- The seminar instantly focuses. It is very easy to 'lose' a large group in the early minutes of settling down.

- The questions relate to pre-set reading. If followed consistently, students will quickly realize that the reading is essential and that participation is impossible without it. (You may have to reinforce this point with some groups by requesting that those who have obviously not done the reading leave the seminar.)
- The questions are also broad and open-ended. This allows particular interests and enthusiasms to be followed up as well as offering space for uncertainties to be voiced. This can be further facilitated through a final question which encourages students to detail the concept which they found the most difficult.

After a suitable discussion period (15–20 minutes) during which the tutor moved around between particular groups, individuals from each group reported back on their findings and thoughts. At this point, it is essential to avoid creating an atmosphere of 'performance'. What is wanted is a forum for discussion. Encourage this by positioning yourself at the side rather than the front of a room so that remarks are not filtered through you. (A useful technique is to take notes from the discussion on an OHP transparency which you can display while remaining in an unobtrusive sitting position.)

After a period of sharing views and general discussion, the seminar then moved on to consider some primary source material. With large classes it is best to offer different materials to each small group so that discussion can be both broad and comparative. Always be aware of how difficult it is to be the last group reporting back – it is useful to swap the speaking order rather than simply going around the room in the same direction.

For this particular seminar, the primary material consisted of a short propaganda film (15 minutes) shown to the entire group, and sufficient examples of newspaper reports, propaganda posters and autobiographical extracts for each small group to look at something different. The discussions this time were less formally structured than previously, with students simply being asked to talk about what they had seen and read, and think about how Joan Scott's theories might be applied to these particular examples. Groups were instructed to appoint a raconteur to summarize their findings. After showing the film and distributing the material, the tutor physically withdrew from the room while the group discussions took place. This is a useful tactic to ensure that discussion does not become a one-to-one dialogue between students and tutor. During the first part of the seminar, the tutor had been moving around between groups and was able to detect any particular problems regarding preparation or uncertainty of the main subject matter at an early stage.

As the discussion itself was less formally structured, this made it easier to impose a more rigid structure on the final part of the seminar which again involved sharing views. The use of respondents ensured that each of the different items distributed was introduced to the entire group. The balance of discussion/reportage was maintained through the tutor's use of carefully inserted questions such as 'what do other groups think of this?', encouraging listeners to formulate responses to all the materials.

The tutor's main input into whole group teaching came at the end of this seminar when a short period of time was set aside for summary and looking ahead to the following week. The tutor's summary both pulled together the main points that had arisen through discussions and also emphasized particular points which may not have featured, but were important to the subject. The final moments of the seminar were devoted to 'housekeeping', especially to reminding students of the requirements for the coming week.

(Dr Krista Cowman)

Final stages

The completion of a large-group seminar brings its own particular problems. Preparing students for assessment takes time. When devising assessments within the arts and humanities, it is vital that the teacher retains familiarity with new developments in technology in order to ensure that assessment continues to evaluate the skills and the knowledge base for which it is designed. The arrival of the Internet and CD ROM as familiar tools within higher education poses particular problems. For example, students have access to far more information than ever before but may be no better equipped to evaluate all that they encounter. Furthermore, plagiarism becomes more difficult to detect. Perhaps even more fundamental is that many arts research projects, for example, have traditionally begun by the building up of annotated bibliographies aimed at encouraging critical reading within a chosen field and evaluating selected texts. However, increasingly students appear to acquire such bibliographies from CD ROMs. The exercise is still valid but the resultant skills are quite different. The production of an annotated bibliography within the arts and humanities thus becomes more of a gauge of students' familiarity with new technology than of critical reading within a discipline.

Interrogating Practice

Does your institution or department have a policy on plagiarism? How is it enforced? Do your students understand what this term means? If not, what could be done to ensure that they do?

Resources

Large groups present particular problems for the provision of resources within the arts and humanities. It is important to ensure that each member of the group has adequate access to necessary resources and that sufficient material is provided for every member of the group. The preparation of the reading list must be thorough and attention given to library availability. Communications and information technologies (**C&IT**), particularly the **World Wide Web**, can ensure students have access to all course hardware as well as selected documents for reading (copyright issues having been attended to), as well as access to on-line discussion groups and, if appropriate, their course tutor.

The majority of programmes in history and English, as has been noted, will be aimed either at familiarizing students with as broad a range of materials as possible or at close textual analysis. When large numbers of students are chasing one book, such work becomes difficult. Increasing financial pressure on students makes it difficult to assume they will buy the necessary texts, especially in the arts and humanities when the number of essential texts for each module can be in double figures. Relying on journal articles, multiple library copies, and short-loan collections, are only partial solutions. Even assuming a 12-hour per day, 6-day a week opening of libraries, within a group of 40, this would allow each student less than two hours in a week with a key text. Many teachers are now taking advantage of the new copyright legislation to produce copyright cleared 'readers' of photocopied articles which the students purchase, the price covering the clearance costs. This has obvious advantages: the teacher can select precisely the most appropriate and up-to-date material and the 'lost' student has no excuse for not preparing for the seminar.

COMMUNICATION AND INFORMATION TECHNOLOGY (C&IT)

As in all disciplines, a current and pressing matter is the extent to which teachers use C&IT (see Chapter 12). It has become less important that students should know specific cultural sequences, for example in archaeology, geography or history, as opposed to the acquisition of the skills and methods by which data are collected and analysed. However, it is essential that if there is heavy use of such methods, the content must not be controlled by the process. Ever burgeoning though material is, it is imperative that teachers do not feel pressured into covering particular areas simply because software exists. Conversely there is, perhaps, a reluctance to engage in the use of C&IT as arts staff may feel they have less knowledge and experience. Arts and humanities staff may feel ever more pressured into providing computer support to students when they feel ill-equipped to do so. Furthermore, access for their students, even to terminals, may be problematic as student numbers grow. Some universities appear to be experiencing serious difficulties in keeping pace with IT demands. And yet, greater use of electronic software can ease access to difficult to obtain primary sources for arts and humanities students and, so long as the downloading of electronic documents does not simply become an excuse for the transference of costs of photocopied course materials to the students, such devices can be immensely helpful to all those concerned. The use of C&IT is a key skill, and students' ability to use and exploit technology will be essential for the majority of students' future employability (Miall, 1990). For example, an essential prerequisite for professional historians is the skill and ability to access and use electronic records, and the situation for many professional geographers is even more pressing.

In the arts and humanities, as perhaps in other disciplines, technology is helping in the borderlands between traditional higher education and types of educational experiences that are becoming increasingly important in that sector, for example in flexible, distance, lifelong and open learning projects. What is clear is that as student numbers, and particularly class sizes, increase in higher education, modes of delivery may well need to replicate patterns traditionally found in other sectors of adult education. Thus **CAL** (computer-assisted learning) distance packages which can be used at a later time may not only be facilitating off-campus learning but also enhancing the educational experiences of those on-campus who are increasingly being taught in large groups. Similarly, packages designed as open learning packages can be used to offer flexibility and variety of pace to traditional higher education arts students (Wisdom and Gibbs, 1994). As yet, Web-based learning seems generally stronger in the social sciences and sciences but, with the aid of initiatives such as the Computers in Teaching Initiative (**CTI**), there is considerable scope for those in the arts to use such methods for innovative teaching. Such an initiative is offered in Case Study 4. What teachers do need to determine is what types and range of outcome can be achieved by which methods, whether they use technology or not.

Interrogating Practice

Consider how you would use an electronic discussion group in the context of a module in which you teach (or how could you improve existing usage)? Would this be a more or less efficient and effective method than a face to face seminar? (You may wish to read Chapter 12 before considering this question.)

Case Study 4: Integrating C&IT: Year One Archaeology Module

University of York

Background

This case study outlines the use of SYASS (Southampton-York Archaeological Simulation System (arising from the CTI). Its aims are twofold. First, to raise students' experience of excavation management through computer simulation and, second, to raise the students' competence in the use of computers.

The process of an archaeological investigation (or excavation) is a multi-stage process which involves:

- the creation of the research design for the investigation;
- dimensioning the problem and its possible solution;
- conducting the detailed investigation, continuously recording and assessing results;
- analysing and report writing.

In York, SYASS was introduced as one element in a year one module on data analysis, involving seven and a half contact hours per week. Students are taught the theoretical aspects of site excavation, context description, the stratigraphic mix, etc. SYASS is an integral part of the course to enable students to explore for themselves practical aspects of data analysis.

The software

SYASS offers a simulation of an archaeological excavation, placing students in an archaeological site about which the SYASS authors knew everything. Its objectives are, first, to introduce the student to some of the basic methods used by the archaeologist in the course of field work and, second, to consider how the archaeologist knows where to dig, what is involved in the process, to include dating techniques. All students are provided with a 'budget', within which they must determine how to allot money to different parts of the project. SYASS can be used in a seminar with direct input from the tutor to highlight certain points, or as a free-standing exercise to allow students to be involved in the different stages of investigation as follows:

1. Research procedure. This involves all the preparation for excavation, to include map and archive analysis, reconnaissance methods such as aerial photography, costing, and gaining funding. Further to this reconnaissance, the student can begin to formulate a suitable research design and goals for the excavation.
2. Excavation procedure. The student is asked to choose how the excavation is to proceed. Recovery is divided into six levels from A to F. Level A is the pre-excavation phase and includes activities such as field walking. Level F is the post-excavation phase and consists of such activities as pit sieving. B to E describe methods from bulldozer to paintbrush.
3. Defining an area for excavation. Further to determination of the recovery level, the student, using a set of X and Y coordinates, is asked to specify where and to what depth to excavate. The software allows the student to excavate an area of any size – from trench to whole site.
4. Excavation. Further to the setting of parameters outlined in 1–3 above, the programme proceeds to 'excavate', which entails the querying and selection of information from the database. This results in the student being told – via a counter – how many archaeological features have been encountered, how much money has been spent, and how much money is remaining.
5. Analysis. This is the core of SYASS in that the student is placed in a position to interpret the data that were generated in the process of this activity.

Conclusions

SYASS has continued to be developed as an aid to ensure students have a full understanding of archaeological methods and terminology. Exposing students to a teaching and learning activity in which they have to manipulate resources provides them with skills of wider applicability, particularly those of data management.

(Dr Julian Richards, Department of Archaeology)

ASSESSMENT

Many generic issues relating to assessment have already been discussed (see Chapter 5) and so this section will pinpoint one or two issues that arise in arts and humanities assessment.

Traditional modes of assessment (eg essays, reports)

An obvious issue of assessment in the arts and humanities arises from the fact that the standardizing and marking of discursive scripts can be time-consuming, subjective and problematic. This makes it all the more important to devise assessment criteria which are as clear as possible to tutors and students. New staff and part-time tutors should ensure that they obtain help in familiarizing themselves with the standards required by the department. Many teachers have probably experienced the perplexities of wondering just what does constitute a 65 per cent or a 'first' in their particular department. Guidance is essential for establishing essay marking criteria and especially for devising standards for a 'top', 'middle' and a 'bottom' in a pile of essays. No staff member should feel inadequate because they do not inherently possess such knowledge, and it is the responsibility of departments to provide training in all facets of assessment policy and practice for new staff.

Arts and humanities staff are not frequently bound by the requirements of professional bodies. Of itself this offers more freedom for such academics to determine the nature of the subject they are teaching, and therefore the criteria upon which it will be assessed. In practice, such freedom can make choice more complex. Academic departments must make their own judgement, for example, upon the extent to which vocational skills will be incorporated and assessed in their subjects, bearing in mind the programme **specification** template of the Quality Assurance Agency (QAA, 1998).

Clearly, the ultimate assessment is the **summative** assessment of the final degree mark, but increasingly, higher education teachers have seen the benefits of emphasizing **formative** assessment. It is only when such diagnostic assessment regularly occurs that a teacher and student can check what learning is taking place. Almost always, learning in the arts and humanities must be concerned with processing and analysing the information which has been presented. Mere transmission of information has a limited place in most arts subjects, with discussion having long been an integral part of learning in this field. Feedback to learners allows them to test and stretch their understanding. In several arts and humanities disciplines, feedback on ideas has often come via the seminar. The opportunity for this is now limited. So too is time for detailed individual comment on essays. Increasingly, alternative approaches to assessment are used to address these concerns, such as peer and oral assessment.

Oral assessment

Alternative methods of assessment to the written examination or essay are increasingly being used. In a number of situations, oral assessment in the arts is becoming more common, and clear criteria must be in place for such assessment. It may be helpful for those new to this form of assessment in the arts and humanities disciplines in higher education to examine criteria established by those for whom oral assessment has long been common practice: there have long been teachers of spoken English, or other language teachers who have examined oral practices, for example. Some of these may offer models to those who are less experienced in this form of assessment.

One almost totally neglected form of assessment and presentation in a number of arts disciplines is that of the 'poster presentation'. Much used in the sciences and social sciences, there appears to be no reason to exclude such practice from arts and humanities workshops. Such a mix of textual and visual display could be a profitable start for consideration of presentational skills prior to any oral assessment.

Arts and humanities teachers need to think particularly carefully about their control and assessment of oral work. Because of the student-centred focus of the seminar, discussion is an integral part of such sessions. Despite minority views on respecting the students' right to silence, and the more commonly found sensitive handling of students who experience difficulties in participating in discussion, the majority of academics would agree that student participation is essential in seminars. However, such a reliance on large group participation does not deny the need for a clear structure to discussion groups. Discussion is sometimes handled less well than other aspects of teaching since it is assumed to be easy and a natural process. The discussion leader needs to be well organized and prepared and to remain in control of the learning, and to make clear to students by what criteria their oral contribution is being assessed.

Interrogating Practice

Select a method of assessment you have used and make a list of: the types of cognitive, affective, interpersonal or psychomotor skill it can assess well; what it can't assess; how high an order level of operating it can assess; some statements about its validity and reliability; its efficiency and effectiveness.

OVERVIEW

This chapter sought to identify some of the distinctive features of teaching and learning in the arts and humanities. Though not exhaustive in its coverage of discipline areas, some common themes were identified and explored, such as the need for careful and considered planning, different strategies (as illustrated in the case studies) for addressing large group teaching, and the need for departmental guidance on assessment criteria and practice.

REFERENCES

Brown, S and Race, P (1997) *Staff Development in Action: A compendium of staff development resources and suggestions on how to use them*, SEDA Paper 100

Jenkins, K (1991) *Rethinking History*, Routledge, London

Miall, D (1990) *Humanities and the Computer*, Clarendon Press, Oxford

NISS (1997) *Quality Assessment Overview Reports*, (http://www.niss.ac.uk/education /hefce/qar/overview.html)

Parsons, S (1993) Feminist challenges to curriculum design, in *Culture and Process of Adult Learning*, eds R Thorpe and A Harrison, Routledge, London

QAA (1998) *Higher Quality*, **1** (3), Quality Assurance Agency, London

Scott, J (1987) Rewriting history, in *Beyond the Lines: Gender and the two world wars*, ed M Higonnet *et al*, Yale University Press, New Haven

Wisdom, J and Gibbs, G (1994) *Course Design for Resource Based Learning: Humanities*, Oxford Centre for Staff Development, Oxford

FURTHER READING

Miall, D (1990) See above. A range of useful chapters offering practical examples of the use of C&IT across the disciplines of the humanities.

NISS (1997) See above. A wealth of suggestions for innovative and good practice is offered in the Subject Overview Reports.

Wisdom, J and Gibbs, G (1994) See above. A useful resource in terms of its offering case studies and insights into varied approaches to resource based learning.

22

Key Aspects of Teaching and Learning in Social Sciences and Law

Helen Garrett

AIMS AND INTRODUCTION

As earlier parts of this volume give advice on student learning and teaching techniques for higher education, this chapter will avoid replication. It will focus instead on approaches to teaching and learning in social sciences and law, particularly at undergraduate level, and show how generic methods can be adapted to best suit these disciplines. The factors that influence approaches to teaching and learning in these disciplines will be explored. Reasons for similarities and differences in approach between the disciplines will be discussed and, from this, general lessons about the nature of teaching and learning in these fields will be drawn. The chapter will conclude with a section on recent developments in teaching and learning in a discipline-specific context.

The chapter is based on the research literature on teaching and learning in higher education generally, but more specifically on the author's own research (largely unpublished) at City University, London, into the particular approaches taken in the social sciences and law. The research has used teaching observations, interviews and student feedback. The chapter includes two illustrative case studies on different teaching methodologies, one in psychology and one in law.

EXPECTATIONS OF TEACHING AND LEARNING IN THE DISCIPLINES

Although groupings of disciplines into faculties or schools can vary across institutions, the definition of social sciences with which this author is most familiar is a school containing sociology, psychology and economics – the linkage being more historical than based on any current imperative. Other institutions would include social policy, politics and/or government or education, and perhaps exclude economics from the social sciences. The developing nature of each subject suggests that the individual disciplines of the social sciences are growing apart and it will be interesting to see whether this is reflected in a divergence of approaches to teaching and learning. It could be said that psychology is increasingly becoming a biological science, economics an increasingly mathematical science, while sociology remains a social science. One could perhaps anticipate therefore that teaching and learning in psychology and economics would focus more on the development of skills (learning by doing) as well as knowledge, while sociology remained a more discursive discipline.

Law, as a discipline with a long history and a large body of 'rules' to be learnt, could perhaps be expected to retain many of the features of traditional university teaching: lectures, **tutorials** and private study. These hypotheses will be explored later in the chapter.

WHAT DETERMINES APPROACHES TO TEACHING AND LEARNING?

One might argue that as far as selecting a particular teaching methodology is concerned, a lecturer in any discipline should be guided by two things: what they know the students have to be taught to cover the contents of the syllabus and what they want the students to learn (although the latter is somewhat less under the lecturer's control than the former). These two factors are usually expressed in the **aims** and **objectives** of the syllabus. The aims indicate generally what will be covered in a teaching session or whole course while the objectives (or **learning outcomes** as they are also known) define what students should know or be able to do at the end of a session or complete course (see Chapter 4).

Defining aims and objectives is a prerequisite for designing any teaching session and should provide the lecturer with some clues about the approach to take. An aim tends to define the content; as in 'to inform students of the key sociological concepts of class, race and gender', and the objectives, through indicating learning, point towards appropriate teaching processes. It is clear that an objective which states 'at the end of the course students will be able to critically evaluate evidence, and its interpretation, from psychological research in cognitive psychology' requires a different approach to teaching to one which says 'by the end of the course students will be able to understand and use enough of the foreign language to hold simple conversations'.

So aims and objectives are key in all disciplines, but are they all that lecturers need to know to embark on their teaching careers? Alas, of course the answer is no. In the rather more muddled realities of university teaching, decisions about teaching and learning are also influenced consciously or unconsciously by a number of other factors. These include:

- the nature of the subject knowledge;
- the academic and cultural norms of the discipline (which include the beliefs about why students choose to study a particular discipline);
- the underlying ideology about the nature of learning and consequently the perceived role of staff and students;
- the nature (and number) of the student body and their expectations of teaching and learning;
- the learning and teaching experiences of academic staff;
- personal preferences for particular styles (the lecturer whose toes curl with embarrassment at the thought of **role play,** for example, is not likely to be the best facilitator of the method);
- the availability of resources.

In addition to these internal variables, the curriculum may be constrained by the validation requirements of professional bodies such as the British Psychological Society.

Interrogating Practice

Which of the discipline-related factors that influence decisions about teaching and learning most affect the approaches to teaching and learning taken in your department?

THE FACTORS WHICH INFLUENCE TEACHING AND LEARNING IN THE SOCIAL SCIENCES AND LAW

Although the weighting of factors will undoubtedly vary from university to university, there is a core of experiences and beliefs that seem to hold true for disciplines in these subject areas. These are rarely articulated in any formal forum but tend to be revealed in conversation with individual academics. These are identified in the following sections and their implications for teaching and learning discussed.

The nature of the subject

The picture of a traditional university some 25 years ago would show relative homogeneity in how subjects were taught. Teaching would normally consist of lectures, tutorials and **laboratory classes**, where this was appropriate, whereas learning was the separate activity which students undertook during private study. In common with traditional school teaching, the nature of the subject made little difference to the approach. This is no longer the case. The changes in higher education, including the growth in student numbers; the availability of **communication and information technology (C&IT)**; the increasing emphasis on learning as well as teaching; and the impact of various quality initiatives (see Chapter 15), have led to a reappraisal of the nature of teaching and learning. This has led to the introduction of some innovative teaching methods and some divergence in disciplinary approaches.

As with many other aspects of university processes, changes in teaching and learning tend to occur incrementally. In the social sciences and law, therefore, although there is an increasing literature (particularly in professional journal articles) about innovative approaches, their adoption is not yet widespread. Many of the more common developments have been within the traditional teaching framework rather than in radical departures from it. This is due in part to the perceived nature of the subjects. The subjects are seen as academic rather than professional or vocational. Most teaching in these disciplines is based on a cognitive/rationalist approach, ie the aim is for students to know that, rather than to know how (Ellis, 1992). At undergraduate level there is little sense that students are being trained as practitioners; the emphasis is consequently less on practice, professionalism and **experiential learning** (see Chapter 11) than on the development of cognitive skills. Learning to understand concepts, critically evaluate evidence and construct arguments are all valued as outcomes of an undergraduate course. As one lecturer at City University said, 'At undergraduate level the social sciences are an education, not a training.' It is during postgraduate study that the 'professional training' element is more usually introduced, with a concomitant increase in skills development.

Because social sciences and law are subjects which 'rely on discussion and disputation as a major forum for learning' (Timms, 1997: 4), the lecture (to set the scene), private study (to develop underpinning knowledge) and the tutorial/**seminar**/laboratory (to discuss, analyze or apply) are still central features of the curriculum. What has changed is the style, content and often the process of each of these activities.

All of us can probably remember the charismatic lecturer who needed no audio-visual aids to keep us enthralled; but few can emulate such individual approaches. The most effective lecturer now is likely to have moved from a 'low-tech', didactic presentation, occasionally enlivened by a few lines written on a board, to conducting an activity which uses a range of media. The main functions of the lecture remain as they ever were; to convey facts in such a way as to make them comprehensible; to provide a framework; to highlight significant theories in the field. However, in recognition of the fact that students have different **learning styles** and limited attention spans, lecturers will use handouts, overhead slides, video, audio or computer equipment to support and add clarity to their oral presentations (see Chapter 7). Short periods of interaction will often be built into the lecture; a quick calculation; a show of hands for or against a particular theory; specific questions put to the students.

Students undertaking private study are more likely to access a greater range of learning resources, self-teaching packages and the Internet being the most common. Guiding them to useful Web sites as well as providing reading lists has become part of all lecturers' roles. **Small group** work of different types (see Chapter 8) has evolved to handle larger numbers and to involve more than the talkative few in discussion. Group work is used more extensively, for example for discussion, to prepare joint student presentations or during the session for work on problems and case studies.

Having said that, there are some common strands in the teaching and learning methods in the social sciences and law, and due to the nature of the subject knowledge there are also differences of degree. This is largely a feature of the type of information being used by students. These differences are most visible when looking at the relative weight given to each of the teaching methodologies used. In sociology and law, the lecture and discussion remain the core of the curriculum because the subjects are very much discursive and socially based. The development of communication and presentation skills is particularly emphasized in these subjects. Economics and psychology, because of their greater mathematical or science base, involve more computer and laboratory-based work, particularly for data analysis. One example that illustrates how the teaching method arises from the nature of the subject knowledge is presented in Case Study 1.

Case Study 1: Description of a Second Year Course in Research Methods in Psychology Course

City University, London (course run by Professor John Gardiner)

An introduction to experiments

Psychology students are introduced to experiments in their first year in two ways. First, they undertake short practical experiments in a range of theoretical areas. These are usually designed by the lecturers and are mainly computer-based simulations. Second, they are required to give 12 hours of their time (for which they gain credits) to be the subjects of third-year or postgraduate students' experiments. The latter exercise introduces them to the research culture in the department and gives them the opportunity to learn first-hand about methodologies and theoretical issues through the debriefing they receive after each study. In the second year they start to conduct experiments themselves.

Course aims

The main aim of the research methods course is to develop their research skills for a major research project in their final year. They therefore need to understand the logic of experimentation in psychology as opposed to that in the pure sciences, the most obvious of which is the variability of human beings. As the students are learning about the complexity of human behaviour, the sound way of doing so is through using real human beings in their research.

The structure of the course

The course is designed in three, four to six week blocks, during which students undertake research in three areas of psychology. As the lecturers can show students how to conduct experiments but not exactly what will result when they do, the course concentrates on keeping the formal input through lectures to a minimum. The main focus is on the process of experimentation itself and feedback from tutors.

The course begins with initial lectures to introduce the key concepts in more complicated experimental design, ie experiments with more than one variable. These are didactic lectures followed by illustrative examples. Students' grasp of the issues is tested by problem-solving exercises and exercises involving critiques of poor research design (usually written with great enjoyment by the lecturers). These exercises are done after the lecture in small groups and de-briefed in a later class.

The students then carry out their own research for the remainder of the block.

They work independently in groups of two or three. First, the group identifies a problem area from within the lecture topic; second, plans and designs their research; third, conducts the research; and fourth, analyses the data and reaches conclusions. Finally they make an oral report at a final plenary session.

During the period of the research there are no formal timetabled sessions; the groups have to organize their own activities and plan their time. During this period, however, they can seek advice and feedback from lecturers and demonstrators and have free access to the computer laboratories.

The first block usually involves research into a cognitive problem; the second, which repeats the pattern, a physiological oriented problem; and the final block, a questionnaire-based investigation of an area of applied psychology. This last area can involve testing a hypothesis on members of the local community as well as on students.

Outcomes

The experience of teamwork, time management and the presentation of technical information clearly and intelligibly are some of the **key**, **personal**, **transferable skills** developed during this process. Students are encouraged by their personal tutors to think not only about the results of their research but to reflect on the process they have gone through. One measure of the success of the approach is that there have been some publications arising from second year projects.

The academic and cultural norms

In talking about teaching and learning in the social sciences and law, one is assuming a greater homogeneity between the subjects than probably exists. Even the same subject taught in two different universities will undoubtedly vary and institutional cultures should be considered when making decisions about teaching and learning. Having said that, there are some general conclusions that can be drawn about cultural influences on teaching and learning.

The first is that social sciences and law share some common beliefs about the nature of teaching and learning, which in turn influence their approach to new developments. Perhaps the most strongly felt one is that the acquisition of knowledge has a strong social dimension. While in no way being Luddite about the role of technology and its place in teaching and learning in social sciences and law, the concept of a virtual university is one which is greeted with dismay by academics in these disciplines (except perhaps in economics). Interactivity is a key aspect of their approach to teaching and learning and **computer-assisted learning (CAL)** for example (in its current state of development) is felt to represent both too simple and too static a view of the world. Even the thought of replacing (rather than supplementing) a lecture with a video-recorded one is felt to adversely affect the dynamic that the learning experience should be a shared venture between staff and students.

A second belief is that research should inform teaching. The social sciences and law are both disciplines that have a relevance to how the broader society or societies outside higher education operate. They are concerned with issues that impact upon human beings. The theoretical models with which students are dealing are enhanced, it is thought, by their being introduced to pertinent real-world issues through individual academics' research. When talking to students, it is clear to see that they enjoy the sense of being close to new developments and respond to the enthusiasm and commitment conveyed by lecturers when they talk about their research. Academics who use their own research selectively to illuminate a subject are appreciated; those who forget that not everyone is quite as excited by their research into the profit-cost margins of corner grocery shops risk inducing terminal tedium. Lecturers should aim to get the student response 'it really brings the subject alive', rather than the reaction ' I thought she was supposed to be helping us to learn, not showing off how clever she is'.

Interrogating Practice

What are your views about the links and relationships in your discipline between teaching, student learning and research?

An extension of the interest in linking theory to real-world activity is to encourage students themselves, in the social sciences in particular, to study the local community. Provided that they are well supervised and any ethical issues are resolved, locally based project work (see Chapter 9) can illuminate academic themes. It is perhaps surprising that these links are not made more, although it is possibly explained by a combination of the view about what is 'academic' and the practical resource problems involved.

The nature of teaching and learning in disciplines

Teaching

Until relatively recently, discussions about teaching in most disciplines have focused on the content of a course rather than the process of teaching. With the introduction of **programme/subject review** (see Chapter 15) and the consequent development of teaching and learning strategies and committees, this is gradually changing.

Subject overview report: law

The subject overview report for law (HEFCE, 1995) was one of the first published documents on the state of teaching in higher education. In general the report comments favourably on the provision available, highlighting good practice such as:

- courses with clearly defined aims and objectives;
- scholarly and stimulating lectures encouraging an independent and critical analysis of the law;
- well-qualified staff with an interest and enthusiasm for their subject;
- encouragement for students to take a self-directed approach through student-led seminars or group presentations;
- comprehensive and thorough pastoral care;
- appropriate assessment with constructive feedback.

Two areas needing development are referred to, the need to develop IT skills and the integration of key transferable skills across the curriculum. These issues are discussed later in this chapter.

However, it is probably still true to say that many academics think more about what they teach than how and why they teach it in a particular way. It is interesting therefore to ask academics to articulate their beliefs about the role of the teacher. Disciplinary differences are quite clear.

On the whole, academics in the social sciences and law tend to espouse a view of teaching that says that it is less about transmitting information than about facilitating students to learn. This, if translated into practice (which is not always the case), suggests a different approach to teaching from that implied by the memorable quote from an academic in a different discipline: 'If I'm not talking I don't feel that I am teaching'. Several researchers have attempted to identify different conceptions of teaching (eg, Ramsden, 1992). Fox (1983) identified four basic concepts of teaching:

- the 'transfer theory', where knowledge is a commodity to be passed from teacher to student;

- the 'shaping theory', where students are moulded to a predetermined pattern;
- the 'travelling theory', where lecturers act as expert guides;
- the 'growing theory', where lecturers focus on the emotional and intellectual development of students.

Although the approach taken to teaching will depend on a number of variables, including which year of the course is being taught, lecturers in social sciences and law tend to describe themselves as 'expert guides' rather than the authoritative source of knowledge.

If this perception of the teaching role is translated into practice it is likely that lectures will be less about transmitting facts (which students can read up) than alerting them to the complexities and contradictions in academic knowledge. The role of lecturer as facilitator is, however, probably best seen outside lectures during the activities that help the student to make sense of the information they gain from lectures and personal study. Although this includes the formal timetabled activities of classes, computer laboratories, seminars and tutorials, social sciences and law lecturers allocate a significant amount of time for individual or small group academic guidance.

Interrogating Practice

What are the main teaching methodologies used in your department? What is the rationale for their choice?

Learning

Having talked about perceptions of the teaching role, it is to be hoped that there would be some correlation with the anticipated learning outcomes. In theory, if not always in practice, the correlation is there. Säljö (cited in Gibbs, 1981) offered five conceptions of learning:

- an increase in knowledge;
- memorizing;
- the acquisition of facts or procedures which can be retained and/or utilized in practice;
- the abstraction of meaning;
- an interpretative process aimed at the understanding of reality.

To these five, Marton (cited in Morgan, 1993) has added a sixth: changing as a person – a fundamental change about seeing oneself and a way of seeing what is learnt.

While most academics would expect any learning to include an increase in knowledge, academics in the social sciences and law tend to favour the 'abstraction of meaning' as being the desired learning in higher education. This again has implications for the way the student learning experience should be designed if beliefs are translated into practice. It would be difficult to see how students could be encouraged to seek for meaning if their teaching and learning experiences regularly put them in the position of being passive recipients of ready-made knowledge. It is even more difficult to see how students can attain the desired learning outcomes if assessment methods emphasize memorizing and reproducing information (see Chapter 5).

One way to illustrate the way this belief in the purpose of learning (and the nature of a particular subject) translates into a teaching approach, is by examining Case Study 2 in the subject of law. It describes learning and teaching in one particular area and then examines the rationale for the approaches used.

Much of law, in common with the social sciences, is taught by the lecture/problem-solving tutorial method. In law, this learning process begins with looking at the rules and principles of a particular area of law, usually in a lecture. Cases are used to illustrate these rules and principles that are then applied to hypothetical situations during the tutorial sessions. This is an appropriate approach for those areas of law which have well established principles and precedents that apply in all cases.

Tort law, which includes such areas as negligence, trespass, deformation and nuisance, has few, if any, general guiding rules or principles. Some areas of tort are relatively recent and are still developing so it is an area of law where judges are frequently faced with novel situations. Decisions in tort cases are developed by analogy with previous cases rather than by looking for the appropriate rule. The key to understanding the subject, therefore, is not to look for the one right answer, but to understand the process by which judges reach their decisions. It is consequently an area of law with high levels of uncertainty.

It is clear then, that the required learning is not a process of identification (from precedent) and then application, but one of analysis: exactly that extraction of meaning which academics describe as their aim. Unless this analytical process occurs, students will not be able to understand tort law. The case method uses the cases themselves, rather than the rules, as the basis for learning the law. Rules are only discussed where they arise out of cases.

Case Study 2: Tort Law – First Year Compulsory Course on LLB Law

City University, London (course run by Dr Yvonne Jacobs)

In this course the students use only case notes, which are the edited records of the facts of a case in tort and the reasoning of the judges leading to their decisions. This is because in tort the reasoning of the judges is as important as the decision. Students are therefore working from primary rather than text book sources. They prepare by reading the cases that will be analysed and discussed in the case method class. It is suggested to them that they conduct their reading by breaking down the case into the facts; the issues; the solution; and the reasons for the solution.

In the class itself, the learning process followed is active and interactive. Students have to think through, individually or in groups, why judges have reasoned in a particular way by responding to carefully posed questions from the lecturer. These start off fairly general and then become increasingly complex as the students explore decisions and legal concepts in more and more detail. Once students are confident in the method, hypothetical facts or cases are introduced to see whether they can apply the reasoning to similar situations.

Rationale for the approach

Marton and Säljö (1976), in their research into the way students tackle a learning task, distinguished between two different approaches to learning. **Surface learning** takes place when a student focuses on memorizing facts and details, whereas **deep learning** involves a search for understanding and meaning (see Chapter 3). A surface learning approach would be of no assistance to students studying tort law, as memorizing the decision in one case is of little help in deciding the likely outcome of apparently similar cases. This exercise is designed to lead students to take a deep learning approach by involving them in active engagement with the material. Assessment focuses less on the students 'getting it right' than on the reasoning process they demonstrate. The assessment process therefore complements the teaching and learning approach.

> ### Interrogating Practice
>
> In your teaching and assessment practices, how can you encourage students to take a deep approach to learning? Are there any areas of teaching where your students work from primary material? Is there any scope for developing this?

Student profile and expectations

In common with all other disciplines in higher education, the student body in social sciences and law has grown and diversified, leading to some re-evaluation of approaches to teaching and learning. Partly because of the pressure of numbers and partly because of an increasing focus on the learning side of the teaching/learning equation, there has been a growth in what are called student-centred teaching methods. These, broadly speaking, are any teaching methods that provide an environment to learn rather than one in which there is a one-way transmission of information. Some examples from the social sciences and law are mentioned above.

It is noticeable, however, that students (particularly those entering university straight from school) who choose to study an academic subject such as the social sciences and law, on their arrival tend to have very traditional expectations of the teaching in a university. They tend to view education as something that will be done to (or for) them rather than something they will help to create for themselves. It is therefore worth spending some time early in a course talking about approaches to teaching and learning, to reduce the risk of a mismatch between expectations and teaching methodologies. Although some departments formalize this process by agreeing **learning contracts**, it can also be done by setting ground rules at the beginning of a course about expectations on both sides. One lecturer always starts her course by conducting a session on students' experiences of a time they learnt successfully and a time when they failed to learn. The students discover the conditions and types of learning that appear to suit them best and discover that there is a wide range of approaches to learning. Another starts his course by getting the students to complete a learning styles questionnaire and then discussing the implications for personal study (see Chapters 3 and 16).

The introduction of any new teaching method needs to be well prepared and the rationale underpinning the reason for changes discussed with the students, if they are going to be used successfully (see Chapter 6). The rapid disappearance of students from a sociology seminar series, when told that they would each have to do a presentation, without any guidance on design or delivery, should act as a warning. Academics attempting to be innovative and introducing student-centred approaches mid-curriculum have found it difficult. They have discovered that it is very hard to change the learning habits of students in their final year when up to that point they have experienced education as a fairly passive activity.

The increasing number of students has led to changes other than in teaching methodologies. One of the most noticeable is the attempt to help students take increasing responsibility for their own learning. In recognizing that students will have limited access to staff on an individual basis, departments have looked for other ways to give guidance and support (see Chapter 14). In one psychology department, for example, this has taken the form of providing all students with a 'personal development file'.

This file has two purposes. The first is to help them to organize their time and keep a record of their academic work and as such contains timetables and record sheets. The second is to help them to identify and record their personal transferable skills (see Chapter 10). The most common skills used as selection criteria by organizations in their graduate recruitment programmes are described and the student prompted by a series of questions to identify and describe their current and developing level of skill. This is taken to each session with their personal tutor for review and discussion. Ultimately it will provide their **record of achievement** for use in job applications.

In other approaches to support, some departments use a mentoring system, with second-year students directing first-year students to information sources. Others use student-led study circles where students divide a learning task between them and then combine the results of their work. Self-teaching software is increasingly used for learning languages and computer software.

Case Study 3: Students' Views

City University, London

The author's research interviews at City University, with students in the social sciences and law, show that when asked to say what they find most conducive to successful learning, students rarely mention the teaching method. The factors they identify are:

- a supportive environment with academics being approachable and patient;
- the provision of formative feedback, both written and verbal;
- a clear understanding of what is expected of them, particularly when preparing essays or presentations;

- a reasonable choice of paths though the curriculum, so they could follow their own interests;
- a reasonable workload with well-spaced and coordinated assessments;
- sufficient access to books and computers;
- interesting lectures and discussions which did not overload them with information or fail to take into account what they already knew;
- clear aims and objectives, so that lectures and discussions were well focused (rambling discussion sessions are identified as a particular waste of time).

The learning and teaching experience of staff

There is a tendency for academics in all disciplines to either teach as they were taught or to stick to a style that suits them. While the first tendency is not necessarily recommended, there is some legitimacy in the second. Teaching, after all, is an art as well as a practice, where the personalities of the lecturer and the students and the relationship between them form part of the process. Also, there is no one ideal model of teaching. Provided that some thought has gone into the selection of a teaching approach, how a session is conducted is usually more important to students than what it is (see this page and the previous).

As far as students are concerned, effective teaching is more about the ability to communicate (and this means listening as well as talking), than providing a technicolor display of dazzling techniques. This is not to suggest that, as with any profession, achieving a level of competence and a grasp of teaching technique should be ignored. An inaudible voice and illegible overhead slides are unforgivable.

To a large extent, academics have a high degree of autonomy in deciding both what and how they teach. They need to feel comfortable with the way they teach and it is reasonable to expect that this will influence individual approaches to teaching and learning. The only danger in this is if it inhibits any consideration of other approaches. An ability to assess what sorts of approaches help students to learn and adapt one's methods accordingly is probably the most valuable contribution a lecturer can make to teaching.

THE FUTURE

In common with every other discipline, social sciences and law are limited in the resources they can devote to developments in teaching and learning. This is one reason why many of the approaches to teaching and learning have been changing in an evolutionary rather than revolutionary way. Consequently the picture painted so far in this chapter is of developments around a fairly traditional core. Can this remain the same? The answer is probably not. Pressure is on, not least from the recommendations in the **Dearing Report** (NCIHE, 1997), to at least explore other approaches.

Professional journals such as the *Psychologist* and the *SocInfo Journal* reflect the debates about the nature of teaching in the 21st century. The key areas discussed are the use of C&IT, and the development of vocationally relevant skills and competencies.

Interrogating Practice

Does your department/school have a teaching and learning strategy that considers these developments?

Communication and information technology

This is certain to be one of the growth areas in teaching and learning (see Chapter 12). The current debate takes for granted that its use will increase and focuses on how best it can serve student learning. It is clear that academics in the social sciences and law see its role in supplementing and enhancing teaching and learning, not supplanting the human activity involved.

Many of the developments in teaching and learning are not universal panaceas nor universally applicable. There is still much research and evaluation work to do. As Hammond and Trapp, heads of a **CTI Centre** in psychology, say: 'There is a healthy wariness of using technology for efficiency gains that might degrade the quality of learning' (1998: 389). New lecturers are recommended to carefully evaluate whether any new development suits the subject and the students before using it. As far as CAL is concerned in the social sciences, it should be no surprise that specialist commercial software is more usually found in the areas of statistical and data analysis, **simulation** and **modelling**. Outside these subjects social science software is relatively underdeveloped, although this is changing.

IT is probably in greater use at present than communication technology. We can be sure we will see its increased use within institutions, for example by lecturers who may post the complete text or summaries of their lectures, reading lists or assessment topics on a home page and provide links to other relevant resources. Data-bases such as LEXIS for legal references, expand the amount of information available and make it faster to access.

The development of communication technology is at present more limited but seems to offer scope for the sort of teaching and learning prized by lecturers in social sciences and law. The examples which follow show how this technology is being used to develop interactive and flexible learning.

Case Study 4: Strategies to Promote Learning in the Social Sciences and Law

Booth, Crompton and Henry (1997) describe developing an electronic discussion group at the University of Stirling to provide a mechanism for sociology students to take part in electronic tutorials. They used Usenet News, rather than e-mail discussion lists (which are probably more common), as the discussion medium and set up five newsgroups each with between four and six students. The students were taught how to use the technology and were told that they had to make contributions to three out of the four tutorials. A postgraduate student monitored the groups during the process.

The evaluation of the programme identified advantages and difficulties that are worth bearing in mind when thinking about introducing communication technology into teaching and learning. Among the advantages were:

- students could participate at a time that suited them;
- students had time to give more thought to their contribution and they could also revisit discussions and refine or develop their views;
- every student, including those who were never heard in face-to-face tutorials, contributed, and the level of the discussion was rated as high;
- it enabled students to develop their computing skills.

The things learnt from the pilot study were:

- that the discussions need to be moderated by an on-line facilitator, to keep the momentum going and to keep the groups feeling involved;
- that technical problems, difficulties with access to computers and differing IT skill levels among students create a disincentive to participation;
- that the use of electronic communication methods changes the role of the lecturer from teacher to on-line moderator/facilitator, with consequent staff development implications.

Tolmie and Anderson (1998) describe a similar example of using computers to assist learning. They used peer-based tutorials to help University of Strathclyde psychology students prepare the research outline for their dissertations. The groups of students met physically in the same place and time and ran the tutorial themselves, aided in structuring the discussion by a computer programme.

At each of the tutorials the computer programme identified important issues and asked the group to discuss them in relation to each student's project. These ranged from helping them to decide on the research question they wanted to ask, to discussions of the appropriate experimental design. Interestingly, to ensure that all the students received their fair share of attention, the software also took over that well-known human tutor's role of telling them when they had exceeded the time for any part of the discussion. The supervisor's role was to conduct a report-back session after each tutorial.

After evaluation, the researchers found that the students' discussions had been focused and purposeful. Students had found it useful to discuss their work with peers in a structured way and this seemed to have been reflected in the quality of their research designs compared with previous years. The lessons learnt were that the students needed to be adequately prepared to make best use of 'their slot' and that they needed de-briefing time.

(adapted from Booth, Compton and Henry, 1997; Tolmie and Anderson, 1998)

Both these examples appear to fulfil the requirement that not only were they efficient in using students' and staff time effectively, they also had positive learning outcomes for the students. For anyone interested in exploring the use of C&IT, there are many other examples of its use in the social sciences and law, many of them developed by the subject specific CTI Centres and detailed in the CTI handbook.

The development of vocationally relevant skills and competencies (key skills)

The concept of embedding key skills in the curriculum is one that is fraught with problems, not least in deciding quite what the skills for employment are. It is generally agreed that it is an area of development that even traditional academic disciplines need to consider (see Chapter 10).

It is probably true to say that the skills needed by students will involve IT skills; communication/social skills such as negotiating and cooperating; technical skills such as researching and presenting information, as well as the cognitive skills like the interpretation of evidence, critical thought and constructing arguments. In the social sciences and law the skills are usually developed through the use of training in basic computer packages, dissertations, exercises, group project work and presentations. These are all valid ways of giving students practical experience of generic skills. There are four things which academics can do to enhance this experience:

- provide guidance or training in the skill;
- encourage students to recognize that they are developing a skill;
- consider which skills fit best at which places within the curriculum;
- explore how far any of them overlap with skills needed in the discipline.

A student presentation undertaken without adequate guidance on construction and delivery can be a de-motivating experience. Doing only one presentation, without an opportunity to improve with practice, can also deter students from developing their skills. The second aspect of the process of skill acquisition is for academic staff to give feedback on the process of the activity as well as the content. Students need to think not only about what they did but how they did it. The example given earlier of a personal development file kept by the student and regularly reviewed with a tutor is one way of encouraging students to reflect on their skills (see page 322).

The Dearing Report (NCIHE, 1997) identifies four key skills which students will need to develop; communication skills, written and oral numeracy, use of C&IT and learning how to learn. While social sciences and law would legitimately claim that communication skills are a central feature of an education in the discipline, the remaining three are probably at a lower stage of development taking the disciplines as a whole.

As a final word on this developing area, some sociology departments, particularly in the post-1992 universities, are developing the idea of work placements or supervised work experience to help students prepare for work (see Chapter 11). Although this is not yet widespread, it may increasingly become a feature of social sciences courses.

OVERVIEW AND CONCLUSION

This chapter has raised issues relevant to the activities of teaching and learning in law and social science disciplines. It has looked at the current state of development in these subject areas and suggested some reasons for the particular approaches taken. The brief glimpse into the future raises questions rather than offers solutions, but it highlights those areas where debate on teaching and learning is likely to be focused in the foreseeable future.

As has been said in many different contexts, change is the only constant in higher education. Academic staff will need to take a critical look at their approach to teaching and learning, question assumptions and be willing to explore and develop best practice across disciplinary areas.

For anyone interested in teaching and learning, it is an exciting if challenging and exhausting time. The outcome for students should make it worth it.

REFERENCES

Booth, S, Crompton, P and Henry, M (1997) Using tutorials to foster student learning: a pilot study, *SocInfo Journal*, **3**, pp 11–22

Ellis, R (1992) An action-focus curriculum for the IP professions, in *Learning to Effect*, ed R Barnett, SRHE and Open University Press, Milton Keynes

Fox, D (1983) Theories of teaching, *Studies in Higher Education*, **8**, 151–63

Gibbs, G (1981) *Teaching Students to Learn*, Open University Press, Milton Keynes

Hammond, N and Trapp, A (1998) Enabling psychology education, *Psychologist*, August issue, 389–90

HEFCE (1995) *QO 1/95 Subject Overview Report – Law* (Quality Assessment of Law 1993–94), HEFCE, Bristol

Marton, F and Säljö, R (1976) Approaches to learning, in *The Experience of Learning*, eds F Marton, D Hounsell and N Entwistle, Scottish Academic Press, Edinburgh

Morgan, A (1993) *Improving Your Students' Learning: Reflection on the experience of study*, Kogan Page and Open University Press, London

NCIHE (1997) (Dearing Report) *Higher Education in the Learning Society*, National Committee of Inquiry into Higher Education, HMSO, London

Ramsden, P (1992) *Learning to Teach in Higher Education*, Routledge, London

Timms, D (1997) C&IT and the learning society: some post-Dearing thoughts, *SocInfo Journal*, **3**, 2–11

Tolmie, A and Anderson, T (1998) Information technology and peer-based tutorials, *Psychologist*, August issue, 381–84

FURTHER READING AND SOURCES OF INFORMATION

Communication and Information Technologies for Teaching and Learning in Higher Education. A handbook of services and resources from the Computers in Teaching Initiative. CTI Support Services, University of Oxford.

Radford, J, Van Laar, D and Rose D (eds) (1998) *Innovations in Psychology Teaching*, SEDA Paper 4, SEDA, Birmingham.

Some discipline-specific journals carry articles about teaching in the discipline, eg *Psychologist* and *SocInfo Journal*.

23 Key Aspects of Teaching and Learning in Languages

Carol Gray and John Klapper

INTRODUCTION

This chapter will discusses issues relevant to the effective learning and teaching of modern languages in higher education. The first sections will consider:

- the changing face of language study in higher education;
- the implications for higher education language learning of changed school curricula and examinations;
- insights from second language acquisition research;
- communicative approaches to language teaching;
- autonomous learning;
- communication and information technology (C&IT);
- translation.

There then follows a case study of a first-year post-A level language course which illustrates many of the recent developments in language learning and teaching, and demonstrates how these can be integrated into a coherent whole. The focus throughout will be on language learning rather than the non-language elements of degree courses, since the latter are covered elsewhere in this volume.

LANGUAGES IN HIGHER EDUCATION

Developments in the teaching of foreign languages over the past 40 years have resulted partly from new methodological perceptions but also from the changing role of the higher education institute as language provider. Higher education language courses were once characterized by a predominantly post-A level intake, by translation into and out of the target language, academic essay writing, the study of phonetics and 'conversation classes'. Nowadays languages are offered *ab initio*; there is considerably less emphasis on translation, especially in the early stages of the undergraduate degree; there have been moves in several institutions towards increased use of the target language as the medium of instruction and towards broadening the range of activities employed to include oral presentations, group discussions, debates, précis, summaries, letters, reviews and reports.

'Non-language' components have also changed, with less pre 20th-century literature, more writing by women, and the addition of socio-cultural, political and media studies and film. The extent to which the foreign language is used here as the medium of tuition is variable; in some cases because modularization has mixed language and non-language students on area studies courses, in others because staff fear a 'watering down' of intellectual content.

There is increasing employment of part-time staff, postgraduate research students and 'colloquial assistants' – now usually called foreign language assistants – in the delivery of key course components. The extent to which these categories of staff receive training and support for this vital role is variable.

The total number of students studying languages increased dramatically in the early 1990s but Thomas's survey (1993) suggested that well over 60 per cent of these were 'non-specialist' linguists. This represents another major agent of change; the mushrooming of language courses for non-specialists, so-called institution-wide language programmes (IWLPs), usually delivered by language centres. These range from one-semester modules to full four-year degrees with a year abroad, and account for anything between 10 per cent and 25 per cent of course credits. It is hard to be sure precisely how many non-specialist linguists there are; growth has slowed considerably since Thomas's survey, which nevertheless remains the most reliable source of statistics. Their proportion of total numbers can, however, only have risen as specialist numbers continue to dwindle. One of the features of provision for non-specialists, in contrast to much language teaching in academic departments, is the use of trained 'dedicated', full or, more likely, part-time language teachers, often operating on non-academic contracts.

THE INCOMING STUDENT

One of the most widely accepted tenets of teaching is 'meet the students on their own ground and build on their strengths and their weaknesses' (Saunders, 1996: 32). This, along with insights into the acquisition of both first and second languages (**L1** and **L2**) as discussed below, has been the driving force behind curricular and examination changes in secondary education over recent decades. Examples of such changes are:

- the spread of comprehensive education;
- the development of the GCSE examination catering for a greater range of ability than the O level;
- the introduction of National Curriculum orders outlining what and how pupils should learn during their compulsory school years;
- legislation requiring all pupils of compulsory school age to study a modern foreign language as part of their National Curriculum entitlement (currently under review);
- a bottom-up rather than top-down reform in education, whereby changes introduced in the early years of secondary education are determining the format of GCSE and ultimately A level examinations, and thus the nature of entrants to higher education.

These are both causes and symptoms of a drive to make language learning accessible and useful to all, rather than to a small academic elite.

These developments have far-reaching consequences for teaching in higher education. Methodologies and assessment procedures used in schools are no longer designed to prepare pupils for an academic career in linguistics and literature, rather to convince a wider clientele that language learning is both feasible and worthwhile, and to equip pupils for their potential and widely differing needs.

The challenge is not easy. The original GCSE examination which attempted to modernize attitudes and skills is often attacked nowadays for shifting the balance too far from accuracy to fluency and for improving neither. In an education system judged by league tables, a topic-led syllabus has inevitably led to a focus on 'getting through the topics' rather than facilitating true language learning. While there is thus some justification for complaints about incoming students' lack of grammatical awareness, higher education language teachers must not underestimate the contribution which GCSE has made to increasing access to languages. The task of higher education is to find imaginative and effective ways to tackle this potential deficiency while simultaneously building upon the skills of incoming students.

The National Curriculum Programme of Study defines pupils' entitlement; it is a process rather than content-based programme which emphasizes enjoyment, spontaneity in use of language for real purposes and the development of positive attitudes towards other cultures. This reflects the principles of a **communicative approach** to language learning which sees language as a means of communication rather than an object of academic study. There is also, however, a recognition of the crucial role of 'pre-communicative' work and the need to re-establish the relationship between communicative skills and more formal language-learning skills.

In practice, pupils' learning is largely determined by public examinations and the numerous but essentially similar textbooks which have been produced to support study towards them. GCSE and A level examinations must conform to the principles of the National Curriculum as interpreted through their various Codes of Practice. The major changes at GCSE level have been the increased use of target language both for examination rubrics and for testing purposes and the associated move towards mixed rather than discrete-skill testing. A cause of controversy is the additional move to allow pupils to use dictionaries in examinations.

Beyond 16, many young people now pursue GNVQs, and sixth-form colleges offer a range of syllabuses and examinations accredited by Royal Society of Arts and City and Guilds, among others. Nevertheless, many of the students continuing their language study into higher education are likely to have followed the traditional route of A and AS levels. These, however, are changing in response to the skills and interests of potential learners and current thinking on teaching and assessment methodologies. Again, there is an emphasis on **mixed-skill** teaching and testing, on the use of the target language as the main medium of communication and upon encouraging the development of real-life language learning skills by provision for the use of dictionaries and texts in examinations as well as individual student control of tapes in listening components. In addition, the 'modular' nature of courses allows for students to follow different pathways, academic, literary, or vocationally focused, and the concept of banking modules over a limited period of time could change the A level course structure. The long-term results of these changes are yet to be seen.

Interrogating Practice

To what extent does your department's current practice take account of the needs and skills of incoming learners? Think of three ways you might improve upon current practice.

INSIGHTS FROM WORK ON SECOND LANGUAGE ACQUISITION

Second language acquisition (SLA) has been the focus of considerable research in recent years. There is still no coherent agreed model owing to the difficulties involved in separating out and evaluating the diverse elements which contribute to second or foreign language (L2) acquisition and disagreements over the role of a learner's mother tongue (L1) in this process.

Nevertheless all language teachers need a basic understanding of the principle aspects of SLA. Towell and Hawkins (1994: 7–16) list these as:

- 'transfer': learners' unconscious application of L1 grammatical features to their L2 grammar;
- 'staged development': learners progress through a series of intermediate stages towards L2 acquisition;
- 'systematicity': the broadly similar way L2 learners develop their ability in the target language; the majority of L2 learners go through the same developmental stages regardless of their L1 or the type of input they receive;
- 'variability': during the developmental stages, learners' 'mental grammars of L2' allow alternative forms which may co-exist for a long period;
- 'incompleteness': the failure of most L2 learners to attain a level of automatic grammatical knowledge of L2 comparable to that of native speakers.

One of the implications of these features of SLA is that error and inaccuracy are both inevitable and necessary. The traditional assumptions of language teaching that learners must master new forms in a conscious manner when they are first presented to them, that error should not be tolerated and indeed should be avoided at all costs, are misguided. SLA research reveals, on the contrary, that L2 competence both generally and in specific grammatical instances is *by its very nature* developmental, that it grows as a function of both conscious and unconscious learning and that error plays a major part at all stages of this process.

L1 acquisition depends on learners interacting with other L1 speakers and engaging with increasing amounts of new information which steadily builds on previous knowledge. It therefore seems reasonable to suggest L2 acquisition will similarly be furthered by interaction with authentic language. **Immersion learning** (eg in Canada) and bilingual programmes in several countries have shown that learners need repeatedly to focus on meaning while being exposed for extended periods to L2. For this reason **target language** use in the classroom and the deployment of a wide range of authentic texts are now both recognized as crucial to the language-learning process at advanced levels. The real benefit of authentic texts is that they help shift the focus on interaction along the continuum of L1/L2 medium-orientated communication towards L2 message-orientated communication (see Dodson, 1985). That is to say, authentic texts and realistic tasks (eg preparing an address in a mock French election based on some aspect of a political party's programme) provide learners with an explicit, content-based learning purpose in which the focus is on the message and the achievement of the task. Such tasks also encourage *implicit* learning of syntactical, morphological and lexical features of the target language.

The above suggests L2 acquisition resembles L1 acquisition in a number of important ways. However, most L2 learners clearly approach the target language with a degree of proficiency and literacy in their L1. This means that they can use reading and writing to help promote their L2 learning. Furthermore, they bring to the L2-learning process a capacity for exploring grammatical forms in a conscious and explicit manner, and are able to talk *about* language. These facts make L2 learning in a formal educational setting a much more deliberate and intentional process.

The difficulty is that knowing formal rules does not by itself guarantee the ability to formulate language which obeys these rules. This is a real problem for many learners, especially those combining languages with other disciplines in higher education: in language learning, **inductive learning** processes are just as important as the more cognitive, **deductive approaches** typical of many other academic disciplines, in which it very often *is* possible to learn things as a result of explicit rule teaching and error correction. Language learning, however, is not always a conscious activity dependent on the availability of explicit knowledge about the language and the way it functions, but rather the product of a complex process of both conscious learning and the gradual, unconscious development of an internal ability to use language naturally and spontaneously without reference to the conscious mind.

It is the challenge of the language classroom to develop learners' internalized linguistic competence, that is their implicit knowledge of and capacity for appropriate language use, in tandem with explicit knowledge of grammatical and phonological rules. This requires the development of an expanding body of interlocking skills through imitation, repetition, drilling and frequent practice in extended contexts to the point where these skills become automatic and unconscious. Little and Ushioda's comparison with piano playing seems most apposite in this context: 'Just as the novice pianist must consciously learn finger placements and pedalling, so the language learner must consciously learn bits of language – words and phrases, pronunciation and patterns of intonation – that become embedded in memory and can be accessed spontaneously' (Little and Ushioda, 1998: 15).

Interrogating Practice

Does current departmental practice take account of evidence from research into second language acquisition? How might the department address this issue in its language curriculum?

TOWARDS A COMMUNICATIVE APPROACH TO LANGUAGE LEARNING

These insights have contributed to the development of a **communicative approach** to the teaching of modern foreign languages which is now to be found in all educational sectors. The past 40 years have seen many different approaches to modern language teaching. Grammar-based language teaching, such as grammar-translation, **audio-visual/audio-lingual** methodology and even direct method, all adopt a rigid, graded approach to structures. Textbooks written in these traditions present items in what is considered a logical sequence (eg present tense before past, nominative case before dative) which is intended to teach learners to acquire certain items before progressing to other, linguistically more complex ones. This approach fails to take account of the insights from SLA outlined above. It precludes, for example, the teaching of such central communicative expressions as 'je voudrais' or 'ich möchte' until learners have covered the conditional and the subjunctive respectively.

An approach to language based on communicative need, on the other hand, starts from a consideration of what learners are likely to have to do in the foreign language and then builds in the vocabulary, expressions and grammar needed to perform these 'functions' (see Wilkins, 1976, for an introduction to functional-notional syllabuses). As a result, the same grammar points are revisited again and again throughout a language course. This acknowledges that grammar is not acquired in a linear fashion or in discrete chunks digested one at a time, but that it is rather a staged developmental process which cannot be regimented or rushed.

The principle aim of the communicative approach is to facilitate independent communication by the learner (Pachler and Field, 1997: 70). The communicative classroom is therefore characterized by the following:

- grammar as a facilitator of communication;
- phased development from pre-communicative to free communicative exercises;
- inductive learning of grammar;

- maximum use of the target language;
- a focus on meaning;
- language used for a purpose;
- the foregrounding of learners' needs;
- personalization of language;
- the creative use of language;
- learner interaction;
- the use of authentic language and materials;
- a mixed-skill approach to teaching and assessment.

This means in practice that instead of being based on a purely structural syllabus which works its way in sequence through a range of grammar points with the aim of building up linguistic knowledge and accuracy, a communication-based course sees form as a necessary tool for expressing and exchanging meaning. This does not preclude or diminish the role of grammar. On the contrary, advanced and skilful communication can only take place when learners have assimilated a range of complex structures together with understanding of their application and potential effects within a wide range of situations. However, grammar and knowledge 'about' language are no longer seen as ends in themselves.

Furthermore, grammar is not taught deductively by artificial isolation and presentation of a series of rules, but inductively by the identification of useful patterns within content-focused language. Attention is drawn to recurrent structures, with subsequent clarification and drilling exercises. However, the emphasis is firmly on the context in which such structures occur and hence the meanings which they have the potential to convey. It is a question of identifying rules from examples rather than creating examples on the basis of a presented rule.

Interrogating Practice

Think of a point of grammar you have taught recently. Did your students learn it successfully? Did they learn it deductively or inductively? Can you think how you might have presented it more effectively?

One of the major tenets of a communicative approach is that of maximum use of the target language for instruction and interaction. If the language is not used whenever viable within the learning process, then not only is its status as a means of communication severely undermined, but learners are also denied their only genuine stimulus for developing coping strategies and learning to negotiate meaning. In addition, being surrounded by examples of the language in real situations exposes them to a far wider range of patterns and vocabulary than they would otherwise experience.

The focus of classroom interaction must be the expression of meaning, for where nothing new or meaningful is being said, communication ceases. Consequently, especially at advanced level, the meanings which learners themselves wish to express should form the core of the learning process. Content, materials and the sequence in which grammatical patterns are introduced therefore need to reflect students' needs and interests, so that they can be encouraged to engage with them and to assimilate language through use.

This also underlines another important aspect of the communicative approach, a personalization of the language taught and learnt so that it becomes the learner's own. Inherent in this is unpredictability about language use, whereby learners are encouraged to create their own meanings with language rather than simply repeat what they have heard or seen. The social context of the seminar room itself provides a rare genuine focus for this communication.

Essential to the development of such a course is the use of real, or 'authentic', materials which reflect the social and cultural context of the language. At early stages of the learning process, texts may need to be adapted to make them accessible; after all, we learn our first language to a large extent through adapted exposure by means of specially written books and carefully tailored adult speech.

Finally, communicative language teaching involves the integration of the four language skills of listening, speaking, reading and writing. Real-life language usage incorporates a mixture of skills: we engage in conversations which require both listening and speaking; we respond to written stimuli by filling in forms, writing letters, or discussing the content of our reading with others. Modern methods of teaching and assessment recognize this interdependence of skills and incorporate it into tasks for learners rather than creating artificial distinctions.

AUTONOMOUS LEARNING

If, as suggested above, the learner is to take increasing responsibility for progress and the teacher aims to facilitate, not control, the language learning process, then autonomous learning becomes crucial. Autonomous learning does not mean self-instruction or learning without a teacher. Rather it is a way of complementing face-to-face tuition which makes learning more productive and develops independence. Educational research has long recognized that learning is less effective the more learners depend on the teacher and the less they take responsibility for their own learning. Therefore the emphasis currently being placed on the role of the learner in the pedagogical process is to be welcomed.

In a world which is changing so rapidly, students need not so much to accumulate a set body of knowledge as to learn how to acquire knowledge both now and in the future ('lifelong learning'). Language teaching thus implies the development of transferable language learning skills based on an understanding of what makes an effective language learner.

There are three essential parts to this: first, students need to discover how languages are learnt; second, they need to identify their own strengths and weaknesses as language learners; and third, they need some involvement in shaping their course.

Providing students with an insight into the nature of language learning means explaining to them the reasons for engaging in particular classroom activities. It also means teaching them techniques and strategies for:

- *learning vocabulary*: eg grouping words semantically or grammatically; using colour coding or word cards; recognizing cognates; using imagery, mind maps or word association;
- *learning grammar*: colour-coding structures; using mnemonics for rules;
- *reading*: activating background knowledge; making use of titles or illustrations; skimming and scanning of texts; spotting cohesive and coherence markers (see Nuttall, 1982: 110–11);
- *listening*: listening with a purpose; practising gist listening by using background knowledge; listening with and without a text;
- *writing*: producing drafts; checking written work, spotting errors;
- *speaking*: reading and repeating after a tape for pronunciation; phrases and techniques for seeking repetition/explanation, etc; ideas for increasing oral interaction outside the classroom;
- making the most of CALL: working in pairs/individually; focusing on personal weaknesses, using FL spell-checkers.

Such techniques can usefully be listed in a course or module guide at the start of the year but should also be integrated into language-learning tasks themselves in order to demonstrate their relevance and applicability and to encourage their transfer to similar tasks beyond the classroom.

Students need to establish how they learn most effectively. A distinction is frequently made between 'field dependent' and 'field independent' learners (Skehan, 1989: 111–13). The latter are thought to be able to structure information more easily and therefore to be more deductive in their learning style and more concerned with accuracy. The former are inductive learners, more sociable and therefore more likely to be good communicators in L2, with a greater concern for fluency than accuracy. Learners' preferred strategies are influenced by their cognitive learning styles and it is important both that they become aware of how they learn and that they be encouraged to practise strategies which depend on their less dominant, natural or 'instinctive' cognitive style.

Important though learning styles are, students' motivation is ultimately the major factor in successful language learning (see also Chapter 6). Lambert and Gardner (1972) distinguish between 'integrative' and 'instrumental' motivation; the former indicates a genuine interest in the foreign country and the speakers of L2, while the latter denotes greater concern for the practical benefits of learning the language, such as gaining a qualification or using it to further one's career. Integrative motivation and close identification with the target culture seem to be more successful in motivating learners to persist with the long, demanding process of L2 learning. The further students move towards the integrative end of this continuum, the more likely they are to succeed. It should moreover be remembered that, unlike other disciplines, language learning requires students to foresake part of their own identity: their sense of self as defined by their relation to a particular language community. They also have to adopt once more the uncertain role of the imperfect speaker with its inevitable sense of insecurity. Success will depend to a considerable extent on how they cope with these two factors. Teachers need to be sensitive to these motivational issues both in the image they present of the foreign country and its people, and in the way they structure classroom activities to handle students' uncertainties.

Involving students in the organization of the course implies some or all of the following:

- seeking student preferences as to topics;
- allowing students some say in the choice of materials;
- engaging students in independent information-gathering;
- involving them in individually-chosen project work;
- linking tuition to a range of activities in open learning facilities.

In summary, learners need to accept responsibility for their language learning, to develop the capacity to reflect on their individual learning style and to use that reflection to shape the content and process of subsequent learning.

Interrogating Practice

In what ways are your students encouraged and provided with the tools to become independent learners with transferable language learning skills?

USING COMMUNICATION AND INFORMATION TECHNOLOGY IN MODERN LANGUAGES

Communication and information technology (C&IT) can be a useful tool in the development of autonomous learning. Language teachers often argue that language means interpersonal communication and interaction, requiring face-to-face contact which allows language support mechanisms such as facial and body language to contribute to meaning. However, the growth of e-mail as a means of interpersonal communication, the expansion of the Internet as a source of information, and the increasing use of intranets within institutions as a means of dissemination and interaction cannot be ignored. The computer has many valuable assets as one of a range of potential learning tools, and it is the teacher's duty to encourage learners to make full use of any appropriate tool.

The key question is: 'What is appropriate?' Any computer-based learning or teaching activity must be assessed according to its contribution to the learner's language skills. The development of C&IT skills is important, but usage needs to be language- rather than C&IT-driven. One also needs to be certain of the specific advantages brought by the use of the computer to ensure that valuable time is not wasted in the development and execution of activities which would be more effective using paper and pen.

There are ways in which appropriate software, both generic and language-specific, can make a unique and valuable contribution to the learning process; for example:

- with tutorial guidance, students can make use of grammar-based programmes to improve their accuracy by drill and test exercises (see the use of SAF in the Case Study 1);
- multimedia CD ROMs can be used to develop pronunciation and fluency;
- standard CD ROMs can be a valuable source of research material for project work;
- with appropriate guidance on where to look and how to evaluate the reliability and validity of information, the Internet can be a useful source of authentic and interesting material (see WELL, 1999);
- institutional intranets can be used as a means of communication and support for learners within a guided self-study scheme;
- e-mail and video conferencing can be used to enhance the language learning environment.

The list is far from complete, and many accounts of innovative usage can be found in language-learning journals (eg, LLJ, 1998). Although in many cases the technological revolution has been thrust upon higher education staff rather than being the result of organic growth, language teachers need to harness its clear potential for enhancing the teaching and learning environment. This is particularly important when, in a climate of diminishing resources, higher education institutes are investing large amounts of money to comply with government ICT directives. Linguists must ensure they are in a position to reap their share of benefits from this development.

TRANSLATION

In many universities 'prose' and 'unseen' translation, ie translation into and out of the foreign language, are still very common teaching and testing techniques. It is difficult to prove whether translation helps students to learn language. Many now have doubts but still argue for the retention of L2 to L1 translation, at least with final-year students, as a **key skill**. Others see some residual benefits; for example: '…it would seem likely that, because the exercise involves scrutinizing bits of language and evaluating equivalents in the target language, there is some increase in the students' mastery of both languages' (Sewell, 1996: 142).

Reservations about the continued use of translation relate particularly to many departments' traditional approach: students write a translation in their own time, hand it in for marking by the lecturer, who then spends most of the class hour going over the piece, highlighting problems and possibly offering a 'fair' version. Such an approach fails to make clear how students are to learn *about* translation. Instead, it treats translation simply as a vague support to general language learning, and the process becomes in effect little more than repeated testing. An alternative approach, offered in Case Study 1, aims to encourage students to learn about translation.

Case Study 1: Making Translation a More Effective Learning Process

---

University of Birmingham

1. For students to approach the text in an effective manner, they need to be told its context within the whole work, the purpose for which it was written and its intended audience.

2. They need to be shown that translation is not about simply transposing items from one language to another at the level of lexis and syntax, but that it is about conveying meaning. In order to take this first step in reconstructing meaning, they should be encouraged to read the whole text thoroughly, actively and critically, addressing such questions as:

- why has this been written this way?;
- why does this sentence or paragraph come first?;
- is there any reason for having this long sentence in the first paragraph or these very short sentences?;
- does it matter if I merge sentences in my translation and what would be the effect of this?

3. Students need to see the translator as a mediator between cultural worlds, ie as someone who helps those unfamiliar with a culture to understand and appreciate all the cultural nuances of the original text. Translation is therefore a communicative act. Far more than a test of ability to de-code, it is a process of en-coding.
4. Students should be encouraged to use a translation dossier, to make a systematic note of possible translations of or strategies for coping with expressions/phrases which recur and are frequently forgotten in the flurry of translating week after week. This could be arranged under alphabetical, structure or key word headings.
5. Students could be required to produce an occasional annotated translation, giving their reasons for the choices made. This forces them to focus consciously on the act of translation, thus helping to make them more reflective. Repeated translation without focus on the process provides no evidence of learning or progress.

In addition to the strategies outlined above, when employing translation into L1 it is important to focus students' minds away from grammar and lexis towards whole-text and translation-task issues in order to avoid literal and 'safe' translations. The following ideas may be useful:

- students provide a summary of an L2 text as a briefing to someone visiting the foreign country for a specific purpose; this helps to focus attention on relevance and appropriateness of material, on the information needs of the target audience as well as on the style of students' English version;
- the teacher supplies a specific brief (eg to translate an article for inclusion in a particular quality British daily) which requires clear explication of cultural references, foreign figures or events;
- students translate a particular passage for inclusion in a specialist English-language journal and adapt their translation to the particular 'house style' (see Fraser, 1996: 128–29);

- students correct an inaccurate translation which, depending on their proficiency, can be at a simple factual level or may include idiom, collocation, metaphor, etc.

Translation into L2 poses particular problems and can be very demotivating and a poor learning experience for many students. Often learners are asked to perform too many simultaneous tasks and there is insufficient focus on individual weaknesses. There are three alternatives:

1. A basic pedagogical principle is to demonstrate how to do something before asking learners to do it themselves. In translation this can be achieved by giving students a parallel text which allows contrastive analysis of the two languages. It reveals how the translator has set about the task and highlights interesting discrepancies and even mistakes, which are a source of fascination to learners. Students can then move beyond lexical and grammatical points to look for differences in tone, style and register. At the end of a class spent working on the parallel texts the L2 text can be withdrawn and students required to translate the L1. Marking then involves a lot less correction and the process is less demotivating for everyone. Feedback using the original L2 text can focus on students' alternative renderings, thus emphasizing that there is always more than one correct version and reinforcing the message that it is meaning translators should be seeking to convey.

2. Two L2 versions could be used and students asked to compare the two translations, focusing on, for example, lexis, grammar or even idiom. This is a demanding task but carries much potential for learning in the form of more sophisticated contrastive analysis. Setting up these tasks is not easy, but a bank can be built up based on versions produced by two different language assistants or Erasmus/Socrates students. It is also sometimes possible to find two L2 translations of English literary texts. (This exercise can, of course, work well the other way, comparing and contrasting two L1 versions of an L2 text.).

3. As an alternative to 'cold' translation, students can be asked to prepare a text in pairs by underlining any potentially problematic structures and circling any unknown vocabulary. Ideas are then pooled in fours, and groups subsequently brought together for plenary discussion. Vocabulary and structures can be shared on an overhead with all acceptable ways of translating a particular expression being listed and dictionaries being consulted collectively to further good reference skills. The text is then set for homework. The advantages of this approach are that the weaker benefit from collaboration with more able peers and marking time is reduced as less correction of common difficulties is required. The diagnosis of individual errors with ensuing provision of targeted advice thus becomes much easier.

Interrogating Practice

Think of three sources of parallel translation texts for the language you teach. In what ways could you make your current teaching of translation more process-orientated?

These approaches to translation focus attention on process, on learning how to translate and avoid using translation as a continual testing mechanism. Many of the points discussed in this chapter so far are illustrated in Case Study 2.

Case Study 2: First-year French Language Course

University of Birmingham

Many of the above points are illustrated in the following description of a newly developed language course aimed at bridging the gap between the skills of school leavers and the needs of university language studies. The course has not yet been formally evaluated and is not therefore held up as a model to emulate in its entirety, but shows how one department is moving towards meeting the changing needs of the post-A level student. It has been positively received by students, and staff are enthusiastic about its progress and hopeful of the eventual outcomes.

Developed as part of a comprehensive review of all four years of the single and joint honours language curriculum, the course addresses the needs and skill profile of first-year students and takes account of contemporary views on SLA and student-centred learning. In particular, it seeks to provide a balance between, on the one hand, advanced interpersonal communicative skills and, on the other, familiarity with key areas of French grammar and the ability to apply them in written work.

The old

The previous language programme consisted of a highly cognitive, knowledge-based grammar syllabus, featuring elements of **grammar-translation** methodology, linked to traditional 'conversation' classes with largely untrained *lecteurs/lectrices*. Very challenging paraphrase exercises figured quite prominently, while both oral-based work and free writing in French played a relatively minor role.

The new

By contrast, the objectives of the new programme are to:

- retain and foster students' enjoyment of language learning and their motivation;
- build on experience and skills acquired at A level by developing the use of oral and written language in real-life communicative situations;
- foster a greater awareness of the need for accuracy by encouraging the development of learning strategies which enable students to increase and apply their grammatical competence;
- extend knowledge of grammatical structures via a carefully graded programme, mixing basic analytical presentation and individual and group research, with repeated opportunities for reinforcement and re-use;
- promote autonomous learning, especially the use of CALL in consolidating basic grammatical competence;
- promote French as the normal language of classroom instruction;
- develop the ability to use dictionaries effectively and to take notes in French;
- extend students' vocabulary acquisition and their awareness of register by systematic exposure to authentic texts.

Structure

The programme is built around three contact hours per week:

- 'Le cours de langue': conducted largely in French with groups of 16 and organized around the advanced communicative text *Le Nouveau Sans Frontières 3* (1990), it features a range of oral and written exercises, often conducted in small groups, and is also used for feedback on and discussion of a weekly written task.
- 'Le cours d'expression orale': groups of eight to nine students are taught by a *lecteur/lectrice* who has attended the university's part-time teacher training course (attendance at this five-day course is compulsory for all new foreign language assistants); it is run entirely in French and features exercises aimed at promoting comprehension and oral skills; students' participation is reflected in the continuous assessment mark awarded for oral work.
- 'Le cours de grammaire': a lecture which assumes that grammar *knowledge* does not necessarily equate with accuracy in oral and written tasks and that grammar is not learned in a linear, 'once-and-for-all' fashion; in contrast to the old grammar lecture which laid considerable emphasis on

the 'what' and the 'why' of the grammar syllabus, this new one stresses much more the 'how'; it is interactive, taught initially in English and then increasingly in French, covers a much reduced and simplified grammar syllabus, and employs formal presentation linked to practical work-sheet adaptation in small groups of the material presented. It also features an extensive scheme of autonomous learning, whereby students are required to research grammar rules, check on usage and apply their findings to suggested tasks and exercises; keys to all exercises and work sheets are available in the self-access resources centre.

Grammar: identifying weakness

All students sit an initial **diagnostic test** designed to indicate grammatical weaknesses. On the basis of this test they are responsible for devising a remedial programme of study in preparation for two subsequent progress checks. The aim is to instil in them from the very beginning good language learning habits, training them to find things out for themselves and to use their own initiative. More able students are also encouraged to move beyond the basic programme.

Grammar: self-assessment

The university's SAF (student assessment facility) enables staff to create computerized assessments using a simple mark-up language which are then mounted on the open learning server and can be accessed from a number of different computer clusters around campus:

- there are 24 French tests, each of between 100 and 250 gapped sentences;
- each assessment consists of 20 such gaps;
- students complete at least three tests on each of eight grammar points by a series of cut-off dates;
- feedback is provided at the end of each test with remedial help if required;
- students can do up to five tests on each grammar point and receive a different selection of items on each occasion since the programme selects new items from the database every time a student logs in;
- results are stored centrally, and following each assessment deadline a report is produced and delivered to the course coordinator who records as a formal coursework mark the average of each student's best three scores for that particular test.

Autonomous learning

Besides the SAF materials, students are given a clearly defined programme of autonomous learning based on:

- reference books, dictionaries, grammars;
- newspapers and magazines;
- satellite TV, audio and video tapes;
- CD ROMs and commercial CALL programmes.

Linked to this autonomous learning strand is the study diary which all students are expected to maintain and in which are kept notes on all work done outside the course which has contributed to their language learning. This includes an initial work plan to revise grammar following the diagnostic test, which students discuss individually with their language tutor. The whole study diary forms the basis of a discussion with the student's personal tutor at the end of the first semester.

Assessment

- coursework: two written tests, one oral task, six written tasks, eight SAF tests (25 per cent);.
- oral/aural examination (25 per cent);
- three-hour written examination (50 per cent).

OVERVIEW

Language teachers in higher education need to respond to recent changes in the understanding of how languages are learned as well as in the secondary education system which provides its raw material. Perhaps the most significant change of focus in recent years has been towards content-based, meaning-driven language learning within which students are encouraged to explore topics relevant to their needs and interests via mixed-skill activities. This is in contrast to the traditional grammar-led approach focusing on the written language, which is now out of step with the prior learning experiences of many incoming students. The strengths and weaknesses of these students need to be addressed within a flexible learning package, which encourages language acquisition, develops transferable learning skills and identifies and tackles individual formal weaknesses. As Case Study 2 shows, C&IT can be a valuable tool in providing individual support for learners in this process, encouraging an independent approach to the all-important grammar drilling. Where translation remains part of the language curriculum, attention needs to be paid as much to the process as the product.

REFERENCES

CLE (1990) *Le Nouveau Sans Frontieres*, Paris

Dodson, CJ (1985) Second language acquisition and bilingual development: a theoretical framework, *Journal of Multilingual and Multicultural Development*, 6, 325–46

Fraser, J (1996) 'I understand the French, but I don't know how to put it into English': developing undergraduates' awareness of and confidence in the translation process, in *Teaching Translation in Universities*, eds P Sewell and I Higgins, pp 121–34, AFLS/CILT, London

Lambert, W and Gardner, R (1972) *Attitudes and Motivation in Second Language Learning*, Newbury House, Rowley, Massachusetts

LLJ (1998) *Language Learning Journal*, **18**

Little, D and Ushioda, E (1998) *Institution-wide Language Programmes*, CILT/Centre for Language and Communication Studies, Trinity College Dublin, London/Dublin

Nuttall, C (1982) *Teaching Reading Skills in a Foreign Language*, Heinemann Educational, London

Pachler, N and Field, K (1997) *Learning to Teach Modern Foreign Languages in the Secondary School*, Routledge, London

Saunders, K (1996) Grammatical accuracy: a response to Derek McCulloch, *German Teaching*, 13, pp 30–32

Sewell, P (1996) Translation in the curriculum, in *Teaching Translation in Universities*, eds P Sewell and I Higgins (1996) pp 135–60, AFLS/CILT, London

Skehan, P (1989) *Individual Differences in Second-Language Learning*, Edward Arnold, London/New York

Thomas, G (1993) *A Survey of European Languages in the United Kingdom*, CNAA

Towell, R and Hawkins, R (1994) *Approaches to Second Language Acquisition*, Multilingual Matters, Clevedon/Philadelphia

WELL (1999) Web-enhanced language learning, FDTL project Web site, www.well.ac.uk

Wilkins, D A (1976) *Notional Syllabuses*, Oxord University Press, Oxford

FURTHER READING

Bygate, M, Tonkyn, A and Williams, E (eds) (1994) *Grammar and the Language Teacher*, Prentice-Hall, Hemel Hempstead. A varied collection of articles on the role of grammar in language teaching.

Coleman, James A (1996) *Studying Languages. A Survey of British and European Students*, CILT, London. A key study of British undergraduate language learners, their skills, motivation and background.

Engel, D and Myles, F (eds) (1996) *Teaching Grammar: Perspectives in higher education*, AFLS/CILT, London. Contains a number of suggestions for integrating grammar.

Hervey, S and Higgins, I (1992) *Thinking Translation: A course in translation method*, Routledge, London. A course available in French (1992), German (1995), Spanish (1995) and Italian (1999) with varied techniques and exercises.

Parker, G and Rouxville, A (eds) (1995), *'The Year Abroad': Preparation, monitoring, evaluation*, Current Research and Development, AFLS/CILT, London. A thorough and practical introduction to all aspects of this central part of the undergraduate degree.

Sewell, P and Higgins, I (ed) (1996) *Teaching Translation in Universities: Present and future perspectives*, AFLS/CILT, London

Towell, R and Hawkins, R (1994) *Approaches to Second Language Acquisition*, Multilingual Matters, Clevedon/Philadelphia. A readable survey of the theoretical principles of SLA.

CILT produces a very useful 'Pathfinder' series on all aspects of language learning. Although often written with a secondary audience in mind, the very practical issues discussed here are relevant to all educational sectors.

Key Aspects of Teaching and Learning in Medicine and Dentistry

Adam Feather and Heather Fry

AIMS AND INTRODUCTION

This chapter aims to build on earlier generic chapters, such as those on student learning, assessment and small group teaching. It reviews some of the distinctive aspects of teaching and learning in medicine and dentistry, seeking to elucidate them for the relatively inexperienced teacher.

It will focus on:

- teaching and learning in contexts where patients are involved;
- skills of teaching in simulated settings;
- **problem-based learning** (PBL);
- approaches to assessment of learning in the clinical context.

Chapter 20 also contains material relevant to those teaching basic medical sciences.

It is a truism to say that educating doctors and dentists is a complex business. Medical and dental education involves:

- remembering a large amount of factual material;
- understanding complex mechanisms;
- competence in a wide range of technical skills;
- understanding and use of the scientific method;
- developing socially responsible attitudes and ethical practice;
- promoting interpersonal skills for working with colleagues and patients;
- developing sophisticated problem-solving and reasoning skills.

Few of those involved in medical and dental education teach all of these aspects, but all should be aware of the spectrum and be discriminating in their choice of appropriate methods. Medical and dental education share many overlapping concerns but also have areas of variation. One of the key differences in the training needs of the two professions is that, at undergraduate level, dental students are more involved in invasive work with patients than their medical counterparts. Another is that, on graduation, the dentist has to be capable of independent practice without supervision.

Context and background

The education of dentists and doctors is embedded in the practices and mores of two large service activities, namely, education and health care provision. These dual and sometimes competing strands are present at all levels: undergraduate, pre- and post-registration as well as specialist training.

In the last decade the UK health service and dental and medical education have undergone major changes. These have shifted the emphasis away from hospitals and towards primary care. The General Dental Council (GDC) and General Medical Council (GMC) have statutory responsibility for approving undergraduate courses for training and have both published recent guidelines for devising courses.

The GMC requirements for undergraduate curricula (1993) were radical and extensive. *Tomorrow's Doctors* emphasized the global expansion of knowledge and the rate at which it becomes obsolete. Like several earlier documents, it criticized factual overload in curricula. It emphasized learning and study skills, being curious and critical in approaching knowledge and acquiring understanding of underlying principles, concepts and mechanisms rather than the teaching and regurgitation of enormous amounts of material. This is in line with contemporary understanding of how students and professionals learn (see Chapter 3). The main outcome of the recommendations has been the moves by UK medical schools to a 'core plus options' approach to curricula, and more problem-based methods of delivery. Assessment has lagged a little behind other curricular reforms.

The publication of the GDC undergraduate curriculum recommendations (1997) also marked a considerable advance. The GDC emphasized its desire to see educationally progressive ideas and improved methods of study incorporated into curricula that exhibited reduced congestion. The document is more prescriptive of 'essential elements' than its medical equivalent and encourages early patient contact.

Postgraduate training has also been examined more closely. In 1997 the GMC set out professional and educational requirements for pre-registration house officers. The Calman Report (1993) made speciality training shorter and more structured, introducing greater formality in appraisal and assessment. The vocational year for newly qualified dentists has now become a requirement prior to independent National Health Service (NHS) practice and speciality registers have been established.

It is likely that the role of dentists and doctors will change further as nurses and dental therapists take on more clinical responsibility and inter-professional practice develops. It is also likely that training for tomorrow's dentists and doctors will include greater preparation for an evidence-based approach to practice, and more training in the use of information technology (IT) and the Internet. The trend to formalize postgraduate education and continuing medical/dental education will continue.

Interrogating Practice

You may wish to check that you are familiar with the national recommendations for undergraduate and postgraduate training operating in your country and speciality.

PATIENT-CENTRED TEACHING AND LEARNING

Clinical, as used by the ancient Greeks, meant 'pertaining to the sick bed'. Modern practices have led to changes in this unique teaching and learning environment. However, the basic principles of teaching at the chairside and bedside remain much the same. With earlier clinical exposure, students may be forced to develop a more balanced approach to the acquisition of knowledge, technical skills and professional attitudes and behaviours.

Clinical teaching is a three-way dynamic between teacher, patient and student. As it occurs in the workplace, it may be a 'hostile' environment for all three. As the controlling factor, the teacher is obliged to maximize the situation from all perspectives.

Interrogating Practice

If you are a clinician, think back to your first days as a student in the clinical environment. What were the features (ie of the environment, situations and types of teachers) of a good learning experience?

The patient

Whether in the clinic, surgery or ward setting, the patient is the most vulnerable of the three parties. Most medical patients find clinical teaching extremely rewarding, often commenting that they feel students 'have to learn'. In dentistry there is a slightly different relationship. The patient is receiving treatment from a novice under instruction. Their vulnerability is magnified and the teacher has added (statutory) responsibilities. The patient must be reassured that a watchful eye is being cast. In both cases, the patient's attitude towards being used in teaching should always be respected and it should be reinforced that, whatever their decision, it will not affect their treatment and care. Within teaching hospitals and surgeries, patients should be made aware that the facility is a teaching environment and that students may be present, or in the case of dental students, carrying out the required treatment. This allows the patient to prepare for the initial encounter and to raise any anxieties they may have. At all times one needs to keep the patient informed, reach mutual agreement about the session, and most importantly, ensure that patient privacy and dignity are maintained. One should explain to the medical patient the number and level of the students who will be in attendance and the patient's proposed role. Common questions include, will they be asked to undress, will the students be performing a procedure on them, will there be a discussion about them or the case? Verbal agreement should be obtained. Dental sessions differ in that the patient is being treated and followed up by the student under the supervision of the teacher. The dental supervisor must approve the proposed treatment, ensure it has been explained correctly to the patient and review its course and outcomes.

The student

With new curricula in the United Kingdom, the challenges of the clinical environment will have to be met by students from a very early stage of their training. As with the patient, good preparation reduces anxieties, and sets out a clear level of professional conduct.

Before students are ready to interact with patients they need to practise basic clinical skills. This should occur in a safe, supportive environment such as that of a clinical skills centre (see page 356). Generic skills, particularly communication, may be slowly introduced and practised in this way. For dental students, competence in core skills will have to be demonstrated prior to their introduction to the clinical arena.

Students should be encouraged to attend clinical sessions in the right frame of mind. The dental student is immediately faced with professional obligations, and the teacher must stress their responsibility to their patients. Punctuality, appearance, background reading and practice of skills need to be emphasized. The teacher should make provision for teaching and learning when patients are unable to attend; **self-directed learning (SDL)** and **computer-assisted learning (CAL)** will allow the student time to test knowledge and skills at their own pace.

For medical students, their clinical experience is all too often a rather less demanding time. However, they too should demonstrate similar professional obligation and be in possession of basic equipment such as a stethoscope. (It may be necessary for the teacher to provide additional equipment such a patella hammer, ophthalmoscope or auriscope.) Before they go on the ward, students should be well briefed.

Students should not be placed in an unsupported environment or pressured into performing tasks that are beyond their level of training or conflict with cultural beliefs. Ethical dilemmas may be encountered by students but they should never be asked to face them without guidance.

The teacher

For the clinician, the clinical environment should be one in which they feel comfortable. They will be familiar with the setting, the staff and hopefully aware of the potential problems that may be encountered while teaching.

Full-time members of university staff perform the majority of dental undergraduate teaching and this removes many of the hazards of the 'part-time' medical teacher. Bedside teaching often involves the teacher, patient and several students. In contrast, teaching in the dental clinic involves several students, each with their own patient, being overseen by one teacher. A teacher/student ratio of about 1:8 is fairly common. Dental students work closely with other health care professionals from an early stage of their training and the supervisor should be aware of this relationship and its development. The teacher's role is one of supervision, guidance and ensuring safety of all participants.

If the clinical setting is new, you should make every effort to familiarize yourself with it. Always introduce yourself to the staff and explain the purposes of your teaching. On the wards it may be necessary to check that the patient(s) you wish to use in teaching are not going to be 'employed' in procedures or investigations. Check that your session does not encroach into ward routines. Locations and times may suddenly need to be changed, but the onus is firmly on the teacher to try to be punctual and prepared, or at least inform students and patients of unavoidable changes. (Medical students often quote lack of information and disregard by the clinical staff as reasons for recurrent non-attendance.)

Whatever the clinical setting, the teacher should not use the session to lecture, or use the patient as a 'chalkboard' or living text. The guiding principle in medicine should be one of demonstration and then observation. In dentistry the chairside role is primarily that of advice and supervision. For the teacher, student–patient interactions may appear routine but for the other parties they are often complex and require a great deal of guidance, particularly in the early stages of training. Opportunistic teaching may present itself in both contexts and should never be overlooked. Good preparation and time for **reflection** and **feedback** should be built into sessions.

Clinical teaching and learning is exciting and rewarding, but lack of essentials within the modern NHS, such as appropriate lighting, routine equipment and even patients make teaching challenging. Within the outpatient, community and dental settings, the potential to regulate, plan and control this environment is very much greater than on the wards. Modern medicine and dentistry may have changed the environment in which we teach and learn, but not the basic principles of care and professionalism.

Points to consider when teaching in a patient-centred environment:

- patient, student and teacher safety and anxieties;
- introduction of students to the clinical environment;
- skills acquisition and practice;
- observation and practice of professional behaviour;
- teaching versus treatment.

Interrogating Practice

Using the suggestions above, how will you develop your teaching practice to improve the learning of your students?

SKILLS AND SIMULATION IN TEACHING AND LEARNING

For many years clinical medicine and dentistry were taught by the principle of 'see one, do one, teach one'. This placed the student and patient into an unsatisfactory partnership, rife with potential embarrassment and harm. The inception and utilization of simulation within clinical teaching and learning has allowed students to confront their anxieties within a safe environment, while providing the teacher with a regulated, reproducible teaching arena. The simulated element will most commonly refer to materials, actors and **role play**. There remains some debate as to the stage at which clinical skills, including communication skills, should be introduced into the undergraduate curriculum. The trend has been for ever earlier introduction.

A clinical skills centre or laboratory, where practical procedures and communication skills may be demonstrated and practised, is now incorporated into the infrastructure of many medical and dental schools. The form that this centre takes, and the equipment within it, vary between institutions, from single rooms to multipurpose 'laboratories' and from latex and plastic manikins to virtual reality simulators. Experience within the medical skills centre at the authors' institution has shown that the siting of the centre should, if possible, be close to the clinical areas. This makes for easier teaching and encourages reflection and practice of skills when they are still fresh in the students' minds. Dundee University Medical School (Scotland) has also stressed the need for timetabling of clinical skills sessions into the student curriculum. The centre may be used for teaching by clinical staff and for SDL and CAL, but we have found that the employment of a dedicated skills teacher has revolutionized the utilization and potential of the centre. An initiative at Leeds University Medical School has also seen the employment of a ward-based skills teacher (Stark, Delmotte and Howdle, 1998) which is helping to bridge the competence/practice divide. While dental schools have commonly abandoned rooms of phantom heads, more sophisticated models and partial operatories fulfil similar functions (Suvinen, Messer and Franco, 1998).

Peyton (1998) describes an excellent, and widely advocated, model for teaching skills, known as the 'four stage approach'. It may be applied in many dental and medical settings.

Stage 1   Demonstration of the skill at normal speed, with little or no explanation.
Stage 2   Repetition of the skill with full explanation, encouraging the learner to ask questions.
Stage 3   The demonstrator performs the skill for a third time, with the learner providing the explanation of each step and being questioned on key issues. The demonstrator provides necessary corrections. This step may need to be repeated several times until the demonstrator is satisfied that the learner fully understands the skill.

Stage 4   The learner now carries out the skill under close supervision describing each step before it is taken (adapted from Peyton 1998, 174–77).

This model may be expanded or reduced depending on the background skills of the learner. Video may be used in stages 1 and 2 but this should also follow the guide above, with little or no explanation in stage 1. As with all teaching, the learner must be given constructive feedback and allowed time for reflection and practice of the skills. Within the medical clinical skills centre, particularly in SDL, we have found the use of itemized checklists useful adjuncts to learning.

Interrogating Practice

How could you adapt Peyton's four-stage approach to your own (simulated/non-simulated) clinical teaching?

Simulation

Through the lead of communication skills' teachers, simulation of clinical scenarios has become increasingly sophisticated, now employing professional actors and actresses. Within the safety of this play-acting, the students can express themselves more freely, while investigating the patient perspective through the eyes of the actors. The teacher must provide a clear brief for both actor and student, including detailed background scripts for the actors. Real patients may also be trained and used in clinical training and assessment. Within the authors' institution their input has been invaluable in helping actors get 'in-role'. It is important that the students feel comfortable within their given role and that the scenario is within their expected capabilities. Clear student learning **objectives** are required at all stages, but excessive demands and expectations are often counterproductive.

Simulated patients (SPs) were first used in the 1960s (Abrahamson, 1994) with their use in dental and medical undergraduate and postgraduate education expanding rapidly since the 1980s (Barrows, 1993). They may be used instead of real patients in difficult clinical scenarios, eg breaking bad news and in the reproduction of acute problems that would not be assessable in traditional clinical examinations. In North America, SPs are also used for training and assessing potentially embarrassing clinical procedures such as vaginal speculum examination. In dentistry, SPs are principally used for communication skills training and in assessment (Davenport *et al*, 1998). Despite many advantages, simulation has its limitations and should be additional to, and not a substitute for, clinical opportunities with real patients.

Role playing is another extremely useful teaching and learning tool. Students are able to investigate and explore both sides of a clinical interaction through their adopted roles. Criticisms of this technique are usually a product of poorly prepared sessions. Clear roles, with demonstration by teachers, or using pre-prepared videos, are useful ways of directing the student learning. Encouraging a supportive but quite formal environment during the sessions also encourages students to maintain their role. Pre-warned, with adequate debriefing and reflection, the students usually find this a useful technique.

Videotaping has long been used in general practice, particularly for postgraduate learners. It is, however, an area that has not been so fully exploited in dentistry. This is a useful tool, particularly for reflection and feedback, and may be employed in simulation, role play and the recording of 'real-life' interactions.

Questions to think about in relation to skills and simulation:

- how does the learning environment of the clinical skills centre differ from that of the clinical arena?;
- what are the positive and negative attributes of simulation?;
- how far can and should patients be used in training?;
- what is the role of 'skills and simulation' in assessment?;
- what is the potential for greater IT usage?

PROBLEM-BASED LEARNING

Problem-based learning is an idea that has had currency since the 1960s (Neufeld and Barrows, 1974), but was not widely used in medical and dental education in the United Kingdom until the middle 1990s. It is now an element in many UK medical and dental undergraduate curricula, in some cases being the main pedagogical method used.

There are many variants of PBL. Boud and Feletti (1996) review the range. However, there are some elements that are usually present, including:

- learning and teaching stemming from, and coming after, exposure to a scenario (the 'problem') which may be written, videotaped or a patient (Aspergren, Blomqvist and Borgstrom, 1998);
- small interactive groups of students exploring the problem in a structured manner and subsequently sharing knowledge and understanding;
- students, not the teacher, making decisions about what they need to learn in relation to the scenario;
- a student 'scribe' recording the deliberations of the group;
- a non-didactic facilitator;
- integration of disciplinary and clinical and non-clinical subject matter.

Interrogating Practice

Check if you understand how PBL differs from problem solving. Examine the list above, rejecting any item that would not generally be a feature of a course using problem solving. The rejected item(s) are what distinguish PBL.

The University of Maastricht version of PBL is probably the most widely known. Each problem or scenario is investigated by students following the 'seven-jump' model, in which they:

1.   Clarify terms and concepts in the problem – students pick out words and phrases not understood and see if any group member can explain them.
2.   Define the problem – students set out/restate the terms and ideas that need to be explained or understood.
3.   Analyse the problem – students generate possible explanations (usually some are incorrect).
4.   Make a systematic inventory of the explanations in step 3 – students do this by linking ideas, showing relationships, etc.
5.   Formulate learning questions – these are the things students think they need to learn to be able to understand or explain the problem.
6.   Collect information – each student does this before the next session, attempting to find the answers to the learning questions.
7.   Synthesize and test the information – students report back and discuss their findings (adapted from Bouhuijs, Schmidt and van Berkel, 1987).

A series of problems sharing a common theme are arranged into blocks, typically lasting four to five weeks. Each block has overall objectives and a title indicating the area of study. A problem is discussed over two sessions. In the first session of the block, steps 1–5 of the first problem are covered. Subsequent sessions share a similar format, with steps 6–7 of the previous problem occupying the first hour, and steps 1–5 of the next problem occupying the second hour (see Table 24.1).

Table 24.1 Typical arrangement of a four-week block of PBL teaching

Weeks	1			2	
Activity	Overview Lecture of Theme	PBL 1	PBL 1 · 2	PBL 2 · 3	PBL 3 · 4
Duration (hours)	1	1	2	2	2

Weeks	3		4		
Activity	PBL 4 · 5	PBL 5 · 6	PBL 6 · 7	PBL 7	Other/ Assess- ment
Duration (hours)	2	2	2	1	1

Case Study 1: A Scenario for Problem-based Learning

Lund University, Malmö, Sweden

Trigger

A coloured photograph showing redness and swelling around the maxillary central incisor, accompanied by the words 'Karin notices bleeding around one of her front teeth of the upper jaw when she brushes her teeth'.

This problem is used in the middle of the first year. Lund University has schematic charts (concept maps) of the content of its whole curriculum and of the individual problems. It is worth noting that a tag such as 'explain these phenomena' rarely follows triggers.

Further details of the Lund curriculum and of the Karin problem can be found in Rohlin, Petersson and Svensäter (1998).

Case Study 2: A Scenario for Problem-based Learning

Faculty of Medicine and Health Sciences, University of Newcastle, Australia

Trigger

Peter Fraser, age 47, is brought to the accident and emergency department at the Mater Hospital, by a friend. They had been driving home from a business dinner at a local club when Peter said he felt sick and asked the taxi driver to pull over to the kerb. Peter got out of the car and a minute or so later he vomited food mixed with fresh blood into the gutter. His friend wasn't sure how much blood he had vomited, but thought it was probably about a cupful. Peter had told him he felt a bit shaky and sweaty, so his friend asked the taxi driver to bring them to the hospital.

This working problem is used in the third term of the first year of the Bachelor of Medicine curriculum at the Newcastle Medical School, Australia. Clinical reasoning is regarded as central to student learning; the process is explicit in the tutor guides and groups learn to approach problems through an hypothesis-based enquiry. Hypotheses are based on basic science mechanisms, rather than 'diseases', as their aim is to achieve learning of basic and clinical science in a clinical context. The process is assessed **formatively** and **summatively** in year one of the course.

The focus of the trigger is acute upper gastrointestinal blood loss and hypotheses will be based on the likely site of blood loss and the likely nature of the lesion. The observation that the patient felt 'shaky and sweaty' leads to consideration of the effects of acute blood loss (previously studied in the first term in relation to blood loss after trauma).

(Dr Jean McPherson)

Further details of the Newcastle curriculum can be found in Henry, Byrne and Engel (1997).

Teachers starting to use PBL often find they need to develop new skills. The following generic guidelines are useful pointers. The facilitator:

• is not there to lecture. The facilitator keeps the process on time, on track, ensures students do not go away from a problem with mis-information, asks non-leading questions as and when appropriate, and (in many versions) assesses the performance of all individuals in the group;

- establishes or reiterates group ground rules when taking a new group;
- assists the student 'officers' to fulfil their roles, but does not usurp their positions;
- assists in creating a learning environment in which students can admit they do not know something;
- makes sure students feel able to question and query each other, using an appropriate manner;
- encourages students to use and formally evaluate a wide variety of information sources;
- assists students to present cogently and avoid rambling 'lectures';
- encourages the involvement of all students;
- asks students periodically to summarize a case or aspects of it;
- at the end of each problem asks students to summarize their findings, evaluate how they tackled the problem and suggest how the process could have been more effective;
- gives feedback to students about their performance in a specific, constructive manner (generally within the group setting).

Interrogating Practice

Think about the ways in which you usually teach (or have been taught). If you were facilitating PBL tutorials, which aspects would you find most difficult? How would you tackle these?

Given that the introduction of PBL into an established school requires a substantial change, why is the effort being made? Several meta-analyses reported in review articles examined evidence of the effectiveness of PBL as an approach to teaching and learning (Schmidt, Dauphinee and Patel, 1987; Norman and Schmidt, 1992; Vernon and Blake, 1993; Albanese and Mitchell, 1993; Berkson, 1993). The five studies cover a wide range of arguments and attributes, although, as with many aspects of education, it has proved hard to produce definitive evidence. However, all five studies find evidence to suggest that PBL students are better able to take a **deep approach** to learning (see Chapter 3). Another well-substantiated aspect is that while students on traditional curricula tend to score slightly higher on conventional tests of knowledge (Schmidt, Dauphinee and Patel, 1987; Norman and Schmidt, 1992; Vernon and Blake, 1993), PBL students retain their knowledge longer (Norman and Schmidt, 1992; Albanese and Mitchell, 1993). Students seem to perceive PBL as more clinically relevant and to rate their programmes positively (Schmidt, Dauphinee and Patel, 1987; Vernon and Blake, 1993; Albanese and Mitchell, 1993).

Issues to consider when introducing PBL

Variable aspects of PBL include: at what stage students are provided with tutor-determined learning objectives; whether each student follows up all the learning objectives; how many sessions are allocated to each problem and if there are supporting layers of information that can be revealed to students. There is also debate about the extent of tutor intervention, how far PBL is usable in the more clinical parts of courses and whether the expert or non-expert makes the best type of PBL tutor. No matter what version is used, it is important to train staff and students in its usage, provide adequate tutorial and study rooms and ensure learning resources are available. On first introduction, time is needed for curriculum planning, writing problems and supporting tutorial material, and developing appropriate assessment. PBL also requires a fresh way of thinking about evaluation.

CLINICAL ASSESSMENT

In common with other assessment, clinical assessment needs to be suited to curriculum intentions, while emphasizing preparation for practice. It should be educationally sound, being **valid**, **reliable**, feasible, defendable and well conceived from the perspective of impact on learning. The challenge is to use appropriate assessment methods, following the basic guidelines of assessment (see Chapter 5).

George Paget at Cambridge formally introduced the assessment of clinical skills as part of the medical final graduating examinations in the 1840s (Poynter, 1966). Traditionally, this assessment took the form of a long case, a series of short cases and a viva voce examination. Dentistry too, has long had traditional graduating clinical examinations that have changed very little until the last few years.

During the past 20 years the changing demographics of admissions to medical and dental schools, public expectation and increasing scrutiny from clinicians and educationalists have forced much needed change into these old systems. The GMC has devoted much time to postgraduate performance appraisal (Southgate and Dauphinee, 1998). Cynics may also point to the emergence of examination litigation, notably within the United States, as a reason for such change. The principal problem with the older clinical assessments was relatively strong validity, but poor reliability. The previous written assessments were weak in both validity and reliability. In most UK schools it was also common practice to allow compensation of borderline grades across subjects and between written and clinical assessment.

Key to the changes introduced have been the increase in objectivity, described as the 'objectification' of medical assessment (Van der Vleuten, Norman and De Graaff, 1991) and with it, the increase in reliability. The introduction of newer assessments claiming to have increased validity also saw the division of clinical and written assessment. Another change has been the move away from a 'big bang' graduating examination toward continuous assessment. This has shifted the emphasis of final examinations to 'fitness to practise'. PBL will also influence future assessment choices. As a result of these changes there are now many, newer types of assessment and strategies.

Updating clinical assessment: (a) the short case

The typical traditional medical and dental short case involved a candidate seeing four or five patients in front of a pair of examiners. The candidate was typically asked to carry out a clinical examination or provide a diagnosis. The first major change in clinical assessment came with the description of the **Objective Structured Clinical Examination (OSCE)** (Harden and Gleeson, 1979). Since the early 1990s the OSCE has become widely used in Europe in both undergraduate and postgraduate assessment. In the United Kingdom, medical short cases are rapidly being usurped by the OSCE, whereas in dentistry the two assessments are more frequently being used alongside one another.

The OSCE consists of a circuit made up of a number of cubicles or stations through which each candidate must pass. At each station the candidate is required to perform a given clinical task. This may be observed and assessed by an examiner, or may require the candidate to answer some questions, usually in a multiple-choice format. The tasks may include communication skills, history taking, informed consent, clinical examination of real and simulated patients, clinical procedures performed on manikins, and data interpretation. Stations may also be developed to assess various attitudes and behaviours. Each student is assessed on the same task by the same examiner. To further objectivity, the observer is provided with a checklist that has a breakdown of the task into its component items. The observer is requested to mark the candidate on each of these items. More recently, global rating scales have been advocated and employed. Despite fears and inferences that their use would be a retrograde step toward the old, subjective marking system, they have been shown to be as reliable as their detailed counterparts (Allen, Heard and Savidge, 1998).

The OSCE remains an assessment in evolution. Debate continues about the maximal duration of the stations, the minimum testing time required for a reliable examination and the number of stations and tasks assessed. In most institutions these details are governed by the practical considerations of the number of students to be examined, the facilities available and, perhaps most importantly, the financial constraints. At present, most UK undergraduate high-stake OSCEs consist of 20 to 30 stations, each of approximately 5 to 10 minutes in length. It should be stressed that OSCEs of less than two and a half hours become increasingly unreliable and should not be used summatively. However, the 5 to 10 minute station format limits the type of task assessed and is probably more applicable to the assessment of students in the earlier clinical years. During this period single tasks need to be assessed in isolation to ensure **competence**. At graduation, and indeed probably earlier in dentistry, one is more interested in a holistic approach and extended or paired stations may be employed, lasting 15 to 20 minutes. These may be used to assess a wider range of skills within a single clinical scenario.

Case Study 3: Dental OSCE Station Used at the Dental School of St Bartholomew's and the Royal London School of Medicine and Dentistry, London

This five-minute, final-year, undergraduate station uses freshly mixed alginate (impression material) to simulate soft tissues. The usual surgical instruments are available to carry out the procedure. There are separate sets of examiner and candidate instructions.

Question

You are going to carry out inverse bevel flap periodontal surgery (modified Widman flap) to treat periodontal pocketing at the misial and distal aspects of the lower first molar tooth.

Make the incisions you would use on the buccal aspect of the model provided, and elevate the flap appropriately.

The examiners' mark-sheet details 10 aspects the candidate needs to perform correctly. For each aspect a single mark is awarded if it is done as detailed on the mark sheet; no mark is given when it is not done as detailed. The 10 points were:

- selects correct instrument for incision (number 15 scalpel blade);
- uses finger rest on tooth;
- preserves gingival contour/'knife edge' papillae;
- makes inverse bevel incision 1 mm from the gingival margin;
- makes incision at correct angle to the long axis of the tooth;

- extends incision down to the alveolar bone;
- makes appropriate extension of the flap by extending flap to distal of second molar and to first premolar *or* uses appropriate relieving incision(s);
- makes second incision in gingival crevice;
- elevates flap with correct instrument (periosteal elevator);
- uses periosteal elevator correctly (convex curvature pointing medially).

Case Study 4: An Example of a Medical OSCE Station

This five-minute station would also include a background script for the simulated patient and a separate set of examiner and candidate instructions.

You are a medical student attached to a general medical outpatient clinic. The next patient is a 72-year-old man complaining of palpitations. Please take a history of the presenting complaint and any further relevant history with a view to making a diagnosis.

The examiners' mark-sheet from this OSCE uses a three-point scale of 'good'; 'adequate'; 'not done' and contains items relating to both communicating with a patient (such as introducing oneself and inviting the patient to ask questions) and to asking the correct questions of a patient with these symptoms. The station concludes with the examiner asking the candidate to offer a differential diagnosis. The simulated patient participates in examining the candidate by being asked to respond to two questions on the mark sheet: Did the candidate treat you in a professional manner? Did the candidate allow you to express your concerns?

(adapted from Feather, Visvanathan and Lumley, 1999)

The main problems with the OSCE format are the financial costs and the manpower required. The administration, logistics and practicalities of running an undergraduate OSCE are comprehensively described in Feather and Kopelman (1997). At St Bartholomew's and the Royal London School of Medicine and Dentistry, we have run undergraduate OSCEs for five years and have calculated that they are approximately 30–50 per cent more expensive than traditional examinations. However, this must be set against their reliability, which is far superior to that of traditional short cases.

Updating clinical assessment: (b) the long case

The traditional long case in both medicine and dentistry was a one-hour unobserved session in which the candidate was required to clerk a patient and formulate a management plan. They were then examined by a pair of examiners. This assessment had remained unchanged since probably before the days of Paget. However, it too has recently been subjected to review and more objective formats have been developed; these include the observed long case (Newble, 1991) and the **Objective Structured Long Examination Record**, the **OSLER** (Gleeson, 1992). A combination of these approaches has been adopted in principle by the Royal College of Physicians and is being evaluated. These changes have led to candidates seeing similar patients with parts or all of the clerking being observed by the examiners and identical aspects being assessed. Performance is graded against a checklist, similar to that used in an OSCE.

The updated long case is a more reliable assessment than in its traditional form but is still not satisfactory for summative purposes. As with the traditional long case, it should only be used in combination with other assessments of clinical competence, eg an OSCE. At present, medical students and postgraduates are rarely observed clerking patients. Formative and summative use of the updated long case should rectify this and be a useful tool, when applied over several disciplines, in picking up common problems. The authors are not aware of publication of a dental equivalent to the updated long case, but it has equal potential in dental assessment, where an observer may objectively assess the full dental consultation and management. Teachers and students alike will have to prepare for this form of assessment.

In North America, a further development has been the **Focused Patient Encounter** (FPE) also known in postgraduate education as mini-**Clinical Examination Exercise** (mini-CEX). This involves the student being asked to focus their history and examination to one key point of the clinical problem, eg dental or chest pain.

Updating clinical assessment: (c) the viva voce

The **viva voce** is often used as a summative assessment tool but is regarded by many as educationally defective and indefensible. It is the least reliable of any form of clinical assessment because it uses only two examiners and its unstructured format can result in a very variable interaction. Its content validity is also questionable. Despite its poor reliability, its use is still widespread in undergraduate and postgraduate assessment within the United Kingdom. It is often used in making pass/fail decisions and decisions of 'excellence'. Its defenders quote it being 'like real life' and 'useful in gauging a candidate's all round knowledge', but much of what is gauged about a candidate is actually covered by other, more reliable forms of assessment. In an attempt to bring its supporters and detractors together, it too has been subject to 'objectification'. The viva voce, structured or otherwise, will no doubt remain entrenched within the UK medical and dental education system, and we should continue to prepare candidates and potential viva examiners.

Updating clinical assessment: (d) log books

Log books have long been used to record clinical practice, exposure and events in both undergraduate and postgraduate education. However, in their traditional form, they were often subject to abuse, even in the more supervised dental environment. This abuse was often a result of poor objectives and unrealistic targets. In response to this criticism, the use of the log book has changed. Students should now be encouraged to use them to reflect upon clinical events in which they have taken part. Entries in the log book should be monitored and commented upon, so directing the student's learning. Thus, they may be used as a formative assessment tool. With the introduction of the Calman recommendations, most senior house officers and specialist registrars are now required to keep training logs. These are used to ensure all trainees are reaching nationally agreed standards but are also useful for the trainees to reflect upon their areas of strength and those that require improvement.

Developing written assessment: extended matching questions

Over the past 30 years, written assessment has also been subject to change. Much of this has been driven by the use of computer-assisted marking schedules and the need for increased reliability and validity. **Multiple-choice (MCQ)** and short answer questions are common to many disciplines, but **extended matching questions (EMQs)**, have been developed to assess higher levels of cognition, including diagnostic reasoning (Case and Swanson, 1996). At present their use is limited in UK undergraduate dental and medical curricula.

Case Study 5: The EMQ Format

Theme: anaemia

Options

A	Acquired non-immune haemolytic anaemia	G	Iron deficiency anaemia
B	Anaemia of chronic disease	H	Leukoerythroblastic anaemia
C	Aplastic anaemia	I	Pernicious anaemia

D	Autoimmune haemolytic anaemia	J	Sickle cell disease
E	Congenital spherocytosis	K	Sideroblastic anaemia
F	Folate deficiency	L	Thalassaemia major

Please select from the list above the most appropriate diagnosis for each of the patients below:

1. A 55-year-old woman presents with lassitude and tingling in her limbs. On examination she is pale and has a peripheral sensory neuropathy. The serum contains autoantibodies to parietal cells and intrinsic factor.
2. A 64-year-old man presents with pain in the upper right quadrant of his abdomen. Ten years earlier he had an aortic valve replacement. Investigations reveal a normochromic, normocytic anaemia with fragmented red cells and a reticulocytosis. A direct Coomb's test is negative.
3. A 44-year-old woman presents with lassitude. Her full blood count reveals a hypochromic, microcytic anaemia. Her serum ferritin is low.

Assessment is one of the fastest changing areas in medical and dental education and one in which continuing professional development is crucial. The innovations within this field may also be generalizable to some other disciplines as they update their teaching and learning process.

OVERVIEW

Medical and dental teaching and learning has recently undergone 'major surgery' with the aim of 'anastamosing' sound educational theory with traditional teaching and learning methods. New curricula, with student driven learning, 'objectification' and innovation within assessment, and the changing postgraduate structure have left much for the 'jobbing' clinician to keep up with. Many in the older schools question whether such revolution is worthwhile. Evidence, although measured on older criteria, suggests that these major changes are not producing a 'better' graduate but are producing a different, perhaps more rounded, individual but one in whom the public can still place confidence. As professionals, we are coming under increasing public scrutiny and this is never truer than in education. We must apply the same evidence-based approach to our teaching practice as we do to our clinical practice. Traditional methods do not need to be thrown away but can be improved and brought into line with modern educational theory and practice.

REFERENCES

Abrahamson, S (1994) The foreword to *A Handbook for Medical Teachers*, 3rd edn, eds D Newble and R Cannon, Kluwer Academic Publishers, London

Albanese, M and Mitchell, S (1993) Problem-based learning: a review of literature on its outcomes and implementation issues, *Academic Medicine*, **68** (1), pp 52–81

Allen, R, Heard, J and Savidge, M (1998) Global ratings versus checklist scoring in an OSCE, *Academic Medicine*, **73** (5), pp 597–98

Aspergren, K, Blomqvist, P and Borgstrom, A (1998) Live patients and problem-based learning, *Medical Teacher*, **20** (5), pp 417–20

Barrows, H (1993) An overview of the uses of standardized patients for teaching and evaluating clinical skills, *Academic Medicine*, **68**, pp 443–53

Berkson, L (1993) Problem-based learning: have expectations been met? *Academic Medicine*, **68** (10), pp S79-S88

Boud, D and Feletti, G (eds) (1996) *The Challenge of Problem-Based Learning*, Kogan Page, London

Bouhuijs, P, Schmidt, H and van Berkel, H (eds) (1987) *Problem-Based Learning as an Educational Strategy*, Network Publications, Maastricht, Netherlands

'Calman Report' (1993) *Hospital Doctors: Training for the future*, Report of Working Group on Specialist Medical Training, Department of Health, London

Case, S and Swanson, D (eds) (1996) *Constructing Written Test Questions for the Basic and Clinical Sciences*, National Board of Medical Examiners, Philadelphia

Davenport, E *et al* (1998) An innovation in the assessment of future dentists, *British Dental Journal*, **184** (4) pp 192–95

Feather, A and Kopelman, P (1997) A practical approach to running an OSCE for medical undergraduates, *Education for Health*, **10**, pp 333–50

Feather A, Visvanathan, R and Lumley, J (1999) *OSCEs for Medical Undergraduates*, Pastest, Cheshire

General Dental Council (1997) *The First Five Years*, GDC, London

General Medical Council (1993) *Tomorrow's Doctors*, GMC, London

General Medical Council (1997) *The New Doctor*, GMC, London

Gleeson F (1992) Defects in postgraduate clinical skills as revealed by the objective structured long examination record (OSLER), *Irish Medical Journal*, **85**, pp 11–14

Harden R, and Gleeson, FA (1979) Assessment of clinical competence using an objective structured clinical examination (OSCE), *Medical Education*, **13**, pp 41–54

Henry R, Byrne, K and Engel, C (eds) (1997) *Imperatives in Medical Education*, Faculty of Medicine and Health Sciences, Newcastle, Australia

Neufeld, V and Barrows, H (1974) 'The McMaster Philosophy': an approach to medical education, *Journal of Medical Education*, **49**, pp 1040–50

Newble, D (1991) The Observed Long Case in Clinical Assessment, *Medical Education*, **25** (5), 369-73

Norman, G and Schmidt, H (1992) The psychological basis of problem-based learning: a review of the evidence, *Academic Medicine*, **67** (9), pp 557–65

Peyton, JWR (1998) *Teaching and Learning in Medical Practice*, Manticore Europe Limited, Rickmansworth, Herts

Poynter F, (ed) (1966) *The Evolution of Medical Education in Britain*, Pitman Medical Publishing Company Limited, London

Rohlin, M, Petersson, K and Svensäter, G (1998) The Malmö model: a problem-based learning curriculum in undergraduate dental education, *European Dental Journal*, **2**, pp 103–14

Schmidt, H, Dauphinee, W and Patel, V (1987) Comparing the effects of problem-based and conventional curricula in an international sample, *Journal of Medical Education*, **62**, pp 305–15

Southgate, L and Dauphinee, D (1998) Maintaining standards in British and Canadian medicine: the developing role of the regulatory bodies, *British Medical Journal*, **316**, pp 697–700

Stark P, Delmotte, A and Howdle, P (1998) Teaching clinical skills using a ward-based teacher, presentation at the ASME Conference, Southampton, September, 1998

Suvinen, T, Messer, L and Franco, E (1998) Clinical simulation in teaching preclinical dentistry, *European Journal of Dentistry*, **2** (1), pp 25–32

Van der Vleuten, C, Norman, G and De Graaff, E (1991) Pitfalls in the pursuit of objectivity: issues of reliability, *Medical Education*, **25**, pp 110–18

Vernon, D, and Blake, R (1993) Does problem-based learning work? A meta-analysis of evaluative research, *Academic Medicine*, **68** (7), 551–63

FURTHER READING

Albanese and Mitchell (1993) See above. The single best place to gain an idea of the usefulness of PBL and possible variations in its use.

Case and Swanson (1998) See above. For different types of examination questions.

Jolly, B and Grant, J (eds) (1997) *The Good Assessment Guide*, Joint Centre for Medical Education in Medicine, London. Probably the best single source of explanation about suitable types of assessment.

Jolly, B and Rees, L (eds) (1998) *Medical Education in the Millennium*, Oxford University Press, Oxford. Many useful chapters, especially student learning and learning with the Internet

Newble, D and Cannon, R (1994) *A Handbook for Medical Teachers*, Kluwer Publishers, London. A basic 'how to do medical education'; also useful for dentistry.

Peyton JWR (ed) (1998) See above. Some aspects helpfully described.

25 Key Aspects of Teaching and Learning in Business and Management Studies

Judith Foreman and Tom Johnston

AIMS AND INTRODUCTION

This chapter focuses on drawing out and considering distinctive features of business and management studies at the undergraduate level. Its emphasis is on the implications of these features for teaching, learning and assessment. The chapter builds upon and refers to several of the generic chapters in Part 1.

Business and management education is not unique in seeking to develop a wide range of skills in its students, but for a long time it has shown concern for aspects of performance, for what students can 'do' as well as what they 'know'. The 'doing' aspect of the projected future career has centred on a set of personal and practical skills, roughly outlined as 'working with people', which are seen to develop alongside, or, ideally, intermingled with the development of knowledge and understanding.

BACKGROUND

Business and management studies in the United Kingdom attract the largest number of applicants for first degree and Higher National Diploma (HND) courses. The number of applicants has increased over several years. In 1996–97 the number of students enrolled on undergraduate business courses was 158,912 or 11.4 per cent of total higher education enrolments (HESA, 1998). Students tend to be young and to come from diverse social and educational backgrounds. For example, although just over half of those admitted to business courses have A levels, students in this area are more likely than other subject groups to have General National Vocational Qualifications (GNVQs). Compared to the overall pattern of ethnic minority participation in higher education, business and management courses attract a high proportion of ethnic minority students. The area is popular with women as well as men, although there is evidence of gender segregation in terms of the specific areas of business and management education studied (UCAS, 1998).

The subject area generally described as business and management is broad and multi-disciplinary. Provision of courses in the area covers many different educational levels and qualifications, designed to meet the needs of both experienced practitioners and those without practical experience. Analysis of data from institutions offering first degree courses in business and management reveals a wide variety of course titles and subject combinations. These include general undergraduate courses in business studies, business administration and management, more specialist courses covering specific aspects of business and management such as human resource management, marketing and operations management, and courses specializing in particular industrial sectors such as public sector management, leisure management, tourism management, and hotel and catering management. There are also many joint and combined honours programmes linking business and management with a wide variety of subject areas including languages, psychology, economics, law, computing science, accounting and finance, engineering and science subjects.

In addition to content, curriculum structures also vary with, for example, some first degrees incorporating a work placement in a three or four-year, full-time programme. Part-time and **distance learning** modes of delivery are also evident. Contents and curriculum structures have also changed in recent years as institutions have forged closer links between traditional academic courses accredited by higher education institutions and courses accredited by external bodies such as the awarding body Edexcel. For example, many institutions now provide one and two-year 'top-ups' to related HND programmes leading to BA and BSc awards in business and management. There are also examples of institutions incorporating guidelines on content and **learning outcomes** in the design of undergraduate courses derived from bodies such as Management Charter Initiative (MCI).

The current debate regarding **quality**, **standards** and **subject benchmarking** for UK higher education, stimulated by the **Dearing Report** (NCIHE, 1997), the **Quality Assurance Agency** (QAA) and the funding councils, may result in the production of guidelines for business and management education in which subject contents and learning outcomes are broadly specified (see Chapters 4 and 15). This may, in turn, provide greater clarity and understanding regarding what is a complex subject area, and provide some reassurance to those concerned with academic standards. (The Association of Business Schools has already produced its own guidelines for the higher degrees of DBA and MBA.)

Whatever the outcome of the current quality debates, the widespread use of **modularity**, and the popularity of business and management studies options to students within other subject areas, will mean that in many institutions business and management subjects will continue to be taught in combination with a wide variety of disciplinary and vocational areas, and to attract diverse groups of students. This raises many issues and challenges for the development of effective learning and teaching in the area.

Interrogating Practice

What subject combinations are represented among the students you teach? Do you think this has any implications for your teaching and their learning?

SKILLS AND KNOWLEDGE IN BUSINESS AND MANAGEMENT EDUCATION

Business and management education is characterized by multiple **aims** and **objectives** that reflect the diversity of the subject area, the variety of courses available to students, and specific disciplinary and institutional needs and philosophies. Despite the obvious vocational orientation of courses in business and management, debates concerning the relationship between theory and practical skills, especially the role of behaviourally-oriented subject matter in business and management curricula, have a long history. Much of this debate has focused on the validity of **competence**-based education as opposed to more theoretically based approaches and on the pedagogical implications of incorporating a skills focus into the curriculum.

Since the 1980s, pressure on business and management education providers to examine their understanding of, and approach to, developing the links between theory and practice and the teaching and learning of practical skills has grown. This pressure largely arose in the wake of widespread claims that business and management schools are failing to produce graduates with the attributes needed by modern organizations.

Numerous studies purporting to identify the qualities of effective managers and organizational practitioners (see, for example, Margerison and Kakabadse, 1984) drew attention to purported deficiencies. In much of this literature is the contention that although specialist subject knowledge and strong analytical skills are important, competence in personal and interpersonal skills and being able to work effectively with people are a critical prerequisite for success in management. In their study of what constitutes effective management, Whetton, Cameron and Woods (1994), for example, identify a number of attributes as the most frequently discussed skills of effective managers. The attributes include: verbal communication – including listening; managing time and stress; managing individual decisions; recognizing, defining and solving problems; motivating and influencing others; delegating; setting goals and articulating a vision; self-awareness; team building; and managing conflict. These attributes are similar to those resulting from several other surveys published in the management literature and, according to Whetton, Cameron and Woods (1994), are generally agreed upon across both the public and private sectors and at all levels of management.

The focus on developing a broad range of skills and knowledge, including personal and interpersonal skills, is also highlighted in current discussion regarding the development of **key, transferable skills** in the curriculum for students on all degree programmes. Debates regarding the skills and abilities that all graduates will need for employment in the organizations of the future are widespread (see Chapter 10). In these debates, many of the skills, aptitudes and attitudes now identified as the keys to employability and lifelong learning for graduates of all disciplines, resemble those also commonly identified as essential for graduates of business and management courses. For example, recent research on skills regarded as desirable by employers indicates that the so-called 'soft-skills' such as oral and written communication, team working, listening and problem solving are as important as academic qualifications in preparing people for employment. In relation to managerial roles specifically, the research suggests that over 90 per cent of human resource professionals consider soft skills as key competencies and a prerequisite for managers (DfEE, 1998).

Despite the enduring reluctance among some individuals and institutions to embrace a more explicitly focused skills approach to business and management education, and continued discussion regarding the educational value and utility of such approaches, analysis of current aims and objectives in relation to intended learning outcomes in UK institutions reveals a combination of subject specific knowledge, critical thinking and analytical skills, as well as personal and transferable skills, as being commonly taught on business and management courses. The **quality assessment** overview report on business and management studies in 47 UK institutions concluded that intended learning outcomes for students 'usually encompass the development of students' intellectual capacities, vocational knowledge and skills, personal and transferable skills, and progress to employment and further study' (HEFCE, 1995). For over half of the institutions assessed, vocational relevance, the needs of industry, capability and responsiveness to the changing nature of organizations and their needs, were emphasized. The commitment to develop students' business skills together with personal and transferable skills was evident in two-thirds of the cases. The report notes, however, that there are a variety of different approaches to defining 'skills', different approaches to their development in the curriculum, and different emphases placed on skills by institutions.

Interrogating Practice

If you are not familiar with it, read the quality assessment report for the subject in your institution. How far have things moved on since it was produced? How would you characterize the approach in programmes you teach on to the development of key skills?

TEACHING AND LEARNING APPROACHES

The best approach to business and management studies learning and teaching must combine a number of aims:

- development of a set of personal and interpersonal skills;
- development of rigorous knowledge and the ability to interrogate models and theories through the application of critical thinking and analytical skills;
- opportunities to practise and apply theoretical and conceptual learning.

Achieving these aims raises many pedagogical issues concerning teaching and learning methods, and assessment of what is learned, and resource implications. Drawing on our own experiences, and the views of others involved in first degree business and management education, the following guidelines and practical examples are offered toward creating an effective and supportive learning environment.

Arguably, the broad range of knowledge, skills and understanding demanded of graduates in business and management necessitates that we go beyond the conventional lecture/**seminar/tutorial** format and explore different types of learning and teaching activity. At the very least, textbook-based, lecture-problem styles of learning associated with the acquisition of 'knowledge' must be augmented with other methods designed to develop a broad range of personal and practical skills. Behind the search for different and more appropriate types of learning is a debate that has been going on in all sectors and levels of education for many decades. It concerns the roles of the teacher and learner and their relationship in terms of expertise, knowledge and experience. The debate can be illustrated by a number of polar descriptions under the headings 'tutor-centred' and 'learner-centred' approaches (see Table 25.1).

Table 25.1   Roles of teacher and learner in different models of education

Tutor-centred	Learner-centred
Expert	Learners draw on and use own experience
Single answer	Diversity of viewpoints
Student passive recipient	Student active in own learning
Led by tutor	Multi-dimensional channels of interaction
Subject/knowledge focus	Analysis and problem solving
Theoretical/abstract	Interrogating theory/practice
Answers	Confessing confusion or even ignorance
	Learns what questions to ask

We would argue that a 'learner-centred' approach in which class members are challenged to become 'learners' rather than 'students' is important. Learners need to take ownership of their own development through self-managed learning, and to be actively involved in the development of their classmates (Serey and Verderber, 1991). Such involvement is a key element in creating a learning environment in which knowledge, understanding and skills can be developed. Chapters 3 and 11 provide further information about the theories and research underpinning these perspectives, and on experiential learning. The emphasis on 'learning to learn' and 'learning to think' has implications for the role of the teacher and the role of the student, and the contribution each makes to the learning environment (see also o Chapter 16). For example, many students in higher education today have work and life experiences that would clearly enhance a particular module or course, especially in the area of business and management, and in these cases students may have as much to contribute to the class as the tutor. This, of course, means that the teacher may have to relinquish some authority and claim to expertise and search for new ways of undertaking the role of educator. It may be that the new role is that of a 'guide', rather than a 'sage', in which the tutor's job is to set the task which requires the search for knowledge, to help students seek it out, and to demonstrate how that knowledge can be used.

Approaches to teaching and learning in business and management include a variety of methods: case studies; **simulations**; projects; small-group work; **computer-assisted learning** and work experience are commonly adopted, both within and in addition to the traditional lecture, seminar and tutorial format. Most of these methods are described in a generic context in chapters earlier in this volume. At first degree level, however, large numbers of students and pressure on resources (classroom time, staff time and student time) often result in heavy reliance on the conventional lecture/seminar format, and may work against the encouragement of a more learner-centred approach and opportunities for the development of a range of personal and practical skills. Nevertheless, there are ways of creating more stimulating and exciting classroom atmospheres within the conventional lecture/seminar framework, where learners can be more actively involved in their own and others' learning, and a broad range of skills can be fostered.

Working with small groups

Case Study 1 is drawn from our experiences in delivering a final year compulsory module on a first degree programme in Organization Studies. Large numbers of students (approximately 80) were required to take the module, so 'seminar' groups tended to be large and to discourage student participation. The seminar tutors often ended up providing a mini-lecture in further explanation of the lecture that had preceded the seminar. As a consequence of growing unhappiness with this situation, a group of tutors set about devising a more dynamic and participatory approach working within the constraints of large student numbers and limited staff resources.

Case Study 1: Reconfiguration of Final-year Undergraduate Module on Organizational Analysis

Bradford Business School, Bradford College

For some time there had been concern that the traditional one-hour lecture followed by the one-hour seminar (which often became a mini-lecture) was encouraging passivity in students. Over a short period, a team of staff devised an approach to the coverage of a compulsory unit in the final year of the BA (Hons) Organization Studies degree. The characteristics of the approach were:

- the unit, Organizational Analysis, was divided up into five topics;
- each topic was delivered over a two-week period;
- in the first week a one-hour lecture was followed by a one-hour seminar;
- for the lecture, the following were provided in handouts: title of topic; brief outline; specific, manageable readings; seminar questions;
- seminar readings were assigned to individuals;
- for each seminar, two roles were assigned to students: (i) that of recorder, who noted the group's discussion and other relevant points with regard to the seminar questions and compiled the list of uncertainties and other questions for the tutor; (ii) that of chair, whose role was to concentrate on the dynamics of the group (and not be a subject specialist), to facilitate discussion and bring in quiet students, etc.

The student discussion in the seminar group was scheduled for 30 minutes, with no tutor present. At the half-hour, the tutor joined the group to receive the summary of the discussions so far and the uncertainties/disagreements. The role of the tutor was to clarify these issues in discussion with the students.

Week 2 pursued the topic in greater depth through a workshop. Each student was allocated reading in advance of the workshop with the expectation that it would be completed; the workshop also had topic questions.

At the beginning of the two-hour session each student was quickly allocated to one of three or four discussion groups with one hour to prepare for a plenary session which took place in the second hour with all students present. The first half-hour was tutor-free. Each plenary session varied. For example, in some instances where the topic and problem permitted, students presented their work in the form of a debate on a proposition.

The programme was reviewed at the end of the year and was judged positively by both students and staff. The positive features were seen to be:

- the development of skills – advocacy, communication, teamwork;
- students were able to express uncertainties without a tutor present;
- the structure prevented a series of mini-lectures which bred student passivity;
- the structure made it difficult for passengers and spongers;
- it forced learners to come to terms with the material.

Some problems also emerged. For example:

- participation of all students was not always easy to achieve;
- some students tended to dominate discussion, making it difficult for others in the group;
- not all students were as committed to this form of learning as others were.

A key element in the development of business and management skills, as with many other skills, is that learners should be given the opportunity to practise their skills (Bigelow, 1991). Practice can take many forms. In Case Study 1, the seminar/workshop structure required not only student participation in group discussion, analysis and problem solving, but also included an element of role play as part of the experience. Students acted as recorders and observers of other learners' deliberations, chaired discussions, and acted as group facilitators. In so doing, students were able to practise a variety of personal and interpersonal skills, including oral communication, leadership, chairing, cooperation, teamwork, negotiation and listening.

For group work to be effective, tutors need training and experience in the effective management of this kind of learning. Planning has to go into such things as the role of the tutor, the layout of the classroom, the expectations and ground rules that will shape the process, and ways in which learner participation can be enhanced. With a diverse group of students, facilitating such participation can be challenging (Entwistle, Thompson and Tait, 1992).

Interrogating Practice

What contribution can this method of working make to the development of students' practical and intellectual skills in business and management? How could group work be more widely used in the courses with which you are involved? What steps may be taken to ensure that students are fully involved in discussion and interaction during group work?

Students also need some preparation and experience. Demands made on students in one module could be stressful and counter-productive if there is little emphasis on developing their self-confidence, teamwork and oral communication skills elsewhere in the programme of study. At Bradford College, students are given the opportunity of undertaking communication skills training through the provision of modules in written and oral communications as part of their degree course. Elsewhere, group work, communication and interpersonal skills are integrated into the learning and teaching approaches of several core modules at all levels of the course, providing opportunities for experience as students progress through their programme of study.

Using case studies

In addition to role play and seminar presentations, opportunities for learners to practise and develop their skills, knowledge and understanding through application can take many other forms. Case studies, originally devised for use in medicine and law, have long been used in business and management education as a way of encouraging students to develop analytical and problem solving skills as well as enhancing their practical managerial knowledge.

Students who are provided with case studies are encouraged to use, work through and apply relevant theoretical and conceptual models to the analysis of real organizations. Case studies can be of varying complexity. They may comprise a basic, simple description of a single incident that raises a problem for discussion. Alternatively they might provide a panoply of information to constitute a full-blown scenario, having information on the broad external context within which an organization operates, together with information about the internal context such as finance, human resource issues, reward systems and work systems.

Case studies can be used in a variety of ways with students. For example, students may be asked to specify solutions to practical managerial problems, or to provide a critical analysis of what is going on in the organization. Some writers on the use of case studies in business and management education criticize what is regarded as a tendency to rely on conventional managerial problem-solving approaches and cases, and the adoption of a narrow managerial perspective at the expense of a more critical analysis, for example Corbett (1994). In working on case studies, students may be required to provide an individual written response to the case study, or may be required to work in groups and to provide both an oral presentation as well as written material as part of their remit. Students may be required to analyse and solve problems, individually or in groups, from particular role positions within the case study organization – for example, from the perspective of a consultant, the director of personnel, the managing director, union representatives, and so on.

Case studies can be derived from a number of sources, including the European Case Clearing House (see Resources and Further Reading, page 390), the tutor's own research and/or consultancy experience, can be based on real events in real organizations (suitably anonymized where appropriate), or describe fictitious situations and organizations. Some books supply useful cases, for example Clegg, Kemp and Legge (1985).

Well thought-out case studies, with careful guidance and sensitive feedback from tutors and other students, have the capacity to interest, motivate and engage learners both intellectually and emotionally. Like all teaching methods, however, the question has to be asked, 'in which situations does a case study approach best enhance learning and help students achieve their learning outcomes?' Consideration also needs to be given to ways in which cases studies may work in conjunction with other learning resources – books, tutors, etc. In addition, tutors may require some guidance on how best to undertake case study analysis (for example Easton, 1982).

Case Study 2: Using Case Studies in Business and Management Education

The following is an example of the use of a case study in an introductory unit, Introduction to Management, with a group of stage one undergraduates at Bradford College who, despite having some labour market experience, have limited managerial knowledge and experience. Class sizes for this core unit are large, typically 80 to 90 students, so the lecture followed by seminar format tends to be used.

The unit is taught across both semesters and aims to introduce students to the study of management and the work of managers as preparation for more in-depth study later in the programme. In the second semester students are introduced to particular aspects of management, including managing information, managing people, marketing, operational and strategic management. Case studies are widely used in this segment of the teaching programme in order to give students the opportunity to examine management issues with reference to situations arising from real-world organizations. Typically the case studies are used in the following way.

The topic area 'managing people' provides an overview of personnel and human resource management and usually includes a lecture on the concept of managing diversity. The lecture seeks to outline the concept, some of the issues relating to diversity in contemporary organizations and what this means in terms of managerial practice. In so doing, the session also introduces the concept of inequality, identifies the groups likely to suffer from unfair treatment and examines briefly some of the internal process and practices that contribute to inequality in organizations. This can be difficult to grasp in the abstract and the importance of the topic to the practice of effective 'people management' in organizations can sometimes be overshadowed by student responses to the issue as of interest only to women or other 'disadvantaged' groups. The use of concrete examples in a case study has aided understanding and has been a useful way of engaging diverse groups of students in debate.

In this particular instance a published case study from a collection edited by Clegg, Kemp and Legge (1985) has proved extremely useful. The case study is only six pages, short enough for student reading and analysis in class, but rich in detail. The case study also provides questions for discussion, although in the time available it is not possible to address all of them. In the seminar following the lecture, students are divided into smaller groups to analyse the case study and prepare answers to the questions. In the second half of the session, students report back to the whole seminar group on their responses to the questions. The tutor facilitates discussion.

In another example of the use of case studies in teaching on the management of diversity, students are asked to draw up an appropriate programme of action to promote equal opportunities, using information contained in a case, and to present their recommendations in the form of a role play. In this instance, small groups of students are asked to assume the role of consultants or a working party and to present their proposals to senior organizational managers using appropriate arguments and means of communication.

Interrogating Practice

Reflect on a particular module or topic area in which you teach and think about (more) ways in which the use of case studies could aid students' understanding and learning. Ask yourself what, in this instance, could a case study achieve that another form of teaching could not? How could the case study be used in conjunction with other teaching and learning approaches and resources?

Use of university learning in the workplace

The predominant purpose of business and management education is to facilitate learning, practice and action outside the programme. Transfer of learning occurs when the learning in one situation influences a person's learning and performance in other situations. The learning in question may concern knowledge, skills, attitudes or behaviours. The manner in which transfer of learning may occur is considerably debated and raises a number of issues about student learning (see Chapter 11). Given that many business and management programmes claim their graduates are able to 'hit the ground running', or have the skills and ability to enable them to make a contribution to their employer from the outset, some specific preparation for the transfer/use of skills and other attributes in the workplace is appropriate.

The classroom provides opportunities for the acquisition of theoretical knowledge and is a relatively safe place to experiment with personal and interpersonal behaviours, make mistakes and receive constructive and supportive **feedback** on performance. However, transferring learning to an actual job setting using classroom-based approaches is limited. Student placements in organizations can provide new and challenging contexts in which to develop skills, and the opportunity to use theory learnt in the classroom to practise in the lived world of business and management.

Many business administration degrees conventionally include a 'sandwich' element in the course structure. This usually takes the form of students undertaking work placement for a year as part of a four-year course of study. On other courses a shorter period of work placement may be included in the course structure. This may take the form of a block of time spent in an organization during part of the academic year. Case Study 3 is derived from our own experience of providing a work placement element on undergraduate programmes in management and organization studies over many years.

> ## Case Study 3: The Professional Semester at Bradford Business School, Bradford College

Background and explanation

The current professional semester at Bradford College has developed over many years. Prior to semesterization and modularization, an organization placement element was included in each of the three years of full-time study on a variety of management and related degrees. This sequential placement was intended to be developmental and to provide students with progressive opportunities to relate theory to practice and to develop a range of vocational and transferable skills. After the introduction of a modularized curriculum structure and semesterization, practicality resulted in the abandonment of the sequenced placement and the introduction of the professional semester. This is located in **level 2** of the full-time programme and comprises the whole of the second semester.

The professional semester is designed to provide students with a structured opportunity to synthesize their studies and relate theory to practice through an extended experience in an organization which matches as far as possible their vocational choice or academic specialization. After a three-week introductory programme, students normally undertake a placement for eight consecutive weeks in a selected organization. During this period, they are expected to perform such duties as are mutually agreed between themselves, their allocated college tutor and a supervisor from within the organization. Students are expected to conform with, insofar as is feasible, the customary working hours and practices of the organization at the level in which they are placed. The terms 'professional placement' or 'organizational placement' are preferred to 'work experience' in order to convey the distinct nature of the placement, which includes a complex range of activities and expectations in addition to providing students with an opportunity to experience 'work'.

The placement semester is fully integrated into the curriculum structure and teaching and learning processes of each degree programme. Lecturers are fully involved in the preparation of students for placement and provide support and supervision for students during their time away from the classroom. Assessment is built into the structure of the placement and relates to both the core and optional areas of students' degree programmes.

Aims

Within the specific context of each degree programme the broad aims of the professional semester are to:

- promote and enhance students' abilities to relate theory and practice within the core and optional elements of their programmes of study;
- promote the active development of students' critical thinking and inter-personal skills through extended, **reflective** practice in organizations;
- allow students to evaluate their own efforts and actions in applying their growing theoretical knowledge, skills and insights to an analytical appraisal of the placement organization;
- promote student **autonomy** in learning, by facilitating individualized experience of value to deepen their understandings and to serve as a basis for their subsequent learning;
- allow students to test themselves against the expectations and demands of a possible future career and assess their own performance as an orga-nizational member at an appropriate level.

Preparation and assessment

Preparation for the placement semester is embedded in each of the preced-ing semesters. For example, core modules in organizational theory and analysis introduce a range of theoretical and conceptual models for the analysis and understanding of organizations and includes a variety of expe-riential and skills based exercises to develop student skills in identifying, analysing, and diagnosing selected issues in organization practice. An introductory module in social psychology and organizational practice includes, as part of its contents and aims, the development of interpersonal skills useful for working with people in various organizational settings, for example, skills of interaction, communication, self-evaluation and group participation. A module in research methods develops students' skills in undertaking independent research in organizational settings. During the three weeks at the beginning of the placement semester, students are given further preparation and support. This takes the form of structured lectures, seminars and tutorials derived from the core and optional elements of their programmes, with a specific focus on the tasks that students are expected to undertake in their placement organization that will count toward meeting the assessment requirements of the course.

Assessments typically take the form of asking students to evaluate critically a particular theory or conceptual model in terms of its applica-tion to their placement organization. Thus, for example, in their studies of organization theory, students may be asked to examine the nature and utility of 'systems theory' as applied to their placement organization and its environment. In their studies of operations management, students may be asked to evaluate the effectiveness of a product or a service or system within the organization, and utilizing the concept of the product life-cycle.

The assessment of the professional semester in the main arises through the submission of a placement **portfolio** at the end of the semester. This consists of written assignments corresponding to the core and optional elements of the student's course of study and the placement preparation sessions. In addition to written assignments, however, students are also required to do an individual oral presentation made to a group of students and tutors on a topic of their choice. The presentation is normally derived from an individual research investigation undertaken by the student within their placement organization. **Peer assessment** forms part of the assessment for this piece of work.

Placement organization, supervision and support

Academic and support staff within the College have, over many years, built up strong links with a network of local private, public service and voluntary organizations. Such staff, in discussion with students, are able to assist in identifying and selecting placement organizations which match students' career and academic aspirations. At the same time, however, students are also expected to be fully involved in the process of finding an appropriate organization and in negotiating the terms of their placement. This involves students in undertaking a qualifications, personal skills and career aims audit. They must also investigate and select a suitable placement, identify self-development needs and devise an action plan to meet self-development needs, make an application for a placement, and participate in selection procedures (eg providing a curriculum vitae, attending interviews) to obtain the placement.

(Craig Docherty, David Dunn and Judith Foreman)

We would strongly argue that in order for organizational placement to be an effective means of enhancing students' knowledge and skills and to provide the basis for further learning, it must be fully integrated into the overall curriculum content and assessment strategy of the course programme.

ASSESSMENT AND FEEDBACK

Assessment methods in business and management are broad in range, reflecting the diversity of teaching and learning approaches in the area and the wide variety of skills and knowledge encompassed by the subject. As with other subject areas, best practice involves ensuring that teaching, learning and assessment methods complement one another and that assessment criteria are well understood by students (see Chapter 5). The assessment methods must be congruent with the skills and knowledge being assessed. In planning assessment, the first stage of the process involves identifying the knowledge, skills and other attributes that students are expected to demonstrate and deciding whether students will be subject to assessment in all of these aspects.

Devising appropriate, **valid**, strategies for assessing business skills – critical, analytical as well as action skills – poses challenges in terms of more familiar forms of assessment such as essays and examinations and may necessitate the development of different approaches. Nevertheless, more conventional assessment methods such as written assignments can, where appropriate to the subject matter, be designed to include criteria relating to the conventions associated with written communications in business and management settings.

Assessment provides a powerful incentive for students to take personal and interpersonal skills seriously, as well as reflecting the important role that such skills play in the curriculum (Gibbs *et al*, 1994). Less familiar methods, such as oral presentation (see Case Study 3) and role play, can be used in appropriate subject contexts and assessed using criteria developed from the conventions and requirements of professional practice. Peer assessment may form an element in all or part of these types of assessment. Business and management may also find approaches used in connection with skills assessment in other disciplines, for example medicine and dentistry (see Chapter 24), to have scope for adaptation.

Case studies can be used as opportunities for students to demonstrate their learning. Care is needed, however, in the selection of cases to ensure they provide an appropriate basis for assessment and enable students to demonstrate their skills. Work/organization placement can also be used as opportunities for students to demonstrate what they know and can do. In Case Study 3, students' abilities to transfer their learning on the course to practice, are assessed in the form of written assignments collected into a portfolio. The assignments are designed to test students' theoretical knowledge, their ability to undertake research activity and analyse the work situations they are in. They also assess students' ability to evaluate the applicability of theoretical and conceptual models to the real world of their placement organization. By completing the work placement, students also demonstrate a variety of additional personal and interpersonal skills necessary for their successful operation in an organizational environment. In this case, however, these skills are not formally assessed.

An essential part of the process of learning is receiving feedback (see Chapter 6). Just as it is important in relation to written work, receiving feedback on performance in communication and team working is essential to learning in these areas. At Bradford, feedback and monitoring are regularly provided for students in cases where their skills are being assessed. Often this takes the form of lecturers giving feedback to an individual student, and will not involve other students in the process. Other models for giving and receiving feedback, however, provide guidelines on monitoring as a fundamental and regular part of the teaching and learning process, and provide examples of the ways in which students can be involved in reflection on their own and other students' performance (see, for example, Gibbs, 1994).

Interrogating Practice

Reflect on ways of giving feedback to students and ways in which students can be involved in giving feedback to each other.

OVERVIEW

This chapter, in addition to showing the importance of cognitive and intellectual skills development in management education, has emphasized the growth of a set of personal and interpersonal practical skills, including self-awareness, which are seen as essential for future business managers and organizational practitioners. The teaching and learning strategy utilized is one that attempts to bring out in the participant an active, exploratory stance to the subject matter, to place her or him in a challenging position where rote answers are often not available for solutions. Much of the approach is incremental, moving from the relative security of the classroom to attempts to explore, assess, appraise and actively experiment with the participant's own skill in real world situations.

REFERENCES

Bigelow, J (ed) (1991) *Managerial Skills: Explorations in practical knowledge*, Sage, California
Clegg, C, Kemp, N and Legge, K (eds) (1985) *Case Studies in Organisational Behaviour*, Harper & Row, London
Corbett, M (1994) *Critical Cases in Organisational Behaviour*, Macmillan, London

DfEE (Department for Education and Employment) (1998) *Skills and Enterprise Executive*, Issue 1, February 1998, Sheffield

Easton, G (1982) *Learning from Case Studies*, Prentice-Hall International, London

Entwistle, N, Thompson, S and Tait, H (1992) *Guidelines for Promoting Effective Learning in Higher Education*, Centre for Research on Learning and Instruction, University of Edinburgh, Edinburgh

Gibbs, G (1994) *Learning in Teams: A student manual*, The Oxford Centre for Staff Development, Oxford

Gibbs, G et al (1994) *Developing Students' Transferable Skills*, The Oxford Centre for Staff Development, Oxford

HEFCE (Higher Education Funding Council for England) (1995) *Quality Assessment of Business and Management Studies 1994*, Subject Overview Report 00 7/95

HESA (Higher Education Statistics Agency) (1998) *Students in Higher Education Institutions 1996/97*, Cheltenham

Margerison, C and Kakabadse, A (1984) *How American Chief Executives Succeed*, AMA Publications, New York

NCIHE (1997) (Dearing Report) *Higher Education in the Learning Society*, National Committee of Inquiry into Higher Education, HMSO, London

Serey, T and Verderber, K (1991) Beyond the wall: resolving issues of educational philosophy and pedagogy in the teaching of managerial competencies, in *Managerial Skills: Explorations in practical knowledge*, ed J Bigelow, pp 3–19, Sage, California

UCAS (1998) *Annual Report 1997 Entry*, UCAS, Cheltenham

Whetton, D, Cameron, K and Woods, M (1994) *Developing Management Skills for Europe*, Harper Collins, London

RESOURCES AND FURTHER READING

Bigelow, J (1991) and Whetton *et al* (1994) See above. Both provide useful explorations of practical knowledge

Heath, J (1998) *Teaching and Writing Case Studies: A practical guide*, European Case Clearing House, is a useful source of case studies and guide to using them.

The European Case Clearing House, based at Cranfield University in the United Kingdom and Babson College in the United States supplies, for a fee, management case studies. It holds thousands of cases, many of which have associated teaching notes, and promotes using case studies in teaching.

Glossary

This glossary provides two types of information. First, it provides the reader with simple explanations and definitions of technical and educational terms used in this book. Second, it provides a dictionary of many commonly-used abbreviations and acronyms used in higher education. The glossary has been carefully assembled by the editors. In the text, glossary entries appear in **bold**. These reflect current usage in higher education in the United Kingdom.

Academic practice   A term used to describe the collective responsibilities of academic staff in higher education, namely those: for teaching, learning and communicating the subject, discipline-specific research/scholarship, academic management activities and for some service requirements.

Accreditation   Certified as meeting required standards; eg an accredited teacher implies the teacher has achieved predetermined and agreed standards or criteria.

Achievement motivation   A desire to succeed at a task; eg obtaining high grades, even when the task does not inspire interest (see also extrinsic motivation, intrinsic motivation).

Achieving approach to learning   *See* strategic approach.

Action learning   An approach to learning involving individuals working on real projects with the support of a group which meets regularly to help members reflect on their experience and to plan next actions.

Active learning   A process of engaging with the learning task at both the cognitive and affective level.

Adult learning theory   A range of theories and constructs claimed to relate specifically to how adults learn. Includes self-directed learning. Much of the work on reflection and experiential learning is also part of this area. Concerns over validity of some of the theories and how far they are applicable to younger learners in higher education.

Affective domain   One of the major areas of learning, the learning of values.

AGCAS   Association of Graduate Careers Advisory Services.

Aims (learning aims)   At the top of the hierarchy of specifications commonly used to define a learning experience. They are intended to provide the student, teacher and other interested parties with an understanding of the most overarching general statements regarding the intended consequences of a learning experience (*see also* objectives, learning outcomes).

Amotivation   Absence of tangible motivation.

Andragogy   The theory of adult learning, associated with the work of Malcolm Knowles.

AP(E)L   Accreditation of prior (experiential) learning. Taking into account previous 'certificated' learning gained either as whole or part of a programme, towards all or part of a new qualification. Also the counting of experience [experiential] towards obtaining a qualification.

Appraisal (as used in higher education)   A formal, regular, developmental process in which the one being appraised is encouraged to review and reflect upon performance in the workplace. Usually based on a focused interview between the one being appraised and the appraiser, who may be a peer, head of department or line manager. At the interview, objectives (linked to strategic aims of the department) are set and development needs identified. Performance against these objectives is reviewed at the next appraisal interview (*see also* performance management).

Approaches to studying inventory A device used to identify student approach to study.

Assessment Measurement of the achievement and progress of the learner.

Audio-visual lingual methodology Structural methodologies in language teaching developed in the 1950s and 1960s based on drilling, the formation of habit and avoidance of error.

Audit (academic/continuation) A verification of academic procedures. The first external audits in the United Kingdom were carried out by the Academic Audit Unit whose function has now been subsumed by the Quality Assurance Agency in their continuation audits.

Autonomy (of student/learning) Commonly refers to students taking more responsibility for and control of themselves and their learning, including being less spoon-fed. May also include elements of students taking more responsibility for determining and directing the content of their learning.

Blueprinting (of assessment) Ensures that assessment tasks adequately sample what the student is expected to have learned.

Buzz group A small group activity, typically within a large group, in which students work together on a short problem, task or discussion. So called because of the noise the activity generates.

C&IT Communication and information technologies.

CAL (computer-assisted learning) Use of computers for education and training, sometimes referred to as computer-assisted instruction (CAI) or computer-based learning (CBL). In this context the computer is usually used for a discrete item of teaching.

CALL Computer-assisted language learning.

CIHE Council for Industry in Higher Education.

CILT Centre for Information on Language Teaching and Research.

Clinical examination exercise (CEX) North American assessment devised in the 1980s to evaluate interns and residents' ability to clerk patients, ie take a history, examine the patient and devise a management plan. The assessor, who is a faculty member, uses a similar checklist/global ratings to an OSCE. Initially cases lasted one to two hours; the tendency now is for shorter and more frequent tests. Also known as a focused patient encounter (FPE).

Cognitive domain The major area of learning in most disciplines, to do with knowledge, understanding and thinking.

Communicative approach An approach to the teaching and learning of languages which emphasizes the primacy of meaning and communication needs.

Competence Most contemporary use in education relates to performing a task or series of tasks, with debate over how far such activities also require underpinning knowledge and understanding. 1. May be used generically to mean demonstrated achievement with respect to any clearly defined set of outcomes. 2. Is used to indicate both a high level of achievement and to denote a just acceptable level of activity (where it represents level 3 of a five-stage classification of progression – *see also* novice, expert). 3. Defined by the National Council for Vocational Qualifications as something which a person in a given occupational area should be able to do.

Computer-mediated learning Derived from a systems view of education, the computer has a role in enabling the learning, rather than being the sole medium for delivering learning. It encompasses a view which puts the learner at the centre of the learning, rather than the teacher.

Constructivist A number of theories attempting to explain how human beings learn. Characterized by the idea of addition to, and amendment of, previous understanding or knowledge. Without such change, learning is not thought to occur. Theories of reflection and experiential learning belong to this school.

Content-based language learning Surrounding and exposing students to examples of language in real situations rather than focusing on the learning of vocabulary and grammar.

Continuing professional development (CPD) Career or lifelong development of a type that goes beyond 'training' (which implies bringing oneself up to a given level of competence to perform a task). The word professional in the context of academic practice implies professionalism in the discipline through scholarship and research, service, professionalism as a teacher and professionalism in the different aspects of being an academic manager.

Course This term is used to refer to both smaller module-sized units of study and, confusingly, to larger units encompassing a set of modules which comprise a programme of study, leading to an academic award (*see also* module).

Courseware Software designed to be used in an educational programme. Refers to programmes and data used in CAL, computer-based learning.

Credit accumulation and transfer (CATS), credit frameworks, credit rated Assigning a numerical value to a portion of learning, often based on a number of notional learning hours earning one credit point. Thus modules can be said to be worth 30 credits and rated at level M (masters). Used as a currency for purposes of transfer and equivalence, with many different schemes in existence.

Criterion-referenced assessment Judges how well a learner has performed by comparison with predetermined criteria.

Critical incident (analysis) An event which, when reflected on, yields information resulting in learning from experience.

CTI (Centre) Computers in Teaching Initiative (Centre) An initiative backed by the UK Funding Councils in the 1990s. Replaced in 2000 by the Learning and Teaching Support Network, with a generic centre and 24 subject centres.

CVCP Committee of Vice-Chancellors and Principals of the Universities of the United Kingdom.

Dearing Report, *see* National Committee of Inquiry into Higher Education.

Deductive teaching/learning Working from general premises; presenting grammar rules in isolation and encouraging learners to generate specific examples based on the rules.

Deep approach to study **(deep learning)** Learning which attempts to relate ideas together to understand underpinning theory and concepts, and to make meaning out of material under consideration (*see also* surface approach, strategic approach).

DENI Department of Education for Northern Ireland.

DfEE Department for Education and Employment.

Diagnostic test A test used (possibly at the start of an undergraduate module) to identify weaknesses, eg in grammatical knowledge or numeracy, and used so that these might be addressed in a more focused manner.

Direct method (of language teaching) A rigid, graded approach to the structure of language that is intended to teach learners to acquire certain items before progressing to the next.

Distance learning Learning away from the institution, as exemplified by the Open University. Most often students work with learning resource materials that can be paper based, on video-tape, available on broadcast TV or accessed through the World Wide Web.

Domain A particular area (type) of learning. Much associated with categorizing learning outcomes and the use of hierarchical taxonomies within each domain. Considerable dispute on the number and range of domains and the hierarchies of learning within them. In the original Bloom taxonomy of 1956, the three domains identified were the cognitive, affective and psychomotor.

EHE (Enterprise in Higher Education) Launched in 1987 and ran until 1996. A scheme of pump-priming funding for projects aimed at bringing about more 'enterprising' qualities in students in higher education. As a result of programmes, students should have developed keys skills, be more informed about world of work, be better prepared to make career choices and able to take responsibility in their professional/working lives.

Electronic journal A learned journal, but not necessarily refereed, on the Internet. Electronic journals offer reduced time to publication, allow hyperlinking to other documents, and in some cases are enhanced by multimedia materials.

EMI/Q (extended matching item/question) A written assessment (eg testing diagnostic investigation and reasoning). Each question has a theme from which lists of possible answers are placed in alphabetical order. The candidate is instructed to choose the best matching answer(s) to each of a series of scenarios, results, etc.

Evaluation Quantitative and qualitative judgement of the curriculum and its delivery, to include teaching.

Experiential learning Learning from doing. Often represented by the Kolb Learning Cycle.

Expert Can be used with either a general or specific meaning, to indicate complete mastery at level 5 of a five-stage classification of progression. The expert practitioner does not rely on rules and guidelines as they have an intuitive grasp of situations based on deep understanding, and an analytical approach to new situations (*see also* novice, competence).

External examiner/examining External examiners are part of universities' self-regulatory procedures and play a key role in maintaining standards between institutions in a particular discipline. Usually distinguished members of the profession who have the respect of colleagues and students alike. For taught courses they typically act for a defined number of years (often three). External examiner reports form the basis of institutional review of courses and programmes for quality assurance purposes. They play a similar role in examination of postgraduate dissertations and theses, leading discussion in viva voce examinations.

Extrinsic motivation Typifies students who are concerned with the grades they get, external rewards, and whether they will gain approval from others (*see also* achievement motivation, intrinsic motivation).

Facilitator As opposed to teacher, tutor or mentor, a role to encourage individuals to take responsibility for their own learning, through the facilitation of this process.

Fair (of assessment) Fair with respect to: 1. Consistency between different markers. 2. Transparency and openness of criteria and procedures. 3. Procedures that do not disadvantage any group of learners in the cohort.

FAQ Frequently asked question.

Feedback Oral or written developmental advice on performance so that the recipient has a better understanding of values, standards, criteria, etc. *See also* formative assessment.

Fieldtrip/coursework Practical or experimental work away from the university designed to develop practical skills, eg observation of natural environments or surveying, which may be for a single session or coherent period of study lasting several days. Most common in life and environmental sciences, geography, civil engineering, construction.

FL(A) Foreign language (assistant).

Flexible learning Often used interchangeably with the term 'open learning', but may be distinguished from it by the inclusion of more traditional modes of delivery (such as the lecture) involving meeting with a tutor. The idea of open access irrespective of prior educational achievement is also often absent.

Focus group   A technique for pooling thoughts, ideas and perceptions to ensure equal participation by all members of a group. Requires a group leader and 8 to 15 participants. Some versions of the method aim to obtain a consensus view, others the weight and thrust of opinion. More accurately called nominal group technique.

Formative assessment   This is assessment that is used to help teachers and learners gauge the strengths and weaknesses of the learners' performance while there is still time to take action for improvement. Typically it is expressed in words rather than marks or grades. Information about learners is used diagnostically (*see* summative assessment).

FPE (focused patient encounter)   *See* CEX.

Functional notional syllabus/approach   A syllabus designed on the basis of an analysis of language 'meanings', ie notions (such as time and place) and functions (such as asking, informing, denying).

Grammar-translation   A structural teaching approach whereby a grammatical point is explained and learners are drilled in its use by means of translation of numerous examples into and out of the target language.

HEFCE   Higher Education Funding Council for England.

HEFW   Higher Education Funding Council for Wales.

HEQC   Higher Education Quality Council – now defunct, *see* QAA.

HERD   Higher Education Regional Development Fund.

Hypermedia   An extension of hypertext for a cross-referenced collection of documents. It is viewed with the aid of an interactive browser programme, which allows the reader to move easily from one document to another. Hypermedia extends this model to include graphics, sound, video and other kinds of data. WWW is a partial hypermedia

system since it supports graphical hyperlinks and links to sound and video files.

ILT   Institute for Learning and Teaching in Higher Education. Professional body created in the United Kingdom in 1999 as an NCIHE recommendation.

Immersion learning   Student interaction with authentic language through long periods of exposure to the second language.

Independent learning (study)   Often used interchangeably with the terms 'open learning', 'self-directed learning' and 'autonomous learning'. Has a flavour of all these. Perhaps most strongly associated with programmes of study created individually for each learner.

Induction   Initial period on joining an organization as an employee or as a new student joining a programme of study/research. During induction, basic information is provided through short courses, small group activities or one-to-one meetings. The purpose is to equip the staff member or student with background information so that they might become effective in their role or in their study as soon as possible.

Inductive teaching/learning   Working from particular cases to general conclusions; learners identify recurrent use and pattern in context and work towards the formulation of rules.

Interpersonal domain   One of the major areas of learning, the learning of behaviour involved in interacting with others.

Intranet   Any network which provides similar services within an organization to those provided on the Internet, but which is not necessarily connected to the Internet. The commonest example is the use by an institution of one of more WWW server on an internal network for distribution.

Intrinsic motivation   Typifies students who enjoy a challenge, want to master a subject, are curious and want to learn (*see also* achievement motivation, extrinsic motivation).

IWLP   Institution-wide language project.

JISC Joint Information Systems Committee.

Key/core/transferable skills Various definitions, eg communication, numeracy, IT and learning to learn ('we see these as necessary outcomes of all higher education programmes', NCIHE, 1997). Values and integrity, effective communication, application of numeracy, application of technology, understanding of work and the world, personal and interpersonal skills, problem solving, positive attitudes to change (Confederation of British Industry).

L1 (of language teaching) Learner's mother tongue.

L2 (of language teaching) A second or foreign language, learnt either in the classroom or naturalistically in the country concerned.

Laboratory/practical class A type of teaching session, usually included in curricula in experimental sciences, biomedical sciences and engineering disciplines, which is broadly intended to offer training in techniques and learning how to carry out experimental investigations.

Learning contract A contract drawn up between teacher and learner, whereby each agrees to take on certain roles and responsibilities, eg the learner to hand in work on time and the teacher to return corrected work within a specified period of time. May specifically concern setting out the learning outcomes the learner undertakes to achieve.

Learning cycle Theory describing the stages of learning from concrete experience through reflection and generalization to experiment towards new experience, often attributed to David Kolb.

Learning objectives *See* objectives

Learning outcomes Specific statements which define the learning students are expected to have acquired on completion of a session, course, programme, module, or unit of study.

Learning style Used to describe how learners differ in their tendencies or preferences to learn. Recognizes learning differences; a mix of personality and cognitive processes which influence approaches to learning.

Level (of award) A classification of awards into a number of different levels, based upon knowledge, skills and behaviour. Various frameworks exist offering benchmarking criteria. One is the Northern Ireland Credit Accumulation and Transfer Consortium (NICATS) which has eight levels arranged in ascending order from 'entry level', with characteristics such as recall, elementary comprehension, exercise of basic practical skills and ability to carry out directed activity under close supervision, to level 8. This requires display of mastery of complex and specialized areas of knowledge and skills, employing advanced skills to conduct research, or advanced technical and professional activity, accepting accountability for decision making.

Live database One or more large structured sets of data, usually associated with software to update and query the data. A simple database might be a single file containing many records, each of which contains the same set of fields where each field is a certain fixed width. A database is one component of a database management system. In a learning context a live database is one which is set up for current real life use.

MCQ Multiple choice question

Mentor Most often a colleague who acts as a supporter and adviser to a new member of an institution, eg by helping them adapt to institutional culture, acting as a sounding board for ideas and encouraging reflection on practice.

Mini-CEX (mini-clinical examination exercise) *See* CEX

Mixed skills teaching/testing The integration of the four language skills (listening, speaking, reading and writing) in tasks which replicate real-life language use, eg relaying written stimuli orally, making a written note of a spoken message.

Modelling calculations A description of observed behaviour, simplified by ignoring certain details. Models allow complex systems to be understood and their behaviour predicted within the scope of the model, but may give incorrect descriptions and predictions for situations outside the realm of their intended use. A model may be used as the basis of simulation.

Module   A discrete unit of study, often credit rated and part of a larger award-bearing course or programme of study. Sometimes the term 'course' is also used in this same sense.

MOO   MUD object-orientated, where MUD stands for 'multi-user dimension' or 'multi-user domain'. It was originally 'multi-user dungeon', and described a system used for collaborative text-based game-playing. MOOs have taken the concept further, providing a virtual environment usually with a visual interface accessed over the WWW. Participants are represented visually, and chat via text in rooms set aside for particular topics. Most frequently used in education as a visually enhanced live conferencing system. Some excellent examples can be reached via http://www.susqu.edu/ac_depts/arts_sci/english/harris/mudsmoos.htm

National Committee of Inquiry into Higher Education (NCIHE)   The Dearing Report, set up under Sir Ron (now Lord) Dearing by the Conservative Government in February 1996 to make recommendations for the next 20 years about the purposes, shape, structure, size and funding of higher education. Essentially a product of the deepening crisis in university funding. Reported in July 1997. The extensive report included aspects such as organization of programmes, quality matters, staff development and funding, etc.

Norm-referenced assessment   Judges how well the learner has done in comparison with the norm established by their peers.

Novice   Can be used with either a general or specific meaning to indicate a beginner. Level 1 of a five-stage classification of progression (*see also* expert and competence).

Objectives   Originally developed by educational psychologists and known as behavioural objectives. Definition and use have become less and less precise in recent years. Their meaning has ranged from exact, measurable outcomes of specific learning experiences to more generalized statements of outcomes for courses of study. The term is often used interchangeably (but loosely) with the term 'learning outcomes'.

OMR (optical mark reader)   A special scanning device that can read carefully placed pencil marks on specially designed documents. OMR is frequently used to score forms, questionnaires and answer-sheets.

Open learning   Learning organized to enable learning at own pace and at time and place of choice. Usually associated with delivery without a tutor being present and may or may not be part of a formal programme of study. Will often allow learning in order of own choice, in a variety of media and may also imply no entry barriers (eg no prior qualifications).

Oral examination   *See* viva voce examination.

OSCE (objective structured clinical examination)   Clinical assessment made up of a circuit of short tasks, known as stations. Several variations on the basic theme. Typically, candidates pass through a station where an examiner grades them according to an itemized checklist or global rating scale.

OSLER (objective structured longer examination record)   Clinical assessment with some similarity to an OSCE, but involving one or more long case. Similar to the CEX, it is a useful formative assessment but may be used in addition to other clinical assessments, eg an OSCE, in a summative manner.

Passive learning/approach   As opposed to active. Learning or an approach to learning that is superficial and does not involve full engagement with the material.

Peer assessment   Assessment by fellow (peer) students, as in peer assessment of team activities.

Peer support   A system whereby students support one another in the learning process.

Students may be in informal groups (sometimes known as learning groups) or more formal, designated groups (as in SI groups) when the course leader divides the class into groups.

Peer tutor/tutorial   Tutorial facilitated by fellow students (peer tutors), eg SI groups.

Performance management   A systematic way of measuring how an organization, unit or individual is doing. It involves objective setting, agreeing methods of delivery, reviewing, amending, evaluation and rewarding success.

Placement   Placing students outside their home institution for part of their period of study, often work-placement in which the student 'learns on the job'.

Portfolio (teaching portfolio)   A personal collection of evidence of an individual's work, eg to demonstrate achievement and professional development as a university teacher.

Probation   The initial phase in employment with a new organization in which a member of staff 'learns the job'. In higher education, this usually involves periods of formal training and development and often the probationer is supported by a mentor. Many institutions set formal requirements that staff are expected to meet for satisfactory completion of probation.

Problem class   Typically a session in the teaching of mathematics and physical science in which students work through problems and derive solutions with the support of a teacher and/or tutor/demonstrator. Not to be confused with PBL sessions.

Problem-based learning (PBL)   A pedagogical method introduced in the 1960s, much used in medicine. Curriculum design involves a large amount of small-group teaching and claims greater alignment with sound educational principles. Learning and teaching come after learners identify their learning needs from a trigger in the form of a scenario ('the problem').

Programme of study   An award-bearing collection of modules or programme of teaching and learning, typically running over a defined period of time (eg BA, MEng).

Programme specification (as defined by the NCIHE, 1997)   Common format for identification of potential stopping off points and specification of intended levels and outcomes of programmes of study in terms of: the knowledge and understanding that a student will be expected to have upon completion; key skills – C&IT, numeracy and learning how to learn; cognitive skills – understanding of methodologies or ability in critical analysis; subject specific skills – such as laboratory skills. Likely to be used to compare courses by students, employers and quality agencies.

Progress file   A term given prominence by the NCIHE. Being developed by the QAA for the whole sector. Likely to contain a transcript, or formal record of academic achievement (with or without a statement of learning outcomes derived from the programme specification), and a developmental aspect enabling students to monitor, plan and reflect on their own development.

Psychomotor domain   One of the major areas of learning, the learning of certain types of skill.

QAA   Quality Assurance Agency for Higher Education.

Quality   The achievement and maintenance of pre-specified standards, used in a generic sense to refer to all those elements that relate to teaching and learning processes, particularly as they impact on students' experiences of higher education and the conditions that support student learning.

Quality assessment overview report   An overview report bringing together main themes and issues from a full round of quality assessment visits, in a single subject area, undertaken by the HEFCE and currently available through their website (www.hefce.ac.uk).

Quality assurance   An ongoing process by which an institution (department, school or faculty) monitors and confirms that the conditions are in place for students to achieve the standards set.

Quality control   Refers to the detailed checks on procedures and activities necessary for the attainment of high quality and standards.

Quality enhancement   Refers to all the activities and processes adopted to improve and develop the quality of higher education and of practice.

Quality specification   Details the requirements and elements for achieving high quality teaching and learning and/or high academic standards.

Record of achievement   File of evidence of a learner's achievement, both qualitative and quantitative (eg grade obtained for each module taken). Increasingly the term is being replaced by the term 'progress file'.

Reflection   Taking time to consider an experience that one has been involved in, or any new piece of learning, and reflecting on the different factors contributing to its success, failure, meaning or otherwise.

Reflective practitioner   Someone who is continually involved in the process of reflecting on experience and is capable of reflecting in action, continually learning from experience to the benefit of future actions.

Reliable (of assessment)   A test which is consistent and precise in terms of factors, such as marking, quality of test and test items. The assessment process would generate the same result if repeated on another occasion with the same group, or if repeated with another group of similar students.

Role play   A planned learning activity where participants take on the role of individuals representing different perspectives (eg a mock interview) to meet specific learning objectives, such as to promote empathy or to expose participants to a scenario in which they will have to take part in the near future.

SAQ (structured answer question)   Also known as modified essay questions or short answers. SAQs test knowledge recall in a directed, but non-cueing manner.

SEDA   Staff and Educational Development Association. Formerly known as the Standing Conference on Educational Development (SCED).

Self-directed learning (SDL)   The learner has control over educational decisions, including goals, resources, methods and criteria for judging success. Often used just to mean any learning situation in which the learner has some influence on some of these aspects.

Semester   A period of study in a modular programme of study, over which a set of modules are taught. Typically the academic year is divided into two semesters of equal length. Of variable length across the sector.

Seminar   Used with different meanings according to discipline and type of institution. May be used to describe many forms of small group teaching. Traditionally one or more students present formal academic work (a paper) to peers and a tutor, followed by discussion.

SHEFC   Scottish Higher Education Funding Council.

SI   Supplemental instruction. Imported from the United States. A means of supporting learners through the use of trained SI instructors who are also students. SI instructors take the role of facilitator and operate within a framework determined initially by the course leader. Usually SI instructors are more senior students selected for the role.

Signpost   Statements in teaching sessions that help students to see the structure and direction of the teaching, and the links. Typically in a lecture, signposts will be used to give the big picture and then to signal the end of one section, the start of the next and where it is going.

Simulated patient (SP)   An actor or other third party who role plays the part of the patient in a clinical encounter with dental, medical or similar student.

Simulation   Often associated with role play, but increasingly used in the context of C&IT, a learning activity that simulates a real life scenario requiring participants to make choices which demonstrate cause and effect.

Situated cognition   Mentoring; support for the learner offered in the context of the learning environment. For example, in the case of language learning, assistance with vocabulary would be offered in the context of the environment rather than the other way around.

SLA Second language acquisition.

Small group teaching A term used to encompass all the various forms of teaching involving 'small' groups of students, ranging from one-to-one sessions to groups of up to 25 (or even more) students. Includes tutorials, seminars, problem classes.

Standards The term used to refer to student attainment in terms of expected and actual levels of attainment.

SToMP Software teaching of modular physics. SToMP is a TLTP project which is a complete multimedia learning environment for some topics in first year undergraduate physics. Study is via units which introduce topics, and describe the relevant concepts. Hyperlinks take users to appropriate physical models, animations, deviations, video clips, interactive graphs and other resources. SToMP can be used in a variety of ways, including self-study, possibly in distance learning role and for lecture demonstrations.

Strategic approach to study (strategic learning) Typifies students who adapt their learning style to meet the needs of the set task. Intention is external to the real purpose of the task, as it focuses on achieving high marks for their own sake, not because they indicate high levels of learning. Also known as the achieving approach.

Subject benchmarking Being developed by QAA. A way of setting standards for subject areas.

Subject Review (*see also* teaching quality assessment) The quality assessment process for higher education provision, at subject level, undertaken by the QAA in England and Northern Ireland since 1998. The method is set out in the *Subject Review Handbook*. There are six aspects of provision: curriculum design content and organization; teaching, learning and assessment; student progress and achievement; student support and guidance; learning resources and quality management

and enhancement. Each provider is given a graded profile by applying a grade (1, 2, 3 or 4) to each aspect of provision. Nature of replacement in 2002 uncertain.

Summative assessment The type of assessment that typically comes at the end of a course/module or section of learning and awards the learner with a final mark or grade for that section. The information about the learner is often used by third parties to inform decisions about the learner's abilities.

Surface approach to study (surface learning) Learning by students which focuses on the details of the learning experience and which is based on memorizing the details without any attempt to give them meaning beyond the factual level of understanding. *See also* deep approach, strategic approach.

Target language The particular foreign language being taught/learnt.

Teaching quality assessment (TQA) The process of quality assessment in higher education provision at the subject level, as first undertaken by the funding councils, under the terms of the 1992 Further and Higher Education Act. Since 1998, known in England and Northern Ireland as Subject Review and currently the responsibility of the QAA.

Team teaching A system whereby learning is designed, delivered and supported by two or more teachers who may share the same session.

TLTP (Teaching and Learning Technology Programme) TLTP was launched in 1992 by the Universities Funding Council and to date funded by the UK Funding Councils. It has supported the development of a wide range of courseware for teaching and learning in higher education.

TONIC An online course on how to use the Internet, produced for the higher education community in the United Kingdom. It provides practical guidance on major Internet topics, from basic to advanced (http://www.netskills.ac.uk/TONIC/cgi-bin/load.cgi).

Tutorial   Used with different meanings according to discipline, type of institution, level, and teaching and learning method. Involves a tutor and one or more students. May focus on academic and/or pastoral matters.

UCoSDA   Universities' and Colleges' Staff Development Agency, an agency of the Committee of Vice-Chancellors and Principals of the UK.

Valid (of assessment)   Adequacy and appropriateness of the task/test in relation to the outcomes/objectives of the teaching being assessed, ie it measures what it is supposed to measure.

Video conference   A discussion between two individuals or groups of people who are in different places but can see and hear each other using electronic communications. Pictures and sound are carried by the telecommunications network, eg ISDN, or the Internet. Such conferences can take place across the world.

Viva voce examination   An oral examination, typically at the end of a programme of study. One part of assessment strategy if used in undergraduate programmes, principal means of assessment of postgraduate degrees. Can be used to test communication, understanding, capacity to think quickly under pressure and knowledge of procedures.

Web site poster board   A learning tool to encourage students to become involved in interacting with ideas and/or other students electronically, usually accessed via intranet, WWW.

Work-based learning   A type of curriculum design allowing content and learning to arise from within real working contexts. Students, usually employees, studying part-time and using their workplace to generate a project. Unlike PBL, work-based learners are working on real problems in real time.

WWW (World Wide Web)   A system of representing information across the Internet. Viewers use a browser programme to view information which is presented via a server. The main use of the WWW is to view documents which use hypertext mark-up language (HTML) to format documents.

INDEX